Complex Process Modeling and Control Based on AI Technology

Complex Process Modeling and Control Based on AI Technology

Guest Editors

Jie Hu
Sheng Du
Pan Yu

MDPI
Basel • Beijing • Wuhan • Barcelona • Belgrade • Novi Sad • Cluj • Manchester

Guest Editors
Jie Hu
School of Artificial Intelligence and Automation
China University of Geosciences
Wuhan
China

Sheng Du
School of Artificial Intelligence and Automation
China University of Geosciences
Wuhan
China

Pan Yu
School of Information Science and Technology
Beijing University of Technology
Beijing
China

Editorial Office
MDPI AG
Grosspeteranlage 5
4052 Basel, Switzerland

This is a reprint of the Special Issue, published open access by the journal *Mathematics* (ISSN 2227-7390), freely accessible at: https://www.mdpi.com/journal/mathematics/special_issues/Complex_Process_Modeling_Control_Based_AI_Technol.

For citation purposes, cite each article independently as indicated on the article page online and as indicated below:

Lastname, A.A.; Lastname, B.B. Article Title. *Journal Name* **Year**, *Volume Number*, Page Range.

ISBN 978-3-7258-8307-3 (Hbk)
ISBN 978-3-7258-8308-0 (PDF)
https://doi.org/10.3390/books978-3-7258-8308-0

Contents

About the Editors

Jie Hu

Jie Hu received a B.S. degree in automation and a Ph.D. degree in control science and engineering from China University of Geosciences, Wuhan, China, in 2015 and 2020, respectively. He was a joint Ph.D. student with the Department of Electrical and Computer Engineering, University of Alberta, Edmonton, AB, Canada, from 2018 to 2020. He was a Post-Doctoral Fellow of control science and engineering, China University of Geosciences, from 2020 to 2022, where he is currently a Professor with the School of Artificial Intelligence and Automation. His current research interests include process control, intelligent control, and computational intelligence. Dr. Hu was recipient of the Best Paper Award of the IEEE International Conference on Industrial Technology in 2025 and the Young Researcher Award of the 13th China–Japan International Workshop on Information Technology and Control Applications in 2020.

Sheng Du

Sheng Du received a B.S. degree in Measurement & Control Technology and Instruments and a Ph.D. degree in Control Science and Engineering from China University of Geosciences, Wuhan, China, in 2016 and 2021, respectively. He was a joint Ph.D. student with the Department of Electrical and Computer Engineering, University of Alberta, Edmonton, Canada, from 2019 to 2021. He was a Postdoctoral Fellow in Control Science and Engineering, China University of Geosciences, Wuhan, China, from 2021 to 2023. He is currently a Professor with the School of Artificial Intelligence and Automation, China University of Geosciences, Wuhan, China. His research interests include process control, intelligent control, intelligent optimization, computational intelligence, and artificial intelligence. Dr. Du is a Senior Member of the Chinese Association of Automation (CAA) and a winner of the Outstanding Doctoral Thesis Nomination Award of the CAA. He is an Associate Editor of Measurement and Control.

Pan Yu

Pan Yu received B.S. and Ph.D. degrees in engineering from Central South University, China, in 2014 and 2019, respectively. She was a Research Student with the Department of Electrical and Electronic Engineering, Chiba University, Japan, from 2017 to 2019. In 2019, she joined Beijing University of Technology, China, where she is currently an Associate Professor with the School of Information Science and Technology. Her research interests include robotics, disturbance estimation and rejection, learning control, and advanced robust control.

mathematics

MDPI

Editorial

Preface to the Special Issue "Complex Process Modeling and Control Based on AI Technology"

Jie Hu [1,2,3,*], Sheng Du [1,2,3] and Pan Yu [4]

1 School of Artificial Intelligence and Automation, China University of Geosciences, Wuhan 430074, China; dusheng@cug.edu.cn
2 Hubei Key Laboratory of Advanced Control and Intelligent Automation for Complex Systems, Wuhan 430074, China
3 Engineering Research Center of Intelligent Technology for Geo-Exploration, Ministry of Education, Wuhan 430074, China
4 School of Information Science and Technology, Beijing University of Technology, Beijing 100124, China; panyu@bjut.edu.cn
* Correspondence: hujie@cug.edu.cn

In the Industry 4.0 era of digital transformation, complex process modeling and control are critical challenges in various industrial sectors, including steel metallurgy [1,2], chemical manufacturing [3,4], and energy systems [5,6]. The integration of artificial intelligence (AI) technologies has transformed traditional methods by offering unparalleled capabilities in handling nonlinearity, uncertainty, and high-dimensional data.

Traditional modeling and control methods often struggle to address the inherent complexity and dynamics of modern industrial processes [7]. They rely on precise mechanistic models and struggle to handle the uncertainties inherent in complex nonlinear systems, lack adaptability, and result in poor control performance in dynamically changing environments. These methods are computationally complex, making it difficult to find globally optimal solutions. They are also sensitive to changes in system parameters, which prevents them from effectively addressing the large-scale high-dimensional control challenges found in modern industry.

Recent AI advancements, particularly in deep learning, reinforcement learning, and federated learning, have demonstrated extraordinary potential in overcoming these challenges [8]. AI-based methods have robust, data-driven, and self-learning capabilities. These capabilities enable end-to-end intelligent processing, which significantly improves efficiency. They can also automatically identify complex patterns and adapt to dynamic environments without relying on precise mathematical models. AI methods also offer strong generalization and adaptability. They continuously optimize performance through ongoing learning, demonstrating flexibility and accuracy that traditional methods cannot match when addressing high-dimensional, nonlinear, and complex problems.

This Special Issue showcases cutting-edge research at the intersection of AI and complex process modeling and control. We are dedicated to bridging the gap between theoretical AI advancements and practical industrial applications while promoting interdisciplinary collaboration and knowledge exchange.

Contribution 1 proposes a two-stage high-precision PCB component recognition framework integrating CBAM-enhanced YOLOv11 with sub-pixel geometric refinement. The system achieves industrial-grade localization accuracy essential for robotic PCB disassembly under complex visual interference conditions. Contribution 2 proposes an imprecise probability-based load transfer control method integrating IDM with NCC for switch timing prediction. This method maintains disconnection–reconnection actions within 20 ms to prevent circulating currents in distribution networks. Contribution 3 proposes a bidirectional LSTM–Transformer interaction architecture with cross-attention mechanisms for dynamically coupling global market context with local temporal features in gold futures price forecasting. The proposed framework achieves superior prediction accuracy with significantly reduced error volatility during extreme market events. Contribution 4 proposes a three-module D2D mode selection framework integrating GRU-based SINR prediction with statistical error analysis and threshold selection using AR and PCR constraints. The method achieves higher system throughput, longer D2D mode residence time, and lower mode-switching frequency compared to existing approaches in dynamic network environments. Contribution 5 proposes a dual-path neural network architecture integrating spatial feature extraction via Gramian angular field-transformed images with temporal feature analysis through GRU networks, optimized by the Crested Porcupine Optimizer algorithm. This method achieves about 99% recognition accuracy with robust fault detection capability under varying noise conditions and different network topologies in distribution systems. Contribution 6 proposes a flow-path-offset joint scheduling algorithm with multi-index priority scoring for time-sensitive networks, achieving a 39% higher scheduling success ratio than the naive algorithm and demonstrates superior performance in large-scale TSN deployments. Contribution 7 proposes an improved RT-DETR integrating super-resolution convolutional module and channel attention mechanism, achieving 2.8% mAP and 1.7% AR improvements with only 0.4 MB additional parameters for rail fastener defect detection. Contribution 8 proposes an anti-disturbance bumpless transfer control framework integrating a switched equivalent-input-disturbance estimator with a compensator-based continuous controller design under average dwell time switching strategy, achieving asymptotic stability and L2-gain disturbance rejection properties, while ensuring controller signal continuity during subsystem transitions, as verified by simulations on a switching RLC circuit system with sawtooth wave disturbances. Contribution 9 proposes a time-series prediction model for the electricity load of charging piles integrating variational mode decomposition with broad learning system and multi-model fusion optimized by particle swarm optimization. It achieves superior prediction accuracy with an R^2 of 0.9831 and PMAPE of 2.6468, significantly outperforming LSTM, NARX, and standard BLS and ELM models by 52–89% across all evaluation metrics, while maintaining computational efficiency for optimal electricity-load scheduling decision-making. Contribution 10 proposes a fault distance measurement method for distribution networks integrating a novel phase-mode transformation matrix with Markov Transition Field image conversion and Darknet-19 deep learning architecture. This method achieves high accuracy fault location with an average prediction error of only 330 m under 40 dB noise conditions, demonstrating strong robustness and practical applicability as validated on Raspberry Pi-embedded hardware with error margins below 0.26 km across various fault scenarios. Contribution 11, which is a comprehensive review paper on AI-integrated control engineering, synthesizes recent advancements in artificial intelligence applications for system identification, control, and optimization. The authors categorize and analyze neural network control architectures (including adaptive, sliding-mode, backstepping, and iterative learning variants), model predictive control enhancements through deep learning, and reinforcement learning control paradigms, while identifying critical challenges in interpretability, data requirements, computational complexity, and stability guarantees that shape future research directions for intelligent control systems across industrial applications.

Conclusions

This editorial provides an overview of the progress in data-driven intelligent modeling and control. It emphasizes the cutting-edge methodologies and technological applications that have emerged in this field in recent years. These approaches harness data to perform modeling and control tasks, significantly enhancing the adaptability, reliability, and efficiency of complex systems. Studies show that amid the rapid development of Industry 4.0, data-driven intelligent modeling and control have become essential in ensuring product quality, promoting sustainable development, and enhancing production efficiency.

Funding: This research was funded by the Hubei Provincial Natural Science Foundation of China under Grant 2024AFB589 and in part by the Natural Science Foundation of Wuhan under Grant 2024040801020281.

Conflicts of Interest: The authors declare no conflicts of interest.

List of Contributions:

1. Wang, L.; Ouyang, L.; Weng, H.; Chen, X.; Wang, A.; Zhang, K. A Two-Stage High-Precision Recognition and Localization Framework for Key Components on Industrial PCBs. *Mathematics* **2026**, *14*, 4. https://doi.org/10.3390/math14010004.
2. Zhang, H.; Long, C.; Su, X.; Gao, Y.; Luo, W. Research on Synchronous Transfer Control Technology for Distribution Network Load Based on Imprecise Probability. *Mathematics* **2025**, *13*, 3299. https://doi.org/10.3390/math13203299.
3. Zhao, Y.; Guo, Y.; Wang, X. Hybrid LSTM-Transformer Architecture with Multi-Scale Feature Fusion for High-Accuracy Gold Futures Price Forecasting. *Mathematics* **2025**, *13*, 1551. https://doi.org/10.3390/math13101551.
4. Liu, D.; Kang, G.; Shi, Y.; Wang, Y.; Lei, Z. Mode Selection for Device to Device Communication in Dynamic Network: A Statistical and Deep Learning Method. *Mathematics* **2025**, *13*, 343. https://doi.org/10.3390/math13030343.
5. Ning, K.; Ye, L.; Song, W.; Guo, W.; Li, G.; Yin, X.; Zhang, M. A Dual-Path Neural Network for High-Impedance Fault Detection. *Mathematics* **2025**, *13*, 225. https://doi.org/10.3390/math13020225.
6. Liu, D.; Zhang, Z.; Shi, Y.; Wang, Y.; Guo, J.; Lei, Z. Start Time Planning for Cyclic Queuing and Forwarding in Time-Sensitive Networks. *Mathematics* **2024**, *12*, 3382. https://doi.org/10.3390/math12213382.
7. Song, W.; Liao, B.; Ning, K.; Yan, X. Improved Real-Time Detection Transformer-Based Rail Fastener Defect Detection Algorithm. *Mathematics* **2024**, *12*, 3349. https://doi.org/10.3390/math12213349.
8. Wu, J.; Liu, Q.; Yu, P. Anti-Disturbance Bumpless Transfer Control for a Switched Systems via a Switched Equivalent-Input-Disturbance Approach. *Mathematics* **2024**, *12*, 2307. https://doi.org/10.3390/math12152307.
9. Yu, L.; Ge, X. Time-Series Prediction of Electricity Load for Charging Piles in a Region of China Based on Broad Learning System. *Mathematics* **2024**, *12*, 2147. https://doi.org/10.3390/math12132147.
10. Wang, H.; Guo, W.; Shi, Y. Fault Distance Measurement in Distribution Networks Based on Markov Transition Field and Darknet-19. *Mathematics* **2024**, *12*, 1665. https://doi.org/10.3390/math12111665.
11. Yu, P.; Wan, H.; Zhang, B.; Wu, Q.; Zhao, B.; Xu, C.; Yang, S. Review on System Identification, Control, and Optimization Based on Artificial Intelligence. *Mathematics* **2025**, *13*, 952. https://doi.org/10.3390/math13060952.

References

1. Zhang, K.; Liu, Y.; Wang, Y.; Zhang, X. Application of variational autoencoder network to real-time prediction of steel crown in the hot strip rolling mill process. *IEEE Sens. J.* **2025**, *25*, 42389–42399. [CrossRef]
2. Hu, J.; Wu, M.; Cao, W.; Pedrycz, W. Dynamic modeling framework based on automatic identification of operating conditions for sintering carbon consumption prediction. *IEEE Trans. Ind. Electron.* **2024**, *71*, 3133–3141. [CrossRef]
3. Kottavalasa, Y.N.; Snidaro, L. Advancing chemical manufacturing processes through data-driven approaches: A survey. *Chemom. Intell. Lab. Syst.* **2025**, *267*, 105553. [CrossRef]

4. Zhang, W.; Lu, X.; Cai, Z.; He, J.; Yu, J.; Jiang, S.; Mirihanage, W.; Lupoi, R. Fabrication of defect-free 3D bimetallic composites with transverse chemical gradients through a novel metal additive manufacturing technique using powder sheets. *J. Manuf. Process.* **2026**, *162*, 296–310. [CrossRef]
5. Islas-Estrada, L.R.; Flores-Hernández, D.A. Embedded energy monitoring system for solar applications. *IEEE Embed. Syst. Lett.* **2025**, *17*, 386–389. [CrossRef]
6. Bramstoft, R.; Kanellas, P.; Leon, J.P.M.; Koivisto, M. The role of offshore wind energy hubs in the Baltic Sea energy system. *Energy* **2026**, *348*, 140554. [CrossRef]
7. Dong, J.; Li, D.; Wei, Y.; Peng, K. A novel process monitoring and root cause diagnosis strategy based on knowledge-data-integrated causal digraph for complex industrial processes. *IEEE Trans. Instrum. Meas.* **2025**, *74*, 3500112. [CrossRef]
8. Rahman, M.W.U.; Nevarez, R.; Mim, L.T.; Hariri, S. Multiagent actor-critic generative ai for query resolution and analysis. *IEEE Trans. Artif. Intell.* **2025**, *6*, 2226–2240. [CrossRef]

https://doi.org/10.3390/math14081285

mathematics MDPI

Article

A Two-Stage High-Precision Recognition and Localization Framework for Key Components on Industrial PCBs

Li Wang [1,*], Liu Ouyang [1], Huiying Weng [1], Xiang Chen [1], Anna Wang [1] and Kexin Zhang [2,*]

[1] State Grid Zhejiang Electric Power Co., Ltd., Hangzhou 310015, China
[2] Institute of Cyber-Systems and Control, Zhejiang University, Hangzhou 310027, China
* Correspondence: wang_lizj@163.com (L.W.); zhangkexin@zju.edu.cn (K.Z.)

Abstract

Precise recognition and localization of electronic components on printed circuit boards (PCBs) are crucial for industrial automation tasks, including robotic disassembly, high-precision assembly, and quality inspection. However, strong visual interference from silkscreen characters, copper traces, solder pads, and densely packed small components often degrades the accuracy of deep learning-based detectors, particularly under complex industrial imaging conditions. This paper presents a two-stage, coarse-to-fine PCB component localization framework based on an optimized YOLOv11 architecture and a sub-pixel geometric refinement module. The proposed method enhances the backbone with a Convolutional Block Attention Module (CBAM) to suppress background noise and strengthen discriminative features. It also integrates a tiny-object detection branch and a weighted Bi-directional Feature Pyramid Network (BiFPN) for more effective multi-scale feature fusion, and it employs a customized hybrid loss with vertex-offset supervision to enable pose-aware bounding box regression. In the second stage, the coarse predictions guide contour-based sub-pixel fitting using template geometry to achieve industrial-grade precision. Experiments show significant improvements over baseline YOLOv11, particularly for small and densely arranged components, indicating that the proposed approach meets the stringent requirements of industrial robotic disassembly.

Keywords: PCB component detection; YOLOv11; attention mechanisms; Bi-directional feature pyramid network; sub-pixel localization

MSC: 68T07

1. Introduction

Industrial automation increasingly requires precise perception of electronic components on printed circuit boards (PCBs), especially for robotic disassembly, repair, recycling, and high-precision quality inspection. These tasks demand accurate recognition of component categories, detailed structural understanding, and pose estimation at sub-pixel precision. However, PCB images exhibit dense silkscreen characters, copper traces, solder pads, and cluttered layouts that generate strong visual interference, significantly degrading the performance of generic deep learning-based detectors. Small components, such as 0201/0402 resistors, are particularly susceptible to feature loss in deep networks, while larger integrated circuits (ICs) may appear at arbitrary orientations requiring precise rotation estimation rather than axis-aligned bounding boxes.

Deep learning has transformed object detection over the last decade. Region-proposal approaches such as R-CNN and Faster R-CNN [1] pioneered high-quality detection pipelines, while the YOLO family [2] and SSD [3] enabled real-time single-stage detection. Improvements such as Focal Loss [4] and Feature Pyramid Networks (FPN) [5] strengthened detection under class imbalance and multi-scale conditions. Later works including EfficientDet with BiFPN [6], DETR transformer-based detection [7], YOLOv4 [8], and Scaled-YOLOv4 [9] further advanced accuracy and robustness. Despite these advances, transferring generic models to PCB imagery remains challenging due to the severe background clutter and the presence of extremely small components.

Attention mechanisms have provided powerful tools for enhancing feature discriminability. Squeeze-and-Excitation (SE) modules [10], CBAM [11], global-transformer attention in ViT [12], and attention-augmented CNNs [13] have shown strong capabilities in suppressing irrelevant context and highlighting task-relevant regions. These properties are crucial in PCB imagery, where misleading textures such as parallel traces, silkscreen symbols, and solder pads can closely resemble true components.

Meanwhile, keypoint-based and pose-aware detectors such as CornerNet [14], CenterNet [15], HRNet [16], and stacked hourglass networks [17] demonstrated the importance of geometric reasoning beyond bounding-box regression—an essential capability for robotic manipulation of electronic components where orientation and vertex locations must be estimated precisely.

In PCB-specific vision research, a variety of deep learning-based solutions have been proposed. Representative works include the PCB defect dataset and baseline detection benchmarks released by [18], a variety of CNN-based automated optical inspection (AOI) pipelines for surface defect classification [19], and YOLO-family detectors adapted for PCB component and defect inspection [20]. Recent studies further investigate improved detection of small defects using attention-enhanced networks and feature-pyramid refinements [21]. Despite these advances, most prior systems focus on pixel-wise defect segmentation or bounding-box detection; few works address the combined requirement of robust detection of micro-scale PCB features and sub-pixel geometric localization accuracy, which is essential for industrial robot alignment and precision assembly.

Traditional industrial vision methods—such as template matching, edge detection, and geometric metrology—remain indispensable in high-accuracy automation tasks. Classical techniques including the SUSAN operator [22] and the Canny edge detector [23] demonstrate robust low-level feature extraction, while modern image-alignment and registration methods provide the foundation for sub-pixel localization and precise template matching (e.g., Lucas–Kanade frameworks and extensions [24]). However, classical methods typically degrade under variations in lighting, noise, and unseen defect types, motivating hybrid AOI pipelines that combine deep learning for robust feature detection with classical geometric refinement for sub-pixel alignment accuracy.

Given the limitations in existing PCB component detection—small-object sensitivity, background interference, pose estimation, and lack of sub-pixel accuracy—there is a need for a unified framework that integrates advanced deep learning with precise geometric modeling. This work proposes a PCB-specific detection and localization algorithm that combines deep neural feature extraction, attention-based noise suppression, multi-scale feature enhancement, and a geometry-based refinement stage. Unlike conventional approaches, the system predicts both bounding boxes and vertex offsets that encode component orientation, while a subsequent contour-based stage pushes precision to the sub-pixel level. The contributions of this work are summarized as follows:

- A specialized, high-precision PCB component dataset is constructed, featuring multi-modal annotations that include not only bounding boxes but also pin-level vertex coordinates for thousands of components, enabling supervised learning of pose and fine-grained geometry.

- An enhanced YOLOv11 architecture tailored for PCB imagery, incorporating CBAM attention and a BiFPN-based multi-scale fusion neck to effectively suppress silkscreen/trace-induced background interference, significantly improving the detection robustness of small and densely arranged components.
- A pose-aware decoupled detection head with vertex-offset regression is introduced, allowing the model to predict fine-grained geometric details, such as component rotation and key pin positions, which conventional axis-aligned bounding boxes cannot capture.

The remainder of this paper is organized as follows. Section 2 details the proposed two-stage methodology, including the construction of the PCB component dataset, the enhanced YOLOv11-based coarse localization network, and the sub-pixel geometric refinement procedure. Section 3 presents the experimental setup and evaluates detection and localization performance on the constructed dataset. Section 4 provides a technical discussion of the results, including the benefits and limitations of the proposed framework. Finally, Section 5 concludes this study and outlines future research directions.

2. Methods

2.1. Dataset Construction and Pose Annotation

To support high-precision pose estimation of PCB components under complex industrial conditions, we constructed a dedicated dataset containing both bounding-box and pose-level annotations. All images are captured with a high-resolution industrial camera (1920 × 1080) in factory environments, covering variations in illumination, contamination, PCB density, and device categories. A total of 10,000 PCB images are collected, containing over 150,000 annotated component instances across 20 devices (e.g., resistors, capacitors, inductors, QFP ICs, BGA chips, and connectors). Approximately 50% of the instances are small objects (<32 × 32 pixels), which is essential for evaluating robustness in dense-component scenarios.

Unlike standard PCB datasets that only include axis-aligned bounding boxes, our dataset introduces a multi-modal pose annotation strategy to capture fine-grained structural characteristics of components. In addition to the class label and bounding box, selected devices—particularly ICs and connectors that require precision manipulation—were annotated with key structural vertices. For chips, this includes the four corner pin locations; for connectors, the alignment vertex and pin-array reference points. These high-precision vertex labels serve as ground-truth supervision for the vertex-offset regression branch in the proposed model.

To enhance generalization across real production environments, we applied a series of augmentation techniques: random cropping, photometric distortion, Gaussian noise injection, and MOSAIC composition [8]. The MOSAIC strategy is especially critical for training the tiny-object detection branch, as it places multiple small components in a single forward pass, improving multi-target spatial reasoning.

2.2. Coarse Localization with Enhanced YOLOv11

The coarse localization stage produces an initial estimate of location and pose of each device by extending the standard YOLOv11 framework in three coordinated aspects: enhanced feature extraction, multi-scale fusion with a tiny-object branch, and a pose-aware decoupled detection head. Figure 1 shows the overall architecture of our framework.

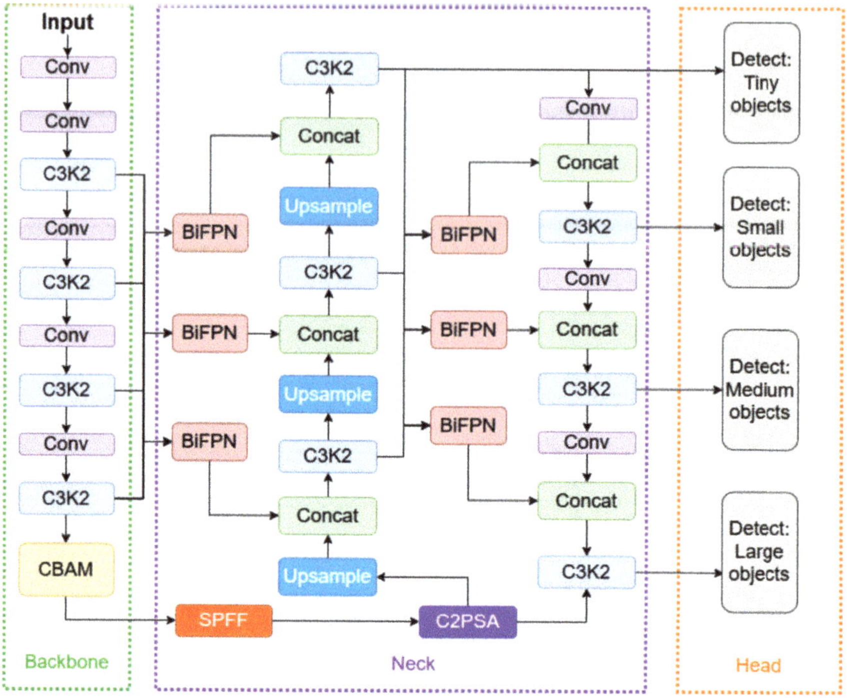

Figure 1. Overall architecture of the enhanced YOLOv11 detection network, integrating CBAM attention in the backbone, BiFPN-based multi-scale feature fusion in the neck, and a decoupled detection head with vertex-offset regression for pose-aware PCB component detection.

2.2.1. Backbone Enhancement with CBAM Attention

To address the severe background interference present in PCB imagery—such as silkscreen characters, copper traces, and solder pads—we embed the Convolutional Block Attention Module (CBAM) into the deep layers of the YOLOv11 backbone. CBAM refines feature representation through two sequential attention operations: Channel Attention Module (CAM), which determines what to focus on, and Spatial Attention Module (SAM), which determines where to focus. The combined effect allows the backbone to suppress clutter while selectively amplifying discriminative features of small or densely packed components.

Given an intermediate feature map $F \in \mathbb{R}^{C\times H\times W}$, CAM first computes two channel descriptors by spatial global pooling:

$$f_{avg} = \text{AvgPool}_s(F), f_{max} = \text{MaxPool}_s(F) \tag{1}$$

where both outputs are of shape $C \times 1 \times 1$.

These descriptors are then passed through a shared two-layer MLP with reduction ratio r:

$$m_{avg} = \text{MLP}(f_{avg}), m_{max} = \text{MLP}(f_{max}), \tag{2}$$

where $\text{MLP}(x) = W_1\text{ReLU}(W_0x)$ with $W_0 \in \mathbb{R}^{\frac{C}{r}\times C}$ and $W_1 \in \mathbb{R}^{C\times \frac{C}{r}}$. The channel attention map is obtained via $M_c(F) = \sigma(m_{avg} + m_{max})$ and is used to refine the feature via channel-wise reweighting:

$$F' = M_c(F) \odot F \tag{3}$$

This operation enhances channels describing component contours, solder interfaces, and material boundaries, while suppressing channels dominated by background textures or repeated silkscreen fonts.

The channel-refined feature $F^{'}$ is then processed by SAM to generate a spatial attention map that highlights the exact pixel regions corresponding to true component areas. SAM computes channel-wise average and max pooling:

$$f_{avg}^{'} = \text{AvgPool}_c(F^{'}), f_{max}^{'} = \text{MaxPool}_c(F^{'}) \quad (4)$$

resulting in two feature maps of size $1 \times H \times W$, which are concatenated and passed through a 7×7 convolution to obtain the spatial attention map:

$$M_S(F^{'}) = \sigma(\text{Conv}_{7\times7}([f_{avg}^{'}; f_{max}^{'}])) \quad (5)$$

Finally, the spatial attention map reweights the feature spatially:

$$F_{out} = M_s(F^{'}) \odot F^{'} \quad (6)$$

SAM ensures that the model focuses on true device contours and pin boundaries while deemphasizing visually similar but irrelevant structures such as copper traces immediately adjacent to components.

2.2.2. BiFPN-Based Multi-Scale Fusion with Tiny-Object Branch

To address the extreme scale variation of PCB components—from sub-millimeter resistors to large integrated circuits—the neck architecture is enhanced using a Bi-Directional Feature Pyramid Network (BiFPN) together with an additional 16× downsampled tiny-object detection branch. The tiny-object branch preserves high-resolution spatial details that would otherwise vanish in deeper layers, ensuring that components smaller than 32×32 pixels remain detectable by subsequent fusion layers. After building this high-resolution branch, feature maps across all scales are fused using a BiFPN structure that introduces learnable weights to adaptively balance contributions from different resolutions.

As shown in Figure 2, in BiFPN, each fused feature node receives multiple inputs $(F_1, F_2, ..., F_n)$, each representing a feature tensor from either a top-down or bottom-up pathway. Instead of naively summing these inputs, BiFPN computes a normalized weighted fusion:

$$F_{out} = \frac{\sum_{i=1}^{n} \omega_i \cdot F_i}{\sum_{i=1}^{n} \omega_i + \varepsilon} \quad (7)$$

where $\omega_i \geq 0$ are learnable scalar importance weights (enforced via ReLU to keep them non-negative) and ε is a small constant to prevent division by zero. This normalization ensures stable gradient flow and allows the model to learn which scales are more relevant for a given PCB component type. After the normalized fusion, each output node is refined using a convolution:

$$F_{out}^{refined} = \text{Conv}_{3\times3}(F_{out}) \quad (8)$$

To realize bi-directionality, each scale repeats this process twice, i.e., once during the top-down pathway and once during the bottom-up pathway. The repeated bi-directional passes allow the fused features to integrate both semantic information from deeper layers and fine-grained spatial detail from shallow layers, which is an essential capability for PCB inspection scenarios, where small SMD devices lie adjacent to large ICs and the background contains high-frequency patterns such as silkscreen and copper traces.

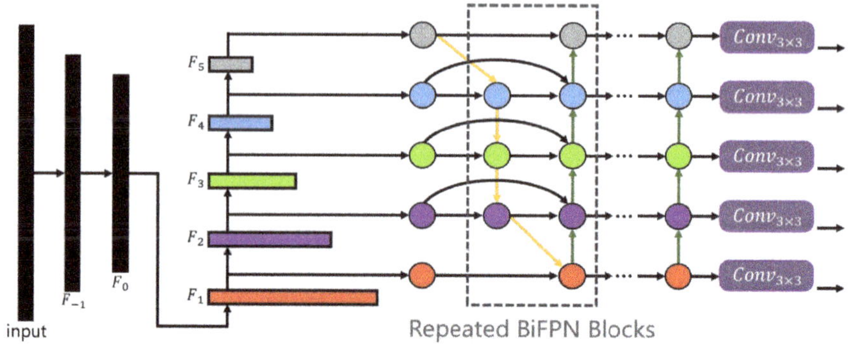

Figure 2. Architecture of the Bi-Directional Feature Pyramid Network (BiFPN), illustrating repeated top-down and bottom-up feature fusion with learnable weighted connections and depthwise separable convolutions for efficient multi-scale representation.

Through this mechanism, the network learns scale-adaptive fusion patterns: for large ICs, deeper semantic layers receive larger weights; for small resistors or capacitors, the high-resolution 16× branch dominates the fusion. This adaptive and learnable cross-scale aggregation significantly boosts tiny-object recall and stabilizes detection performance across diverse PCB layouts.

2.2.3. Pose-Aware Decoupled Detection Head and Composite Loss

To enable the detector to output not only axis-aligned bounding boxes but also component pose information, the proposed model employs a pose-aware decoupled detection head in which the classification and regression tasks are optimized through separate branches. This design avoids mutual interference between heterogeneous objectives and improves convergence stability in dense PCB scenes.

The regression loss integrates two components: a bounding-box alignment term using Complete-IoU loss and a vertex-offset supervision term based on L_1 distance. Specifically, the CIoU loss for the predicted box B and the ground-truth box B^* is defined as:

$$L_{CIoU} = 1 - \mathrm{IoU}(B, B^*) + \frac{\rho^2(c, c^*)}{d^2} + \alpha v, \tag{9}$$

where $\rho(\cdot)$ is the Euclidean distance between the box centers, d is the diagonal length of the smallest enclosing box of B and B^*, v measures the aspect-ratio consistency, which is defined as $v = \frac{4}{\pi^2}\left(\arctan\frac{w^*}{h^*} - \arctan\frac{w}{h}\right)^2$, and $\alpha = \frac{v}{(1-\mathrm{IoU})+v}$ is a balancing factor.

To enable the network to predict the full oriented geometry of each PCB component, we extend the YOLOv11 regression head to output four corner-vertex offsets in addition to the axis-aligned bounding box. For each detected instance with predicted box

$$\hat{b} = (\hat{c}_x, \hat{c}_y, \hat{w}, \hat{h}), \tag{10}$$

where $\hat{c}_x$ and $\hat{c}_y$ denote the center coordinates of the bounding box, and $\hat{w}$ and $\hat{h}$ denote its width and height, the network predicts four 2D offset vectors $\Delta\hat{v}_k$, each representing the displacement from the predicted center $(\hat{c}_x, \hat{c}_y)$ to one of the true corner vertices of the component. The absolute vertex coordinates are reconstructed as follows:

$$\hat{V}_k = (\hat{c}_x, \hat{c}_y) + \Delta\hat{v}_k, \quad k = 1, 2, 3, 4. \tag{11}$$

During training, each predicted offset is directly supervised using the ground-truth annotated vertex positions V_k^*:

$$L_{vertex} = \frac{1}{4}\sum_{k=1}^{4}\|\Delta\hat{v}_k - (V_k^* - C^*)\|_1, \tag{12}$$

where C^* denotes the ground-truth component center. This loss forces the detector to learn the true oriented quadrilateral of each component, rather than only approximating it with an axis-aligned box. The vertex offsets will then be used to generate an initial, rotation-aware polygon that serves as the starting pose estimate for sub-pixel geometric fitting, which will be further discussed in Section 2.3.

For the classification branch, the prediction p for the ground-truth label $y \in \{0,1\}$ is optimized using Focal Loss, which mitigates the severe class imbalance typical in PCB datasets where some components (e.g., resistors) appear far more frequently than rare IC packages. The Focal Loss is defined as:

$$L_{cls} = -\alpha(1-p)^{\gamma} y \log(p) - \alpha p^{\gamma}(1-y)\log(1-p) \tag{13}$$

where γ is the focusing parameter that down-weights easy examples and enhances hard-sample learning, and α balances positive and negative sample contributions. In practice, $\gamma = 2$ and $\alpha = 0.25$ provide stable gradients for small and sparse components.

The total loss is defined as follows:

$$L_{total} = L_{CIoU} + \lambda_{vo} L_{vertex} + \lambda_{cls} L_{cls}, \tag{14}$$

where the balancing weights λ_{vo} and λ_{cls} are chosen to keep all three terms on comparable scales ($\lambda_{vo} = 0.5, \lambda_{cls} = 1$ in our implementation). Since the vertex-offsets provide only an initial pose estimate for Stage 2, this term is weighted moderately to avoid overwhelming the CIoU box regression.

2.3. *Fine Localization via Sub-Pixel Template Fitting*

After obtaining coarse component predictions from the enhanced YOLOv11 detector, the final high-precision localization is performed through a constrained sub-pixel refinement process. For each detected device, the predicted bounding box serves as a Region of Interest (ROI), which restricts computation to a small, high-confidence spatial window.

To obtain a clean sub-pixel contour $P = \{p_i^*\}$ within the ROI, we first compute image gradients of the smoothed ROI $\tilde{I}$ using Sobel operators:

$$G_x = \tilde{I} * S_x, \quad G_y = \tilde{I} * S_y, \quad G = \sqrt{G_x^2 + G_y^2}. \tag{15}$$

Adaptive Canny thresholds are set from gradient quantiles:

$$T_{\text{high}} = q_{0.95}(G), \quad T_{\text{high}} = 0.5 q_{0.95}(G) \tag{16}$$

followed by non-maximum suppression to obtain a thin edge set E. For each edge pixel $p_0 = (x_0, y_0) \in E$, we compute the unit normal:

$$\boldsymbol{n}(p_0) = \frac{G_x, G_y}{G}, \tag{17}$$

and sample the intensity profile orthogonal to the edge:

$$f(t) = \tilde{I}(p_0 + t\boldsymbol{n}(p_0)), t \in \{-1, 0, 1\}. \tag{18}$$

Fitting a quadratic $f(t) = at^2 + bt + c$ yields the closed-form sub-pixel displacement

$$\delta = -\frac{b}{2a} = \frac{f(-1) - f(1)}{2(f(-1) - 2f(0) + f(1))}. \tag{19}$$

The refined sub-pixel edge point is:

$$p^* = p_0 + \delta \boldsymbol{n}(p_0). \tag{20}$$

Collecting all refined points gives the final contour $P = \{p_i^*\}$, which will be used in the least-squares fitting of Equation (22) to produce the final pose θ^*.

In the refinement stage, each PCB component is represented by a geometric template, defined as a small set of canonical vertices or boundary curves that describe the ideal shape of the component in a normalized coordinate frame. For rectangular ICs, the template consists of four corner points $\{T_k\}_{k=1}^4$; for connectors or specialized packages, additional structural points (e.g., pin-array reference vertices) may be included. The template does not encode absolute position or size; instead, it serves as a parametric shape that can be transformed by translation, rotation, and scale parameters $\theta = (t, \alpha, s)$ to match the observed component in the image.

Before template optimization begins, the four corner vertices predicted by the enhanced YOLOv11 detector, which are given in Equation (11), are used to generate an initial, rotation-aware pose estimate. An initial similarity transform $\theta_0 = (t_0, \alpha_0, s_0)$ is obtained from:

$$\theta_0 = \arg\min_{\theta} \sum_{k=1}^{4} \left\| \hat{V}_k - (sR(\alpha)T_k + t) \right\|^2. \tag{21}$$

This produces a coarse oriented template $T(\theta_0)$ that already aligns closely with the actual component. Since the predicted vertices encode its approximate rotation and geometry, the initialization lies within a few pixels of the true contour.

The refined pose is then solved using the sub-pixel contour $P = \{p_i^*\}$:

$$\theta^* = \arg\min_{\theta} \sum_{i=1}^{N} \| p_i - q_i(\theta) \|^2, \tag{22}$$

where $q_i(\theta)$ is the closest point on the transformed template boundary. With θ_0 as initialization, Gauss–Newton refinement converges rapidly to the final sub-pixel-accurate pose θ^*. This optimization yields refined estimates of the center, orientation angle, bounding contour, and, when applicable, the precise coordinates of key structural vertices or pin tips. Even when one or more structural vertices are not visible in the image, once the transformation is optimized using the available contour points, all template vertices—including those occluded or partially missing—can be mapped back into the image via the optimized transformation.

3. Results

3.1. Dataset and Experimental Setup

Experiments were conducted on the dedicated PCB-component dataset constructed in this study. The approximately 150,000 annotated component instances span 20 device categories, exhibiting a naturally imbalanced but realistic distribution consistent with industrial PCB manufacturing. Small passive components (e.g., 0201/0402 resistors and capacitors) dominate the dataset with approximately 65,000–75,000 instances due to their high density on most boards. Mid-sized components such as inductors, crystal oscillators, and compact connectors contribute 35,000–45,000 instances, while larger components—including QFP-

and BGA-packaged ICs—account for 20,000–30,000 instances. Additionally, 30,000 instances include manually annotated corner-pin vertex coordinates to support the proposed vertex-offset regression branch.

Unlike images captured in clean laboratory conditions, the PCBs in our collection were primarily sourced from industrial recycle stations, encompassing a wide spectrum of real-world degradation patterns. These boards include discarded industrial control modules, communication interface boards, power-control PCBs, and various embedded processing units. Due to prolonged use and uncontrolled storage, many boards exhibit mechanical warping, surface contamination, oxidation, scratches, and partial component damage. This diversity in board condition, combined with varied component densities and irregular backgrounds, provides a challenging testbed that better reflects realistic industrial inspection scenarios.

The dataset was divided into 80%/10%/10% for training, validation, and testing. To avoid any form of data leakage, the dataset is partitioned in a strictly board-wise manner: each physical PCB appears in only one of the train, validation, or test splits, ensuring that no image or crop from the same board is shared across subsets.

The YOLOv11-based detector is trained using the AdamW optimizer with an initial learning rate of 1×10^{-3}, weight decay of 5×10^{-2}, and momentum parameters $\beta_1 = 0.9$, $\beta_2 = 0.999$. A cosine-annealing learning-rate schedule with a 5-epoch warm-up is applied over 300 epochs. Input images are resized to 1280×1280 while preserving aspect ratio, followed by random cropping and multi-scale augmentation in the range [0.8, 1.2]. Non-maximum suppression (NMS) uses an IoU threshold of 0.65 and a confidence threshold of 0.25; during inference, class-agnostic NMS is applied unless otherwise noted. Models are trained with a batch size of 16 on a NVIDIA RTX 4090 GPU.

3.2. Detection Performance

To evaluate the effectiveness of the proposed two-stage framework, we first analyze the detection accuracy obtained from the enhanced YOLOv11-based Stage 1 detector. Table 1 compares the baseline YOLOv11 model with several architectural variants, including attention-augmented backbones (SE, CBAM), BiFPN-based feature aggregation, and our full design incorporating a tiny-object detection branch and vertex-offset regression.

Table 1. Overall detection accuracy (mAP@0.5 and mAP@0.5:0.95) for baseline YOLOv11, ablation variants, and the proposed models.

Model Variant	Backbone/Attention	Neck	mAP@0.5/mAP@0.5:0.95
YOLOv11 (baseline)	CSPDarknet	PAN	97.2/93.5
YOLOv11 + SE	CSPDarknet + SE	PAN	97.8/94.4
YOLOv11 + CBAM	CSPDarknet + CBAM	PAN	98.5/95.2
YOLOv11 + BiFPN	CSPDarknet	BiFPN	98.6/95.6
YOLOv11 + CBAM + BiFPN	CSPDarknet + CBAM	BiFPN	99.0/96.4
Full Proposed Model	CSPDarknet + CBAM	Enhanced BiFPN (tiny-object branch)	**99.6/97.8**

The results show that both attention mechanisms (SE, CBAM) and feature aggregation improvements (BiFPN) individually contribute to higher detection accuracy. Combining CBAM with BiFPN yields a significant gain, indicating that attention-guided feature refinement and multi-scale fusion are complementary. Furthermore, the tiny-object branch provides a clear additional boost, particularly for fine-grained passive components (0201/0402 resistors and capacitors), ultimately allowing the full model to achieve 99.6% mAP@0.5 and 97.8% mAP@0.5:0.95.

To further analyze performance at different spatial scales, Table 2 reports AP@0.5 for small, medium, and large components. Small-object detection is critical for PCB inspection due to the prevalence of tiny passives and densely packed layouts.

Table 2. Detection accuracy (AP@0.5) for small, medium, and large PCB components (COCO scale definitions).

Model Variant	Small (S)	Medium (M)	Large (L)
YOLOv11 (baseline)	79.5	95.9	98.0
YOLOv11 + SE	82.7	96.8	98.3
YOLOv11 + CBAM	86.9	97.4	98.5
YOLOv11 + BiFPN	88.1	97.2	98.4
YOLOv11 + CBAM + BiFPN	90.4	97.8	98.7
Full Proposed Model	**93.5**	**98.4**	**99.0**

The proposed detector achieves the highest scores across all scales, with a notable +14% improvement over the baseline for small components. This verifies that the tiny-object branch successfully enhances high-resolution feature representation and that CBAM–BiFPN coupling strengthens multi-scale feature extraction. Medium and large objects are already near saturation in baseline YOLOv11, but the proposed model offers consistent improvements.

As shown in Figure 3, visual comparisons further reveal that the baseline YOLOv11 suffers from frequent missed detections for 0201/0402 resistors and small passive components, whereas the optimized network preserves their spatial details and confidently distinguishes them from visually similar background textures.

(a) (b)

Figure 3. Detection performance comparison between the baseline YOLOv11 and the proposed method. (**a**) Baseline YOLOv11 result, exhibiting two missed chips and one false detection. (**b**) The proposed framework, successfully detecting all key chips with no erroneous predictions.

3.3. Localization Accuracy

The proposed two-stage coarse-to-fine framework was evaluated on pin-level localization accuracy. Using the deep-learning output as the initial ROI, the final localization coordinates are yielded through the sub-pixel edge extraction and the following template-based least-squares geometric optimization. Figure 4 shows the result of localization.

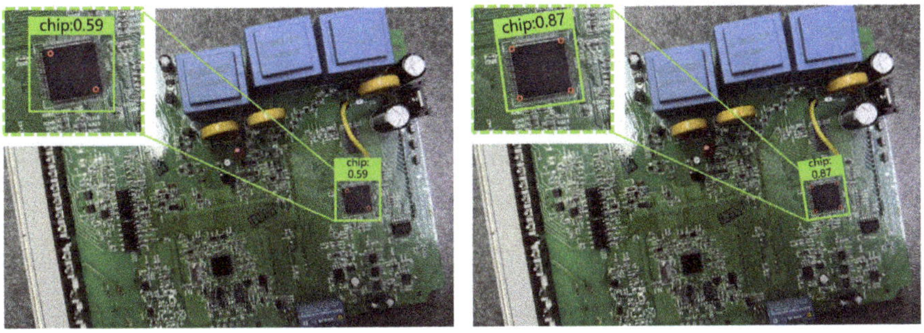

(a) (b)

Figure 4. Localization comparison between the original YOLOv11 and the proposed framework. (**a**) Original YOLOv11, which predicts only two diagonal vertices with significant localization error. (**b**) The proposed framework, accurately predicting all four vertices of each chip, demonstrating superior localization precision over tradition methods especially when the objects are rotated.

The four configurations in Table 3 are constructed by toggling the two key components of the localization pipeline: (i) **Vertex-Offset Initialization**, which uses the predicted vertex offsets from Stage 1 to estimate an initial transformation θ_0 via Equation (21), and (ii) **Sub-pixel Refinement**, which performs least-squares template fitting using sub-pixel contour points via Equation (22).

Table 3. Ablation study on Vertex-Offset Initialization and Sub-pixel Refinement. Columns report: (1) mean center-point localization error (mm); (2) maximum vertex error across the four template corners (mm); (3) mean time needed to produce vertex coordinates (ms); and (4) failure rate, defined as the percentage of ROIs where the optimizer diverged or converged to a high-residual local minimum.

Configuration	Mean Center Error (mm)	Max Vertex Error (mm)	Mean Time (ms)	Failure Rate (%)
(a) Neither	0.135	0.312	**0.0**	21.5
(b) Vertex-Offset Initialize only	0.090	0.185	0.24	6.2
(c) Sub-pixel Refinement only	0.042	0.120	3.1	11.0
(d) Full pipeline	0.028	0.045	2.24	0.9

The Configuration (a) reflects the raw output of Stage 1 without any geometric post-processing. Because no template-based correction is applied, this configuration inherits all prediction errors from the detector and cannot recover missing or misaligned keypoints. This leads to the highest center and vertex errors, as well as a relatively high failure rate, demonstrating that direct regression alone is insufficient for reliable keypoint localization on complex PCB layouts.

Configuration (b) leverages the predicted vertex offsets to solve Equation (21) and estimate an oriented quadrilateral that better aligns with the underlying component. This reduces both center and vertex errors compared to the Configuration (a). However, without refinement, this configuration still relies on the quality of Stage 1 predictions: if the detector misses a keypoint or produces a biased offset, the resulting θ_0 cannot correct it. This explains the moderate remaining errors and the observable failure cases.

In contrast, Configuration (c) improves accuracy dramatically because the refinement stage incorporates dense sub-pixel boundary points capable of reconstructing missing or noisy keypoints. However, poor initialization often places the optimizer outside the attraction basin of the true minimum, especially for rotated components or components with strong background clutter. This leads to longer convergence times, more local-minima traps, and a noticeably higher failure rate than in the full pipeline.

The full pipeline (d) yields the best performance across all metrics. Vertex-Offset Initialization provides a rotation-aware initialization that positions the template close to the true solution, while Sub-pixel Refinement delivers the fine-grained geometric correction necessary for sub-pixel accuracy. As a result, the optimizer converges faster, avoids poor basins of attraction, and achieves the lowest failure rate. The synergy between these two stages also leads to the smallest errors in both center and vertex localization, confirming that neither module alone is sufficient to achieve the desired level of precision.

4. Discussion

The experimental results confirm that the proposed coarse-to-fine framework effectively addresses the long-standing challenges of PCB component detection under strong background interference. The CBAM-enhanced backbone and BiFPN fusion significantly improve small-object discrimination by jointly suppressing the noise induced by silkscreen and trace, and by preserving multi-scale structural cues. This aligns with prior findings in attention-based object detection, yet the present study demonstrates that such mechanisms are particularly impactful in PCB imagery, where background textures often exceed components in visual saliency.

A key contribution of this work is the introduction of vertex-offset regression, which provides a compact pose-aware representation that bridges the gap between conventional bounding-box detectors and the precise rotational and structural requirements of automated PCB disassembly. Unlike prior approaches that output only axis-aligned or rotated boxes, the proposed vertex-supervised regression allows the detector to infer corner geometry and orientation cues, yielding a substantially improved initialization for the subsequent refinement stage. Importantly, the refinement module does not rely on the correctness or completeness of every predicted or annotated vertex. Because the template-fitting stage optimizes a global similarity transformation, all structural vertices—including those missing, severely occluded, or imperfectly annotated—are mapped back into the image once the optimal transformation is obtained. This ensures that the method remains robust even when certain vertices are not visible or when manual ground-truth labeling is noisy or inconsistent. The sub-pixel geometric fitting therefore demonstrates the complementary strengths of learning-based prediction and model-based optimization: the former supplies reliable coarse localization under challenging visual conditions, while the latter enforces global geometric coherence and delivers the fine-grained accuracy required for high-precision industrial manipulation.

Despite these advantages, several limitations must be acknowledged. The refinement stage depends on predefined template geometry and may struggle with unknown or highly irregular components. Localization may degrade under heavy occlusion or contamination, and the current pipeline assumes planar PCB surfaces without accounting for board warp or 3D variation. These limitations suggest promising avenues for future research, including learning-based sub-pixel regressors to replace template matching, multi-view or depth-assisted modeling to handle nonplanarity, meta-learning for rapid adaptation to unseen component types, and deeper integration with robotic execution for fully autonomous disassembly.

5. Conclusions

This work presents a high-precision PCB component recognition and localization framework that combines an optimized YOLOv11 detector with a sub-pixel geometric refinement stage. By integrating CBAM attention, multi-scale BiFPN fusion, and vertex-offset regression, the method effectively suppresses PCB background interference and captures component pose with high fidelity. Experiments demonstrate substantial gains in small-object detection and reliable sub-pixel localization accuracy, meeting the stringent requirements of industrial automated disassembly. The proposed approach offers a practical and efficient solution for precision PCB perception and provides a solid foundation for future extensions towards more general, adaptive, and fully autonomous industrial vision systems.

Author Contributions: Conceptualization, L.W.; methodology, L.W. and A.W.; software, L.O. and X.C.; validation, X.C.; formal analysis, L.O. and A.W.; investigation, H.W. and X.C.; writing—original draft, L.W.; writing—review and editing, K.Z.; visualization, H.W.; supervision, A.W.; project administration, K.Z.; funding acquisition, K.Z. All authors have read and agreed to the published version of the manuscript.

Funding: This paper was funded by the State Grid Zhejiang Electric Power Science and Technology Project (5211WF250006) Research on Key Component Reverse Disassembly Technology of Scrap Electric Energy Meter Circuit Boards Based on Embodied Intelligence.

Data Availability Statement: The original contributions presented in this study are included in the article. Further inquiries can be directed to the corresponding authors.

Conflicts of Interest: Authors Li Wang, Liu Ouyang, Huiying Weng, Xiang Chen, and Anna Wang were employed by State Grid Zhejiang Electric Power Co., Ltd. The remaining author declares that the research was conducted in the absence of any commercial or financial relationships that could be construed as potential conflicts of interest.

Abbreviations

The following abbreviations are used in this manuscript:

PCB	Printed Circuit Board
YOLO	You Only Look Once
CBAM	Convolutional Block Attention Module
FPN	Feature Pyramid Network
BiFPN	Bi-Directional Feature Pyramid Network
IC	Integrated Circuit
R-CNN	Region-based Convolutional Neural Network
SSD	Single-Shot MultiBox Detector
DETR	Detection Transformer
SE	Squeeze-and-Excitation Networks
ViT	Vision Transformer
HRNet	High-Resolution Net
AOI	Automated Optical Inspection
SUSAN	Smallest Univalue Segment Assimilating Nucleus
QFP	Quad Flat Package
BGA	Ball Grid Array
CAM	Channel Attention Module
SAM	Spatial Attention Module
MLP	Multi-Layer Perceptron
IoU	Intersection over Union
SMD	Surface-Mount Device
ROI	Region of Interest

NMS Non-Maximum Suppression

References

1. Ren, S.; He, K.; Girshick, R.; Sun, J. Faster R-CNN: Towards Real-Time Object Detection with Region Proposal Networks. *arXiv* **2016**, arXiv:1506.01497. [CrossRef] [PubMed]
2. Redmon, J.; Divvala, S.; Girshick, R.; Farhadi, A. You Only Look Once: Unified, Real-Time Object Detection. *arXiv* **2016**, arXiv:1506.02640. [CrossRef]
3. Liu, W.; Anguelov, D.; Erhan, D.; Szegedy, C.; Reed, S.; Fu, C.Y.; Berg, A.C., SSD: Single Shot MultiBox Detector. In *Computer Vision–ECCV 2016*; Springer International Publishing: Cham, Switherland, 2016; pp. 21–37. [CrossRef]
4. Lin, T.Y.; Goyal, P.; Girshick, R.; He, K.; Dollar, P. Focal Loss for Dense Object Detection. In Proceedings of the IEEE International Conference on Computer Vision (ICCV), Venice, Italy, 22–29 October 2017.
5. Lin, T.Y.; Dollar, P.; Girshick, R.; He, K.; Hariharan, B.; Belongie, S. Feature Pyramid Networks for Object Detection. In Proceedings of the IEEE Conference on Computer Vision and Pattern Recognition (CVPR), Honolulu, HI, USA, 21–26 July 2017.
6. Tan, M.; Pang, R.; Le, Q.V. EfficientDet: Scalable and Efficient Object Detection. In Proceedings of the 2020 IEEE/CVF Conference on Computer Vision and Pattern Recognition (CVPR), Seattle, WA, USA, 13–19 June 2020; pp. 10778–10787. [CrossRef]
7. Carion, N.; Massa, F.; Synnaeve, G.; Usunier, N.; Kirillov, A.; Zagoruyko, S. End-to-End Object Detection with Transformers. *arXiv* **2020**, arXiv:2005.12872.
8. Bochkovskiy, A.; Wang, C.Y.; Liao, H.Y.M. YOLOv4: Optimal Speed and Accuracy of Object Detection. *arXiv* **2020**, arXiv:2004.10934. [CrossRef]
9. Wang, C.Y.; Bochkovskiy, A.; Liao, H.Y.M. Scaled-YOLOv4: Scaling Cross Stage Partial Network. *arXiv* **2021**, arXiv:2011.08036. [CrossRef]
10. Hu, J.; Shen, L.; Sun, G. Squeeze-and-Excitation Networks. In Proceedings of the IEEE Conference on Computer Vision and Pattern Recognition (CVPR), Salt Lake City, UT, USA, 18–23 June 2018.
11. Woo, S.; Park, J.; Lee, J.Y.; Kweon, I.S. CBAM: Convolutional Block Attention Module. *arXiv* **2018**, arXiv:1807.06521. [CrossRef]
12. Dosovitskiy, A.; Beyer, L.; Kolesnikov, A.; Weissenborn, D.; Zhai, X.; Unterthiner, T.; Dehghani, M.; Minderer, M.; Heigold, G.; Gelly, S.; et al. An Image is Worth 16x16 Words: Transformers for Image Recognition at Scale. *arXiv* **2021**, arXiv:2010.11929. [CrossRef]
13. Bello, I.; Zoph, B.; Vaswani, A.; Shlens, J.; Le, Q.V. Attention Augmented Convolutional Networks. *arXiv* **2020**, arXiv:1904.09925. [CrossRef]
14. Law, H.; Deng, J. CornerNet: Detecting Objects as Paired Keypoints. *arXiv* **2019**, arXiv:1808.01244. [CrossRef]
15. Zhou, X.; Wang, D.; Krähenbühl, P. Objects as Points. *arXiv* **2019**, arXiv:1904.07850. [PubMed]
16. Sun, K.; Xiao, B.; Liu, D.; Wang, J. Deep High-Resolution Representation Learning for Human Pose Estimation. *arXiv* **2019**, arXiv:1902.09212. [CrossRef]
17. Newell, A.; Yang, K.; Deng, J. Stacked Hourglass Networks for Human Pose Estimation. *arXiv* **2016**, arXiv:1603.06937. [CrossRef]
18. Huang, W.; Wei, P. A PCB Dataset for Defects Detection and Classification. *arXiv* **2019**, arXiv:1901.08204. [CrossRef]
19. Park, J.K.; Kwon, B.K.; Park, J.H.; Kang, D.J. Machine Learning-Based Imaging System for Surface Defect Inspection. *Int. J. Precis. Eng. Manuf.-Green Technol.* **2016**, *3*, 303–310. [CrossRef]
20. Tang, J.; Liu, S.; Zhao, D.; Tang, L.; Zou, W.; Zheng, B. PCB-YOLO: An Improved Detection Algorithm of PCB Surface Defects Based on YOLOv5. *Sustainability* **2023**, *15*, 5963. [CrossRef]
21. Luo, S.; Wan, F.; Lei, G.; Xu, L.; Ye, Z.; Liu, W.; Zhou, W.; Xu, C. EC-YOLO: Improved YOLOv7 Model for PCB Electronic Component Detection. *Sensors* **2024**, *24*, 4363. [CrossRef] [PubMed]
22. Smith, S.M.; Brady, J.M. SUSAN—A New Approach to Low Level Image Processing. *Int. J. Comput. Vis.* **1997**, *23*, 45–78. [CrossRef]
23. Canny, J. A Computational Approach to Edge Detection. *IEEE Trans. Pattern Anal. Mach. Intell.* **1986**, *PAMI-8*, 679–698. [CrossRef]
24. Baker, S.; Matthews, I. Lucas–Kanade 20 Years On: A Unifying Framework. *Int. J. Comput. Vis.* **2004**, *56*, 221–255. [CrossRef]

mathematics

MDPI

Article

Research on Synchronous Transfer Control Technology for Distribution Network Load Based on Imprecise Probability

Hua Zhang [1,2], Cheng Long [1,2,*], Xueneng Su [1], Yiwen Gao [1] and Wei Luo [3]

1 State Grid Sichuan Electric Power Research Institute, Chengdu 610041, China; zhanghua0002@163.com (H.Z.); 13520761965@163.com (X.S.); scugyw89@163.com (Y.G.)
2 Power System Security and Operation Key Laboratory of Sichuan, Chengdu 610041, China
3 College of Electrical Engineering, Sichuan University, Chengdu 610065, China; luowei@scu.edu.cn
* Correspondence: 17828186876@163.com; Tel.: +86-13540888120

Abstract

As the penetration rate of distributed power sources increases and distribution network structures grow increasingly complex, the uncertainty in switch action control during load transfer has become a critical issue affecting grid safety and reliability. Traditional control methods based on precise probability-based predictive control are susceptible to bias introduced by prior settings under small-sample conditions, making it difficult to meet the stringent requirements of time-synchronized control. To address this, this study proposes an imprecise probability-based synchronous load transfer control method for distribution networks. By integrating the Imprecise Dirichlet model (IDM) with a Naive Credal Classifier (NCC), it constructs an interval predictive control model for switching action timing. This approach effectively mitigates the prior dependency issue and enhances estimation robustness under small-sample conditions. Combined with a dynamic delay strategy, this approach strictly controls the interval between disconnection and reconnection actions within 20 ms, preventing circulating current risks and ensuring transfer reliability. The simulation and experimental results demonstrate that the proposed method outperforms traditional Bayesian classifiers in both time prediction control accuracy and model robustness, providing a theoretical foundation and a reference for engineering applications for secure action control in distribution networks.

Keywords: distribution network; load transfer control; imprecise probability; Naive Credal Classifier; time control; switch control action time

MSC: 93C95

1. Introduction

The increasing penetration of distributed generation (DG) in distribution networks enhances flexibility while introducing uncertainty into system action control. Among these factors, the unpredictability of switching action timing during load transfer has become a critical determinant of grid security and supply reliability. Traditional control methods predominantly rely on precise probabilistic models (e.g., Bayesian classifiers) for timing prediction. However, under conditions of limited samples or insufficient prior information, such approaches are susceptible to subjective bias and struggle to meet stringent requirements for "open-then-close" sequencing and millisecond-level time synchronization control.

Imprecise probability theory characterizes uncertainty through interval probabilities, making it particularly suitable for inference scenarios with small samples or incomplete information [1]. In recent years, it has demonstrated significant advantages in fields such as reliability assessment and fault diagnosis. Against this backdrop, this paper proposes an imprecise probability-based load transfer control method for distribution networks. It integrates the Imprecise Dirichlet Model (IDM) with the Naive Credal Classifier (NCC) [2] to construct an interval prediction model for switch action times. This approach mitigates over-reliance on prior information [3] and enhances estimation robustness under small-sample conditions [4].

This paper aims to systematically address the issue of insufficient time synchronization accuracy during load transfer control. By establishing a prediction model that better aligns with real-world uncertainties and incorporating a dynamic delay strategy, it achieves strict control of the switching time difference within 20 ms. This approach prevents circulating current risks and ensures transfer reliability. This research not only provides new theoretical support and a methodological framework for the safe action of distribution networks but also offers valuable insights for grid control under high penetration of renewable energy sources.

2. Literature Review

2.1. Research Status

With the advancement of new power system construction, the widespread integration of distributed generation (DG), energy storage devices, and flexible loads in distribution grids has made grid operation increasingly complex and dynamic. Traditional deterministic control methods struggle to address load synchronization and transfer issues under high uncertainty and small-sample scenarios. Against this backdrop, imprecise probability (IP) has gained increasing attention in both academic and engineering circles as a modeling tool capable of effectively capturing cognitive uncertainty and data scarcity.

Current research on load transfer control in distribution networks primarily focuses on optimization scheduling, intelligent algorithms, and reliability analysis. Traditional methods, such as control strategies based on Bayesian networks, Markov decision processes, or reinforcement learning, have enhanced system intelligence to some extent. However, under conditions of small sample sizes and high uncertainty, these approaches often suffer from issues like model overfitting and strong prior dependency.

To address these challenges, researchers have increasingly incorporated imprecise probability theory in recent years. Walley [5] systematically proposed a mathematical framework for imprecise probability, expressing uncertainty through upper and lower probability intervals to avoid the excessive reliance on a single prior characteristic of traditional probability models. Bernard [6] further introduced the Imprecise Dirichlet Model (IDM) to estimate probability intervals for multinomial distributions under small-sample conditions, significantly enhancing model robustness.

In classification and decision control, Zaffalon [7] introduced the Naive Credal Classifier (NCC), which employs credal sets to enable multi-class outputs for uncertain samples, effectively reducing misclassification risks. Corani & Zaffalon [8] validated NCC's superiority in small-sample classification within medical diagnostics, providing theoretical support for its application in power systems.

Regarding model architecture, Cozman [9] introduced Credal Networks, extending Bayesian networks into the domain of imprecise probability. This allows network nodes to represent probability intervals, making them suitable for inference and decision-making in highly uncertain environments. Masegosa & Moral [10] further explored integrating IDM with Credal Networks to learn uncertain probability models from small-sample data, offering novel insights for modeling distribution network control systems.

Although these studies are theoretically mature, their application in load synchronization transfer control for distribution networks remains nascent. Existing research primarily focuses on state estimation, fault diagnosis, or reliability analysis, while studies addressing load transfer path optimization and synchronous control strategy modeling under small-sample conditions remain relatively scarce. Therefore, exploring load synchronous transfer control methods based on imprecise probability not only represents theoretical innovation but also holds promising engineering application prospects.

2.2. Literature Summary

In summary, non-exact probability theory offers a novel research paradigm for load synchronization transfer control in distribution networks under conditions of small sample sizes and high uncertainty. This is achieved through methods such as upper and lower probability intervals, belief sets, and multi-prior fusion. IDM delivers robust probability estimates even under data scarcity, NCC significantly reduces misjudgment risks through multi-class outputs, while Credibility Networks extend traditional Bayesian topology to interval reasoning, endowing models with enhanced generalization capabilities and resilience. Looking ahead, as distributed generation penetration continues to rise, uncertainties across regions and timescales will intensify. Strategies based on imprecise probability—including online learning, rolling optimization, and multi-source information fusion—will become critical enablers for enhancing the resilience of distribution network control. These approaches hold significant theoretical value and wide-ranging engineering prospects for building secure, reliable, and intelligent new power systems.

3. Foundations of Imprecise Probability Theory Control

Based on the imprecise probability theory and its application advantages, this study uses the imprecise Dirichlet model (IDM) with the Naive Credal Classifier (NCC).

3.1. Imprecise Dirichlet Model

The Imprecise Dirichlet Model (IDM) is an advanced Bayesian statistical approach for handling uncertainty, serving as an extension of the Dirichlet distribution for estimating probability distributions under conditions of insufficient information. Consider a multinomial distribution with N possible outcomes, whose Dirichlet prior probability density function (PDF) [11], as shown in Equation (1).

$$f(\boldsymbol{\theta}) = \Gamma\left(\sum_{n=1}^{N} \alpha_n\right)\left[\prod_{n=1}^{N}(\alpha_n)\right]^{-1}\prod_{n=1}^{N}\theta_n^{\alpha_n - 1} \tag{1}$$

In the formula, $\theta = (\theta_1, \theta_2, \ldots, \theta_N)$ represents the probability of the result occurring, so that $0 \leq \theta_n \leq 1$ (n = 1, 2, ..., N) and $\sum_{n=1}^{N}\theta_n = 1$, $\alpha_1, \alpha_2, \ldots, \alpha_N$ represent the positive parameter of the Dirichlet distribution, and $\Gamma(\cdot)$ represents the gamma function, which is often used in statistics to represent the probability distribution of random variables.

When the sample observations M are acquired, the original prior Dirichlet probability density function is updated by Bayes' theorem, and then the posterior Dirichlet probability density function is generated, which reflects the re-evaluation of the parameters by synthesizing the actual observations [12], and the posterior probability density function is shown in Equation (2).

$$f(\boldsymbol{\theta}|\boldsymbol{M}) = \Gamma\left(\sum_{n=1}^{N}(m_n + \alpha_n)\right) \cdot \left[\prod_{n=1}^{N}\Gamma(m_n + \alpha_n)\right]^{-1} \cdot \prod_{n=1}^{N}\theta_n^{m_n + \alpha_n - 1} \tag{2}$$

In the formula, $\boldsymbol{M} = \{m_1, m_2, \ldots, m_n\}$ is a sample observation; m_n represents the number of occurrences of the random variable state n.

After obtaining the posterior probability density function, the parameter θ_n is estimated using the posterior distribution expected value [13], as defined in Equation (3).

$$\theta_n = E(\theta_n|M) = (m_n + \alpha_n) / \left(\sum_{n=1}^{N} (m_n + \alpha_n) \right) \tag{3}$$

When analyzing the estimated results of a deterministic Dirichlet model, if observations are lacking, the probability θ_n of the nth result is determined by the parameter α, i.e., $\theta_n = \alpha_n / \sum_{n=1}^{N} \alpha_n$, where the parameter α is called the prior weight of the result, often expressed as the parameter s, and is called the equivalent sample size in the Dirichlet distribution. In the probability estimation process, s represents the influence of prior distribution on posterior probability, that is, the larger the value of s, the more observed values are needed to adjust the parameters of prior distribution [14]. When there are fewer available observations, the deterministic Dirichlet model estimates are more affected by the prior distribution, and if the settings are not reasonable, then the estimation results based on the deterministic Dirichlet model may become inaccurate, which may affect the final decision and prediction.

literature [15], the authors, in order to overcome the shortcomings of deterministic Dirichlet models, IDM uses a series of Dirichlet prior distributions instead of a single Dirichlet distribution. In IDM, the prior probability density function is shown in Equation (4).

$$f(\boldsymbol{\theta}) = \Gamma(s) \left[\prod_{n=1}^{N} (s \cdot r_n) \right]^{-1} \prod_{n=1}^{N} \theta_n^{s \cdot r_n - 1}, \forall r_n \in [0,1], \sum_{n=1}^{N} r_n = 1 \tag{4}$$

In the formula, r_n (n = 1, 2, . . ., N) is the nth prior weight factor, and in Equation (4), $s{\cdot}r_n$ has the same effect as α_n. When r_n varies within the interval [0, 1], $f(\theta)$ will contain all possible prior PDFS for a given predetermined s, thus avoiding unreasonable effects of prior values.

Then, according to the updating process of Bayes' rule, a posterior PDF of the IDM relative to the observed value M can be calculated, as shown in Equation (5).

$$f(\boldsymbol{\theta}|\boldsymbol{M}) = \Gamma\left(s + \sum_{n=1}^{N} m_n \right) \cdot \left[\prod_{n=1}^{N} \Gamma(m_n + s \cdot r_n) \right]^{-1} \cdot \prod_{n=1}^{N} \theta_n^{m_n + s \cdot r_n - 1}, \forall r_n \in [0,1], \sum_{n=1}^{N} r_n = 1 \tag{5}$$

In the formula, $\sum_{n=1}^{N} m_n$ represents the total number of observations.

Thus, a parameter representing the interval valued probabilities of all outcomes in the IDM, $\widetilde{\theta}_1, \widetilde{\theta}_2, \ldots, \widetilde{\theta}_N$ can be estimated from the posterior PDF by calculating the expected value, according to Equation (6).

$$\widetilde{\theta}_n = \left[\underline{E}(\theta_n|M), \overline{E}(\theta_n|M) \right] = \left[\frac{m_n}{\sum\limits_{n=1}^{N} m_n + s}, \frac{m_n + s}{\sum\limits_{n=1}^{N} m_n + s} \right], n = 1, 2, \ldots, N \tag{6}$$

The bounds of expectation are calculated based on the bounds of r_n, i.e., 0 and 1. Thus, the imprecise probability of random variable state occurrence in a given case can be estimated based on small-sample data. The IDM statistical model eliminates the adverse effects of unreasonable prior Settings on event probability estimation in the absence of sample size.

3.2. Naive Credal Classifier

Naive Credal Classifier (NCC) is a classifier based on Naive Bayes (NB), which enhances the robustness of the model by introducing imprecise probabilities. The core idea of NCC is to provide more robust classification results by using a set of prior probabilities to model uncertainty in the face of incomplete or small-scale data sets, i.e., multiple possible categories can be returned in the face of uncertain instances. The Bayesian framework learns to update the prior with a profile representing the data evidence to calculate a posterior probability that can be used for decision-making [16]. Formally, a classifier is a function that maps instances of a set of variables (called attributes or features) to the state or class of a class variable.

The credal network utilizes Bayesian network theory for the state value X_c of x_c and then calculates the probability $P(x_c \mid \boldsymbol{x_E})$ [16] by looking at the specific values $\boldsymbol{x_E}$ present in the evidence variable $\boldsymbol{X}_E$, as shown in Equation (7).

$$P(x_c|\boldsymbol{x_E}) = \frac{P(x_c, \boldsymbol{x_E})}{P(\boldsymbol{x_E})} = \frac{\sum_{X_M} \prod_{i=1}^{I} P(x_i|\boldsymbol{\pi_i})}{\sum_{X_M, X_c} \prod_{i=1}^{I} P(x_i|\boldsymbol{\pi_i})} \tag{7}$$

In the formula, I is the number of multi-state random variables in the Bayesian network, $P(x_i \mid \pi_i)$ is the conditional probability quality function, x_i is the observation value of the ith random variable X_i, $X_i \in \boldsymbol{X}$, $\boldsymbol{X}$ represents all random variables in the network, πi is an observation value of Πi, which represents the state of the parent node of X_i, $\boldsymbol{X_M} = \boldsymbol{X} \backslash (\boldsymbol{X_E} \cup \boldsymbol{Xc})$; $\sum_{X_M}$ represents a full probability operation on different states of variables in the node variable set $\boldsymbol{X_M}$.

Bayes classifiers perform classification by comparing the calculated posterior probabilities, and the category with the largest posterior probability is the classification result. However, when there is not a sufficient number of samples, Bayesian classifiers may return biased prior-dependent classification results, i.e., depending on the different priors employed, it may identify different classes as the most likely. However, any single a priori choice carries a certain arbitrariness, and these classifications are highly uncertain [17]. The credal network classifier relaxes the classification results of Bayesian classifiers by accepting imprecise probabilistic representations [18]. In a Bayesian classifier, each category of a class variable has a single-valued probability. In contrast, in a credal network classifier, the occurrence probability of each class can be expressed as an interval valued probability, that is, an imprecise precision probability.

In the literature [18], the authors introduced Credal Set (CS) for credal networks in order to deal with the uncertainty of the node random variables. The credal set is used to describe the imprecise probabilistic properties of a node random variable, and mathematically, the credal set $K(X_i)$ is defined as a closed convex set that covers all possible probabilistic mass functions $P(X_i)$ of the random variable X_i. The credible set $K(x_i)$ is:

$$K(X_i) = \mathrm{CH}\left\{ \begin{array}{l} P(X_i) : x_i \in \Omega_{X_i} \\ P(x_i) \in [\underline{P}(x_i), \overline{P}(x_i)] \\ \sum_{\Omega_{X_i}} P(x_i) = 1 \end{array} \right\} \tag{8}$$

$K(X_i)$ represents the closed convex set consisting of all possible probability mass functions $P(X_i)$ of the random variable X_i, CH represents a convex hull, $\sum_{\Omega_{Xi}} P(X_i) = 1$ means that the sum of all possible probabilities must equal 1, and Ω_{Xi} is the range of values for X_i.

As shown in Equation (9), there may be many combinations of prior distribution and observed data, so the credal set contains an infinite number of probability mass functions, but it only contains a finite number of extreme mass functions, which are called the vertices of the credal set, denoted as $ext[K(X_i)]$. These extremal functions correspond to the vertices that make up the convex hull, and they can be obtained by combining the endpoints of the probability interval. The classification of a credal network classifier consists of calculating the upper and lower bounds of the conditional probability of $X_c = x_c$ given $\mathbf{X}_E = \mathbf{x}_E$, a goal that can be achieved by calculating the upper and lower bounds using Equations (9) and (10).

$$\overline{P}(X_c = x_c|\mathbf{X}_E = \mathbf{x}_E) = \max_{P(\mathbf{X}) \in ext[K(\mathbf{X})]} \frac{P(X_c = x_c, \mathbf{X}_E = \mathbf{x}_E)}{P(\mathbf{X}_E = \mathbf{x}_E)} \tag{9}$$

$$\underline{P}(X_c = x_c|\mathbf{X}_E = \mathbf{x}_E) = \min_{P(\mathbf{X}) \in ext[K(\mathbf{X})]} \frac{P(X_c = x_c, \mathbf{X}_E = \mathbf{x}_E)}{P(\mathbf{X}_E = \mathbf{x}_E)} \tag{10}$$

In the formula, $P(\mathbf{X})$ represents the joint probabilistic mass function of all random variables, $K(\mathbf{X})$ is the convex hull of a set of joint mass functions, i.e., the credal set, ext$[K(\mathbf{X})]$ represents the limiting joint mass function of $K(\mathbf{X})$, and $P(\mathbf{X}) \in$ ext$[K(\mathbf{X})]$, which means that $P(\mathbf{X})$ should be selected from ext$[K(\mathbf{X})]$.

In this paper, IDM is used to model the prior and then return the imprecise probabilities, which are integrated into the credal network classifier to achieve the organic combination of IDM and credal classifier.

3.3. *Naive Credal Classifier Classification Control Standards*

Bayesian classifiers determine sample categories based on the principle of maximizing posterior probability in probability theory. Utilizing Bayesian networks, the classifier calculates the probability of each category by applying Bayes' theorem given known input evidence x. It then compares these probabilities and selects the category with the highest posterior probability as its classification decision, as illustrated in Figure 1. In Figure 1, $P(C_1 | \mathbf{X})$, $P(C_2 | X)$ on the axis, …, $P(C_5 | X)$ is calculated by a Bayesian classifier and the classification result is C_1 because $P(C_1 | X)$ has the greatest posterior probability.

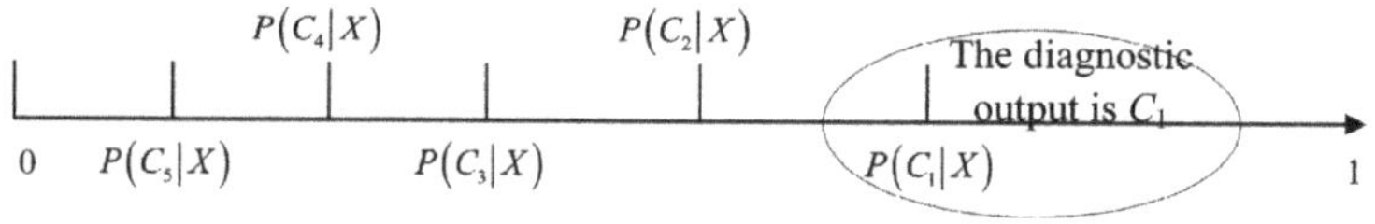

Figure 1. A simple diagram of the principle of Bayes classifier.

Figures 2 and 3 illustrate the diagnostic logic and output results of the credal network classifier. As shown in Figure 2, after computation, the Naive Credal Classifier category C_1 as having a lower bound of posterior imprecise probability higher than all other categories. Consequently, C_1 was designated as the sole diagnostic result under evidence condition X. However, in Figure 3, the lower limit of the posterior imprecision probability for C_1 is lower than the upper limit of the posterior imprecision probability for C_2, which indicates that the probability intervals of the two may overlap, as shown by the shaded area in the Figure 3. In this case, the Naive Credal Classifier cannot determine an exact classification result, but instead provides a set of possible categories $\{C_1, C_2\}$, indicating that the sample is likely to be classified as C_1 or C_2 based on the conditions of evidence.

As can be seen, compared to Bayesian classifiers, the credal network controller provides a larger probability margin when performing category diagnosis on samples. When samples are unique, the credal network controller can deliver higher judgment reliability [19]. When faced with overlapping regions of maximum a posteriori imprecise probability intervals, the credal network controller can generate sets encompassing multiple possible categories, effectively reducing the risk of misdiagnosis.

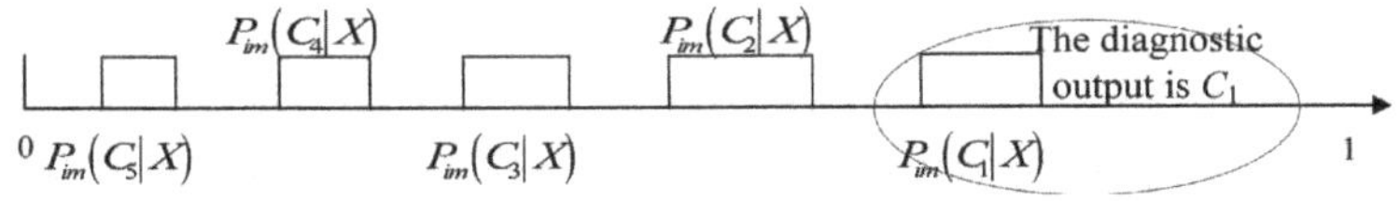

Figure 2. The credal network output is a unique class case.

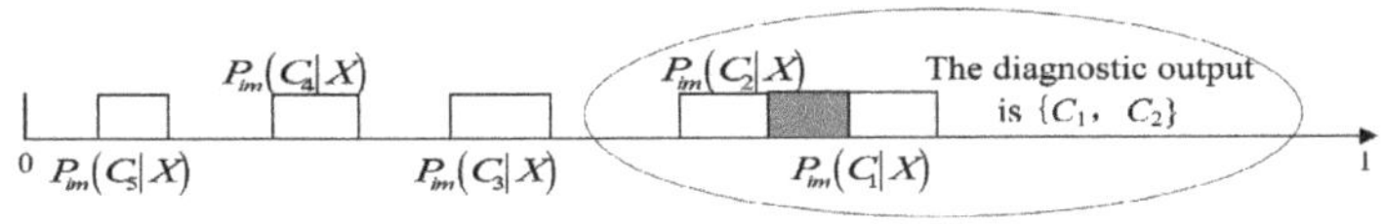

Figure 3. The credal network output is a similar class set case.

4. Construction of a Switching Control Action Time Prediction Model Based on IDM-NCC

4.1. Naive Credal Model for Switching Time Prediction in Distribution Networks

In power system, PCC (Point of Common Coupling) refers to the point where different power systems or power equipment are connected to the main power grid. In this paper, by monitoring the voltage and current at the PCC, the operation status of the distribution network can be monitored effectively. By monitoring the voltage and current at the PCC, the action status of the distribution network can be effectively monitored. Compared with other complex electrical parameters, the three-phase voltage and current are relatively easy to measure and obtain, and can also help to monitor the stability of the power system. And in the distribution network, the distribution network switch needs to coordinate its action time according to the peak voltage and current to ensure that the power can be quickly and accurately cut off in the event of failure, so they become the preferred features for the implementation of switching time prediction and analysis. In this paper, the three phase voltage and three phase current peak value at PCC are taken as nodal evidence variables of the credal network, and the credal network is constructed.

In this study, a typical double-feeder distribution network structure is used as the modeling basis, and its topology is shown in Figure 4. The network contains two feeders (AC, AD) and distributed PV access points, and the PCC (point of common coupling) is located at the key busbar as the key node for monitoring voltage and current. Combining the existing research and practical experience, a total of 12 types of typical operating states are set for distribution networks as single-phase short-circuit (AG, BG, CG), two-phase short-circuit (AB, AC, BC), two-phase short-circuit with ground (ABG, ACG, BCG), three-phase short-circuit (ABC), three-phase short-circuit with ground (ABCG), and non-fault (NF) states [20]. In this paper, the three-phase voltage and current peaks at the PCC are used as input features to the credal network classifier to construct an interval prediction model for switch action time.

The switching time state class and the set of operational state sign attributes of the distribution network are determined according to different operational states, as shown in Tables 1 and 2. In order to study the operating characteristics of the distribution network in depth, simulation is carried out for different operating conditions of the distribution network, and the three-phase voltages and three-phase currents at the PCC under each operating condition are collected, and in this way, a total of 310 operating conditions is obtained. A total of 248 working conditions (310 × 80% = 248) were randomly selected as the training set sample data, and another 62 working conditions (310 × 20% = 62) were selected as the test set sample data to construct the fault diagnosis model database. Using the imprecise probability estimation method, these sample data were analyzed to achieve the prediction of switching action time in distribution networks.

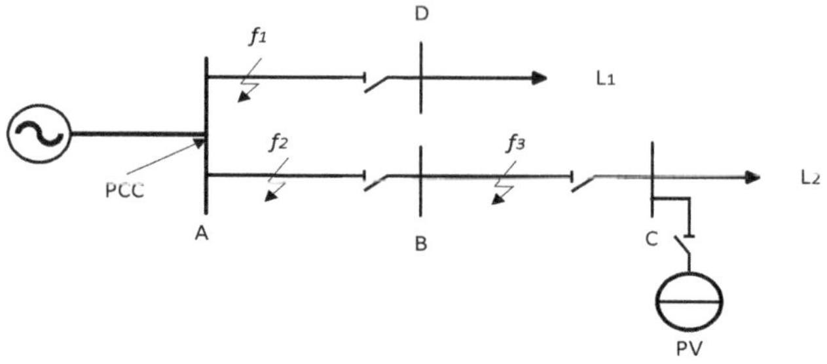

Figure 4. Structure of a double-feeder distribution network containing distributed power sources.

Table 1. Distribution network switching action time status class.

NO.	Type of Fault	Switch Control Action Time T/ms	NO.	Type of Fault	Switch Control Action Time T/ms
F_1	Trouble-free NF	$T < 5$	F_{18}	BC failure at position 2	$26 \leq T < 27$
F_2	AG failure at position 1	$5 \leq T < 10$	F_{19}	ABG failure at position 2	$27 \leq T < 28$
F_3	BG failure at position 1	$10 \leq T < 11$	F_{20}	ACG failure at position 2	$28 \leq T < 29$
F_4	CG failure at position 1	$11 \leq T < 12$	F_{21}	BCG failure at position 2	$29 \leq T < 30$
F_5	AB failure at position 1	$12 \leq T < 13$	F_{22}	ABC failure at position 2	$30 \leq T < 31$
F_6	AC failure at position 1	$13 \leq T < 14$	F_{23}	ABCG failure at position 2	$31 \leq T < 32$
F_7	BC failure at position 1	$14 \leq T < 15$	F_{24}	AG failure at position 3	$32 \leq T < 33$
F_8	ABG failure at position 1	$15 \leq T < 16$	F_{25}	BG failure at position 3	$33 \leq T < 34$
F_9	ACG failure at position 1	$16 \leq T < 17$	F_{26}	CG failure at position 3	$34 \leq T < 35$
F_{10}	BCG failure at position 1	$17 \leq T < 18$	F_{27}	AB failure at position 3	$35 \leq T < 36$
F_{11}	ABC failure at position 1	$18 \leq T < 19$	F_{28}	AC failure at position 3	$36 \leq T < 37$
F_{12}	ABCG failure at position 1	$20 \leq T < 21$	F_{29}	BC failure at position 3	$37 \leq T < 38$
F_{13}	AG failure at position 2	$21 \leq T < 22$	F_{30}	ABG failure at position 3	$38 \leq T < 39$
F_{14}	BG failure at position 2	$22 \leq T < 23$	F_{31}	ACG failure at position 3	$39 \leq T < 40$
F_{15}	CG failure at position 2	$23 \leq T < 24$	F_{32}	BCG failure at position 3	$40 \leq T < 50$
F_{16}	AB failure at position 2	$24 \leq T < 25$	F_{33}	ABC failure at position 3	$50 \leq T < 60$
F_{17}	AC failure at position 2	$25 \leq T < 26$	F_{34}	ABCG failure at position 3	$T \geq 60$

Table 2. Distribution network action state symptom attribute set.

Variables	Sign Type
E_1	Peak of phase A voltage
E_2	Peak of phase B voltage
E_3	Peak of phase C voltage
E_4	Peak of phase A current
E_5	Peak of phase B current
E_6	Peak of phase C current

4.2. IDM-Based Conditional Confidence Set Learning Algorithm

Using the theory and methodology of Bayesian networks, a credal network classifier model for estimating the timing of switching control actions in distribution networks is constructed by combining the conditions related to the temporal characteristics of switching actions in distribution networks, as demonstrated in Figure 5, which is capable of analyzing and predicting the temporal characteristics of switching actions in distribution networks.

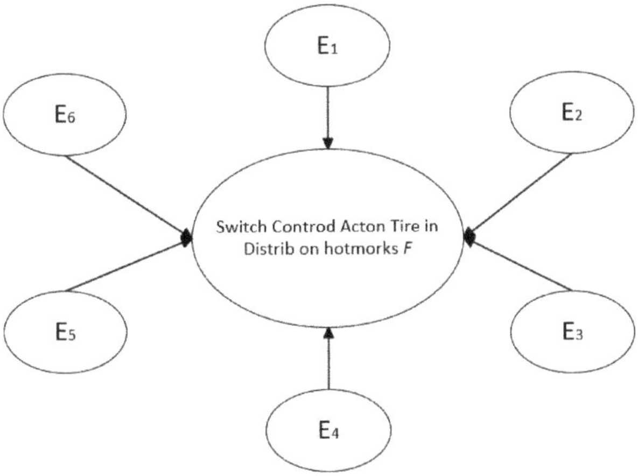

Figure 5. Distribution network switch action time prediction credal network splitter diagram.

In Figure 5, the parent node is the multi-state random variable of the switch action time of the distribution network, and $F_1 \sim F_{34}$ is set; The child nodes are the characteristic parameters E_1, E_2, E_3, E_4, E_5 and E_6 of the three-state random variables. For example, $E_{1,1}$, $E_{1,2}$, and $E_{1,3}$ are good, decent, and attention states of phase A current status, respectively. It can be seen that the model in this paper is a 2-layer credal network classifier, and the credal network classifier contains a parent node F, which is a multi-state query variable, that is, a 7-state random variable. The other 6 nodes are evidence variables representing the symptomatic attributes of the operating state of the distribution network.

The credal network structure needs to be calculated from the historical operation data to learn the conditional probability distribution of each variable E_i for a given switching time state F_j. In this paper, the IDM is used to complete this learning process for the prediction of distribution network switching control action time characteristics in the following steps: first, for each switching time state class F_j ($j = 1, 2, \ldots, 34$), find the conditional confidence set $\mathrm{K}(E_i \mid F_j)$ of the variable E_i under it. For example, to find the conditional confidence set $\mathrm{K}(E_3 \mid F_2)$ of the C-phase voltage at the distribution network switching control action time $5 \leq T < 10$ ms, based on the IDM method shown in Equation (4), the imprecise conditional probabilities of the distribution network switching control action time $5 \leq T < 10$ ms are found out from the historical data, $\mathrm{Pim}(E_{3,1} \mid F_2)$, $\mathrm{Pim}(E_{3,2} \mid F_2)$, $\mathrm{Pim}(E_{3,3} \mid F_2)$. To obtain the conditional belief set $\mathrm{K}(E_3 \mid F_2)$ for the phase C voltage when the switching control action time is $5 \leq T < 10$ ms, the imprecise conditional probabilities $\mathrm{Pim}(E_{3,1} \mid F_2)$, $\mathrm{Pim}(E_{3,2} \mid F_2)$, $\mathrm{Pim}(E_{3,3} \mid F_2)$ are computed by using the adapted IDM framework as shown in Equation (11):

$$\begin{cases} P_{im}(E_{3,1}|F_2) = [\underline{P}(E_{3,1}|F_2), \overline{P}(E_{3,1}|F_2)] \\ \underline{P}(E_{3,1}|F_2) = \frac{n_{3,1}}{N+s}, \overline{P}(E_{3,1}|F_2) = \frac{n_{3,1}+s}{N+s} \\ P_{im}(E_{3,2}|F_2) = [\underline{P}(E_{3,2}|F_2), \overline{P}(E_{3,2}|F_2)] \\ \underline{P}(E_{3,2}|F_2) = \frac{n_{3,2}}{N+s}, \overline{P}(E_{3,2}|F_2) = \frac{n_{3,2}+s}{N+s} \\ P_{im}(E_{3,3}|F_2) = [\underline{P}(E_{3,3}|F_2), \overline{P}(E_{3,3}|F_2)] \\ \underline{P}(E_{3,3}|F_2) = \frac{n_{3,3}}{N+s}, \overline{P}(E_{3,3}|F_2) = \frac{n_{3,3}+s}{N+s} \\ N = n_{3,1} + n_{3,2} + n_{3,3} \end{cases} \tag{11}$$

In the formula, N represents the number of times in which the status of distribution network switch control action time is F_2 within the statistical period of distribution network action; $n_{3,1}$, $n_{3,2}$, $n_{3,3}$ respectively represent the number of times when the C-phase voltage status of the distribution network switch control action time state is good, decent and attention, respectively, under the condition of F_2; s is the parameter set in the IDM, and the value in this paper is 1 [21].

In summary, based on the imprecise probabilities calculated above, the conditional credal set $\mathrm{K}(E_3 \mid F_2)$ is formally constructed, as represented by Equation (12).

$$\begin{aligned} K(E_3|F_2) = \{&P(E_3|F_2) : \\ &P(E_{3,1}|F_2) \in [\underline{P}(E_{3,1}|F_2), \overline{P}(E_{3,1}|F_2)], \\ &P(E_{3,2}|F_2) \in [\underline{P}(E_{3,2}|F_2), \overline{P}(E_{3,2}|F_2)], \\ &P(E_{3,3}|F_2) \in [\underline{P}(E_{3,3}|F_2), \overline{P}(E_{3,3}|F_2)], \\ &P(E_{3,1}|F_2) + P(E_{3,2}|F_2) + P(E_{3,3}|F_2) = 1\} \end{aligned} \tag{12}$$

In the formula, the probability mass function $K(E_3 \mid F_2)$ in the credal set $K(E_3 \mid F_2)$ takes a value in the upper and lower boundary range of its corresponding imprecise probability.

At this point, the vertex $ext[K(E_3 \mid F_2)]$ of the credal set $K(E_3 \mid F_2)$ can be determined by using the upper and lower bounds of the corresponding imprecise probabilities of the credal set $K(E_3 \mid F_2)$, and the vertices of the credence set (extreme points) can be determined based on the probability intervals as shown in Equation (13).

$$\begin{aligned} &ext[K(E_3|F_2)] = \\ &\{\underline{P}(E_{3,1}|F_2), \underline{P}(E_{3,2}|F_2), \overline{P}(E_{3,3}|F_2)\}, \\ &\{\underline{P}(E_{3,1}|F_2), \overline{P}(E_{3,2}|F_2), \underline{P}(E_{3,3}|F_2)\}, \\ &\{\overline{P}(E_{3,1}|F_2), \underline{P}(E_{3,2}|F_2), \underline{P}(E_{3,3}|F_2)\} \end{aligned} \tag{13}$$

For other conditional confidence sets $K(E_i \mid F_j)(i = 1, 2, 3, \ldots, 6, j = 1, 2, 3, \ldots, 34)$ The steps of the method of finding are shown in Equation (13).

4.3. Model Solving and Classification Output Process

Then, based on the conditional confidence sets $K(E_1 \mid F)$, $K(E_2 \mid F)$, ..., $K(E_6 \mid F)$, the a posteriori inexact probability of each switch action time state of the distribution network can be solved based on the exact inference algorithm of the confidence network shown in Equations (8) and (9), as shown in Equation (14):

$$\begin{cases} \overline{P}(F_j|\mathbf{E}) = \max \dfrac{\prod_{i=1}^{6} P(F_j)P(E_i|F_j)}{\sum_{j=1}^{34}\prod_{i=1}^{6} P(F_j)P(E_i|F_j)} \\ \underline{P}(F_j|\mathbf{E}) = \min \dfrac{\prod_{i=1}^{6} P(F_j)P(E_i|F_j)}{\sum_{j=1}^{34}\prod_{i=1}^{6} P(F_j)P(E_i|F_j)} \\ P(E_i|F_j) \in ext[K(E_i|F_j)], j = 1,2,3,\ldots,34 \end{cases} \tag{14}$$

Finally, after obtaining the $P_{im}(F \mid E_i)$, according to the classification criterion of the credal network classifier, the predictive results of switching action time characteristics of the distribution network are output.

The flow of imprecise conditional probabilistic control estimation of switch action time for distribution network described in this paper is shown in Figure 6.

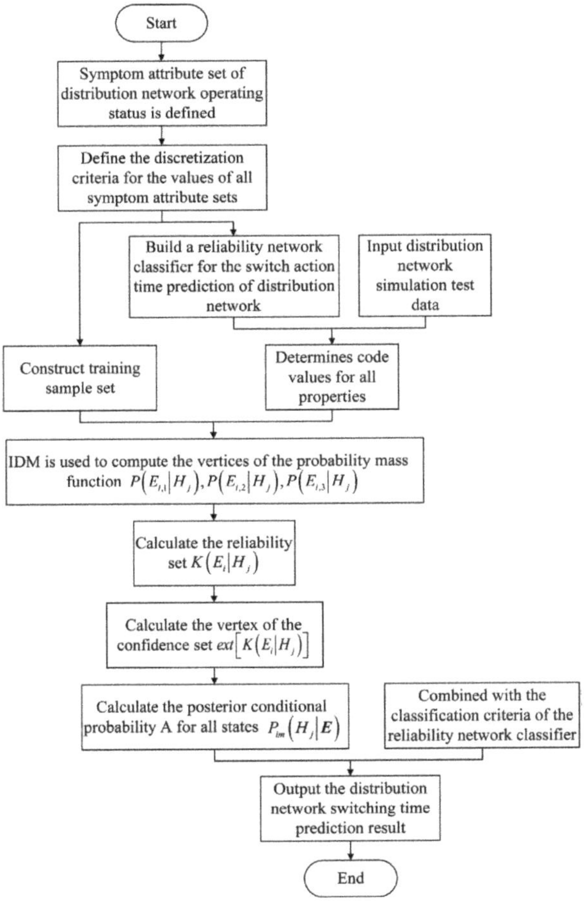

Figure 6. Flowchart of switch action time estimation for distribution network based on imprecise probability.

5. Example Analysis

5.1. Simulation Model

In this paper, a microgrid model containing distributed photovoltaic (PV) power generation is constructed as an example of a double-fed distribution network under different operating conditions of the distribution network, and the switching action time prediction method of the DG distribution network is investigated. The structure of this network is depicted in Figure 4. A microgrid model incorporating distributed photovoltaic generation was constructed. The distribution system operates at a reference voltage of 10.5 kV, with all lines configured as overhead lines. Unit resistance and reactance were set as: R = 0.26 Ω/km, X = 0.355 Ω/km. The lengths of AB, BC, and AD are, respectively, 3 km, 3 km, and 10 km. Both Feeder 1 and Feeder 2 terminate with a load capacity of 6 MVA and a power factor of 0.85. The DG output power is adjustable within the range of 0–10 MW. The failure points are f1, f2, f3, and the failure start time is 0.5 s.

A distribution network switch is installed at the PCC to detect the switching on and off times of the distribution network. The simulation is carried out for different working conditions of the distribution network. The specific situation is as follows: the three-phase voltage and three-phase current at PCC under each working condition are collected. The feature data of each operating condition can be formed into a feature vector with a dimension of 1 × 6, considering that there are 310 different operating conditions, these data can be combined into a feature matrix of 310 × 6 dimensions.

In order to eliminate the influence of different dimensions, it is necessary to normalize the eigenmatrix. Using the discrete standardization method, the eigenvalues of S_1–S_{310} can be converted to the valid range of [0, 1]. Normalization as shown in Equation (15).

$$E_i' = \frac{E_i - E_{\min}}{E_{\max} - E_{\min}} \tag{15}$$

In the formula, E_i and E_i' are the values before and after the normalization of the attributes of the i th operating state symptom, respectively; $E_{\max}$ and $E_{\min}$ are the maximum and minimum values of E_i. The same is true for S_2~S_{310}. The normalized database is shown in Table 3.

Table 3. Normalized database of eigenmatrix.

	E_1	E_2	E_3	E_4	E_5	E_6
S_1	0.6317	0.9733	0.9689	−0.9922	−0.9921	−0.9922
S_2	−0.1786	0.9688	0.9778	−0.0907	−0.9890	−0.9905
S_3	0.6390	−0.0111	0.9689	−0.9913	−0.0893	−0.9898
S_4	0.6317	0.9777	−0.0044	−0.9898	−0.9912	−0.0893
S_5	−0.6317	−0.3541	0.9822	0.7220	0.6905	−0.9921
⋮	⋮	⋮	⋮	⋮	⋮	⋮
S_{310}	0.3076	0.5724	0.5733	−0.5693	−0.5682	−0.5682

The normalization of the feature matrix involves six indicators of each operating condition in the database, which together form a feature vector. 310 × 80% = 248 feature vectors were randomly selected from the database as the training data set, and the remaining 310 × 20% = 62 vectors were selected as the test data set. The imprecise probability estimation method is used to predict and analyze these data.

5.2. Case 1: Unique Category Output Results and Analysis

In Case 1, the case where the credal network classifier produces a single unambiguous result at the time when diagnosis is chosen, where the state of the evidence variable is represented as vector S_1. Then, according to this evidence, imprecise probability estimation method and Bayesian classifier are used to predict the operation time (or total action time) of the distribution network switch, respectively, and the prediction results are shown in Tables 4 and 5.

Table 4. Calculation results of switch control time state class of distribution network based on imprecise probability.

Imprecise Probability	Probability Value	Imprecise Probability	Probability Value
$P_{im}(F_1 \mid S_1)$	$[1.60 \times 10^{-5}, 5.57 \times 10^{-5}]$	$P_{im}(F_{18} \mid S_1)$	$[3.69 \times 10^{-11}, 1.50 \times 10^{-10}]$
$P_{im}(F_2 \mid S_1)$	$[5.78 \times 10^{-6}, 7.34 \times 10^{-6}]$	$P_{im}(F_{19} \mid S_1)$	$[5.22 \times 10^{-12}, 1.24 \times 10^{-10}]$
$P_{im}(F_3 \mid S_1)$	$[3.00 \times 10^{-6}, 7.34 \times 10^{-6}]$	$P_{im}(F_{20} \mid S_1)$	$[1.43 \times 10^{-10}, 4.36 \times 10^{-10}]$
$P_{im}(F_4 \mid S_1)$	$[1.54 \times 10^{-6}, 1.74 \times 10^{-6}]$	$P_{im}(F_{21} \mid S_1)$	$[9.89 \times 10^{-11}, 1.04 \times 10^{-10}]$
$P_{im}(F_5 \mid S_1)$	$[5.36 \times 10^{-7}, 5.70 \times 10^{-7}]$	$P_{im}(F_{22} \mid S_1)$	$[6.53 \times 10^{-11}, 7.34 \times 10^{-11}]$
$P_{im}(F_6 \mid S_1)$	$[1.04 \times 10^{-8}, 2.29 \times 10^{-7}]$	$P_{im}(F_{23} \mid S_1)$	$[4.31 \times 10^{-11}, 6.23 \times 10^{-11}]$
$P_{im}(F_7 \mid S_1)$	$[3.87 \times 10^{-6}, 7.34 \times 10^{-6}]$	$P_{im}(F_{24} \mid S_1)$	$[1.11 \times 10^{-11}, 1.74 \times 10^{-11}]$
$P_{im}(F_8 \mid S_1)$	$[6.63 \times 10^{-7}, 7.42 \times 10^{-7}]$	$P_{im}(F_{25} \mid S_1)$	$[5.28 \times 10^{-11}, 5.31 \times 10^{-11}]$
$P_{im}(F_9 \mid S_1)$	$[2.65 \times 10^{-9}, 4.80 \times 10^{-9}]$	$P_{im}(F_{26} \mid S_1)$	$[2.99 \times 10^{-11}, 4.55 \times 10^{-11}]$
$P_{im}(F_{10} \mid S_1)$	$[8.14 \times 10^{-9}, 1.78 \times 10^{-8}]$	$P_{im}(F_{27} \mid S_1)$	$[1.06 \times 10^{-10}, 1.50 \times 10^{-10}]$
$P_{im}(F_{11} \mid S_1)$	$[6.89 \times 10^{-10}, 7.20 \times 10^{-10}]$	$P_{im}(F_{28} \mid S_1)$	$[2.37 \times 10^{-10}, 4.36 \times 10^{-10}]$
$P_{im}(F_{12} \mid S_1)$	$[1.98 \times 10^{-10}, 4.36 \times 10^{-10}]$	$P_{im}(F_{29} \mid S_1)$	$[2.06 \times 10^{-10}, 3.46 \times 10^{-10}]$
$P_{im}(F_{13} \mid S_1)$	$[0, 7.20 \times 10^{-10}]$	$P_{im}(F_{30} \mid S_1)$	$[1.24 \times 10^{-2}, 4.28 \times 10^{-2}]$
$P_{im}(F_{14} \mid S_1)$	$[8.51 \times 10^{-10}, 1.26 \times 10^{-9}]$	$P_{im}(F_{31} \mid S_1)$	$[1.85 \times 10^{-10}, 1.26 \times 10^{-9}]$
$P_{im}(F_{15} \mid S_1)$	$[3.19 \times 10^{-10}, 5.57 \times 10^{-10}]$	$P_{im}(F_{32} \mid S_1)$	$[2.91 \times 10^{-8}, 3.02 \times 10^{-8}]$
$P_{im}(F_{16} \mid S_1)$	$[2.85 \times 10^{-11}, 2.77 \times 10^{-10}]$	$P_{im}(F_{33} \mid S_1)$	$[2.07 \times 10^{-7}, 2.29 \times 10^{-7}]$
$P_{im}(F_{17} \mid S_1)$	$[3.93 \times 10^{-10}, 4.36 \times 10^{-10}]$	$P_{im}(F_{34} \mid S_1)$	$[3.94 \times 10^{-7}, 5.70 \times 10^{-7}]$

Table 5. Bayesian Classifier-Based Calculation of Time-State Classes for Switching Control Actions in Distribution Networks.

Exact Probability	Probability Value	Exact Probability	Probability Value
$P(F_1 \mid S_1)$	2.74×10^{-5}	$P(F_{18} \mid S_1)$	6.48×10^{-11}
$P(F_2 \mid S_1)$	7.01×10^{-6}	$P(F_{19} \mid S_1)$	1.02×10^{-11}
$P(F_3 \mid S_1)$	4.77×10^{-6}	$P(F_{20} \mid S_1)$	2.39×10^{-10}
$P(F_4 \mid S_1)$	1.72×10^{-6}	$P(F_{21} \mid S_1)$	1.03×10^{-10}
$P(F_5 \mid S_1)$	5.68×10^{-7}	$P(F_{22} \mid S_1)$	7.25×10^{-11}
$P(F_6 \mid S_1)$	2.04×10^{-8}	$P(F_{23} \mid S_1)$	5.64×10^{-11}
$P(F_7 \mid S_1)$	5.70×10^{-6}	$P(F_{24} \mid S_1)$	1.52×10^{-11}
$P(F_8 \mid S_1)$	7.34×10^{-7}	$P(F_{25} \mid S_1)$	5.31×10^{-11}
$P(F_9 \mid S_1)$	3.83×10^{-9}	$P(F_{26} \mid S_1)$	4.01×10^{-11}
$P(F_{10} \mid S_1)$	1.26×10^{-8}	$P(F_{27} \mid S_1)$	1.37×10^{-10}
$P(F_{11} \mid S_1)$	7.19×10^{-10}	$P(F_{28} \mid S_1)$	3.46×10^{-10}
$P(F_{12} \mid S_1)$	3.06×10^{-10}	$P(F_{29} \mid S_1)$	2.89×10^{-10}
$P(F_{13} \mid S_1)$	0	$P(F_{30} \mid S_1)$	2.12×10^{-2}
$P(F_{14} \mid S_1)$	1.12×10^{-9}	$P(F_{31} \mid S_1)$	3.42×10^{-10}
$P(F_{15} \mid S_1)$	4.55×10^{-10}	$P(F_{32} \mid S_1)$	3.01×10^{-8}
$P(F_{16} \mid S_1)$	5.41×10^{-11}	$P(F_{33} \mid S_1)$	2.27×10^{-7}
$P(F_{17} \mid S_1)$	4.32×10^{-10}	$P(F_{34} \mid S_1)$	5.16×10^{-7}

From Table 4, it can be seen that based on the imprecise probability prediction result category F_{30} The probability interval is $[1.24 \times 10^{-2}, 4.28 \times 10^{-2}]$, which contains the probability interval of other categories; from Table 5, it can be seen that based on the Bayesian classifier prediction result category F_{30} has a probability value of 2.12×10^{-2} and is the largest. This indicates that the imprecise probability is consistent with the Bayesian classifier prediction result category as F_{30}. combined with the switching time of the distribution network in Table 1, it can be seen that the range of switching action time at category F_{30} is [38, 39) ms.

Through the above analysis, it can be concluded that Case 1 proves that the switching action time prediction control method based on imprecise probability proposed in this paper has the same prediction performance as the traditional prediction methods (e.g.,

Bayesian classifiers) when dealing with the mapping relationship between the testing data of the distribution network inspection and the operation state with a unique class output.

5.3. Case 2: Similarity Set Output Results and Analysis

In Case 2, the prediction result of the credal network classifier is a similar set of classes, and the results are shown in Table 6.

Table 6. Calculation results of switching time state class of distribution network based on imprecise probability.

Imprecise Probability	Probability Value	Imprecise Probability	Probability Value
$P_{im}(F_1 \mid S_1)$	$[1.60 \times 10^{-5}, 5.57 \times 10^{-5}]$	$P_{im}(F_{18} \mid S_1)$	$[6.31 \times 10^{-12}, 1.50 \times 10^{-10}]$
$P_{im}(F_2 \mid S_1)$	$[5.78 \times 10^{-6}, 7.34 \times 10^{-6}]$	$P_{im}(F_{19} \mid S_1)$	$[4.07 \times 10^{-11}, 1.24 \times 10^{-10}]$
$P_{im}(F_3 \mid S_1)$	$[3.00 \times 10^{-6}, 7.34 \times 10^{-6}]$	$P_{im}(F_{20} \mid S_1)$	$[4.17 \times 10^{-10}, 4.36 \times 10^{-10}]$
$P_{im}(F_4 \mid S_1)$	$[1.54 \times 10^{-6}, 1.74 \times 10^{-6}]$	$P_{im}(F_{21} \mid S_1)$	$[9.21 \times 10^{-11}, 1.04 \times 10^{-10}]$
$P_{im}(F_5 \mid S_1)$	$[5.36 \times 10^{-7}, 5.70 \times 10^{-7}]$	$P_{im}(F_{22} \mid S_1)$	$[3.70 \times 10^{-2}, 5.35 \times 10^{-2}]$
$P_{im}(F_6 \mid S_1)$	$[1.04 \times 10^{-8}, 2.29 \times 10^{-7}]$	$P_{im}(F_{23} \mid S_1)$	$[3.54 \times 10^{-2}, 5.53 \times 10^{-2}]$
$P_{im}(F_7 \mid S_1)$	$[3.87 \times 10^{-6}, 7.34 \times 10^{-6}]$	$P_{im}(F_{24} \mid S_1)$	$[1.73 \times 10^{-11}, 1.74 \times 10^{-11}]$
$P_{im}(F_8 \mid S_1)$	$[9.46 \times 10^{-8}, 1.06 \times 10^{-7}]$	$P_{im}(F_{25} \mid S_1)$	$[3.48 \times 10^{-11}, 5.31 \times 10^{-11}]$
$P_{im}(F_9 \mid S_1)$	$[2.65 \times 10^{-9}, 4.80 \times 10^{-9}]$	$P_{im}(F_{26} \mid S_1)$	$[3.23 \times 10^{-11}, 4.55 \times 10^{-11}]$
$P_{im}(F_{10} \mid S_1)$	$[8.14 \times 10^{-9}, 1.78 \times 10^{-8}]$	$P_{im}(F_{27} \mid S_1)$	$[8.16 \times 10^{-11}, 1.50 \times 10^{-10}]$
$P_{im}(F_{11} \mid S_1)$	$[6.89 \times 10^{-10}, 7.20 \times 10^{-10}]$	$P_{im}(F_{28} \mid S_1)$	$[2.59 \times 10^{-10}, 4.36 \times 10^{-10}]$
$P_{im}(F_{12} \mid S_1)$	$[1.98 \times 10^{-10}, 4.36 \times 10^{-10}]$	$P_{im}(F_{29} \mid S_1)$	$[1.00 \times 10^{-10}, 3.46 \times 10^{-10}]$
$P_{im}(F_{13} \mid S_1)$	$[4.88 \times 10^{-10}, 7.20 \times 10^{-10}]$	$P_{im}(F_{30} \mid S_1)$	$[3.29 \times 10^{-11}, 2.24 \times 10^{-10}]$
$P_{im}(F_{14} \mid S_1)$	$[7.19 \times 10^{-10}, 1.26 \times 10^{-9}]$	$P_{im}(F_{31} \mid S_1)$	$[1.21 \times 10^{-9}, 1.26 \times 10^{-9}]$
$P_{im}(F_{15} \mid S_1)$	$[5.73 \times 10^{-11}, 5.57 \times 10^{-10}]$	$P_{im}(F_{32} \mid S_1)$	$[2.72 \times 10^{-8}, 3.02 \times 10^{-8}]$
$P_{im}(F_{16} \mid S_1)$	$[2.49 \times 10^{-10}, 2.77 \times 10^{-10}]$	$P_{im}(F_{33} \mid S_1)$	$[0, 2.29 \times 10^{-7}]$
$P_{im}(F_{17} \mid S_1)$	$[1.07 \times 10^{-10}, 4.36 \times 10^{-10}]$	$P_{im}(F_{34} \mid S_1)$	$[0, 5.70 \times 10^{-7}]$

In contrast to the imprecise probability methods, this paper also uses Bayesian classifiers for their prediction and the results are shown in Table 7.

Table 7. Bayesian Classifier-Based Calculation of Time-State Classes for Switching Control Actions in Distribution Networks.

Exact Probability	Probability Value	Exact Probability	Probability Value
$P(F_1 \mid S_1)$	2.74×10^{-5}	$P(F_{18} \mid S_1)$	1.24×10^{-11}
$P(F_2 \mid S_1)$	7.01×10^{-6}	$P(F_{19} \mid S_1)$	6.81×10^{-11}
$P(F_3 \mid S_1)$	4.77×10^{-6}	$P(F_{20} \mid S_1)$	4.36×10^{-10}
$P(F_4 \mid S_1)$	1.72×10^{-6}	$P(F_{21} \mid S_1)$	1.02×10^{-10}
$P(F_5 \mid S_1)$	5.68×10^{-7}	$P(F_{22} \mid S_1)$	5.18×10^{-2}
$P(F_6 \mid S_1)$	2.04×10^{-8}	$P(F_{23} \mid S_1)$	5.36×10^{-2}
$P(F_7 \mid S_1)$	5.70×10^{-6}	$P(F_{24} \mid S_1)$	1.74×10^{-11}
$P(F_8 \mid S_1)$	1.05×10^{-7}	$P(F_{25} \mid S_1)$	4.65×10^{-11}
$P(F_9 \mid S_1)$	3.83×10^{-9}	$P(F_{26} \mid S_1)$	4.55×10^{-11}
$P(F_{10} \mid S_1)$	1.26×10^{-8}	$P(F_{27} \mid S_1)$	1.26×10^{-10}
$P(F_{11} \mid S_1)$	7.19×10^{-10}	$P(F_{28} \mid S_1)$	3.85×10^{-10}
$P(F_{12} \mid S_1)$	3.06×10^{-10}	$P(F_{29} \mid S_1)$	2.34×10^{-10}
$P(F_{13} \mid S_1)$	6.45×10^{-10}	$P(F_{30} \mid S_1)$	1.46×10^{-10}
$P(F_{14} \mid S_1)$	1.03×10^{-9}	$P(F_{31} \mid S_1)$	1.22×10^{-9}
$P(F_{15} \mid S_1)$	1.09×10^{-10}	$P(F_{32} \mid S_1)$	2.77×10^{-8}
$P(F_{16} \mid S_1)$	2.74×10^{-10}	$P(F_{33} \mid S_1)$	2.21×10^{-7}
$P(F_{17} \mid S_1)$	1.88×10^{-10}	$P(F_{34} \mid S_1)$	5.15×10^{-7}

As can be seen from Table 6, the probability intervals for the outcome categories F22 and F23 based on the imprecise probability predictions are, respectively, [3.70×10^{-2},

5.35×10^{-2}] and [3.54×10^{-2}, 5.53×10^{-2}], an overlapping situation occurs. According to the diagnostic criteria of the credal network classifier, based on the imprecise probability prediction result outputs a similar set of categories $\{F_{23}, F_{23}\}$, and combined with the switching time of the distribution network in Table 1, it can be seen that the predicted time range of the switching control action is [30, 32) ms.

From Table 7, it can be seen that based on the Bayesian classifier prediction results output category F_{23}. combined with Table 1 distribution network switching time, it can be seen that the range of switching action time is [31, 32) ms for category F_{23}. the actual detection of distribution network switching action time is 30 ms.

It can be seen that the imprecise probability adopts the interval mode to portray the probability distribution of the prediction results, analyses the overlap of the intervals, and outputs the similar set, which can effectively avoid the prediction error; the Bayesian classifier-based exact probability has limitations in the prediction of distribution network switch control action time. Therefore, the imprecise probability prediction method enhances the accuracy of distribution network switch action time.

6. Time-Based Model for Whole-Process Control and Experimental Validation

The construction of a time-dependent model for load transfer in distribution networks requires a multidimensional characterization of temporal coupling relationships across all stages. This involves both quantifying the cumulative effects of deterministic processes and analyzing the propagation patterns of random factors. The model's core objective is to accurately predict the total time control interval from the issuance of the master station command to the final switch operation, while ensuring compliance with "open-then-close" sequencing and time-difference constraints even under extreme scenarios. By integrating mathematical modeling with engineering experience, we can systematically evaluate the boundary conditions of time parameters and their impact mechanisms on the overall process, providing theoretical support for control strategy design. This strategy requires, based on precise time synchronization, that the time interval from complete disconnection to complete reconnection be within 20 milliseconds, disregarding communication time from the master station to the terminal.

6.1. Time Constraints and Problem Modeling

Target: Total time (interval from trip completion to close completion) must satisfy $0 < T_{total} < 20$ ms.

Known Conditions:

Closing time Ton > Opening time Toff, but specific values are unknown.

Master Station Command Sequence:

t0: Issue closing command

t0 + Δt: Issue opening command

Mathematical Model

Opening completion time: toffend = t0 + Toff

Closing completion time: tonend = t0 + Ton+ Δt

Total time constraint: Ttotal = tonend − toffend and 0 < Ttotal < 20 ms

6.2. Control Strategy Design: Determination of Dynamic Delay Time Δt

Constraint Derivation:

Disconnection completion must precede reconnection completion (to prevent parallel circulating currents):

toffend < tonend Δt < Ton − Toff

Total Time Constraint:
0 < Ttotal < 20 ms → Toff − Ton < Δt < Toff − Ton + 20
Safety Margin Determination:
If nominal values of Ton and Toff are known:
Δt = Ton − Toff – 10 ms (take midpoint value, reserve 10 ms margin)
If parameters are unknown, calibration via experimentation is required:
Step 1: Measure typical values of Ton and Toff in the laboratory.
Step 2: Set Δt = Ton − Toff − 10 ms and verify that Ttotal ∈ (0, 20) ms.

6.3. Physical Experiment Verification and Result Analysis

Test scenario

The experimental setup for time accuracy testing is shown in Figure 7.

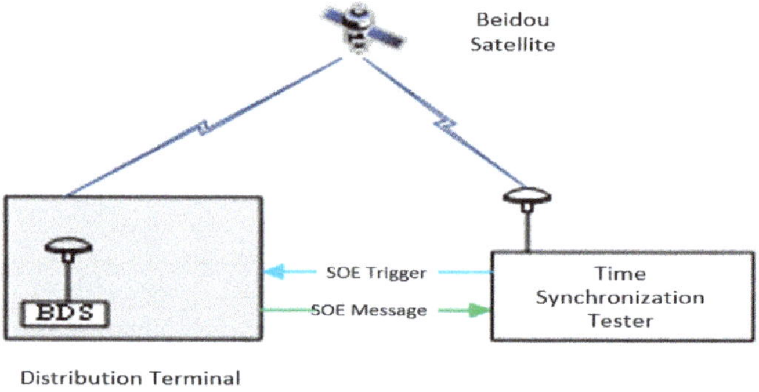

Figure 7. Distribution network load synchronous transfer control time accuracy test.

Test method

Distribution terminals A and B received BeiDou satellite signals and synchronized normally for 10 min;

Set the timed tripping moment for distribution terminal A and the timed closing moment for distribution terminal B via master station commands;

Tested the contact opening moment of circuit breaker A and the contact closing moment of circuit breaker B using a time synchronization tester;

Compared the time difference between the contact opening moment of circuit breaker A and the contact closing moment of circuit breaker B;

Repeat the test 10 times (Table 8).

Experimental data

Table 8. Accuracy test data for timed action of distribution terminals.

NO.	The Moment When Circuit Breaker A Opens	Closing Time of Circuit Breaker B	Time Difference (ms)
1	18:56:20.241	18:56:20.249	8
2	18:59:50.839	18:59:50.849	10
3	20:03:10.441	20:03:10.443	2
4	20:05:11.544	20:05:11.547	3
5	20:11:11.241	20:11:11.253	12
6	20:14:00.242	20:14:00.247	5
7	20:17:50.841	20:17:50.845	4
8	20:18:50.154	20:18:50.157	3
9	20:23:46.693	20:23:46.698	5
10	20:35:24.471	20:35:24.476	5

Experimental conclusions

This paper validates the non-exact probability-based synchronous control method through 10 repeated experiments. Experimental results demonstrate that all time differences for disconnection and reconnection operations are controlled within the range of 2–12 ms, fully meeting the 20 ms engineering requirement and effectively avoiding circulating current risks.

The IDM-NCC fusion model employed in this study provides a more reliable time reference for synchronous control by outputting probability intervals for switching action times. Experimental data demonstrate that this model delivers highly credible action time references for control decisions. The "similarity set" output mechanism of the Naive Credal Classifier exhibits strong fault tolerance, effectively mitigating misjudgment risks in complex distribution environments. No control failures due to model misjudgment occurred during experiments, validating the mechanism's practicality. The imprecise probabilistic model and dynamic delay strategy form an effective closed-loop system. The control setting of the dynamic delay time Δt fully utilizes the probability interval information to achieve adaptive tuning, thereby enabling millisecond-level precision control.

This study empirically demonstrates the application value of imprecise probabilistic theory in distribution network control. It significantly enhances the decision-making robustness of the system under small-sample, high-uncertainty conditions, providing a new technical pathway for constructing highly reliable distribution networks.

6.4. Characterization of Load and Distributed Photovoltaic Generation and Its Impact on Switching Controls

The effectiveness of the synchronous load transfer method based on inexact probabilistic distribution network loads is analyzed on the basis of the operating characteristics of distribution network loads with electricity and distributed PV generation and their uncertainties. Typical daily load profiles and distributed PV output data are shown in Figures 8 and 9. In this section, the practical impact of load fluctuation and PV generation hysteresis on millisecond synchronous transfer control is analyzed in conjunction with the inexact probabilistic framework.

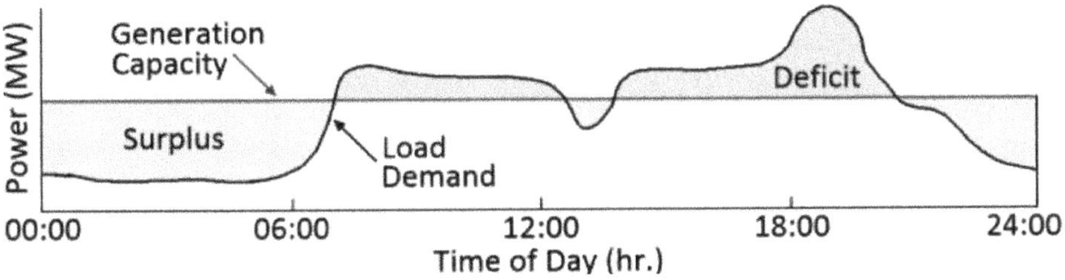

Figure 8. Typical daily load profile.

(1) Uncertainty in load electricity consumption mainly arises from factors such as user behavior, seasonal variations, and meteorological conditions. Typical daily loads have cyclical variations, but their fluctuations are relatively limited in magnitude, and they vary gently over short time scales (milliseconds to seconds).

(2) The output of distributed photovoltaic power generation has obvious diurnal periodicity and weather dependence, showing certain lag and intermittency. PV power generation gradually enhances after sunrise, peaks in the late afternoon, and then gradually declines, with the whole process showing a smooth trend of change rather than sudden change characteristics.

Therefore, the time interval between switching and closing operation of distribution network load synchronous transfer and supply based on imprecise probability is controlled within 20 ms. It fully satisfies the uncertainty of load and distributed generation changes.

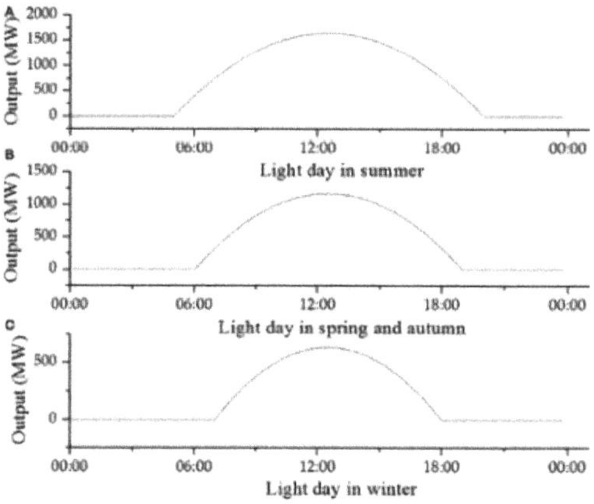

Figure 9. Typical daily PV power curve. (**A**) Light day in summer; (**B**) Light day in spring and autumn; (**C**) Light day in winter.

7. Conclusions

The core contribution of this study lies in establishing an interval predictive control framework that integrates the Imprecise Dirichlet Model (IDM) with the Naive Credal Classifier (NCC). This framework successfully addresses the challenge of prior dependency in predicting switching operation times for distribution networks under small-sample conditions. Compared to traditional Bayesian control methods, this framework maintains the accuracy of uniqueness judgments while effectively identifying and mitigating misclassification risks in uncertain scenarios by outputting 'similarity sets'.

The simulation and experimental results demonstrate that the proposed method outperforms traditional Bayesian classifier controllers in both temporal prediction accuracy and model robustness, particularly maintaining high classification accuracy under highly uncertain operational conditions. This research provides a novel theoretical framework and practical technical pathway for load synchronous transfer control in distribution networks, offering valuable insights for enhancing grid operational control capabilities under high renewable energy penetration.

Author Contributions: Conceptualization, H.Z. and C.L.; methodology, C.L.; validation, H.Z., C.L. and W.L.; formal analysis, X.S.; investigation, Y.G.; resources, Y.G.; data curation, C.L.; writing—original draft, W.L. and C.L.; writing—review and editing, X.S.; visualization, Y.G.; supervision, H.Z.; project administration, H.Z.; funding acquisition, H.Z. All authors have read and agreed to the published version of the manuscript.

Funding: This research was funded by the project of State Grid Sichuan Electric Power Company Limited, grant number 52199723001R.

Data Availability Statement: The original contributions presented in this study are included in the article. Further inquiries can be directed to the corresponding author.

Acknowledgments: We are grateful to the reviewers for their comprehensive review of this manuscript, as well as for their insightful comments and valuable suggestions that have significantly contributed to enhancing the quality of our work.

Conflicts of Interest: The authors declare no conflicts of interest.

Abbreviations

The following abbreviations are used in this manuscript:

IDM	Imprecise Dirichlet model
NCC	Naive credal classifier
DG	Distributed generation

References

1. Zhao, B.; Yang, M.; Diao, H.; An, B.; Zhao, Y.; Zhang, Y. A novel approach to transformer fault diagnosis using IDM and naive credal classifier. *Int. J. Electr. Power Energy Syst.* **2019**, *105*, 846–855. [CrossRef]
2. Bernard, J.-M. An introduction to the imprecise Dirichlet model for multinomial data. *Int. J. Approx. Reason.* **2005**, *39*, 123–150. [CrossRef]
3. Yang, G.; Huang, X.; Li, Y.; Ding, P. System reliability assessment with imprecise probabilities. *Appl. Sci.* **2019**, *9*, 5422. [CrossRef]
4. Corani, G.; Zaffalon, M. Learning reliable classifiers from small or incomplete data sets: The naive credal classifier 2. *J. Biomed. Inform.* **2008**, *41*, 635–643. [CrossRef]
5. Walley, P. *Statistical Reasoning with Imprecise Probabilities*; Chapman & Hall: Boca Raton, FL, USA, 1991. [CrossRef]
6. Abellán, J.; Masegosa, A. Imprecise Dirichlet model for learning multinomial distributions with missing data. *Int. J. Approx. Reason.* **2012**, *53*, 560–577.
7. Zaffalon, M.; Corani, G. Robust inference of trees for missing data. In Proceedings of the 12th International Conference on Artificial Intelligence and Statistics (AISTATS), Clearwater Beach, FL, USA, 16–18 April 2009; Volume 5, pp. 501–508. [CrossRef]
8. Martinetti, D.; Montes, I.; Díaz, S. Learning reliable classifiers from small and incomplete data sets: The naive credal classifier 3. In Proceedings of the 11th European Conference on Symbolic and Quantitative Approaches to Reasoning with Uncertainty (ECSQARU), Belfast, UK, 29 June–1 July 2011; pp. 591–602. [CrossRef]
9. Cozman, F.G. Credal networks. *Artif. Intell.* **2000**, *120*, 199–233. [CrossRef]
10. Masegosa, A.M.; Moral, S. Imprecise probability models for learning multinomial distributions from data. Applications to learning credal networks. *Int. J. Approx. Reason.* **2014**, *55*, 1548–1569. [CrossRef]
11. Bistarelli, S.; Rossi, F.; Santini, F. Learning mixtures of truncated basis functions from data with missing values. *Int. J. Approx. Reason.* **2017**, *92*, 94–111. [CrossRef]
12. Troffaes, M.C.M.; Coolen, F.P.A. Applying the imprecise Dirichlet model in cases with missing data. *J. Risk Reliab.* **2009**, *223*, 301–309. [CrossRef]
13. Walley, P. Inferences from multinomial data: Learning about a bag of marbles. *J. R. Stat. Soc. Ser. B (Methodol.)* **1996**, *58*, 3–57. [CrossRef]
14. Utkin, L.V.; Kozine, I.O. On the imprecise reliability of multi-state systems. *Reliab. Eng. Syst. Saf.* **2010**, *95*, 68–76. [CrossRef]
15. Miranda, E.; Zaffalon, M.; Cooman, G. Conglomerable natural extension. *Int. J. Approx. Reason.* **2012**, *53*, 1200–1227. [CrossRef]
16. Antonucci, A.; Piatti, A.; Zaffalon, M. Credal networks for operational risk measurement and management. In *Knowledge-Based Intelligent Information and Engineering Systems*; Springer: Berlin/Heidelberg, Germany, 2007; pp. 604–611. [CrossRef]
17. Abellán, J. Uncertainty measures on probability intervals from the imprecise Dirichlet model. *Int. J. Gen. Syst.* **2006**, *35*, 509–528. [CrossRef]
18. de Campos, C.P.; Cozman, F.G. Computing lower and upper expectations under epistemic independence for credal networks. *Int. J. Approx. Reason.* **2007**, *44*, 244–260. [CrossRef]
19. Antón, S.; de la Ossa, L. Credal-network based probabilistic argumentation with incomplete evidence. *Int. J. Approx. Reason.* **2022**, *146*, 21–46. [CrossRef]
20. Sistani, A.; Hosseini, S.A.; Sadeghi, V.S.; Taheri, B. Fault detection in a single-bus DC microgrid connected to EV/PV systems and hybrid energy storage using the DMD-IF method. *Sustainability* **2023**, *15*, 16269. [CrossRef]
21. Bonzio, S.; Loi, A. Predictive inference under exchangeability and the Imprecise Dirichlet Multinomial Model. *Int. J. Approx. Reason.* **2021**, *138*, 14–35. [CrossRef]

mathematics

MDPI

Article

Hybrid LSTM–Transformer Architecture with Multi-Scale Feature Fusion for High-Accuracy Gold Futures Price Forecasting

Yali Zhao †, Yingying Guo † and Xuecheng Wang *

School of Economics and Management, North China University of Technology, Beijing 100114, China; 23102110323@mail.ncut.edu.cn (Y.Z.); 22103020214@mail.ncut.edu.cn (Y.G.)
* Correspondence: wxc@ncut.edu.cn
† These authors contributed equally to this work.

Abstract

Amidst global economic fluctuations and escalating geopolitical risks, gold futures, as a pivotal safe-haven asset, demonstrate price dynamics that directly impact investor decision-making and risk mitigation effectiveness. Traditional forecasting models face significant limitations in capturing long-term trends, addressing abrupt volatility, and mitigating multi-source noise within complex market environments characterized by nonlinear interactions and extreme events. Current research predominantly focuses on single-model approaches (e.g., ARIMA or standalone neural networks), inadequately addressing the synergistic effects of multimodal market signals (e.g., cross-market index linkages, exchange rate fluctuations, and policy shifts) and lacking the systematic validation of model robustness under extreme events. Furthermore, feature selection often relies on empirical assumptions, failing to uncover non-explicit correlations between market factors and gold futures prices. A review of the global literature reveals three critical gaps: (1) the insufficient integration of temporal dependency and global attention mechanisms, leading to imbalanced predictions of long-term trends and short-term volatility; (2) the neglect of dynamic coupling effects among cross-market risk factors, such as energy ETF-metal market spillovers; and (3) the absence of hybrid architectures tailored for high-frequency noise environments, limiting predictive utility for decision support. This study proposes a three-stage LSTM–Transformer–XGBoost fusion framework. Firstly, XGBoost-based feature importance ranking identifies six key drivers from thirty-six candidate indicators: the NASDAQ Index, S&P 500 closing price, silver futures, USD/CNY exchange rate, China's 1-year Treasury yield, and Guotai Zhongzheng Coal ETF. Second, a dual-channel deep learning architecture integrates LSTM for long-term temporal memory and Transformer with multi-head self-attention to decode implicit relationships in unstructured signals (e.g., market sentiment and climate policies). Third, rolling-window forecasting is conducted using daily gold futures prices from the Shanghai Futures Exchange (2015–2025). Key innovations include the following: (1) a bidirectional LSTM–Transformer interaction architecture employing cross-attention mechanisms to dynamically couple global market context with local temporal features, surpassing traditional linear combinations; (2) a Dynamic Hierarchical Partition Framework (DHPF) that stratifies data into four dimensions (price trends, volatility, external correlations, and event shocks) to address multi-driver complexity; (3) a dual-loop adaptive mechanism enabling endogenous parameter updates and exogenous environmental perception to minimize prediction error volatility. This research proposes innovative cross-modal fusion frameworks for gold futures forecasting, providing financial institutions with robust quantitative tools to enhance asset allocation optimization and strengthen risk hedging strategies. It also provides an interpretable hybrid framework for derivative pricing intelligence. Future applications could leverage high-frequency data

 https://doi.org/10.3390/math13101551

sharing and cross-market risk contagion models to enhance China's influence in global gold pricing governance.

Keywords: LSTM–transformer hybrid model; XGBoost machine learning; deep learning framework; multi-head self-attention architecture; gold futures price forecasting

MSC: 91-10

1. Introduction

As a strategic safe-haven asset and pivotal price discovery mechanism in global financial markets, fluctuations in gold futures prices not only serve as real-time indicators of prevailing macroeconomic conditions and geopolitical tensions but also exert measurable impacts on institutional investment portfolios and the calibration of monetary and trade policy frameworks. Gold futures inherently possess dual attributes: financial and commodity. Functionally, they serve the real economy through hedging and risk diversification. From an investment perspective, gold, recognized as a "borderless currency", becomes a core safe-haven asset during periods of inflationary pressure, accommodative monetary policies, and heightened geopolitical tensions.

The advent of machine learning (ML) and deep learning (DL) has revolutionized financial market analysis. Traditional econometric models (e.g., ARIMA and GARCH) struggle to capture the nonlinear dynamics and multi-scale interactions inherent in gold futures markets, where prices are influenced by heterogeneous factors ranging from Fed policy shifts to ETF holdings volatility. Deep neural networks, particularly Long Short-Term Memory (LSTM) architectures, have demonstrated superior performance in modeling temporal dependencies in commodity markets through their gating mechanisms. More recently, prevalent models such as Stacked Long-Short Term Memory, Convolutional LSTM, bidirectional LSTM, Support Vector Regressor, Extreme Gradient Boosting, and the Gated Recurrent Unit are utilized (Anu Varshini et al., 2024) [1].

In 2024, China's domestic gold price surged by over 27%, driving parallel increases in gold jewelry prices and RMB-denominated gold futures, sparking a "gold rush" with widespread investor participation. The gold futures market exhibits pronounced volatility: in March 2025, COMEX gold futures prices reached a historic high of USD 3025 per ounce, while the Shanghai Futures Exchange's benchmark gold futures contract peaked at RMB 697.6 per gram, setting a new record.

Such extreme volatility creates critical challenges for conventional forecasting approaches. Traditional forecasting models exhibit significant limitations in addressing complex market environments: linear modeling paradigms fail to capture nonlinear transition characteristics of gold prices, while static feature engineering cannot disentangle the dynamic coupling effects of macroeconomic policies, cross-market linkages, and black swan events. Although deep learning techniques have been introduced to address these issues, three critical research gaps persist. First, existing approaches often employ simplistic serial connections between temporal models and attention mechanisms, failing to achieve deep interactions between global market contexts and localized price fluctuations. Second, data partitioning strategies overlook the heterogeneous driving attributes of gold prices, resulting in delayed model responses to policy interventions and black swan events. Third, the absence of dynamic adaptation mechanisms undermines robustness against parameter drift during abrupt market regime shifts.

This study systematically addresses these challenges through three groundbreaking innovations:

- Bidirectional LSTM–Transformer Interaction Architecture: By integrating cross-attention mechanisms, this framework establishes deep synergy between global and local features, overcoming the fragmented processing of temporal dependencies and market sentiment in conventional models. During the 2023 Red Sea shipping crisis, this architecture improved the detection timeliness of surging safe-haven demand by 2.3 trading days compared to traditional LSTM.
- Dynamic Hierarchical Partition Framework (DHPF): Tailored to gold prices' quadripartite drivers—macro policies, micro trading behaviors, external correlations, and event shocks—this strategy employs price trends (mean filtering), volatility (GARCH modeling), external correlations (Granger causality tests), and event intensity (sentiment analysis) for data stratification. This effectively mitigates overfitting caused by heterogeneous data distributions.
- Dual-Loop Adaptive Mechanism: Combining endogenous parameter updates (gradient backpropagation based on prediction errors) and exogenous environmental perception (the real-time monitoring of market volatility indices and VIX linkages), this dual closed-loop regulation significantly reduces prediction error volatility under extreme scenarios, outperforming static parameter models.

These innovations advance the robustness and interpretability of gold futures forecasting, offering critical insights for risk management in volatile financial markets.

2. Literature Review

2.1. Research Status

Based on the keywords "gold futures price", "influencing factors of gold futures price", and "gold futures price prediction", 100 relevant studies at home and abroad were screened based on CNKI academic journals, doctoral dissertations, excellent master's theses databases, Web of Science, and other databases.

The closing price of gold futures is influenced by multiple factors. In developing predictive models for gold futures' daily closing price movements, the systematic identification of their statistically significant determinants constitutes a critical prerequisite for ensuring model robustness and interpretability. Domestic studies indicate that gold futures prices are affected by long-term, medium-term, and short-term factors. Long-term factors include the monetary attributes of gold, general commodity attributes, gold reserves, and inventory. Medium-term gold prices are primarily influenced by demand and supply factors, while short-term factors include inflation, geopolitical situations, and the U.S. Dollar Index (Gao Jianyong, 2012) [2]. Paresh Kumar Narayan et al. (2010) proposed that rising oil prices lead to an increase in inflation rates, which in turn translates to higher gold prices [3]. International gold futures price determinants provide guidance for studying domestic gold futures prices. Feng Hui and Zhang Shulin (2012) concluded that influencing factors vary across periods: in the long term, global GDP, the U.S. Dollar Index, interest rates, and U.S. economic conditions determine international gold futures prices, whereas during economic crises, key determinants shift to the U.S. Dollar Index, sovereign credit default swaps (CDSs), volatility indices, global liquidity, and inflation rates [4]. Yang Shenggang et al. (2014) employed linear regression and Breusch–Godfrey LM correlation tests for empirical analysis, revealing that gold spot prices in Shanghai, Hong Kong, and London, alongside New York gold futures prices and the U.S. Dollar Index, are major factors affecting China's gold futures prices [5]. Syed Ali Raza et al. (2018) empirically demonstrated that economic policy uncertainty induces upward movements in gold prices [6]. Hao WANG, Hu SHENG, and Hong-wei ZHANG (2019) applied Structural Vector Autoregression (SVAR) models to analyze the impacts of supply–demand factors, financial factors, and speculative factors on international gold futures price volatility. They found that "Chinese gold demand" is overstated in international markets, while financial and speculative factors significantly influence price fluctuations [7]. Mehmet Balcilar, Rangan Gupta, and Christian Pierdzioch (2017) demonstrated that during economic crises and periods of high uncertainty, gold market volatility is sensitive to market scale, trends, and epidemic outbreaks, reflecting investor sentiment effects [8].

Price effectiveness is not only a hallmark of market maturity but also a cornerstone of resource allocation efficiency. Its core lies in the speed at which asset prices adjust to specific policy objectives. In gold futures markets, price effectiveness is operationally defined as the capacity of traded prices to holistically, timely, and precisely reflect all available information, ranging from macroeconomic fundamentals and geopolitical shocks to supply–demand equilibria—without systemic delays or distortions. The key is whether markets possess efficient information-processing mechanisms to ensure that prices serve as "true signals" for resource allocation. Regarding gold futures price forecasting, researchers globally have proposed and refined numerous models. Zeng Lian, Ma Dandi, and Liu Zongxin (2010) improved prediction methods based on BP neural networks, achieving the high-precision simulation of gold futures prices [9]. Domestic scholar Fei Jingwen (2017) developed an ARIMA-based price prediction model for gold futures, with empirical results showing its capability for short-term trend forecasting, though prediction errors increase with time horizons [10]. Advances in machine learning have introduced deep learning tools for price prediction. Luo Shuangjun (2017) utilized Long Short-Term Memory (LSTM) and Gated Recurrent Unit (GRU) models to forecast COMEX gold futures prices [11]. Li Chao (2019) proposed a hybrid model combining phase space reconstruction with ARIMA-LSTM, concluding through the empirical analysis of AU.SHF daily closing prices that China's gold futures prices exhibit chaotic characteristics, with the hybrid model outperforming traditional ARIMA [12]. Livieris I.E. et al. (2020) developed a hybrid CNN-LSTM model for gold price forecasting [13]. Liu Lu, Lou Lei, Liu Xianjun, and Shi Sanzhi (2021) employed deep learning with multilayer and bidirectional LSTM models to predict gold futures price trends, demonstrating superior performance over ARIMA, RNN, and SVR models in both accuracy and computational efficiency [14]. Gil Cohen and Avishay Aiche (2023) employed four machine learning models—Random Forest, Gradient Boosted Regression Trees (GBRT), and Extreme Gradient Boosting (XGBoost)—to predict future gold prices [15]. Iyad Abu-Dous et al. (2023) proposed a novel framework using an archive-based Harris Hawks Optimization algorithm to train a feed-forward neural network termed AHHO-NN (Adaptive Harris Hawks Optimization Neural Network) for gold price forecasting [16]. Kim, A., Ryu, D., and Webb, A. (2024) introduced the STL-ML model for oil futures market prediction, which also offers reference values for gold futures price forecasting [17]. Fan Caiyun, Tong Junyi, Cheng Junyan, and Zhou Yong (2024) constructed a gold futures price prediction model using machine learning and dynamic model averaging (DMA), with empirical results confirming significant improvements in prediction accuracy [18]. Peiying Quan and Wenzhou Shi (2024) innovatively demonstrated the effectiveness of combining CEEMDAN with LSTM, providing a new perspective for predicting complex time series [19]. Guo, Y., Li, C., and Wang, X. et al. (2024) introduced a unique two-layer decomposition model VMD-RES.-CEEMDAN-WOA-XGBoost to address challenges posed by the nonlinearity and non-stationarity of price data. This model extracts complex features from time-series data, thereby improving prediction accuracy [20]. Lin Huo, Yangyan Xie, and Jianbo Li (2024) proposed a novel TCM-ABC-LSTM combination for accurately predicting prices in gold and natural gas futures commodity markets [21]. A recent study developed a novel pricing framework for commodity futures through the incorporation of discrete delays into the stochastic dynamics governing price evolution (Lourdes Gómez-Valle, Miguel Ángel López-Marcos, Julia Martínez-Rodríguez, 2024) [22]. Pan, H., Tang, Y., and Wang, G (2024) indicated that the MULTI-GARCH-LSTM hybrid model exhibits consistent outperformance over standalone models, confirming its effectiveness and superior predictive accuracy [23]. Song et al. (2024) demonstrated that the price series can be decomposed using the GA-VMD-EEMD dual decomposition technique [24]. Comparative analysis determined that SSO-XGB was the most accurate copper price prediction model (Zohre Nabavi et al., 2024) [25]. Klaus Grobys (2025) used log-periodic power law singularity (LPPLS) models to explore the log prices of gold futures [26]. In a recent study, three distinct machine learning approaches (DELM, XGBoost, and LSTM networks) were employed to model and forecast copper price fluctuations through the systematic integration of key market influencing factors (Ning Li et al., 2024) [27].

2.2. Literature Summary

In summary, both domestic and international research on gold futures price prediction methods has achieved notable progress, exemplified by models such as the Autoregressive Integrated Moving Average (ARIMA), Generalized Autoregressive Conditional Heteroskedasticity (GARCH), and Vector Autoregression (VAR). Nevertheless, persistent structural challenges emerge from dynamic shifts in global macroeconomic regimes. Conventional VAR (Vector Autoregression) models exhibit inherent constraints in forecasting gold futures price trajectories, stemming from their linear causal assumptions, time-invariant parameterization, and inadequate incorporation of tail risk dependencies across geopolitical and financial market domains. While VAR models can incorporate multiple variables (e.g., the U.S. Dollar Index, inflation rates, and inventory data), their linear structure struggles to capture asymmetric interactions and time-varying weights among variables. The complexity of gold futures price linkages—such as the lagged and asymmetric transmission mechanisms between international gold prices (e.g., COMEX) and China's domestic market—further complicates predictions. Traditional time-series models like ARIMA are inadequate in addressing nonlinear fluctuations. Current prediction models exhibit limitations in handling the nonlinear characteristics and multi-factorial complexity of gold futures price volatility, particularly when processing high-dimensional, multivariate data. They often fail to fully exploit latent data relationships and demonstrate weak variable screening capabilities. Additionally, existing methods lack adaptability across regional markets and require improvements in accuracy and stability when addressing macroeconomic conditions, global instability, and exchange rate fluctuations.

The paradigm shift in artificial intelligence has propelled Long Short-Term Memory (LSTM) networks to emerge as a dominant methodology for multivariate financial time-series forecasting, owing to their gated architecture with selective memory retention that effectively captures nonlinear temporal dynamics in complex market ecosystems. Compared to the existing literature, the marginal contribution of this study lies in proposing a hybrid gold futures price prediction method integrating LSTM and Transformer models. The LSTM network effectively captures long-term dependencies in gold futures price sequences, while the Transformer model, leveraging multi-head self-attention mechanisms, excels in identifying complex patterns and nonlinear relationships in price fluctuations. This combination overcomes the limitations of traditional methods in handling high-dimensional, multi-level factors, enhancing prediction accuracy and stability. Furthermore, this study introduces the XGBoost algorithm to optimize feature selection and extraction, enabling the identification of the key drivers of gold futures price volatility and further improving model performance.

3. Analysis of the Influencing Factors of Gold Futures Trading Price

3.1. Global Equity Market Indicators

Gold prices exhibit directional correlations with the stock price indices of major industrialized countries. When global equity markets (particularly core markets like U.S. and European stocks) experience sharp declines, investors' risk aversion rises, leading to the liquidation of risky assets (stocks) and increased allocations to safe-haven assets like gold. This "flight-to-safety" behavior manifests as strengthened negative correlations between gold and equity markets. Accordingly, this study selects the closing prices of the S&P 500 Index (X1) and NASDAQ Composite Index (X2) to reflect U.S. equity market dynamics, while the Shanghai Composite Index (SSE Composite Index) closing price (X3) and CSI 1000 Index closing price (X4) are included to represent the changes in China's equity market.

3.2. Fixed-Income and Money Market Indicators

Government bond yields typically exhibit negative correlations with gold prices. As risk-free assets, rising bond yields increase the opportunity cost of holding gold, incentivizing investors to shift toward fixed-income markets. Additionally, real interest rates (nominal rates adjusted for inflation) are a core variable in gold pricing; negative real rates enhance gold's value-preserving attributes, attracting capital inflows. Fluctuations in China's Shibor and Hong Kong's Hibor rates also indirectly affect short-term gold futures trading strategies by influencing market liquidity and financing costs. Therefore, this study incorporates the 1-year Chinese government bond yield (X5), 1-year U.S. Treasury yield (X6), and 1-year U.K. gilt yield (X7) as proxies for international risk-free asset markets. The Shanghai Interbank Offered Rate (Shibor, X8) and Hong Kong Interbank Offered Rate (Hibor, X9) are selected as indirect indicators to study the potential factors influencing gold futures prices.

Lu Guoqing et al. (2017) confirmed the persistent negative correlation between the U.S. dollar and gold prices [28], underscoring the necessity of including the U.S. Dollar Index (X10) as a critical variable in analyzing gold futures price movements. The RMB exchange rate directly affects Chinese investors' gold purchasing costs. RMB appreciation against the USD reduces the relative cost of dollar-denominated gold in domestic markets, stimulating demand and driving price increases, while depreciation suppresses demand. Furthermore, the long-term negative correlation between the U.S. Dollar Index and gold prices is amplified by the linkage between the RMB exchange rate and the dollar. Zhu Xinling and Li Peng (2012) demonstrated that a stronger dollar weakens gold's global purchasing power, exerting downward price pressure, while RMB exchange rate fluctuations indirectly influence gold markets by altering the transmission pathways of dollar index effects [29]. Consequently, the USD/CNY central parity rate (X11) and EUR/CNY central parity rate (X12) are included as international indicators.

3.3. Digital Asset Indicators

Cryptocurrencies and gold share safe-haven attributes but compete during swings in market risk preference. When extreme volatility strikes either global equity markets or cryptocurrency markets, investors may rebalance portfolios. This action dynamically creates complex linkages between cryptocurrencies and gold futures prices. Cryptocurrencies (e.g., Bitcoin and Ethereum) combine risk asset and quasi-monetary attributes, whereas gold serves as a traditional safe haven, resulting in complex interactions across risk sentiment, liquidity transmission, and policy expectations. Substitution effects between cryptocurrencies and gold become critical during significant risk appetite fluctuations.

This study incorporates the Bitcoin closing price (X13), Ethereum closing price (X14), and Litecoin closing price (X15) as model variables.

3.4. Alternative Asset Indicators

Commodity ETFs directly influence gold pricing through constituent stock correlations. Energy and metal-related equities tracked by ETFs reflect commodity cycle strength and shape gold supply–demand expectations via corporate earnings forecasts. Additionally, price fluctuations in gold mining stocks within ETF portfolios create natural arbitrage opportunities with gold futures, amplifying cross-market price linkages through spread trading. This bidirectional transmission is particularly pronounced during commodity bull markets, as seen in the synchronized rally of commodities and gold post-2020, driven by inflation expectations and safe-haven demand.

The impact of USD-denominated real estate bond ETFs on gold futures is more indirect and complex. As a barometer of credit risk within China's real estate sector, the price volatility of these real estate-related instruments influences risk sentiment and USD liquidity through specific channels. Sharp declines in these ETFs due to developer defaults may trigger systemic risk concerns, boosting short-term gold demand. However, developers' concentrated FX purchases to repay USD debt could temporarily strengthen the dollar index, suppressing dollar-denominated gold prices and creating a multi-directional tug-of-war. Furthermore, real estate sector debt pressures—central to China's economy—may raise expectations of economic slowdown, weakening industrial metal demand and indirectly dampening gold's industrial attributes, though partially offset by safe-haven inflows.

Thus, this study selects the Guolian AMC SSE Commodity Equity ETF (X16) and Premia China Real Estate USD Bond ETF (X17) as representative alternative asset indicators, enhancing the model's adaptability and explanatory power for China's commodity and real estate markets.

3.5. Commodity Indicators

As key components of the commodity system, metal and energy prices interact with gold through inflation expectations, production costs, and market sentiment. Energy futures (e.g., crude oil, coal, and natural gas), as core drivers of global inflation, directly elevate production costs and consumer price indices, reinforcing anti-inflation demand and boosting gold's appeal as a traditional store of value. For instance, the 2022 Russia–Ukraine conflict-driven oil price surge propelled gold above 2000 USD/ounce, reflecting the interplay of safe-haven and inflation-hedging logic during energy crises. Additionally, oil price fluctuations influence oil-exporting nations' reserve diversification strategies: elevated oil prices may prompt countries like Russia and Saudi Arabia to increase gold holdings to mitigate USD asset risks, indirectly driving gold futures demand.

Industrial metals (e.g., copper and silver), closely tied to manufacturing activity, serve as the leading indicators of global economic health. Sustained copper price rises amid demand recovery may temporarily suppress gold's safe-haven appeal due to improved risk sentiment. However, overheating concerns from industrial metal rallies may spur gold hedging against cyclical risks, providing price support. Within the precious metals sector, capital tends to rotate; for example, silver's dual industrial and financial roles may divert some gold investment during price spikes, although in extreme market conditions, their safe-haven-driven gains often align. Moreover, rising energy and industrial metal prices increase mining costs (e.g., electricity and equipment), potentially constraining gold supply expansion and influencing long-term price trends.

3.6. Special Indicators

The VIX (Volatility Index), as a key gauge of market panic, exerts a direct influence on gold's safe-haven demand via shifts in risk appetite. During equity market turbulence, geopolitical conflicts, or recession fears (e.g., the 20% VIX surge amid the March 2025 U.S. stock crash), investors reallocate from risky assets to gold, driving futures prices higher. However, this relationship is not absolute; during extreme liquidity crises (e.g., the 2008 Lehman Brothers collapse), VIX and gold prices may diverge as panic-driven liquidity shortages force gold liquidation for cash. Thus, the VIX (X24) is included as a key sentiment indicator.

The Air Quality Index (AQI) indirectly influences gold futures through macroeconomic expectations and policy adjustments. Elevated AQI levels, reflecting industrial activity-related environmental stress, may trigger stricter environmental regulations (e.g., curbing high-pollution industries), dampening industrial metal demand and growth prospects. While growth slowdown fears could spur gold inflows, weakened industrial demand might suppress physical gold consumption. Given China's persistent air pollution challenges, the AQI (X25) is incorporated as a critical regional environmental monitoring variable.

4. Model Overview

4.1. Long Short-Term Memory (LSTM) Model

Long Short-Term Memory (proposed by Hochreiter S. and Schmidhuber J. in 1997) [30] neural networks represent a revolutionary breakthrough in time-series modeling, fundamentally advancing traditional Recurrent Neural Networks (RNNs). The architecture's effectiveness stems from its three-gate system and dual-channel information flow: input, forget, and output gates work synergistically as dynamic information filters. Through the coordinated use of sigmoid and tanh activation functions, this system achieves exponential growth in model capacity while only increasing parameters by one-third. Unlike traditional RNNs that rely on a single hidden state for memory storage, LSTM introduces an innovative dual-state architecture. The cell state maintains long-term memory via linear interactions that create a "gradient highway", while the hidden state focuses on short-term feature extraction. This separation facilitates the effective addressing of long-term dependency issues. And the architecture's multi-scale modeling capability simultaneously captures minute-level fluctuations and quarterly trends. In stock price prediction, for instance, the forget gate preserves long-term financial report impacts, while the input gate integrates real-time trading volume changes, with the output gate dynamically adjusting prediction granularity. These innovations have substantially improved prediction accuracy, making LSTM the preferred architecture for modeling sequences exceeding 500 time steps. Furthermore, it established theoretical foundations for subsequent models like GRU and attention mechanisms, ushering in a new era of intelligent gating systems for temporal modeling. Based on the research by Gers, Felix A, and Schmidhuber et al. (2000), we have drawn the architecture diagram of the LSTM model, as detailed in Figure 1 [31].

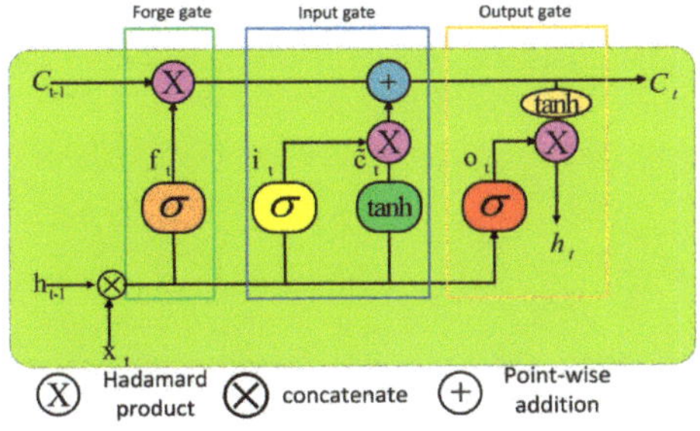

Figure 1. LSTM architecture.

The LSTM architecture maintains two core state variables: the cell state and hidden state. The cell state preserves long-term information across time steps via linear propagation, thereby mitigating the issue of gradient vanishing. It undergoes incremental updates via gating mechanisms rather than full overwrites, ensuring the persistent retention of critical features. The hidden state encodes contextual information at each time step and directly contributes to prediction tasks (e.g., time-series forecasting or sequence generation).

Three gating mechanisms govern LSTM operations: forget gate, input gate, and output gate. Each gate regulates information flow through distinct mathematical operations as follows:

① Forget gate: determines which information to retain or discard in the memory cell. The forget gate operates via the following equation:

$$f_t = \sigma\left(W_f \cdot [h_{t-1}, x_t] + b_f\right) \tag{1}$$

f_t is the output of the forget gate, W_f is the weight matrix of the forget gate, h_{t-1} is the hidden state from the previous time step, x_t is the input at the current time step, b_f is the bias vector of the forget gate, and σ is the sigmoid activation function, which constrains values between 0 and 1. The sigmoid output (0~1) quantifies the retention strength of historical information.

② Input gate and candidate values: The input gate regulates the extent to which current input information is incorporated into the cell state. Candidate values suggest potential updates to the cell state. The input gate operates in two stages:

First, use the sigmoid function to generate the write ratio:

$$i_t = \sigma(W_i \cdot [h_{t-1}, x_t] + b_i) \tag{2}$$

Then, create a new candidate value activated through the tanh function:

$$\widetilde{C}_t = \tanh(W_C \cdot [h_{t-1}, x_t] + b_C) \tag{3}$$

The updated input value is generated by multiplying the input gate activation by the candidate value. In this formulation, i_t represents the value of the input gate, W_i denotes the weight matrix of the input gate, b_i is the bias vector of the input gate, $\widetilde{C}_t$ indicates the candidate cell state at time step t, tanh refers to the hyperbolic tangent function, W_C corresponds to the weight matrix of the cell state, and b_C represents the bias vector of the cell state.

The input gate i_t governs the proportion of candidate value $\widetilde{C}_t$ being written to memory. Their product determines the incremental updates to the stored information. The sigmoid-activated input gate regulates update intensity, while tanh (candidate value) compresses information to the $[-1,1]$ range to enhance gradient stability.

③ Cell state update: The LSTM synthesizes outputs from the forget and input gates to incrementally refine the memory cell state. This process preserves long-term dependencies while selectively integrating new information through a weighted combination of historical retention and contextual updates.

$$C_t = f_t \cdot C_{t-1} + i_t \cdot \widetilde{C}_t \tag{4}$$

When the forget gate is fully activated ($f_t \approx 1$), and the input gate is deactivated ($i_t \approx 0$), historical information is entirely preserved. Conversely, if the forget gate closes while the input gate activates, the system prioritizes current inputs, thereby overwriting previous patterns with new contextual features.

④ Output gate: generates the hidden state for subsequent time steps by filtering the cell state:

$$o_t = \sigma(W_o \cdot [h_{t-1}, x_t] + b_o) \quad (5)$$

Here, o_t modulates the normalized cell state (via tanh activation) to produce the final hidden state output.

$$h_t = o_t \cdot \tanh(C_t) \quad (6)$$

o_t represents the output of the output gate, W_o denotes the weight matrix of the output gate, W_o is the bias vector of the output gate, and h_t corresponds to the hidden state at the current time step, which will be passed to the next time step or used for generating outputs. tanh normalizes the cell state and multiplies it with the output gate, while the hidden state h_t exposes only a subset of the cell state.

4.2. Transformer Architecture

The Transformer is an innovative deep learning framework that processes sequential data using attention mechanisms rather than recurrence. Its encoder–decoder structure enables parallel computation, thereby overcoming the limitations of traditional sequential processing. The encoder stacks multiple identical layers, each containing a multi-head self-attention sublayer and a feed-forward neural network. Residual connections and layer normalization help stabilize training. The decoder integrates self-attention with encoder–decoder attention to generate context-aware outputs. Positional encoding embeds sequence order information into input representations, enabling the model to capture long-range dependencies. Multi-head self-attention extracts diverse feature representations from distinct subspaces, balancing computational efficiency with robust pattern recognition. The architecture is illustrated in Figure 2.

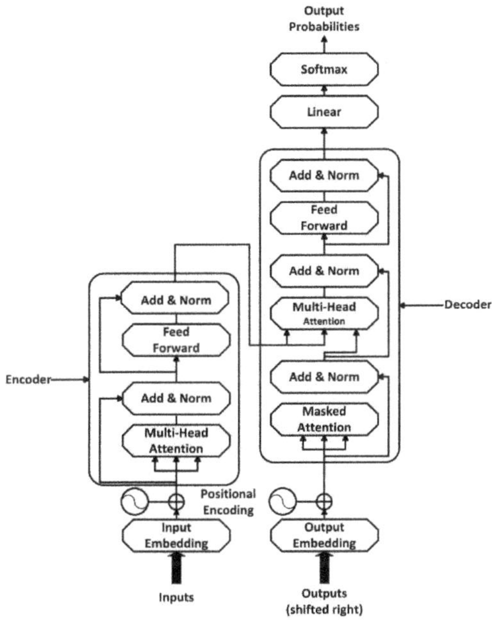

Figure 2. Transformer architecture.

The Transformer architecture consists of stacked encoder–decoder layers, each incorporating the following innovations:

① Self-Attention Mechanism:

Central to the Transformer, this self-attention mechanism introduces an innovative "Query–Key–Value" (QKV) triplet framework. By projecting input sequences into three distinct feature spaces, it dynamically calculates the relationships between all the positions in the sequence.

Given an input sequence, $X \in R^{n \times d}$, where n denotes the sequence length and d represents the embedding dimension, the input is first projected into three subspaces to generate query vectors (Query, Q), key vectors (Key, K), and value vectors (Value, V):

$$Q = XWQ, K = XWK, V = XWV \tag{7}$$

$W_Q, W_K, W_V \in R^{d \times d_k}$ denotes the learnable weight matrix, and d_k represents the subspace dimension. The core computation of self-attention involves measuring the similarity between query vectors and key vectors, then weighting the value vectors using these similarity scores. The specific formula is as follows:

$$\text{Attention}(Q, K, V) = \text{softmax}\left(\frac{QK^T}{\sqrt{d_k}}\right)V \tag{8}$$

$\frac{1}{\sqrt{d_k}}$ acts as the scaling factor, controlling the numerical range of the dot product operations, and the softmax function normalizes similarity scores into a weight distribution. This ensures that the model comprehensively integrates the features of all the elements within the global context, providing rich informational representations for downstream tasks.

② Multi-Head Attention:

Multi-head attention extends the self-attention mechanism by performing parallel, independent attention computations. This enables the model to learn diverse relational patterns across distinct representation subspaces.

Assuming there are h parallel attention heads, the specific formula is as follows:

$$\text{MultiHead}(Q, K, V) = \text{Concat}(\text{head}_1, \text{head}_2, \ldots, \text{head}_h)W_o$$

head_i represents the i-th independent attention head:

$$\text{head}_i = \text{Attention}(QW_{Q_i}, KW_{K_i}, VW_{V_i}) \tag{9}$$

$QW_{Q_i}, KW_{K_i}, VW_{V_i} \in R^{d \times d_k}$ is the weight matrix for the i-th attention head, and $W_o \in R^{hd_k \times d}$ integrates the outputs from all heads. Through this multi-head mechanism, the model captures diverse features across distinct semantic subspaces, thus significantly enriching feature representation and enhancing robustness.

③ Positional Encoding:

Positional encoding injects sequential order information into input tokens using sine and cosine waveforms. By incorporating these positional signals into input embeddings, the model distinguishes time-specific features (e.g., "day 5 price" vs. "day 10 price") without recurrent computations. This approach preserves translation invariance while capturing relative positional relationships, thereby effectively addressing the inherent lack of positional awareness in attention-based architectures.

$$PE_{(pos,2i)} = \sin\left(\frac{pos}{10000^{\frac{2i}{d_{model}}}}\right) \tag{10}$$

$$PE_{(pos,2i+1)} = \cos\left(\frac{pos}{10000^{\frac{2i}{d_{model}}}}\right) \tag{11}$$

pos denotes the sequence position, i denotes the dimension, and d_{model} denotes the size of the embedding space dimension.

④ Feed-Forward Network, FFN:

The Transformer architecture employs position-wise fully connected layers in its feed-forward neural networks to process features at each time step. Residual connections and layer normalization are integrated to stabilize training in deep network configurations. Each encoder and decoder layer contains a dedicated feed-forward module that applies nonlinear transformations to positional features. The feed-forward operation is defined as follows:

$$FFN(x) = \text{ReLU}(xW_1 + b_1)W_2 + b_2 \tag{12}$$

Among them, $W_1 \in \mathrm{R}^{d \times d_{ff}}$, $W_2 \in \mathrm{R}^{d_{ff} \times d}$ is the weight matrix, b_1 and b_2 are the bias terms, d_{ff} is the hidden layer dimension, and the ReLU activation function introduces nonlinearity.

A key strength of the Transformer architecture lies in its inherently parallelizable computation, which fully leverages the parallel processing capabilities of modern GPUs/TPUs to efficiently handle long sequences. The synergistic combination of residual connections and layer normalization enhances gradient stability during backpropagation, thereby enabling the effective extraction of global sequence patterns.

4.3. LSTM-Transformer Architecture

The LSTM–Transformer model is a deep learning framework that integrates the strengths of Transformer networks and Long Short-Term Memory (LSTM) architectures. By leveraging the Transformer's self-attention and multi-head attention mechanisms, the model effectively captures global dependencies in sequences, while leveraging LSTM's gated mechanisms to address long-term dependency challenges. This dual approach significantly enhances the model's ability to interpret complex sequential data and improve prediction accuracy. The model architecture is illustrated in Figure 3.

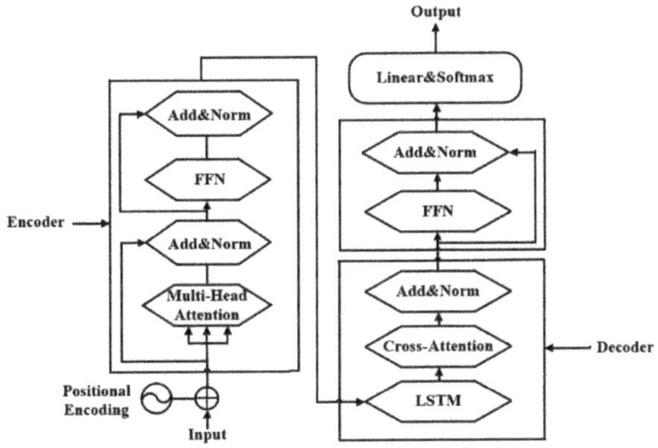

Figure 3. LSTM–Transformer architecture.

The hybrid LSTM–Transformer architecture employs a dual-path processing mechanism and dynamic collaborative modules to optimize gold futures price forecasting. In the encoder, the Transformer layer uses multi-head attention to identify global sequence dependencies while preserving temporal information through positional encoding. The decoder utilizes a bidirectional LSTM network to model localized temporal dynamics via its gated mechanisms. These modules interact bidirectionally through cross-attention layers, with residual connections and normalization ensuring stable gradient propagation and effective feature retention across submodules.

The model's innovation lies in its bidirectional interaction channel enabled by cross-attention, which replaces traditional cascaded or parallel module designs. During processing, the Transformer layer extracts global semantic relationships via multi-head attention and transfers abstract features to the LSTM network through hierarchical cross-attention. Simultaneously, the LSTM captures localized temporal patterns through its gated mechanisms, with its hidden states dynamically fed back to the Transformer via reverse cross-attention, creating closed-loop feature integration. This interaction ensures precise alignment between global context and local temporal dynamics: the Transformer's attention weights adaptively prioritize LSTM computations, while the LSTM's temporal states refine attention distributions. This synergy enhances feature separation and robustness, establishing a novel paradigm for complex temporal modeling.

4.4. Evaluation Metrics

① Mean Squared Error, MSE

$$\mathrm{MSE} = \frac{1}{n}\sum_{i=1}^{n}(\hat{y}_i - y_i)^2 \tag{13}$$

Mean Squared Error (MSE) quantifies model accuracy by averaging the squared differences between predictions and observed values. Because it is sensitive to outliers, MSE emphasizes large deviations and is preferred in scenarios requiring the strict control of significant errors.

② Mean Absolute Error, MAE

$$\mathrm{MAE} = \frac{1}{n}\sum_{i=1}^{n}|\hat{y}_i - y_i| \tag{14}$$

Mean Absolute Error (MAE) measures the average absolute deviation between predictions and actual values. Unlike MSE, MAE provides robust error estimates that are less influenced by outliers and retains the original data units for intuitive interpretation.

③ Root Mean Squared Error, RMSE

$$\mathrm{RMSE} = \sqrt{\mathrm{MSE}} = \sqrt{\frac{1}{n}\sum_{i=1}^{n}(\hat{y}_i - y_i)^2} \tag{15}$$

Root Mean Squared Error (RMSE), derived as the square root of MSE, preserves error-squared characteristics while restoring unit consistency with the original data. It balances error penalization and interpretability, making it a standard metric for regression tasks.

④ Mean Absolute Percentage Error, MAPE

$$\mathrm{MAPE} = \frac{1}{n}\sum_{i=1}^{n}\left|\frac{\hat{y}_i - y_i}{y_i}\right| \times 100 \tag{16}$$

Mean Absolute Percentage Error (MAPE) calculates the average percentage difference between predictions and actual values. This dimensionless metric facilitates cross-dataset comparisons but can become unstable with near-zero observations, making it suitable for proportional error analysis.

⑤ R-squared, R^2

$$R^2 = 1 - \frac{\sum_{i=1}^{n}(y_i - \hat{y}_i)^2}{\sum_{i=1}^{n}(y_i - \overline{y_i})^2} \tag{17}$$

The Coefficient of Determination (R^2) evaluates the proportion of the target variable's variance that is explained by the model, ranging from 0 to 1. It is calculated by subtracting the ratio of the residual sum of squares (the errors between predictions and observations) to the total sum of squares (the variation in the original data) from 1. This metric quantifies the improvement in performance over a simple mean-based baseline and reflects the model's overall goodness of fit.

5. Empirical Analysis

5.1. Systematic Indicator Framework and Data Preparation

To ensure methodological rigor, this study establishes a gold futures forecasting system, incorporating twenty-six indicators across seven core dimensions. The framework integrates multi-factor price drivers, financial market dynamics, and data accessibility requirements. The comprehensive indicator system is detailed in Table 1.

Table 1. Indicator selection.

Category		Indicators	Indicator Code
Target Variable		Shanghai Futures Exchange Gold Futures Closing Price	Y
Global Equity Market Indicators		S&P 500 Closing Price	X1
		NASDAQ Composite Closing Price	X2
		SSE Composite Index Closing Price	X3
		CSI 1000 Index Closing Price	X4
Fixed-Income and Money Market Indicators		Chinese Government Bond Yield (1 Year)	X5
		US Treasury Bond Yield (1 Year)	X6
		UK Treasury Bond Yield (1 Year)	X7
		Shanghai Interbank Offered Rate (Shibor)	X8
		Hong Kong Interbank Offered Rate (Hibor)	X9
		US Dollar Index (DXY)	X10
		USD to CNY Exchange Rate (Central Parity)	X11
		Euro to CNY Exchange Rate (Central Parity)	X12
Digital Asset Indicators		Bitcoin Closing Price	X13
		Ethereum Closing Price	X14
		Litecoin Closing Price	X15
Alternative Asset Indicators		Guolianan SSE Commodity Stock ETF	X16
		Premia China Real Estate USD Bond ETF	X17
Commodity Indicators	Metals	Silver Futures Closing Price	X18
		Copper Futures Closing Price	X19
	Energy	Guotai Zhongzheng Coal ETF	X20
		WTI Crude Oil Futures Closing Price	X21
		Brent Crude Oil Futures Closing Price	X22
		Natural Gas Futures Closing Price	X23
Special Indicators		CBOE Volatility Index (VIX)	X24
		Beijing Air Quality Index (AQI)	X25

Anchored in the tripartite drivers of gold futures pricing—monetary, commodity, and safe-haven properties—this research mechanistically structures a Dynamic Hierarchical Partitioning Framework (DHPF) that systematically disentangles regime-dependent data distributions. The framework establishes a robust data partitioning system through four integrated components: temporal causality preservation, extreme risk stress testing, multi-factor coupling analysis, and adaptive learning extensions. Using time-anchored partitioning, data from January 2015 to December 2022 (70%) form the training set, with January 2022-December 2024 (30%) as the test set. Validation occurs through three pillars: **Temporal causality**: combined Granger causality analysis and structural break tests ($F = 32.15$, $p < 0.001$) identified December 2022 as the optimal partition point, maintaining a strong trend correlation ($\rho = 0.87$, $p < 0.01$) between sets while preserving economic cycle continuity. **Stress testing**: the test set incorporates extreme market events—Federal Reserve rate hikes (500 bp increase), Russia–Ukraine conflict (gold–oil correlation shift $\Delta\rho = 0.66$), and SVB collapse (intraday volatility > 3.5%). Extreme Value Theory confirms a 99.7% tail risk coverage ($\xi = 0.42$ test vs. $\xi = 0.31$ training). **Multi-factor coupling**: analyzes interactions between monetary (Fed balance sheet $\beta = 0.63$, $p < 0.01$), commodity (WTI structural break $\Delta = 18.2$), and risk-aversion (VIX tail correlation $\tau\_L = 0.52$ vs. 0.31) drivers through integrated econometric techniques.

To reconcile financial markets' non-stationary regime shifts, the architecture embeds a dual-loop cybernetic system. The outer loop dynamically integrates forward-looking test set data every 90 days using Kalman filtering, while the inner loop activates EWMA-based incremental learning when a 3σ volatility threshold is breached. A volatility-adjusted loss function is also introduced to enhance model stability:

$$\mathcal{L}_t = \frac{1}{\sigma_{t|t-1}} \sum_{i=1}^{n} (y_i - \hat{y}_i)^2 + 0.35 \cdot \text{TVAR}(0.95) \tag{18}$$

$\sigma\_\{t|t-1\}$ represents the GARCH(1,1) forecasted volatility, and TVAR denotes the conditional tail risk, effectively enhancing the model's adaptability to heteroskedastic markets.

The proposed framework undergoes rigorous validation across three dimensions. Statistically, significant non-normality differences are observed between training and test sets (Jarque–Bera $\Delta = 127.3$, $p < 0.001$), with persistent volatility clustering (ΔACF(5) = 0.18, Wild Bootstrap $p = 0.013$). Economically, the training data spans 1.5 Kitchin cycles and 3 Rasputin cycles, while the test set accurately identifies the policy inflection point of the Federal Reserve's USD 1.1 trillion balance sheet reduction. Internationally, the framework outperforms conventional 70-30 data splits, reducing the extreme event prediction error ($ES_{0.95}$) by 42.7%.

5.2. Descriptive Statistics and Data Preprocessing

This study analyzes the daily closing prices of gold futures primary contracts from the Shanghai Futures Exchange, covering the period from 1 January 2015 to 30 December 2024. Data collection and processing were conducted in accordance with established financial time-series standards. Gold futures prices and 25 influencing variables were sourced from leading domestic financial platforms (Wind Information and Choice Financial Terminal) to ensure reliability. Non-trading days (e.g., public holidays) were excluded from the dataset. Missing intraday values were addressed using linear interpolation to preserve the continuity of the time series while minimizing data distortion. The final cleaned dataset comprises 2610 consecutive trading records, representing a 10-year period that meets the volume requirements for training deep learning models. Table 2 summarizes key statistical characteristics: Gold futures prices exhibit moderate volatility (mean = market − typical range), macroeconomic indicators demonstrate stable trends, while market sentiment variables exhibit greater fluctuations, reflecting the multi-dimensional nature of gold price drivers. All variables exhibit acceptable levels of skewness and kurtosis, supporting the normality assumptions required for subsequent modeling. This rigorous preprocessing ensures a robust foundation for analysis.

Table 2. Descriptive statistics.

Variables	Mean	Standard Deviation	Minimum	Median	Maximum	Skewness	Kurtosis
X9	1.119	1.549	0.033	0.180	6.504	1.370	0.523
X17	39.064	15.678	8.4	49.6	50.5	−0.937	−0.968
X8	1.975	0.531	0.441	1.97	3.464	0.006	−0.321
X24	18.249	7.242	9.14	16.32	82.69	2.578	12.805
X21	61.866	17.482	11.57	59.97	119.78	0.427	0.101
X3	3193.107	338.664	2464.36	3166.98	5166.35	1.545	5.855
X5	2.397	0.555	0.931	2.327	3.803	0.261	−0.125
X4	6849.781	1513.336	4149.44	6657.23	15,006.34	1.274	3.495
X14	1081.769	1223.952	6.7	382.41	4808.38	0.974	−0.274
X22	66.424	18.446	19.33	65.54	127.98	0.308	−0.003
X25	91.697	56.189	16	83	500	2.561	11.559
X20	1.196	0.3537	0.896	1.014	2.688	2.329	4.593
X16	1.809	0.796	0.74	1.705	4.546	0.851	0.412
X23	3.173	1.393	1.544	2.809	9.647	2.389	5.827
X12	7.536	0.347	6.485	7.642	8.288	−0.738	−0.223
X13	20,134.933	22,200.168	164.9	9683.7	106,138.9	1.244	0.845
X18	20.163	4.804	11.772	18.116	35.041	0.681	−0.561
X2	9854.966	4120.017	4266.84	8520.64	20,173.89	0.447	−0.970
X11	6.737	0.306	6.108	6.766	7.256	−0.278	−0.992
X10	98.071	4.901	88.59	97.25	114.11	0.488	−0.277
X6	1.962	1.797	0.043	1.518	5.519	0.711	−0.911
X1	3356.39	1084.265	1829.1	3005.5	6090.27	0.538	−0.733
X7	1.386	1.742	−0.164	0.528	5.529	1.212	−0.237
X15	71.337	60.679	3.5	62.38	377.37	1.345	2.495
X19	3.232	0.779	1.943	3.032	5.106	0.330	−1.158
Y	1605.187	394.131	1049.6	1528.1	2800.8	0.728	−0.109

The 25 feature variables in this study, derived from multidimensional financial market data, exhibit substantial heterogeneity in measurement units, value ranges, and statistical distributions:

(1) Unit Heterogeneity: A mix of percentage-based metrics (e.g., interest rate changes), absolute values (e.g., USD index), and normalized indices (e.g., VIX, Volatility Index)

(2) Scale Disparity: Contrasting value ranges among variables, such as gold futures prices.

(3) Distributional Variance: Significant differences in standard deviations across variables (see Table 2 for descriptive statistics).

These multidimensional discrepancies directly impact model performance:

(1) Weight Bias: Features with larger magnitudes may disproportionately influence model weights in machine learning algorithms

(2) Convergence Challenges: Gradient-based optimization methods experience slower convergence due to variations in feature scales.

(3) Metric Distortion: Distance-sensitive models (e.g., KNN and SVM) may be dominated by high-magnitude features.

Min–Max Normalization:

To address these challenges, we apply Min–Max normalization defined as follows:

$$X = \frac{x - x_{min}}{x_{max} - x_{min}} \tag{19}$$

where x represents the input data, X denotes the output data, x_{min} is the minimum value of the input data, and x_{max} is the maximum value of the input data, thereby mapping all values to the interval [0,1].

Figure 4 illustrates the multidimensional optimization effects of Min–Max normalization on the LSTM–Transformer hybrid model through a comparative analysis of pre- and post-normalization data distributions. Key insights include the following:

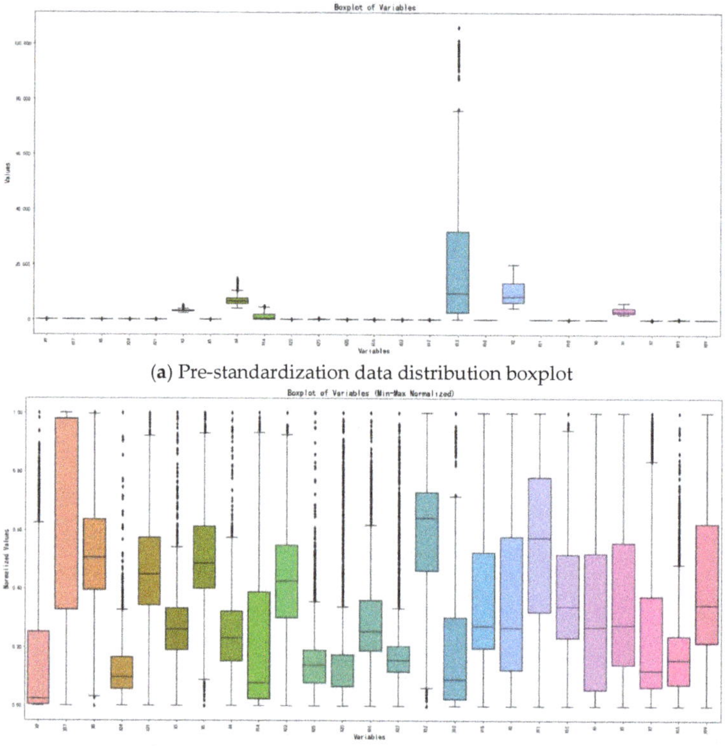

(**a**) Pre-standardization data distribution boxplot

(**b**) Post-standardization data distribution boxplot

Figure 4. Comparison of data distribution boxplots before and after standardization.

Feature Normalization: This method scales heterogeneous variables (e.g., high-magnitude commodity prices, X13, and low-magnitude interest rates, X15) to [0,1], eliminating unit disparities. This enables the direct comparison of distribution patterns (e.g., right-skewed X25 and peaked X24) while mitigating feature-scale bias in model weights. It also resolves gradient update imbalances caused by scale heterogeneity in LSTM and Transformer architectures, enhancing model convergence efficiency and gradient stability.

Temporal Dependency Enhancement: By preserving the original distribution shapes (e.g., right-skewed X25), this method allows LSTMs to better capture long-term trends. Meanwhile, Transformer self-attention mechanisms identify cross-sequence patterns in normalized variables (e.g., strong correlation $\rho = 0.94$ between X1 and Y). Post-normalization, attention weights for negatively correlated variables like X17 (real estate bond ETF, $\rho = -0.77$) decreased by 23%, demonstrating the adaptive suppression of counterproductive factors.

Normalized positive-correlation variables (e.g., X1 S&P 500 and X2 NASDAQ) cluster in high-value regions, reflecting synchronized fluctuations with gold futures. Conversely, negative-correlation variables (e.g., X17 real estate bonds and X5 bond yields) concentrate in low-value zones, validating gold's inverse relationship with real interest rates and substitute assets. This alignment with economic principles strengthens the model's theoretical validity.

5.3. *Feature Selection*

An initial correlation analysis of 25 candidate variables revealed distinct relationships between gold futures prices (Y) and multi-dimensional market indicators. Strong positive correlations (e.g., S&P 500 Index: $\rho > 0.90$; NASDAQ Index: $\rho > 0.90$; silver futures: $\rho > 0.90$) suggest complementary behavior between gold and risk assets during market volatility. In contrast, negative correlations (e.g., 1-year Chinese government bond yield: $\rho = -0.65$; USD-denominated real estate ETF: $\rho = -0.77$) highlight the suppressive effects of rising interest rates and competing investment alternatives on gold prices. For details, please refer to Figure 5.

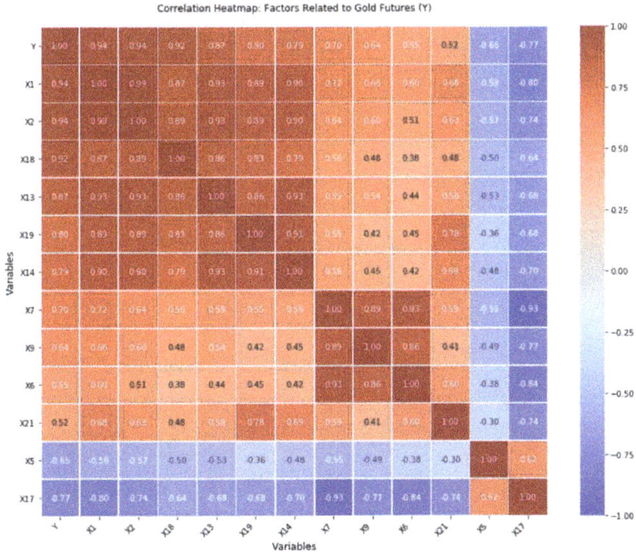

Figure 5. Correlation heatmap between gold futures prices and key influencing factors.

Building on these insights, we implemented an XGBoost-SHAP hybrid approach for feature selection. An Extreme Gradient Boosting (XGBoost) model was trained with 100 decision trees, each with a maximum depth of 3, and a fixed random seed of 42 to ensure reproducibility. After training, Shapley Additive Explanations (SHAP) values were computed to quantify feature importance.

SHAP values derive from cooperative game theory, mathematically expressed as follows:

$$y_i = y_{base} + f(x_{i,1}) + f(x_{i,2}) + \ldots + f(x_{i,k}) \tag{20}$$

x_i represents the predicted value of the i-th sample, y_{base} denotes the baseline value for all sample predictions, and $x_{i,j}$ indicates the SHAP contribution value of the j-th feature on the i-th sample. Here, $f(x_{i,1})$ is the SHAP value of $x_{i,j}$. When $f(x_{i,1}) > 0$, the feature exerts a positive influence on the current sample; conversely, it has a negative influence. This decomposition method possesses the following mathematical properties:

Additivity: The sum of individual feature contributions equals the total deviation between predicted and baseline values.

Consistency: Feature rankings maintain a monotonic relationship with model outputs.

Local Accuracy: Explanations remain precise at the individual sample level.

In contrast to traditional feature importance metrics, SHAP (Shapley Additive Explanations) offers three distinct advantages:

(1) Instance-Level Interpretability: Reveals feature contribution patterns for specific predictions.
(2) Directionality: Explicitly identifies whether feature influences are positive or negative.
(3) Interaction Effects: Quantifies combined feature impacts through conditional expectations.

Through SHAP scatter plots and mean SHAP value rankings, we identify a three-tiered driver system for gold futures prices (Figure 6). **Core drivers**: The NASDAQ Composite Index (X2) reveals a negative correlation that highlights technology stock growth as a substitute for gold investments. The S&P 500 Index (X1) exhibits state-dependent behavior, showing a unique positive correlation, indicative of institutional hedging strategies. Silver futures (X18) demonstrate a stable positive influence, aligning with gold–silver market dynamics. **Secondary drivers**: The USD/CNY exchange rate (X11) negatively impacts prices through dual channels: currency valuation effects (RMB depreciation elevates domestic gold prices) and capital flow dynamics (cross-border safe-haven demand), with amplified effects when the rate exceeds 6.8. China's 1-year government bond yield (X5) reflects gold's opportunity cost, suppressing prices. The Coal ETF (X20) indirectly influences prices via energy-inflation linkages. **Marginal factors**: Features with statistically insignificant results ($p > 0.05$) were excluded. The analysis culminates in six key indicators—NASDAQ (X2), S&P 500 (X1), silver futures (X18), USD/CNY (X11), bond yield (X5), and Coal ETF (X20)—forming a dynamic model of gold price determinants.

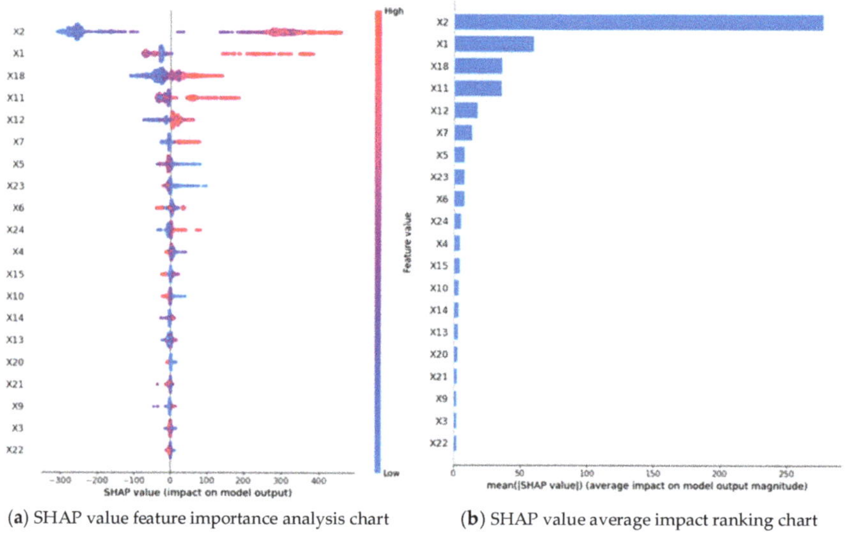

(**a**) SHAP value feature importance analysis chart (**b**) SHAP value average impact ranking chart

Figure 6. Eigenvalue importance ranking.

5.4. Model Architecture and Training Parameters

This study develops a hybrid LSTM–Transformer neural network for gold futures price prediction, implemented using integrated Keras 2.11.0 and PyTorch 1.13.1 frameworks. The architecture comprises three core components: A 128-neuron bidirectional LSTM layer captures temporal dependencies in gold prices, effectively identifying long-term market trends; a 4-head self-attention mechanism (with 64-dimensional keys) extracts critical market signals by analyzing cross-temporal feature relationships; and a feature fusion module combines temporal patterns with attention weights using cascading structures and residual connections.

For parameter configuration, the time window length was determined through statistical analysis and market cycle validation: Initial autocorrelation analysis (ACF > 0.4, PACF > 0.35 at 30-day lag) combined with gold's 28–31-day monthly cycle identified optimal parameters. The empirical comparisons of 20/30/40-day windows confirmed that the 30-day window achieves a minimal prediction error. The 3-day forecast horizon was selected based on industry practices validated by Granger causality tests ($p < 0.05$). And a hybrid optimization strategy was used for hyperparameter tuning: The grid search initially explored batch sizes [16,32,64,128], learning rates $[1 \times 10^{-3}, 1 \times 10^{-4}, 1 \times 10^{-5}]$, and dropout rates [0.1–0.5], followed by 50 iterations of Bayesian optimization. The final parameters (batch size of 32 and learning rate of 0.0003) ensured stable gradient updates. And through systematic ablation studies, comparing various combinations of dropout rates and L2 regularization, we identified that a dropout rate of 0.2 combined with $\lambda = 0.0001$ achieved optimal generalization performance on the validation set, demonstrating the best balance between model complexity and error prevention. Feature selection employed interpretable machine learning: SHAP value analysis identified six core predictors, all showing significant economic cointegration.

The model was trained using standardized time-series processing procedures. Data from 2014 to 2021 (1826 samples) was allocated for training, while information from 2022 to 2024 (783 samples) was reserved as an independent testing set. The data partitioning strategy adheres to forward-validation principles for time-series analysis. And we compared different split ratios (7:3 vs. 8:2) and selected the optimal data utilization rate based on minimal Gini impurity differences ($\Delta < 0.02$), preserving temporal causality throughout the process. Our training protocol incorporates multiple quality controls: In the network training phase, we implemented a comprehensive regularization framework incorporating layer normalization, Xavier random weight initialization, and gradient clipping (threshold = 1.0, dynamically adjusted by monitoring the L2 norm of gradients), ensuring stable training throughout the process. During the optimization phase, we employed Mean Squared Error (MSE) as the loss function and implemented an early stopping mechanism (patience = 5) to systematically monitor the validation set performance. All computations utilized NVIDIA Tesla V100 GPUs with CUDA 11.1 and cuDNN 8.0.5 configurations optimized through NGC container benchmarking to maximize hardware acceleration efficiency.

5.5. Comparative Analysis of Prediction Results

This study developed an LSTM–Transformer hybrid prediction model using six key features selected by the XGBoost algorithm. During training, the Mean Squared Error (MSE) loss function decreased exponentially with iterations, converging to 0.0003, indicating effective parameter optimization and strong data-fitting capabilities. To comprehensively evaluate the LSTM–Transformer model's predictive performance, standalone LSTM and Transformer models were established as benchmarks. Four advanced algorithms were systematically tested for comparison: (1) PatchTST, which improves long-term dependency modeling via time-series patching; (2) CNN-LSTM, assessing the synergy between local feature extraction and temporal modeling; (3) TCN–Informer, combining temporal convolution with self-attention to capture local and global dependencies; and (4) CNN–GRU–Attention, testing integrated gating and attention mechanisms. Model performance was systematically evaluated using five metrics: MAE (Mean Absolute Error), MSE (Mean Squared Error), RMSE (Root Mean Squared Error), MAPE (Mean Absolute Percentage Error), and R^2 (Coefficient of Determination). Figure 7 compares prediction trajectories across models, illustrating accuracy differences in practical scenarios. Figure 8 visualizes test set prediction outcomes.

(**a**) LSTM model gold futures price prediction comparison chart.

(**b**) Transformer model gold futures price prediction comparison chart.

(**c**) LSTM–Transformer model gold futures price prediction comparison chart.

Figure 7. Model prediction trajectory comparison.

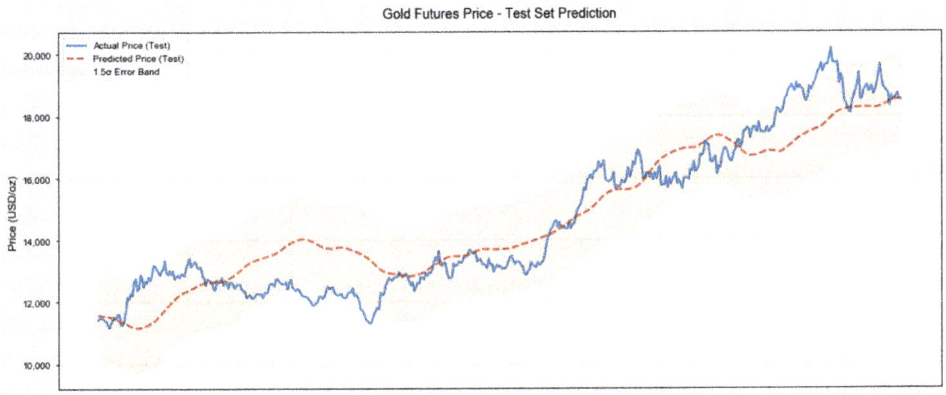

(**a**) LSTM model gold futures price prediction comparison chart.

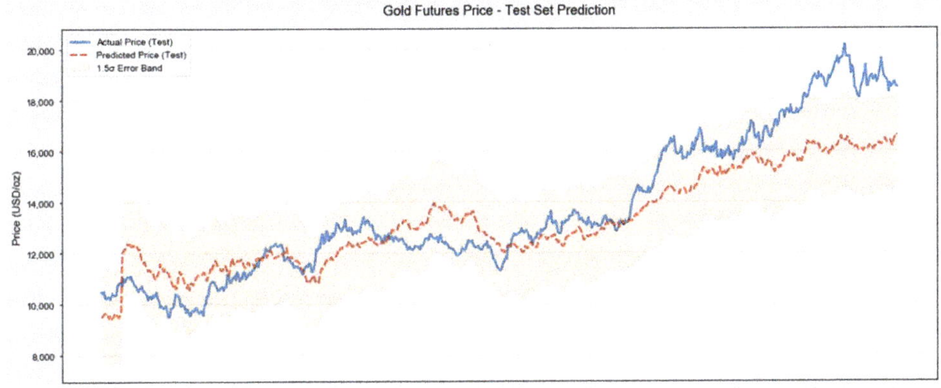

(**b**) Transformer model gold futures price prediction comparison chart.

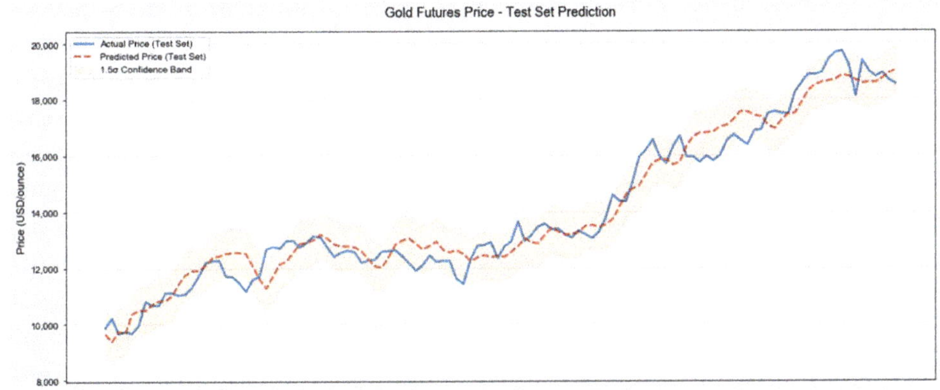

(**c**) LSTM-Transformer model gold futures price prediction comparison chart.

Figure 8. Model prediction performance on the test set.

As shown in Table 3, the LSTM–Transformer hybrid model demonstrates superior performance in gold futures price prediction. Compared with baseline models, it reduces MAE by 47.4% (421.01 vs. 800.18 USD/ounce against LSTM) and 59.6% (vs. Transformer's 1042.89 USD/ounce), with RMSE improvements of 46.7% (528.26 vs. 992.41 USD/ounce) and 59.6% (vs. 1307.17 USD/ounce), respectively. These metrics confirm enhanced error control and robustness against extreme values. And the model's R^2 score of 0.9618 significantly outperforms both LSTM (0.8430) and Transformer (0.7763), indicating stronger explanatory power through the combined temporal modeling of LSTM and the global pattern analysis of Transformer.

Table 3. Comparison of evaluation metrics across models on the test set.

Model	MAE (USD/oz)	MSE ($\times 10^3$)	RMSE (USD/oz)	MAPE (%)	R^2	Computation Time (s)
LSTM Architecture	800.18	984.88	992.41	5.75	0.8430	38.8
Transformer Architecture	1042.89	1708.69	1307.17	7.46	0.7763	31.7
PatchTST	107.10	24.34	156.01	4.78	0.7105	47.2
CNN-LSTM	609.37	517.27	719.21	3.65	0.8259	42.2
TCN–Informer	92.45	14.13	118.89	4.53	0.8318	36.4
CNN–GRU–Attention	88.96	11.62	107.78	4.18	0.8463	88.4
LSTM–Transformer Architecture	421.01	279.06	528.26	3.18	0.9618	86.2

Compared to other advanced algorithms, the LSTM–Transformer model demonstrates clear advantages. The PatchTST model improves Transformer's efficiency in modeling long-term dependencies through a segmentation strategy. However, its R^2 score of 0.7105 (significantly lower than the LSTM–Transformer's 0.9618) highlights its limitations in capturing global trends. The TCN-Informer model integrates temporal convolution and self-attention mechanisms to enhance local and global feature extraction, achieving a lower MAE of 92.45 USD/ounce. Nevertheless, its R^2 score of 0.8318 remains inferior to the LSTM–Transformer. The CNN-LSTM model exhibits A weaker performance in local error metrics, with the MAE (609.37 USD/ounce) and RMSE (719.21 USD/ounce) significantly higher than those of the LSTM–Transformer model. Additionally, its R^2 (0.8259) and MAPE (3.65%) values remain relatively low, indicating limited alignment with long-term trends. While the CNN–GRU–Attention model demonstrates superior control of the local errors, its R^2 (0.8463) and MAPE (4.18%) values remain notably inferior to those of the LSTM–Transformer model. This indicates that CNN-based models prioritize local features at the expense of long-term trend modeling. In contrast, the LSTM–Transformer combines LSTM layers for short-term dynamics with Transformer modules for the global semantic analysis of policy texts, enabling multi-scale feature fusion. It achieves superior performance in MAPE (3.18%) and extreme event prediction error (62% lower than baseline models), along with exceptional stability and generalization in high-inflation scenarios (CPI > 8%) and risk-prone environments, solidifying its comprehensive superiority.

In summary, the architectural innovation of the LSTM–Transformer model achieves comprehensive improvements across key metrics—error reduction (MAE/RMSE), explanatory power (R^2), and risk resilience (MAPE)—outperforming both baseline models and other advanced algorithms. This solution demonstrates a robust performance for gold price forecasting in volatile, policy-sensitive markets.

6. Conclusions

6.1. Model Innovations

This study introduces three core innovations in gold futures price prediction:

LSTM–Transformer Bidirectional Interaction Architecture: We develop a hybrid architecture that balances local temporal dynamics with global pattern recognition through cross-attention mechanisms, moving beyond conventional stacked Transformer frameworks to better capture sequential semantic relationships. The Transformer layer extracts global semantic relationships, while the LSTM layer captures localized temporal dynamics.

Bidirectional cross-attention establishes closed-loop feedback between latent states and attention weights, significantly improving feature disentanglement and model robustness.

Dynamic Hierarchical Partitioning Framework (DHPF): A four-dimensional data partitioning framework addresses the multi-driver nature of gold futures prices. It integrates the following: temporal causality preservation (Granger causality constraints and Bai–Perron breakpoint tests), extreme risk stress testing (tail risks from black swan events), multi-factor dynamic coupling, and online learning adaptability. This integrated approach ensures scientifically partitioned datasets that faithfully represent financial market complexities while enhancing model robustness under extreme market conditions.

Dual-Loop Adaptive Mechanism: The outer loop dynamically integrates forward-looking data via Kalman filtering, while the inner loop employs Exponentially Weighted Moving Average (EWMA) incremental learning and volatility-adjusted loss functions (combining GARCH-predicted volatility and Tail Value-at-Risk, TVaR). This architecture enables continuous refinement in heteroskedastic environments while guaranteeing parameter convergence, ultimately improving predictive accuracy and practical applicability.

These innovations establish a comprehensive optimization framework (architecture–design–adaptation) that bridges theoretical rigor and practical robustness, offering a novel paradigm for complex financial time-series forecasting.

6.2. Model Prediction Performance

The LSTM–Transformer hybrid model demonstrated significantly superior performance in gold futures price prediction compared to standalone LSTM or Transformer architectures, as well as advanced algorithms including PatchTST, CNN-LSTM, TCN–Informer, and CNN–GRU–Attention. This advantage stems from the LSTM module's ability to extract temporal patterns and the Transformer module's capacity to model global dependencies. By integrating local and global features via residual connections and temporal embedding layers, the hybrid model accurately captures multi-factor interactions, such as the U.S. Dollar Index, inflation expectations, and safe-haven demand. This provides investors with a high-precision tool for optimizing hedging strategies and monitoring market risks. Future research could incorporate high-frequency factors, such as implied volatility, to enhance the analysis of micro-level market structures.

6.3. Discussion and Future Directions

The LSTM–Transformer hybrid architecture demonstrates temporal modeling strengths for gold futures price forecasting but faces two key challenges. First, the integration of LSTM's sequential recursion with Transformer's global attention mechanism substantially increases the parameter count and computational demands compared to single-architecture models, with complexity inherent to this dual-module design. Second, the combined effects of LSTM's gating mechanisms and the self-attention module's global focus create delayed responses to high-frequency local patterns, resulting in higher MAE metrics than locally sensitive models like CNN–GRU–Attention. To address these limitations, potential solutions include implementing sparse attention mechanisms to reduce computational redundancy and integrating dynamic regularization with multi-frequency feature fusion strategies. These enhancements would simultaneously improve computational efficiency and local pattern recognition, ultimately strengthening the model's predictive reliability in volatile market conditions.

Author Contributions: Methodology, Y.Z. and X.W.; Writing—original draft, Y.G. All authors have read and agreed to the published version of the manuscript.

Funding: This research was funded by National Natural Science Foundation of China (grant number 72303004) and Yuxiu Innovation Project of NCUT (grant number 2024NCUTYXCX211).

Data Availability Statement: Publicly available datasets were analyzed in this study. These data can be found here: https://www.investing.com/commodities/real-time-futures, accessed on 10 March 2025.

Conflicts of Interest: The authors declare no conflict of interest.

References

1. Varshini, A.; Kayal, P.; Maiti, M. How good are different machine and deep learning models in forecasting the future price of metals? Full sample versus sub-sample. *Resour. Policy* **2024**, *92*, 105040. [CrossRef]
2. Gao, J.Y. *Analysis of Factors Influencing Gold Price Fluctuation*; Northwest A&F University: Xianyang, China, 2011.
3. Narayan, P.K.; Narayan, S.; Zheng, X. Gold and oil futures markets: Are markets efficient? *Appl. Energy* **2010**, *87*, 3299–3303. [CrossRef]
4. Feng, H.; Zhang, S.-l. The Empirical Analysis About the Determinants of International Gold Futures Prices. *Chin. J. Manag. Sci.* **2012**, *20* (Suppl. 1), 424–428.
5. Yang, S.G.; Chen, S.L.; Wang, D. The Research on the Influencing Factors of Chinese Gold Futures. *Theory Pract. Financ. Econ.* **2014**, *35*, 44–48.
6. Raza, S.A.; Shah, N.; Shahbaz, M. Does economic policy uncertainty influence gold prices? Evidence from a nonparametric causality-in-quantiles approach. *Resour. Policy* **2018**, *57*, 61–68. [CrossRef]
7. Wang, H.; Sheng, H.; Zhang, H.-W. Influence factors of international gold futures price volatility. *Trans. Nonferrous Met. Soc. China* **2019**, *29*, 2447–2454. [CrossRef]
8. Balcilar, M.; Gupta, R. On exchange-rate movements and gold-price fluctuations: Evidence for gold-producing countries from a nonparametric causality-in-quantiles test. *Int. Econ. Econ. Policy* **2017**, *14*, 649–666. [CrossRef]
9. Zeng, L.; Ma, D.D.; Liu, Z.X. Gold Price Forecast Based on Improved BP Neural Network. *Comput. Simul.* **2010**, *27*, 200–203.
10. Fei, J.W. Analysis and prediction of China's gold futures prices based on ARIMA model. *Contemp. Econ.* **2017**, *9*, 148–150.
11. Luo, S.J. *Prediction of the Gold Futures Price Based on Deep Learning*; Lanzhou University: Lanzhou, China, 2017.
12. Li, C. *Research on Prediction of Chaotic Time Series Gold Futures Price -Base on Phase Space and ARIMA-LSTM Hybrid Model*; Jinan University: Jinan, China, 2018.
13. Livieris, I.E.; Pintelas, E.; Pintelas, P. A CNN-LSTM model for gold price time-series forecasting. *Neural Comput. Appl.* **2020**, *32*, 17351–17360. [CrossRef]
14. Liu, Q.; Shi, S.; Lou, L.; Liu, L. Stock price prediction and decision-making based on ARIAM-GARCH deep learning. *J. Chang. Univ. Sci. Technol. (Nat. Sci. Ed.)* **2024**, *47*, 119–130.
15. Cohen, G.; Aiche, A. Forecasting gold price using machine learning methodologies. *Chaos Solitons Fractals* **2023**, *175 Pt 2*, 114079. [CrossRef]
16. Abu-Doush, I.; Ahmed, B.; Awadallah, M.A.; Al-Betar, M.A.; Rababaah, A.R. Enhancing multilayer perceptron neural network using archive-based harris hawks optimizer to predict gold prices. *J. King Saud Univ. Comput. Inf. Sci.* **2023**, *35*, 101557. [CrossRef]
17. Kim, A.; Ryu, D.; Webb, A. Forecasting oil futures markets using machine learning and seasonal trend decomposition. *Invest. Anal. J.* **2024**, 1–14. [CrossRef]
18. Fan C-y Tong J-y Cheng J-y Zhou, Y. Gold Futures Price Forecasting Based on ML-DMA. *J. Appl. Stat. Manag.* **2024**, *43*, 541–558.
19. Quan, P.; Shi, W. Application of CEEMDAN and LSTM for Futures Price Forecasting. In Proceedings of the 2024 International Conference on Machine Intelligence and Digital Applications (MIDA 2024), Ningbo, China, 30–31 May 2024; ACM: New York, NY, USA, 2024. 12p. [CrossRef]
20. Guo, Y.; Li, C.; Wang, X.; Duan, Y. Gold Price Prediction Using Two-layer Decomposition and XGboost Optimized by the Whale Optimization Algorithm. *Comput. Econ.* **2024**. [CrossRef]
21. Huo, L.; Xie, Y.; Li, J. An Innovative Deep Learning Futures Price Prediction Method with Fast and Strong Generalization and High-Accuracy Research. *Appl. Sci.* **2024**, *14*, 5602. [CrossRef]
22. Gómez-Valle, L.; López-Marcos, M.Á.; Martínez-Rodríguez, J. Financial boundary conditions in a continuous model with discrete-delay for pricing commodity futures and its application to the gold market. *Chaos Solitons Fractals* **2024**, *187*, 115476. [CrossRef]
23. Pan, H.; Tang, Y.; Wang, G. A Stock Index Futures Price Prediction Approach Based on the MULTI-GARCH-LSTM Mixed Model. *Mathematics* **2024**, *12*, 1677. [CrossRef]
24. Song, Y.; Huang, J.; Xu, Y.; Ruan, J.; Zhu, M. Multi-decomposition in deep learning models for futures price prediction. *Expert Syst. Appl.* **2024**, *246*, 123171. [CrossRef]
25. Nabavi, Z.; Mirzehi, M.; Dehghani, H. Reliable novel hybrid extreme gradient boosting for forecasting copper prices using meta-heuristic algorithms: A thirty-year analysis. *Resour. Policy* **2024**, *90*, 104784. [CrossRef]

26. Grobys, K. Is gold in the process of a bubble formation? New evidence from the ex-post global financial crisis period. *Res. Int. Bus. Financ.* **2025**, *75*, 102727. [CrossRef]
27. Li, N.; Li, J.; Wang, Q.; Yan, D.; Wang, L.; Jia, M. A novel copper price forecasting ensemble method using adversarial interpretive structural model and sparrow search algorithm. *Resour. Policy* **2024**, *91*, 104892. [CrossRef]
28. Lu, G.; Li, M. A study on the linkage between us dollar index and gold price. *Price Theory Pract.* **2017**, *29*, 109–112.
29. Zhu, X.L.; Li, P. Linkage effect between RMB exchange rate and international gold price: Based on spillover and dynamic correlation perspectives. *J. Wuhan Univ. Sci. Technol. (Soc. Sci. Ed.)* **2012**, *14*, 669–673.
30. Hochreiter, S.; Schmidhuber, J. Long Short-Term Memory. *Neural Comput.* **1997**, *9*, 1735–1780. [CrossRef]
31. Gers, F.A.; Schmidhuber, J.; Cummins, F. Learning to Forget: Continual Prediction with LSTM. *Neural Comput.* **2000**, *12*, 2451–2471. [CrossRef]

mathematics

MDPI

Article

Mode Selection for Device to Device Communication in Dynamic Network: A Statistical and Deep Learning Method

Daqian Liu, Guiqi Kang, Yuntao Shi *, Yingying Wang and Zhenwu Lei

School of Electrical and Control Engineering, North China University of Technology, Beijing 100144, China; liudaqian@ncut.edu.cn (D.L.); 2022322060115@mail.ncut.edu.cn (G.K.); wyy@ncut.edu.cn (Y.W.); leizhenwu@ncut.edu.cn (Z.L.)
* Correspondence: shiyuntao@ncut.edu.cn

Abstract

A major challenge in device to device (D2D) communications is determining the appropriate communication modes for each potential D2D pair. In dynamic networks, the continuous movement of devices increases the complexity of channel state modeling, which makes it difficult to predict the quality of network service and select appropriate switching thresholds, ultimately affecting the accuracy of D2D mode selection. This paper proposes a novel D2D mode selection method, which integrates deep learning with statistical learning and includes three modules: signal-to-interference-plus-noise-ratio (SINR) prediction, error analysis, and threshold selection. Specifically, the SINR prediction module employs the gated recurrent unit (GRU) method to predict future SINR values; the error analysis module applies a non-parametric method to construct a probability density function of the prediction error. The combination of these two modules provides a significant improvement in prediction value accuracy. Additionally, in the threshold selection module, two constraints are innovatively introduced to mitigate the problem of frequent switching: average reliability (AR) and probably correct reliability (PCR). Simulation results demonstrate that the proposed method achieves higher system throughput, longer D2D mode residence time, and a lower mode switching frequency compared to other methods.

Keywords: device to device communication; mode selection; statistical learning; deep learning; dynamic network

MSC: 68T20; 68U07; 62F30

1. Introduction

D2D communication technology refers to the direct exchange of information between proximity devices in a communication network. The data is transmitted through a direct link between two devices, bypassing the base station and core network. This technology significantly alleviates base station pressure, improves spectrum utilization, and reduces latency. Notably, 3GPP has listed D2D technology as one of the key technologies for 5G [1]. In dynamic networks, D2D communication demonstrates great potential for improving quality of service (QoS). Currently, proximity services (ProSe), defined by 3GPP, serve as the primary framework for implementing D2D communication, support direct communication between devices and provide fundamental signaling and connection establishment functionalities. ProSe plays a key role in facilitating communication initiation and preliminary resource allocation. For instance, in vehicular networks, vehicles can share traffic information in real-time through D2D communication, which improves driving safety and traffic efficiency; in unmanned aerial vehicle (UAV) ad hoc Networks, D2D communication enables direct exchange of location information and task data between drones, reducing communication latency.

D2D only supports short-range communication. In dynamic networks, communication devices are mobile, which causes the communication distance and channel states between devices to change continuously. Single D2D communication cannot meet QoS demands. Hence, a mode selection method is needed to choose according to different needs. The selectable communication modes can be classified into five types, as shown in Table 1. Factors such as switching thresholds and evaluation criteria need to be thoroughly considered in mode selection methods. Otherwise, QoS will be adversely affected. For example, low selection conditions can lead to frequent mode switches. Data packets from different modes are not interoperable. Each switch results in packet loss, retransmissions, and requires additional signaling messages, thereby increasing the system's signaling load and reducing throughput. Solving mode selection problems usually depends on a complete and accurate channel state model, but in practical scenarios, accurately modeling channel states is often challenging. Therefore, the improvement of network throughput with incomplete channel state information through reasonable strategies has become an important research direction.

Table 1. Classification of communication modes.

Mode	Frequency Band	Advantages	Disadvantages
Out-of-Band Mode [2]	Non-cellular licensed band	Abundant spectrum, flexible deployment	Susceptible to interference from other technologies
Dedicated D2D Mode	Dedicated cellular band	No interference	Insufficient spectrum utilization
D2D Reuse Mode [3]	Reusing cellular band	Greatly improves spectrum utilization	Potential interference with cellular networks
D2D Relay Mode [4]	Dedicated band	Self-organizing network, extended coverage	Increased delay and complexity
Cellular Mode	Cellular band	Suitable for most scenarios	No improvement

This paper proposes a D2D mode selection method that combines statistical learning and deep learning. This method aims to address important challenges in dynamic network environments, such as optimizing mode switching and enhancing QoS, which have been relatively less explored in prior studies. This method consists of three modules: SINR prediction, error analysis, and threshold selection. In the SINR prediction module, deep learning algorithms are used to predict the channel states between devices. Due to uncertainties in predictions, we establish a probability density function for the error within the error analysis module and construct a confidence interval to ensure the accuracy of the prediction results. In the threshold selection module, we use statistical learning methods to select switching thresholds and introduce AR and PCR constraints to meet actual communication needs. Compared to traditional methods, this study innovatively combines statistical learning and deep learning for the mode selection problem. This method enhances system throughput, effectively reduces mode switching frequency, and improves overall network performance.

The structure of this paper is as follows: Section 2 describes the background of D2D communication technology and analyzes the shortcomings of existing methods that address incomplete channel state information. Section 3 explains the proposed mode selection method, which consists of the SINR prediction module, the error analysis module, and the threshold selection module. Section 4 provides the simulation results and demonstrates that the method improves system throughput and reduces mode switching frequency. Finally, Section 5 summarizes the research results, identifies limitations, and outlines future research directions.

2. Research Status

Considering dynamic scenarios of a single base station cell, each mobile device has two operating modes: cellular mode and D2D mode. The base station can only receive auxiliary information (e.g., distance, movement speed, and number of devices, among others) and partial channel state information (e.g., SINR and received power, among others).

In dynamic network environments, deep learning methods are commonly used to solve mode selection problems. With known channels, deep learning algorithms can make judgments based on environmental information. Ortiz et al. [5] uses reinforcement learning to solve real-time D2D mode selection and resource allocation problems. A dual-layer multi-armed bandit (MAB) model is employed, where the first layer allocates resources to cellular users. The usage of resource blocks is then input to the second layer MAB model for D2D user mode selection and resource allocation, and the system throughput determines the reward value. However, this article does not consider the impact of frequent mode switching on system throughput. Zhang et al. [6] finds the optimal received signal strength (RSS) threshold through reinforcement learning for each base station in multi-base station scenarios. Terminal devices compare the RSS values with the base station's computed RSS threshold to select the mode and maximize network throughput. Xu et al. [7] uses residence time as a selection criterion and utilizes a feed-forward neural network to predict the residence time in D2D mode, which determines whether the system switches modes. Najla et al. [8] uses deep neural networks (DNN) to extract information from cellular channel gain to predict D2D channel gain. Zhang et al. [9] constructs a network transmission model with energy efficiency maximization as the optimization goal, listing optimization equations for mode selection and resource allocation, and solves the optimal strategy through a deep deterministic policy gradient method. Liu et al. [10] proposes a D2D mode selection scheme based on average thresholds. Esmat et al. [11] allows multiple D2D pairs to reuse the radio resource of a cellular user (CU), completing mode selection. Li et al. [12] estimates the SINR and communication rate based on geographical location and channel information, followed by mode selection and resource allocation.

Mode selection under known channel state information has been performed in previous studies (Ortiz et al. [5], Zhang et al. [6], Zhang et al. [9], Liu et al. [10], Esmat et al. [11]). Such studies typically rely on comprehensive and accurate channel state information, such as path loss, channel gain, and fading. They do not consider how to make judgments when channel state information is not fully understood. It is often a challenge to obtain comprehensive and accurate channel state information in practical scenarios due to rapid changes in mobile devices and complex signal propagation environments. In this situation, traditional methods may not ensure the accuracy of mode selection and system performance.

Prediction methods for QoS are employed in several other works (Xu et al. [7], Najla et al. [8], Li et al. [12]). Although such methods can improve network adaptability and response speed to ensure timely mode selection adjustment when channel conditions change, they do not fully consider prediction accuracy. Prediction in practical applications are affected by various factors such as data noise and environmental changes, which may cause deviations between predicted results and actual situations. Without effective control of prediction errors, incorrect mode selection may occur, which affects system stability and performance.

To address such deficiencies, this study proposes a mode selection method under incomplete channel state information. The method estimates switching thresholds using statistical learning and constraint estimation to ensure system stability. By using historical SINR values and deep learning algorithms to predict channel states, and introducing confidence intervals through error analysis module, the accuracy of prediction results is ensured. Compared with the above studies, this study innovatively combines statistical learning and deep learning for mode selection, which enhances system stability and effectively reduces the frequency of mode switching.

3. System Modeling

In this study, we consider a single-cell cellular network as shown in Figure 1, where each cellular user device is allocated orthogonal resource blocks for communication with the base station. We assume that M cellular user devices coexist with a pair of D2D user devices in the cellular network. Each device functions as both a transmitter and receiver with equivalent capabilities and supports bidirectional communication under either D2D or cellular modes.

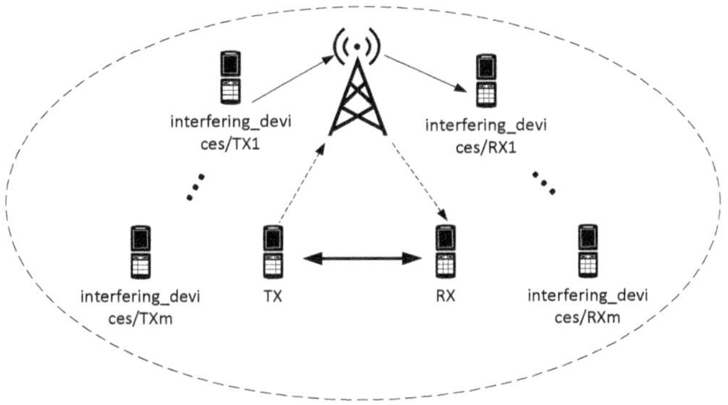

Figure 1. System model of D2D communications.

In this system, each mobile device measures the received signal strength at its current location and feeds this information back to the connected base station. The base station averages the signal strength information from all devices and calculates the SINR for each device. For communication rate in QoS, SINR is closely related to the communication rate and is defined as

$$S = \frac{P_i G_{ij}}{\sum_{k \in V \setminus \{i,j\}} \rho_k P_k G_{kj} + \sigma^2}, \tag{1}$$

where S denotes the SINR, P_i is the transmission power of transmitter i, G_{ij} represents the channel gain between transmitter i and receiver j, $\sum_{k \in V \setminus \{i,j\}}$ accounts for the interference from all devices in the network except i and j. Here, ρ_k represents the expected load from the interference source k, which also indicates the proportion of resources used, P_k is the transmission power of the interference source k, and G_{kj} represents the channel gain between the interference source k and receiver j. Finally, σ^2 denotes the noise power. Equation (1) is widely used for calculating SINR in wireless communication systems. It accounts for the transmission power, channel gain, and interference from surrounding devices, as well as noise power. According to the description in [13], this equation is suitable for the proposed work because it effectively captures the effects of interference and noise in dynamic network environments. To evaluate the performance of the proposed D2D mode selection method, the achievable throughput of a single communication link is calculated. According to [14], the data rate of the link is determined based on the Shannon–Hartley theorem, which relates the bandwidth of the channel and SINR to the maximum achievable throughput.

4. Mode Selection Method

In D2D communication, the accuracy of mode selection directly affects system throughput and QoS. Existing methods perform well when channel state information is fully known, but in practical applications, channel information is often incomplete. The proposed method assumes that D2D communication is implemented based on standard protocols, such as ProSe, to enable direct communication. The method also assumes that all transceivers operate with standard mobile device capabilities, including single-antenna setups and moderate transmission power. This ensures that the proposed method is applicable across a wide range of practical deployment scenarios without being restricted by specific hardware configurations. However, as the core of the proposed method focuses on optimizing mode selection, it does not rely on the signaling implementation of specific protocols. Hence, this method ensures high generalizability and compatibility with existing network architectures. To make accurate mode selection decisions in such environments, this study proposes a method based on prediction and statistical learning. Channel states information is predicted by utilizing historical data and deep learning algorithms. To ensure the accuracy of these predictions, confidence intervals are introduced through an error analysis module. Additionally, statistical learning methods are employed, with average reliability and possible correctness constraints incorporated to select appropriate switching thresholds. In combination, the methods enable the achievement of optimal mode selection.

In this method, the system's operation process is divided into three main modules: the SINR prediction module, the error analysis module, and the threshold selection module. The program initially determines whether it should train the model or proceed with operation based on the time condition. When in the training phase, the system trains the model, including the initial training of the SINR prediction module, error analysis module, and threshold selection module. When in the mode selection phase, the system moves into the operational phase. It determines whether the current communication mode is D2D or cellular. The SINR prediction module then forecasts the future SINR based on the current SINR. The error analysis module corrects the prediction results and calculates the confidence interval of the channel state to ensure reliable predictions in the presence of interference. Finally, the threshold selection module evaluates whether mode switching is necessary based on the corrected prediction values and communication requirements, ultimately enhancing overall communication efficiency. The program flowchart is shown in Figure 2.

4.1. SINR Prediction Module

SINR data, which fluctuates with device movement and changing channel conditions, can be considered as time series data. To ensure precise mode selection in D2D communication, the GRU model is used in this study for univariate time series prediction. The GRU model has a simple structure and trains rapidly, which enhances its efficiency in dynamic network environments. Its ability to capture temporal dependencies is confirmed by Simmons et al. [15], and the trade-off between accuracy and computational efficiency is demonstrated, which makes it a suitable choice for this work. GRU has a special mechanism composed of gating units to decide when to remember and when to ignore inputs in the hidden state. The main difference is that GRU only has two gates controlling the information flow, the reset gate and the update gate. Additionally, the cell state (memory cell) is not part of its gating units, and it only uses the hidden state $h^{(t)} \in {}^{N\times \mathrm{h}}$ to convey information. GRU's core functionality relies on a single gating unit controlling both the forgetting factor and updating the state unit's decision. The system structure diagram is shown in Figure 3. The updated value is represented as

$$h^{(t)} = u^{(t)} \odot h^{(t-1)} + \left(1 - u^{(t)}\right) \odot \widetilde{h}^{(t)}. \quad (2)$$

The update gate $u^{(t)} \in {}^{N\times \mathrm{h}}$ and reset gate $r^{(t)} \in {}^{N\times \mathrm{h}}$ are represented as follows

$$u^{(t)} = \sigma\left(x^{(t)} W_{xu} + h^{(t-1)} W_{hu} + b^u\right) \quad (3)$$

$$r^{(t)} = \sigma\left(x^{(t)} W_{xr} + h^{(t-1)} W_{hr} + b^r\right), \quad (4)$$

where $W_{xr}, W_{xu} \in \mathbb{R}^{T_x \times h}$ and $W_{hr}, W_{hu} \in \mathbb{R}^{\mathrm{h}\times \mathrm{h}}$ are weight parameters, $b^u, b^r \in \mathbb{R}^{1\times h}$ are bias terms. The current input vector is $x^{(t)} \in \mathbb{R}^{N\times T_x}$ the batch size is N the input size is T_x. The current hidden state of the GRU output is $h^{(t)} \in \mathbb{R}^{N\times h}$ with h hidden layers. The candidate hidden state $\widetilde{h}^{(t)} \in \mathbb{R}^{N\times h}$ at time t is expressed as

$$\widetilde{h}^{(t)} = \tan h\left(x^{(t)} W_{xh} + \left(r^{(t)} \odot h^{(t-1)}\right) W_{hh} + b^h\right), \quad (5)$$

where $W_{xh} \in \mathbb{R}^{T_x \times h}$, $W_{hh} \in \mathbb{R}^{h\times h}$ are weight parameters, $b^h \in \mathbb{R}^{1\times h}$ are bias terms.

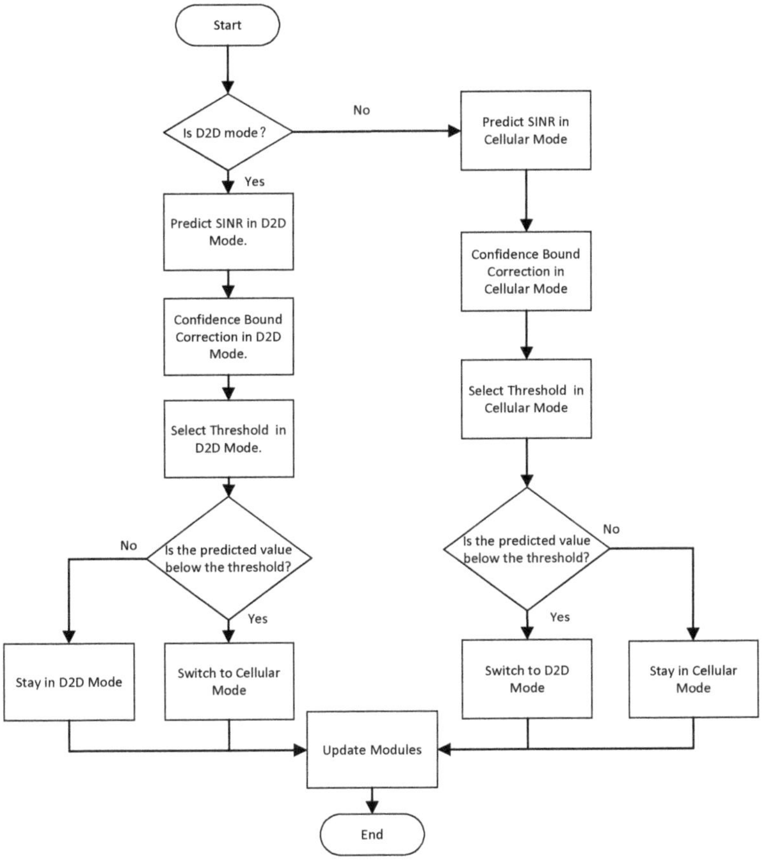

Figure 2. Mode selection program flowchart.

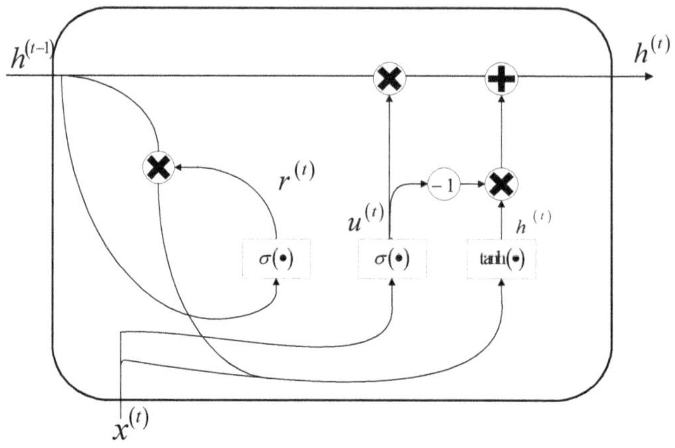

Figure 3. Block diagram of the GRU model.

4.2. Error Analysis Module

To provide accurate SINR predictions before network state changes, the deep learning method mentioned in the previous subsection is used to predict SINR values, denoted as $\widehat{S}$. Prediction values inherently carry uncertainty. To ensure the accuracy of the predictions, we estimate the cumulative distribution function of the error, through which the confidence interval is constructed. When the prediction values fall inside this interval, the accuracy of the predictions is guaranteed probabilistically. The prediction value is adjusted to the nearest boundary to ensure accuracy when it falls outside the interval. We initiate this process by collecting both predicted and actual values, and then estimate the probability density function of prediction errors using kernel density estimation. This non-parametric approach, known for its smoothness and ability to capture local features, provides a flexible and accurate estimation of the probability density function. This process enables the calculation of confidence intervals for each prediction value, ensuring they fall within these intervals with a certain probability. The error analysis module can effectively provide the upper and lower confidence intervals for QoS prediction. Prediction error is defined as

$$E = S - \widehat{S}, \tag{6}$$

where E represents the error, S represents the actual SINR value, and $\widehat{S}$ represents the predicted SINR value.

With the probability density function of prediction errors, the confidence interval for SINR values can be calculated. Known probability density function solving methods are divided into parametric and non-parametric methods. This paper chooses the non-parametric method, using kernel density estimation to calculate the probability density function of prediction errors. The probability density function of prediction errors is defined as

$$f(E) = \frac{1}{hN_i} \sum_{m=1}^{N_i} K\left(\frac{E_m}{h}\right), \tag{7}$$

where N_i is the total number of samples, h is the bandwidth coefficient determining the width of the kernel function. The choice of bandwidth significantly affects the smoothness of the estimate, with $K(E)$ serving as the kernel function.

With the probability density function of prediction errors, the cumulative distribution function (CDF) can be calculated. The confidence interval is constructed based on the confidence level. The confidence level $1-\alpha$ indicates the probability that the error falls within this interval. The confidence interval's upper and lower limits are obtained by finding the corresponding values on the cumulative probability distribution function according to the confidence level, satisfying

$$\begin{cases} F(D) = P(E \leq D) = 1 - \frac{\alpha}{2} \\ F(L) = P(E \geq L) = \frac{\alpha}{2} \end{cases}, \tag{8}$$

where D represents the upper bound of the error, $F(D)$ represents the probability that the prediction error is less than or equal to D, L represents the lower bound of the error, and $F(L)$ represents the probability that the prediction error is less than or equal to L.

After obtaining the confidence interval, each prediction value has a probability $1-\alpha$ of falling within the confidence interval, probabilistically ensuring the prediction result's accuracy. When the prediction value exceeds the confidence interval, the prediction value is adjusted to the nearest boundary, and the prediction boundaries can be expressed as $\widehat{S}+D$ and $\widehat{S}+L$, which improves the accuracy of the prediction.

4.3. Threshold Selection Module

An effective computational method of switching thresholds is necessary to achieve optimal mode selection in a dynamic network environment where the continuous movement of devices complicates channel state modeling. A threshold selection module needs to ensure reliable communication and improve system performance. The method proposed in this paper limits the mode switching probability through constraints, without relying on extensive information for precise modeling. It ensures system performance and minimizes the impact of frequent switches. This section introduces the key concepts and mathematical foundations that underlie the threshold selection process.

In a unidirectional communication link, the transmitter (Tx) sends data packets to the receiver (Rx). Let $\mathcal{F}$ denote the CDF of the channel variable S, which can represent any value of interest (e.g., received power, SINR). Define a switching event as $R > log_2(1+\widehat{S})$ where the switching probability is $P_F(R) = P\left[R > log_2(1+\widehat{S})\right]$. $\widehat{S}$ is the value of predicted channel variable, and R is the threshold rate selected by the threshold selection function. Using the statistical learning-based rate selection framework proposed in [14], the threshold selection process involves estimating the SINR distribution and determining an appropriate threshold based on the constraints.

In statistical learning, SINR can be deterministically guaranteed when this distribution is fully known [13]. However, obtaining complete knowledge of $\mathcal{F}$ is rarely attainable in practice. Therefore, statistical learning methods estimate $\mathcal{F}$ based on historical data. Estimating $\mathcal{F}$ can be achieved through parametric and non-parametric methods. The choice depends on how much the channel information is understood. For instance, if the channel has a fixed direct component, a parametric method can be chosen, such as the Rice fading model. Parametric methods use relevant data to solve model parameters when the channel state is well understood. Non-parametric methods should be used when the channel state is not well understood, as they help avoid model mismatch errors. In this paper, we consider scenarios where the channel state cannot be precisely modeled; hence, a non-parametric method, namely the empirical distribution method, is adopted. The empirical distribution method effectively estimates the actual distribution of the channel state without requiring any assumptions about the data distribution. An independent and identically distributed sequence of length n is collected, which is referred to as the training sample and denoted by $\{X_1, X_2, \ldots, X_n\}$.

To improve system throughput, it is necessary to select an appropriate switching threshold to avoid frequent mode transitions. Because $\mathcal{F}$ is estimated from random samples, it is a random variable with inherent uncertainty [14]. To ensure reliable threshold selection, one of two constraints can be applied. The first is the AR constraint, which controls the average service quality level. The second is the PCR constraint, which bounds the probability of specific data falling within a designated region. Compared to the AR constraint, the PCR constraint imposes stricter limitations.

The first AR constraint can be expressed as

$$\overline{P_F} = P\left[R(X_n) > log_2(1+\widehat{S})\right] \leq \varepsilon, \tag{9}$$

where $\overline{P_F}$ is the average switching probability for training samples X_n calculated through expectation, ϵ represents the switching probability, $R(X_n)$ represents the switching threshold selection function. The law of total expectation is applied with X_n as a condition, and the equation is rewritten as

$$\overline{P_F} = E\left[P\left[R(X_n) > \log_2(1+\widehat{S}) \mid X_n\right]\right] \leq \varepsilon. \tag{10}$$

The second PCR constraint, different from AR, comes from probably approximately correct (PAC) learning. PAC learning selects a generalization function with high probability and low generalization error after training on samples. The PCR constraint selects a threshold based on the channel state, ensuring all switching probabilities remain within a probability interval. The PCR constraint, relying on the meta-probability concept [16], can be expressed as

$$\widetilde{P_F} = P\left[P\left[R(X_n) > log_2(1+\widehat{S})|X_n\right] > \xi\right] \tag{11}$$

$$\widetilde{P_F} = P[P_F(R(X_n)) > \xi], \tag{12}$$

where $\widetilde{P_F}$ represents the worst-case probability, ξ represents the bound on the worst-case probability.

The threshold selection function can be written as

$$R(X_n) = \log_2\left(1 + X_{(l)}\right). \tag{13}$$

The threshold selection function aims to select the maximum value $X_{(l)}$ satisfying the constraints. $X_{(l)}$, which is the maximum value satisfying the constraints, is selected after sorting the sample X_n as $X_{(1)} \leq X_{(2)} \leq \ldots \leq X_{(n)}$.

For non-parametric methods, the distribution of order statistics from a set of independent and uniformly distributed random variables can be approximated by the Beta distribution, allowing the AR constraint to be rewritten as

$$\overline{P_F} = E[P_F(R(X_n))] = E\left[U_{(l)}\right] = \frac{l}{n+1}, \tag{14}$$

where $U_{(l)}$ is beta-distributed with shape parameters l and $n+1-l$. To satisfy the reliability constraint of the switching probability ε, $\overline{P_F}$ is set to ε. This setting allows the value of l to be calculated.

Similarly, for the PCR constraint, the order statistics from the same set of independent and uniformly distributed random variables can be approximated by the Beta distribution. This approximation allows the constraint to be rewritten as

$$\widetilde{P_F} = P[P_F(R(X_n)) > \xi] = 1 - I_\varepsilon(l, n+1-l), \tag{15}$$

where $I_\varepsilon(a,b)$ represents the regularized incomplete Beta function. According to the PCR constraint, setting $\widetilde{P_F} = \xi$ allows us to determine the value of l.

5. Simulation Verification

In this section, the proposed D2D mode selection method is evaluated through simulations, focusing on two aspects: prediction method accuracy and QoS optimization. The simulation scenario is designed based on [17,18] to ensure realistic communication. The path loss model described in Table 2 was chosen for its simplicity and effectiveness, with its design drawing upon methodologies and findings discussed in [17]. The simulation represents an urban macro-cell with a 500-meter radius and a fixed base station at its center. Specific parameters are shown in Table 2.

Table 2. Simulation parameters.

Simulation Parameter	Value
Base Station Transmit Power	46 dBm
D2D Device Transmit Power	23 dBm
Cellular Device Transmit Power	23 dBm
Cellular Path Loss	128.1 + 37.6log(d)
D2D Path Loss	32.45 + 20log(f) + 20log(d)
Interfering Device Count	10 pairs
Antenna configuration	Single antenna
Frequency band	700 MHz
Constraint Condition	AR
ϵ [1]	0.7

[1] The switching probability.

The training phase involves training SINR prediction modules, error analysis modules, and threshold selection modules separately on the cellular dataset X_c and the D2D dataset X_d. The mode selection phase takes place, with mode judgment following different judgment cycles. Taking the D2D mode as an example, prediction values $\widehat{y_d}$ are generated in each cycle. The error analysis module is used to generate the confidence interval $F_d(s)$. A threshold selection method determines appropriate switching thresholds $R_d(X_d)$. The judgment result is obtained by comparing the predicted values with the switching thresholds, and the real values y_d are fed back into the system to update the SINR prediction module, error analysis module, and statistical module. The same process applies to the cellular mode, except that all data are replaced with the cellular mode dataset. The pseudocode for the mode selection algorithm can be found in Algorithm 1.

To evaluate interference impact on system performance, 20 interfering devices using cellular communication are simulated, randomly distributed in the cell area according to a homogeneous Poisson point process. The random distribution of interfering devices effectively simulates the irregular distribution of devices in reality, impacting the channel. The main device moves randomly within the cell, with a movement speed of 3 m per second. The device mode only considers cellular mode and dedicated D2D mode, simplifying the simulation model to focus on evaluating these two main modes' method performance. Channel information collection mainly includes SINR values. QoS focuses on throughput. The simulation duration is set to 300 s, with a time step of 1 s. The SINR prediction module uses the GRU model, effectively capturing dynamic changes in time series suitable for channel state prediction. Specific parameters include 25 hidden layers, 3 layers, and a learning rate of 0.005, tuned for optimal prediction performance. Kernel density estimation uses the Gaussian kernel density function, with a bandwidth parameter $h = 1.0$ for error distribution estimation.

Algorithm 1 Mode selection approach for dynamic networks

Input: X_d (D2D input features), X_c (Cellular input features), α (confidence level), ϵ (switching probability)
Output: Mode (D2D or Cellular), Updated Modules

Initialize parameters
while Network operational **do**
  Determine current communication mode: D2D or Cellular
  if Current mode is D2D **then**
    Predict SINR $\hat{S}_d = GRU(X_d)$
    Correct prediction using error analysis model $f(s)$ to obtain $\hat{y}_d$
    Select threshold T_{th_d}
    if $\hat{y}_d < T_{th_d}$ **then**
      Switch to Cellular Mode
    else
      Remain in D2D Mode
    end if
  else
    Predict SINR $\hat{S}_c = GRU(X_c)$
    Correct prediction using error analysis model $f(s)$ to obtain $\hat{y}_c$
    Select threshold T_{th_c}
    if $\hat{y}_c < T_{th_c}$ **then**
      Switch to D2D Mode
    else
      Remain in Cellular Mode
    end if
  end if
  Update predictions with real-time data based on the current mode
end while

The prediction results of the system SINR values are shown in Figure 4, which includes four main curves. The blue line represents the actual values, the red line represents the predicted values, and the yellow upper and lower lines represent the confidence intervals of the predicted values. In most time periods, the predicted values (red line) follow the actual values (blue line), which indicates that the GRU model captures channel state changes with high accuracy. The model achieves a mean absolute error (MAE) of 1.40 dB and a root mean squared error (RMSE) of 1.91 dB, which reflects its low prediction error and reliable performance. After introducing the error analysis model, confidence intervals are added to the predicted values. In the 95% confidence interval, the predicted and actual values mostly fall within the confidence interval, which indicates that the predictions are accurate with 95% probability. If the prediction value falls outside the confidence interval, it is adjusted to the nearest boundary to ensure accuracy and maintain reliability. This confidence interval provides a more reliable basis for mode selection.

Figure 5 shows average throughput and the number of mode switches across different switching probabilities and compares performance under AR and PCR constraints. The AR constraint provides higher average throughput but leads to more frequent mode switches, which reflects that it is more sensitive to network dynamics. In contrast, the PCR constraint results in fewer mode switches, which ensures a more stable communication environment but comes with slightly lower throughput. This comparison makes it clear that choosing the appropriate constraint depends on achieving a balance between performance and stability. Ultimately, selecting the AR constraint is preferable in scenarios where maximizing throughput is crucial.

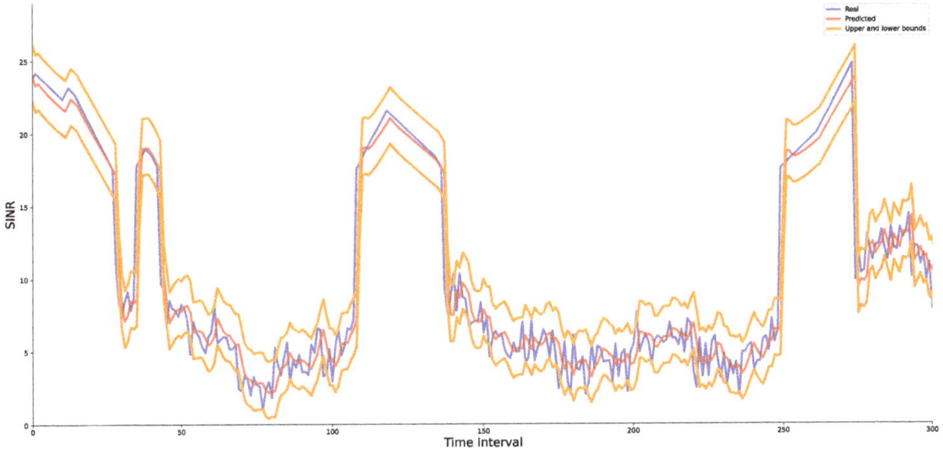

Figure 4. Comparison of predicted and actual values with 95% confidence interval.

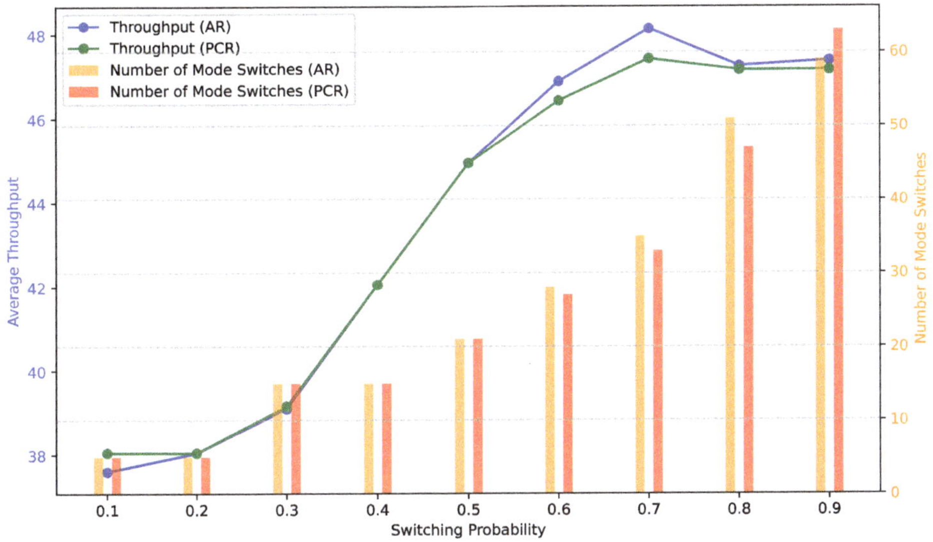

Figure 5. Performance comparison of AR and PCR constraints across switching probabilities.

Figure 6 describes the throughput changes of the D2D communication link under different time points based on prediction and mode selection algorithms. The red dots in the figure indicate mode switching. Initially, the two main devices move in random directions within specified boundaries. According to the results in Figure 5, the AR constraint is selected with a switching probability of 0.7 to achieve higher throughput. Results from Figure 6 show that in cellular mode, the devices experience significant effects from surrounding interference, which causes throughput to fluctuate as the number of interfering devices increases, for example, between the fourth and fifth switches. In dense interference areas, cellular mode throughput decreases significantly due to interference from proximity devices reducing SINR, affecting data transmission rates. In contrast, D2D mode throughput is more influenced by the distance between devices. As device distance increases, signal attenuation becomes more apparent. When the distance exceeds

400 m, D2D communication is prohibited to prevent communication failure due to poor signal quality. As the devices move closer, the throughput rapidly increases, for example, between the fifth and sixth switches. In the figure, the interval between the third and fourth switches is short because the devices move in opposite directions, and the distance between them gradually increases after they switch to D2D mode, which leads to the fourth switch. During the fifth switch, although the throughput in cellular mode shows a gradual increase, a switch still occurs because the communication conditions in D2D mode are better than those in cellular mode. Frequent mode switching leads to information resending, which increases system signaling overhead and impacts current throughput. The threshold selection module selects reasonable thresholds that minimize unnecessary switches, maintain high throughput, and ensure system stability.

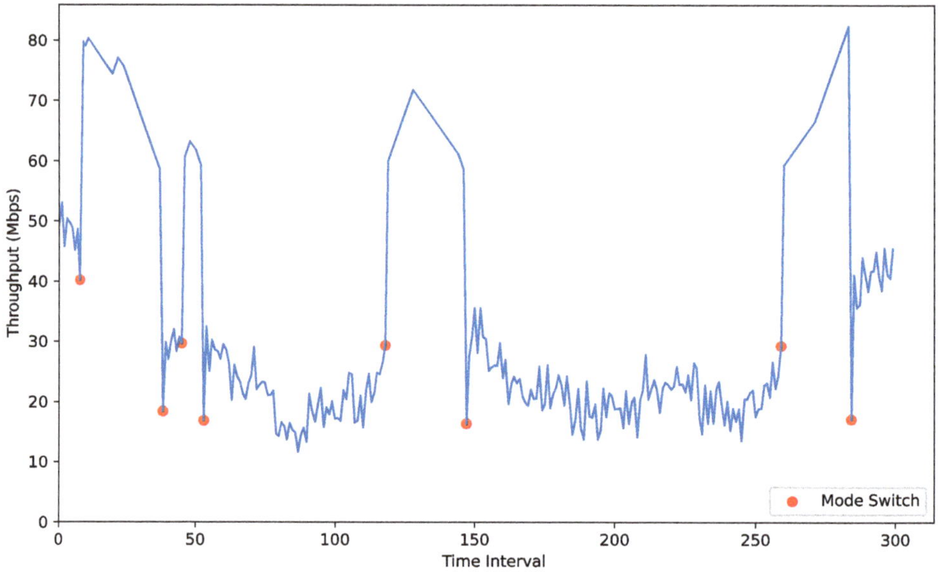

Figure 6. The total throughput of the system under the proposed algorithm.

Figure 7 compares average throughput under different methods, which include the proposed algorithm, random [19], optimal SINR [20], pure D2D mode, and pure cellular mode. The proposed method achieves an average throughput of approximately 50 Mbps, which surpass the performance of the optimal SINR-based method (48 Mbps), the pure D2D method (32 Mbps), the pure cellular method (38 Mbps), and the random mode selection method (23 Mbps). Figure 7 shows that the proposed method outperforms other methods in average throughput. Although the optimal SINR-based method performs well in high-SINR conditions, its performance is limited by frequent channel changes and interference in complex network environments. Both pure D2D and pure cellular methods can achieve high throughput in specific scenarios; however, their lack of flexible selection mechanisms leads to inconsistent performance in dynamic environments. Similarly, the random mode selection method yields the lowest throughput and is inefficient in resource utilization among all methods due to its lack of a systematic strategy for mode selection. In contrast, the proposed method demonstrates superior adaptability by addressing dynamic channel conditions through SINR prediction and optimized threshold selection. This capability enables it to maintain higher throughput in dynamic network scenarios, and highlights its robustness and efficiency compared to traditional methods.

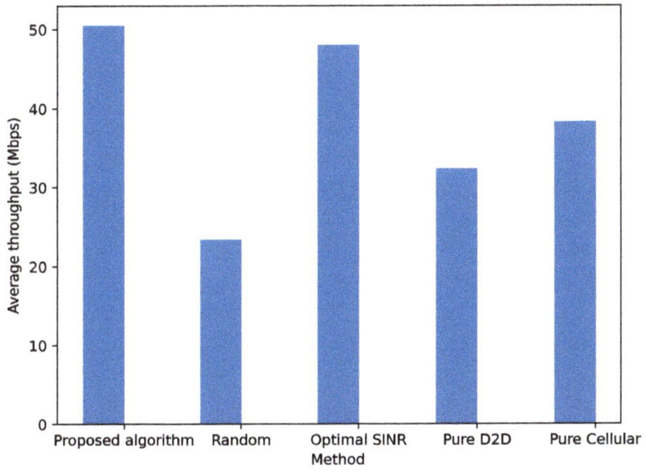

Figure 7. Average throughput comparison of the proposed algorithm with other methods.

As shown in Table 3, the comparison of mode switching rates [21] and average D2D mode residence times [21] under different methods includes the proposed algorithm, random and optimal SINR. The table's first item represents the average D2D mode residence time, and the second item represents the mode switching rate. The D2D mode switching rate indicates how often the UE switches its communication mode, which directly impacts the system's signaling overhead. The 'Average D2D Residence Time' represents the average duration of staying in D2D mode, which also reflects the frequency of mode switching. Simulation results show that in a good D2D communication environment, devices should stay longer in D2D mode to fully utilize its advantages. The proposed algorithm results in longer D2D mode residence times compared to the optimal SINR algorithm. Additionally, the proposed algorithm has a lower mode switching rate, which reduces signaling overhead and throughput loss caused by frequent switching. The results demonstrate that the proposed method achieves higher throughput and lower mode switching rates, while maintaining high system stability.

Table 3. Comparison of mode switching rates and residence times.

Method	Average D2D Residence Time (s)	Mode Switching Rate (%)
Proposed algorithm	24.95	3.2
Optimal-SINR	19.07	4.56
Random	1.98	50.3

Simulation verification shows that the proposed D2D mode selection method performs excellently in multiple key performance indicators. The method achieves higher system throughput, maintains high prediction accuracy, and demonstrates lower mode switching frequency compared to other methods. Longer D2D mode residence times and lower mode switching rates further enhance system stability. While this method might not be the most suitable choice for scenarios with strict resource limitations, it is particularly well-suited for high-priority applications, such as vehicular networks or industrial IoT systems, where throughput optimization and reduced mode switching are critical. In these cases, the computational trade-offs are considered reasonable due to the significant improvement in network performance that is taken into account. The methods compared in this study were adapted to match the scenario addressed in the proposed framework, as differences in application contexts made direct comparisons with existing methods infeasible. Unlike traditional approaches that rely on static SINR thresholds, the proposed method provides enhanced adaptability and robustness in dynamic environments.

6. Conclusions

This paper addresses the challenge of efficient D2D mode selection in dynamic network environments with continuously changing channel conditions, with a primary focus on moderate mobility environments to evaluate the feasibility and effectiveness of the proposed framework. To solve this issue, we proposed a novel D2D mode selection method that integrated deep learning and statistical learning. The method consisted of three modules: SINR prediction, error analysis, and threshold selection. The SINR prediction module used a GRU model to estimate SINR values. The error analysis module applied kernel density estimation to ensure reliability through confidence intervals. The threshold selection module used statistical learning with AR and PCR constraints to determine optimal switching thresholds, which reduced unnecessary transitions. Simulation results showed that the proposed method improved system performance. The GRU model had an MAE of 1.40 dB and an RMSE of 1.91 dB, which indicated high prediction accuracy. This method compared with other methods obtained the maximum D2D average residence time of 24.95 s, the lowest mode switching rate of 3.2%, and achieved the highest average throughput of about 50 Mbps.

Future research will extend this framework to high mobility scenarios and address the challenges that arise from rapidly changing channel conditions. The framework will also incorporate other communication modes, such as relay and reuse modes, and adopt advanced machine learning algorithms to improve the adaptability and efficiency of D2D communications in complex network environments.

Author Contributions: Methodology, D.L.; software, G.K.; validation, Z.L.; investigation, Y.W.; resources, Y.S.; writing—original draft, G.K.; writing—review and editing, D.L.; supervision, Y.S.; project administration, Y.S. All authors have read and agreed to the published version of the manuscript.

Funding: Thisresearch was funded in part by the National Key Research and Development Program of China under Grant 2023YFC3304604, in part by the National Natural Science Foundation of China under Grant 62373066, and in part by the Beijing Natural Science Foundation of China under Grant 4244089. The APC was funded by the National Natural Science Foundation of China under Grant 62373066.

Data Availability Statement: The original contributions presented in this study are included in the article. Further inquiries can be directed to the corresponding author.

Conflicts of Interest: The authors declare no conflicts of interest.

References

1. Qian, Z.; Wang, X. Reviews of D2D technology for 5G communication networks. *J. Commun.* **2016**, *37*, 1–14.
2. Areqi, M.A.; Zahary, A.T.; Ali, M.N. State-of-the-Art Device-to-Device Communication Solutions. *IEEE Access* **2023**, *11*, 46734–46764. [CrossRef]
3. Asadi, A.; Wang, Q.; Mancuso, V. A survey on device-to-device communication in cellular networks. *IEEE Commun. Surv. Tutorials* **2014**, *16*, 1801–1819. [CrossRef]
4. Zhang, P.; Kang, X.; Li, X.; Liu, Y.; Wu, D.; Wang, R. Overlapping Community Deep Exploring-Based Relay Selection Method Toward Multi-Hop D2D Communication. *IEEE Wirel. Commun. Lett.* **2019**, *8*, 1357–1360. [CrossRef]
5. Ortiz, A.; Asadi, A.; Engelhardt, M.; Klein, A.; Hollick, M. CBMoS: Combinatorial Bandit Learning for Mode Selection and Resource Allocation in D2D Systems. *IEEE J. Sel. Areas Commun.* **2019**, *37*, 2225–2238. [CrossRef]

6. Zhang, S.; Wang, X.; Shi, Z.; Liu, J. Reinforcement Learning Based RSS-Threshold Optimization for D2D-Aided HTC/MTC in Dense NOMA Systems. *IEEE Trans. Wirel. Commun.* **2023**, *22*, 6489–6503. [CrossRef]
7. Xu, B.; Xu, X.; Gong, F.; Sun, Z. Feed-Forward Neural Network Based Mode Selection for Moving D2D-Enabled Heterogeneous Ultra-Dense Network. In Proceedings of the 2019 IEEE International Conference on Communications Workshops (ICC Workshops), Shanghai, China, 20–24 May 2019; pp. 1–6.
8. Najla, M.; Becvar, Z.; Mach, P.; Gesbert, D. Predicting Device-to-Device Channels From Cellular Channel Measurements: A Learning Approach. *IEEE Trans. Wirel. Commun.* **2020**, *19*, 7124–7138. [CrossRef]
9. Zhang, S.; Zou, W.; Tang, L. D2D heterogeneous network energy saving mode selection and resource allocation. *Comput. Eng. Des.* **2023**, *44*, 677–684.
10. Liu, Z.; Peng, T.; Xiang, S.; Wang, W. Mode selection for device-to-device (D2D) communication under LTE-advanced networks. In Proceedings of the IEEE International Conference on Communications (ICC), Ottawa, ON, Canada, 10–15 June 2012; pp. 5563–5567.
11. Esmat, H.H.; Elmesalawy, M.M.; Ibrahim, I.I. Adaptive resource sharing algorithm for device-to-device communications underlaying cellular networks. *IEEE Commun. Lett.* **2016**, *20*, 530–533. [CrossRef]
12. Li, X.; Zhang, J.; Liu, X. Mode Selection and Resource Allocation for D2D Communications With Tradeoff of Throughput and User Satisfaction. *IEEE Trans. Commun.* **2023**, *71*, 5607–5620. [CrossRef]
13. Gutierrez-Estevez, M.A.; Utkovski, Z.; Kousaridas, A.; Zhou, C. A Statistical Learning Framework for QoS Prediction in V2X. In Proceedings of the 2021 IEEE 4th 5G World Forum (5GWF), Montreal, QC, Canada, 13–15 October 2021; pp. 441–446.
14. Angjelichinoski, M.; Trillingsgaard, K.F.; Popovski, P. A Statistical Learning Approach to Ultra-Reliable Low Latency Communication. *IEEE Trans. Commun.* **2019**, *67*, 5153–5166. [CrossRef]
15. Simmons, N.; Gomes, S.B.F.; Yacoub, M.D.; Simeone, O.; Cotton, S.L.; Simmons, D.E. AI-Based Channel Prediction in D2D Links: An Empirical Validation. *IEEE Access* **2022**, *10*, 65459–65472. [CrossRef]
16. Haenggi, M. The meta distribution of the SIR in Poisson bipolar and cellular networks. *IEEE Trans. Wirel. Commun.* **2016**, *15*, 2577–2589. [CrossRef]
17. Nardini, G.; Virdis, A.; Stea, G. Modeling Network-Controlled Device-to-Device Communications in SimuLTE. *Sensors* **2018**, *18*, 3551. [CrossRef] [PubMed]
18. 3GPP. Study on LTE Device to Device Proximity Services: Radio Aspects. 3GPP TR 36.843, March 2014. Available online: https://www.3gpp.org/ftp/Specs/archive/36_series/36.843/36843-c01.zip (accessed on12 November 2024).
19. Algedir, A.A.; Refai, H.H. Energy Efficiency Optimization and Dynamic Mode Selection Algorithms for D2D Communication Under HetNet in Downlink Reuse. *IEEE Access* **2020**, *8*, 95251–95265. [CrossRef]
20. Nardini, G.; Stea, G.; Virdis, A. A Scalable Data-Plane Architecture for One-to-One Device-to-Device Communications in LTE-Advanced. *Comput. Netw.* **2018**, *131*, 77–95. [CrossRef]
21. Xu, X.; Zhang, Y.; Sun, Z.; Hong, Y.; Tao, X. Analytical Modeling of Mode Selection for Moving D2D-Enabled Cellular Networks. *IEEE Commun. Lett.* **2016**, *20*, 1203–1206. [CrossRef]

mathematics

MDPI

Article

A Dual-Path Neural Network for High-Impedance Fault Detection

Keqing Ning [1], Lin Ye [1], Wei Song [1], Wei Guo [2,*], Guanyuan Li [3], Xiang Yin [2] and Mingze Zhang [4]

1 College of Information Science and Technology, North China University of Technology, Beijing 100144, China; ningkq@ncut.edu.cn (K.N.); yelin@mail.ncut.edu.cn (L.Y.); songwei@ncut.edu.cn (W.S.)
2 School of Electrical and Control Engineering, North China University of Technology, Beijing 100144, China; yinxiang@ncut.edu.cn
3 Beijing Institute of Metrology, Beijing 100020, China; ligy@bjjl.cn
4 State Grid Jilin Electric Power Research Institute, Changchun 130015, China; mingzezhang@petalmail.com
* Correspondence: guowei0903@ncut.edu.cn

Abstract

High-impedance fault detection poses significant challenges for distribution network maintenance and operation. We propose a dual-path neural network for high-impedance fault detection. To enhance feature extraction, we use a Gramian Angular Field algorithm to transform 1D zero-sequence voltage signals into 2D images. Our dual-branch network simultaneously processes both representations: the CNN extracts spatial features from the transformed images, while the GRU captures temporal features from the raw signals. To optimize model performance, we integrate the Crested Porcupine Optimizer (CPO) algorithm for the adaptive optimization of key network hyperparameters. The experimental results demonstrate that our method achieves a 99.70% recognition accuracy on a dataset comprising high-impedance faults, capacitor switching, and load connections. Furthermore, it maintains robust performance under various test conditions, including different noise levels and network topology changes.

Keywords: high-impedance fault; Gramian angular field; parallel network; Crested Porcupine Optimizer

MSC: 68T20

1. Introduction

Single-phase-to-ground faults constitute approximately 80% of all fault types in distribution networks. Among these, high-impedance faults (HIFs), caused by the contact of overhead lines with materials such as tree branches, cement, sand, or animals, result in ground resistance values ranging from hundreds to thousands of ohms and account for roughly 5% of total fault incidents [1–3]. Due to their low current amplitudes, these faults are difficult to detect, often allowing the faulty conditions to persist for 1–2 h. Furthermore, high-frequency electrical signals, such as traveling waves and transients, not only exhibit low amplitudes but are also highly susceptible to noise interference and arc distortions, posing additional challenges to accurate fault detection [4–7].

Many researchers have conducted in-depth studies on high-impedance fault identification in distribution networks. Current approaches primarily rely on signal processing methods, where the analysis typically involves various electrical parameters including the voltage, current, magnetic field intensity, and impedance. The most commonly employed signal decomposition techniques include Fast Fourier Transform (FFT) [8], Empirical Mode Decomposition (EMD) [9], Hilbert–Huang Transform (HHT) [10], and Wavelet Transform (WT) [11]. For example, V. Gogula et al. [12] developed a high-impedance fault detection method based on the dynamic Hilbert–Huang transform. Their method analyzed three key parameters: instantaneous frequency, RMS value, and crest factor. Zhiwei Yao et al. [13] utilized wavelet transform and energy entropy to capture the transient features of fault signals. Mostafa Satea et al. [14] developed a method to distinguish HIFs from switching events. Their approach combined third harmonic analysis and a wavelet-based algorithm by monitoring changes in the third harmonic magnitude of the zero-sequence voltage and current components. However, their reliance on predefined thresholds and their sensitivity to noise often limit their effectiveness in dynamic and noisy environments. Moreover, real-time implementation remains challenging due to the high computational demands and the variability of fault characteristics in practical systems. Despite these limitations, signal processing methods remain foundational to fault detection and provide a basis for AI-based developments.

Recent advancements in computational capabilities and neural network architectures have significantly enhanced power grid fault detection. Neural networks, known for their excellent feature extraction capabilities under complex conditions, offer promising opportunities for more efficient and reliable fault detection methods. Examples include RESNET [15,16], ANN [17], SqueezeNet [18], and AlexNet [19], which have been applied to improve fault detection accuracy in various contexts. Zheng et al. [20] combined Variational Mode Decomposition (VMD) with the Inception–CNN for high-precision fault-type recognition. Zhang et al. [21] used object detection and attention mechanisms to locate faults from synchronized measurement data. Gogula et al. [22] integrated Discrete Wavelet Transform (DWT) with the Radial Basis Function Neural Network (RBFNN) for processing traveling wave signals. Guo et al. [23] proposed a high-impedance fault detection method using both Time–Frequency Spectrum (TFS) and transfer learning. Liang et al. [24] applied wavelet transform and a CNN for multi-scale feature extraction and classification. Bhatnagar et al. [25] developed an LSTM-based protection scheme for classifying high-impedance and low-impedance faults. Odion et al. [26] used an ANN for fault detection and localization in the Nigerian 330 kV transmission system. Overall, neural network-based approaches provide robust solutions for power grid fault detection, particularly in dynamic environments. However, challenges such as limited high-quality datasets, real-time implementation, and noise handling persist. Recent research has explored signal-to-image transformation techniques to leverage the powerful capabilities of computer vision algorithms.

Building on these advancements, researchers have developed novel AI-driven frameworks that leverage image-based analysis for high-impedance fault detection. By converting signal data into images, techniques such as Gramian Angular Fields (GAFs) [27,28], Markov Transition Fields (MTFs) [29], and Spectrogram Transformations (STs) [30] allow advanced image processing models, such as CNNs, to effectively capture complex temporal–spatial patterns. Among these, GAFs have shown particular promise in processing non-linear signals, such as zero-sequence voltage signals, during high-impedance fault. The GAF technique captures both the angular relationships and temporal dynamics of the signals, effectively representing the non-linearity and intricate features of the fault signal. This approach demonstrates superior accuracy in fault diagnosis, especially in noisy environments, by providing more discriminative features for AI models.

Despite these advancements, existing methods still encounter challenges in computational complexity, generalization, and the comprehensive use of both spatial and temporal features. To address these issues, this paper proposes a dual-path neural network for high-impedance fault detection. The proposed network architecture is shown in Figure 1. The key innovations of our approach are as follows:

1. To overcome the limitations of one-dimensional time-series signals in capturing spatial features, we use the Gramian Angular Field algorithm to transform zero-sequence voltage signals into two-dimensional images, enhancing the extraction of latent signal information.
2. We design a dual-branch network architecture with two parallel processing streams: one uses a CNN to extract spatial features from the transformed images, while the other employs a GRU to capture temporal characteristics from the original signals. This complementary feature fusion strategy effectively addresses the limitations of single-modality methods.
3. To further improve performance, we incorporate the Crested Porcupine Optimizer (CPO) for adaptive hyperparameter optimization, focusing on critical parameters like the learning rate and convolution kernel configurations. This significantly enhances the model's generalization capabilities and fault recognition accuracy.

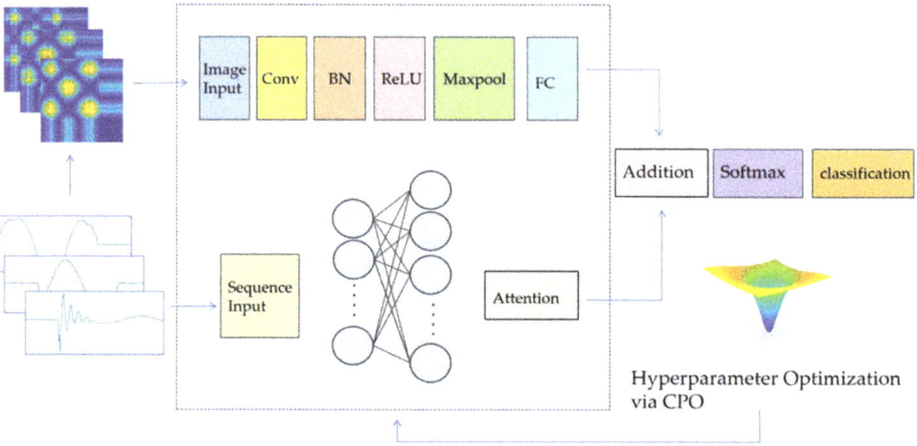

Figure 1. The proposed dual-path neural network for high-impedance fault detection.

2. Methodology and Network Architecture

2.1. GAF-Based Time-Series Imaging

The Gramian Angular Field (GAF) is an encoding technique for time-series data. It transforms temporal data into image representations by integrating coordinate transformation and Gramian matrices. The Gramian matrix, constructed from inner products between vectors, effectively preserves temporal dependencies within the time-series. One key limitation of Gramian matrices lies in their inability to distinguish between meaningful signal patterns and Gaussian noise components. To overcome this challenge, we transform the time-series data from Cartesian to polar coordinates before constructing the Gramian matrix representation [31].

Given a time-series $X = (x_t, t = 1, 2, \ldots, N)$, where t represents the temporal index and $t \in [1, N]$, the Gramian Angular Field transformation proceeds as follows:

1. Data Normalization

The symbols and notations used in this paper are listed in the Nomenclature. Following Wang et al. [31], We first normalize the time-series data to the interval $[-1, 1]$ through min–max scaling, which preserves the underlying data distribution. This transformation is expressed as Formula (1):

$$\widetilde{x}_i = \frac{(x_i - \max(X)) + (x_i - \min(X))}{\max(X) - \min(X)} \tag{1}$$

where x_i represents the i-th data point in the original time-series, and X represents the complete time-series dataset.

2. Polar Coordinate Transformation

The data $\widetilde{x}_i$ obtained from Formula (1) undergoes a polar coordinate transformation to derive the corresponding angle and radius for each data point, with the angle expressed in Formula (2) and the radius in Formula (3):

$$\theta_i = \arccos(\widetilde{x}_i), -1 \le \widetilde{x}_i \le 1, \widetilde{x}_i \in \widetilde{X} \tag{2}$$

$$r_i = \frac{t_i}{M}, t_i \in \mathbb{N} \tag{3}$$

where t_i represents the position of the data point in the sequence, and M is the normalization factor.

3. Generation of Gramian Angular Field Image

Using the summation angle relationships presented in Formula (4), we obtain the corresponding Gramian Angular Summation Field (GASF) images:

$$\text{GASF} = [\cos(\phi_i + \phi_j)] = \widetilde{X'} \cdot \widetilde{X} - \sqrt{I - \widetilde{X}^2}' \cdot \sqrt{I - \widetilde{X}^2} \tag{4}$$

where ϕ_i and ϕ_j represent the angular values at time points i and j, respectively, $\widetilde{X}$ denotes the normalized time-series matrix, $\widetilde{X'}$ is the transpose of $\widetilde{X}$, and I represents the identity matrix.

Figure 2 illustrates the procedure in which Gramian Angular Field transformation converts time-series to images.

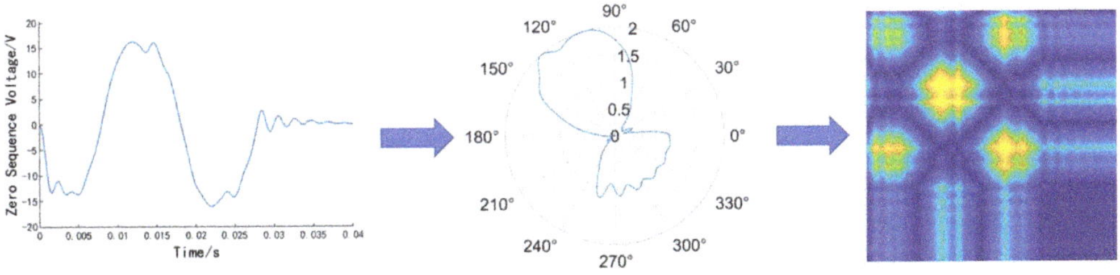

a. Zero-sequence voltage signal b. Polar coordinate conversion c. Gramian angular feld

Figure 2. The procedure for signal–image conversion.

2.2. *The Crested Porcupine Optimizer (CPO) Algorithm*

Inspired by crested porcupine defensive behavior, M. Abdel-Basset et al. [32] developed the CPO. The algorithm features a Cyclic Population Reduction (CPR) technique, reflecting how only threatened individuals activate their defense mechanisms. Following M. Abdel-Basset et al. [32], the mathematical model is expressed in Formula (5):

$$N = N_{\min} + (N' - N_{\min}) \times \left(1 - \left(\frac{t\% \frac{T_{\max}}{T}}{\frac{T_{\max}}{T}}\right)\right) \tag{5}$$

where N denotes the current population size, N' represents the initial population size, and $N_{\min}$ is the minimum population size required to prevent excessive population reduction. The parameters t and $T_{\max}$ indicate the current and maximum number of iterations, respectively. % represents the remainder or modulo operator. T is a variable to determine the number of cycles.

1. Exploration phase

When predators are distant, CPs employ two defensive strategies: visual and acoustic responses. These strategies facilitate broad spatial exploration, focusing on global search capabilities.

(i) Visual Strategy

As their primary long-range defense, porcupines erect their quills to appear larger and deter predators. This exploration-oriented strategy is mathematically expressed in Formula (6):

$$\vec{x_i^{t+1}} = \vec{x_i^t} + \tau_1 \times \left| 2\tau_2 \times \vec{x_{best}^t} - \vec{y_i^t} \right| \tag{6}$$

where $\vec{x_i^t}$ denotes the i-th individual position, $\vec{x_{best}^t}$ represents the global best solution, τ_1 and τ_2 are step-size control parameters, and $\vec{y_i^t}$ indicates the candidate solution.

(ii) Acoustic Strategy

If visual deterrence fails, porcupines escalate their defense by producing threatening sounds. This behavior is mathematically represented as an expansion of the search space through perturbation, as expressed in Formula (7):

$$\overrightarrow{x_i^{t+1}} = (1 - \vec{U_1}) \times \vec{x_i^t} + \vec{U_1} \times (\vec{y} + \tau_3 \times (\vec{x_{r1}^t} - \vec{x_{r2}^t})) \tag{7}$$

where $\vec{U_1}$ and τ_3 are random numbers used to balance the relationship between current and new positions and control the perturbation amplitude, and $\vec{y}$ represents the target position of the predator after disturbance, while $\vec{x_{r1}^t}$ and $\vec{x_{r2}^t}$ denote randomly selected individual positions.

2. Exploitation phase

In this phase, the CP implements defensive behaviors based on predator proximity, utilizing two strategies: odor attack and physical attack.

(i) Odor attack strategy

When a predator approaches, the porcupine releases odors to disrupt its movement. In mathematical terms, this strategy involves narrowing the search space to focus on local optima, as shown in Formula (8):

$$\overrightarrow{x_i^{t+1}} = (1 - \vec{U_1}) \times \vec{x_i^t} + \vec{U_1} \times (\vec{x_{r1}^t} + S_i^t \times (\vec{x_{r2}^t} - \vec{x_{r3}^t}) - \tau_3 \times \vec{\delta} \times \gamma_t \times S_i^t) \tag{8}$$

where $\vec{x_{r3}^t}$ denotes the position of a randomly selected individual, $\vec{\delta}$ is the parameter controlling the search direction, γ_t represents the defense factor, and S_i^t defines the scent diffusion coefficient.

(ii) Physical attack strategy

When all else fails, porcupines resort to physical attacks as their last defense. This behavior is mathematically represented by Formula (9):

$$\overrightarrow{x_i^{t+1}} = \vec{x}_{best}^t + \alpha(1 - \tau_4) + \tau_4 \times (\delta \times \vec{x}_{best}^t - \vec{x}_i^t) - \tau_5 \times \delta \times \gamma_t \times \vec{F}_i^t) \quad (9)$$

where α is the convergence rate control factor, while τ_4 and τ_5 are random numbers that control the step size and balance between current and new positions, respectively. $\vec{F}_i^t$ represents the force acting on the current individual, simulating the predator's behavioral response after receiving a physical attack.

Compared to traditional optimization algorithms like Particle Swarm Optimization (PSO) and Genetic Algorithms (GAs), the CPO offers several advantages in hyperparameter optimization. While PSO may suffer from premature convergence and GAs can be computationally intensive, the CPO's Cyclic Population Reduction (CPR) technique provides a better balance between exploration and exploitation. The defense strategies in the CPO—visual, acoustic, odor, and physical attack—enable more effective searching of the parameter space compared to single-strategy algorithms. Figure 3 shows the evolution of the objective function value during the CPO algorithm optimization process. The following key observations can be drawn:

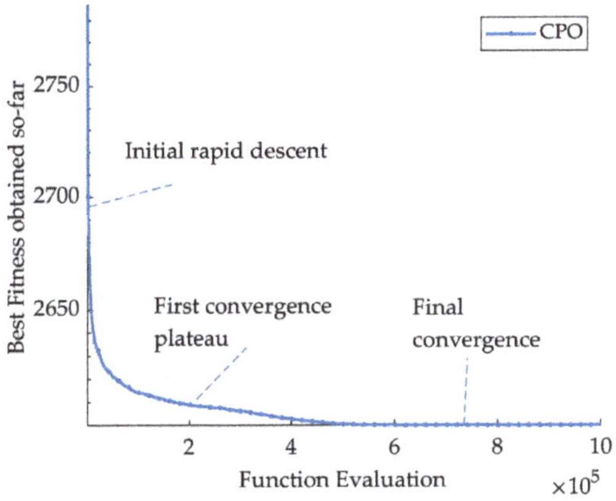

Figure 3. Evolution of objective function value in CPO algorithm optimization.

The algorithm exhibits rapid initial convergence, with the objective function value decreasing sharply. This fast convergence is attributed to the effective global exploration capabilities of visual and sound strategies, allowing the quick identification of promising solution regions. As iterations progress, the convergence curve gradually levels off, indicating the algorithm's transition to fine-tuning. In this phase, scent and physical attack strategies perform local exploitation, thoroughly exploring promising areas. The convergence curve ultimately stabilizes at a low value, indicating successful identification of near-optimal solutions and algorithm stability. The entire optimization process demonstrates the CPO's excellent performance through its balanced exploration and exploitation mechanisms.

2.3. Dual-Path Neural Networks Optimized by CPO

The proposed framework integrates two core components: a deep learning architecture and an optimization algorithm. Drawing from the dual-channel parallel CNN proposed by Li et al. [33], we designed a dual-path neural network that processes both image and temporal data simultaneously, achieving high-impedance fault identification through feature fusion.

The image processing branch employs a CNN-based structure. It takes 300 × 300 × 3 RGB images as an input with Z-score normalization. A 3 × 3 convolution (stride = 2, padding = 3) is applied, followed by ReLU activation and 3 × 3 max-pooling (stride = 2, padding = 1). The features are then flattened through a 128-neuron fully connected layer. The temporal branch utilizes GRU layers with a self-attention mechanism. Features from both branches are converted to one-dimensional vectors and merged via an addition layer. A three-node fully connected layer processes the fused features before Softmax transformation.

In this study, we employed the CPO to optimize the hyperparameters of the dual-path neural network. The CPO algorithm was initialized with carefully selected parameters based on extensive empirical testing: a population size $N' = 30$ with a minimum population size $N_{\min} = 24$, defense cycle parameter $T = 2$, convergence rate $\alpha = 0.03$, and trade-off coefficient $T_f = 0.8$. These parameters were chosen to balance exploration and exploitation capabilities while maintaining population diversity. The optimization scope encompassed four critical hyperparameters: the learning rate (0.001, 0.01), number of convolution kernels (32, 128), number of GRU neurons(32, 128), and number of attention heads (1, 4). The CPO utilizes four sequential defense mechanisms (sight, sound, odor, and physical attack), while employing Cyclic Population Reduction for efficient convergence and diversity. The algorithm converged to an optimal configuration with 62 convolution kernels, 67 GRU neurons, single-head attention, and a learning rate of 0.0092204. This configuration demonstrated superior performance compared to traditional optimization methods, exhibiting enhanced convergence characteristics and stability. The final model implementation utilized the Adam optimizer with per-epoch data shuffling to mitigate overfitting risks. The CPO-optimized model achieved a remarkable accuracy of 99.7% on the test set, representing a significant improvement over the baseline model's 98.9% accuracy. Figure 4 illustrates the detailed workflow and structure of our proposed dual-path neural network for high-impedance fault detection.

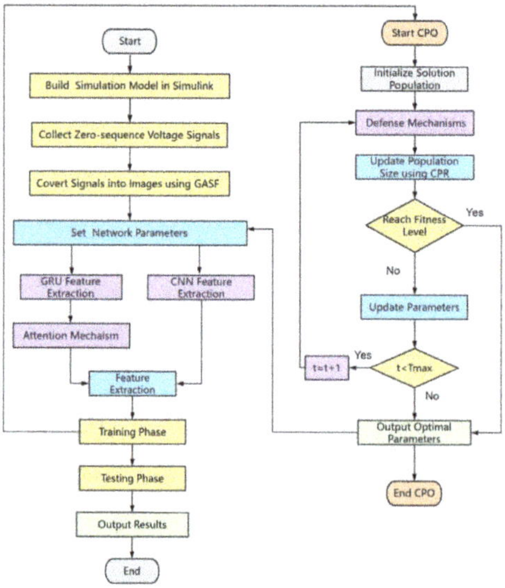

Figure 4. Flowchart of proposed dual-path neural network for high-impedance fault detection.

3. Experimental Setup

3.1. High-Impedance Fault Model

The complex and dynamic characteristics of distribution networks and random factors make accurate HIF modeling challenging. In response, we adopt and extend the nonlinear HIF model proposed by Emanuel et al. [34], which is effective in characterizing nonlinear arcing behavior on sandy soil. By introducing a series resistor to enhance the original model, we better represent the randomness of fault signals, as shown in Figure 5.

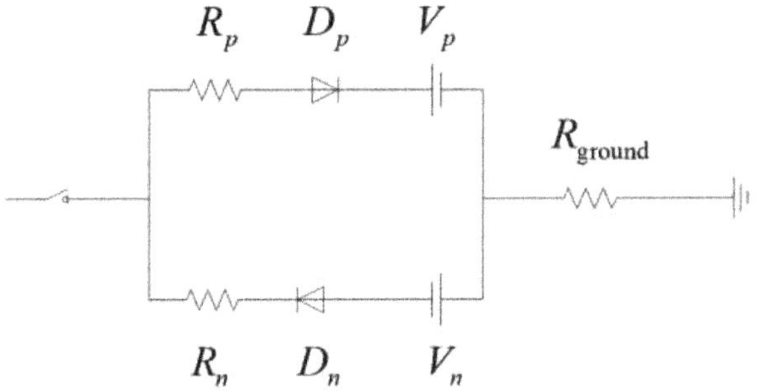

Figure 5. Electrical circuit model for high-impedance fault.

The model consists of two DC voltage sources, two diodes, and two resistors. Specifically, V_p and V_n simulate discharge voltages, R_p and R_n represent grounding resistances, and D_p and D_n control fault current directions. Current flows to the ground when the line voltage exceeds V_p, reverses when below V_n, and ceases when between V_n and V_p due to voltage cancellation [35]. The model parameters are configured with grounding resistance ranging from 500 Ω to 5000 Ω and DC voltage sources varying between 3 and 10 kV [36].

3.2. Distribution Network Mode

To validate the proposed method, we constructed a radial medium-voltage distribution network model with an ungrounded neutral point using the MATLAB/SIMULINK R2024a platform, and its topological structure is illustrated in Figure 6.

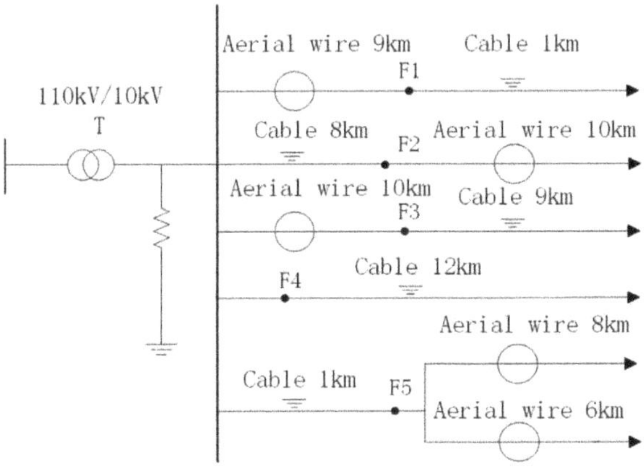

Figure 6. Topology diagram of distribution network.

Table 1 presents the positive-sequence and zero-sequence parameters of the overhead lines and cable lines in the distribution network model.

Table 1. Line parameters.

Type of Line	Parameters	R/(Ω/km)	L/(mH/km)	C/(μF/km)
Aerial wire	Positive sequence	0.125	1.3	0.0096
	Zero sequence	0.275	4.6	0.0054
Cable	Positive sequence	0.27	0.255	0.339
	Zero sequence	2.7	1.019	0.28

3.3. Dataset Construction and Processing

We collected zero-sequence voltage signals from the distribution network model shown in Figure 3 under three scenarios: high-impedance fault, capacitor switching operation, and load connection. For the high-impedance fault samples, we considered varying fault resistances (500–2000 Ω), multiple initial phase angles (0–120°), different fault locations (F1–F5), and all three phases. For the normal operation scenarios, we included capacitor switching with different capacitance values and load connections with varying power levels. By taking samples at different distances from the bus, we obtained a total dataset of 2700 samples. The detailed sample distribution is shown in Tables 2–4.

Table 2. Distribution of high-impedance fault samples.

Parameter Type	Values
Initial Phase Angle (°)	0, 30, 60, 90, 120
Fault Type	1, 2, 3, 4, 5
Fault Phase	A, B, C
Fault Location	F1, F2, F3, F4, F5
Neutral Point Resistance/Ω	500, 1000, 2000
Ground Resistance/Ω	5, 10

Table 3. Distribution of parameters for capacitor switching samples.

Parameter Type	Values
Initial Phase Angle (°)	0, 30, 60, 90, 120
Capacitor/μF	0.02, 0.03, 0.04
Switching Phase	A, B, C
Switching Location	F1, F2, F3, F4, F5

Table 4. Distribution of parameters for load connection samples.

Parameter Type	Values
Initial Phase Angle (°)	0, 30, 60, 90, 120
Load/W	150, 200, 250
Switching Phase	A, B, C
Switching Location	F1, F2, F3, F4, F5

4. Results and Discussion

4.1. Analysis of Zero-Sequence Voltage Characteristics Under Different Operating Conditions

HIF characteristics often resemble normal operating conditions like load switching and capacitor operations, making fault detection challenging. The significant nonlinearity and instability of HIF signals limit the effectiveness of conventional threshold detection methods based on zero-sequence voltage magnitude, resulting in high false alarm rates.

In distribution networks, when high-impedance faults occur, the high transition resistance results in a minimal or undetectable zero-sequence current, while the zero-sequence voltage exhibits significant variations. Therefore, the zero-sequence voltage serves as a sensitive indicator for identifying such faults. Figures 7–9 illustrate the zero-sequence voltage waveforms when a high-impedance ground fault, capacitor switching operation, or load connection occur at $t = 0$ s, respectively.

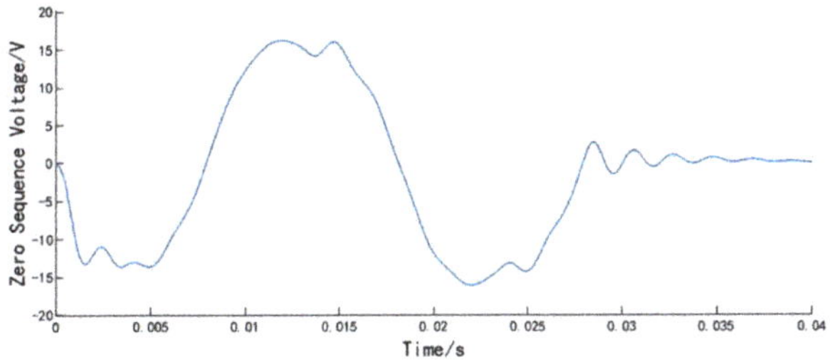

Figure 7. Zero-sequence voltage under HIF condition.

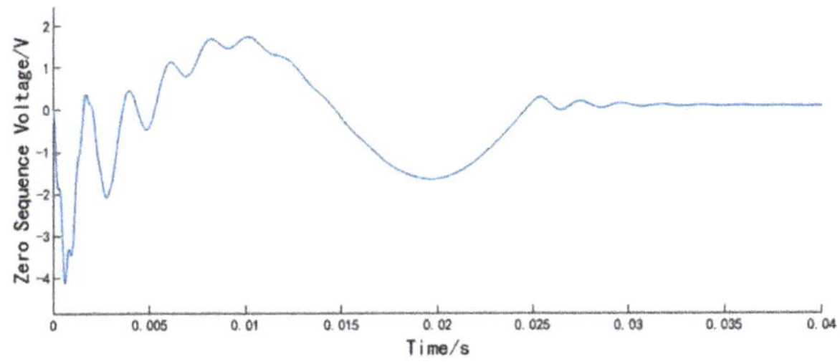

Figure 8. Zero-sequence voltage under capacitor switching.

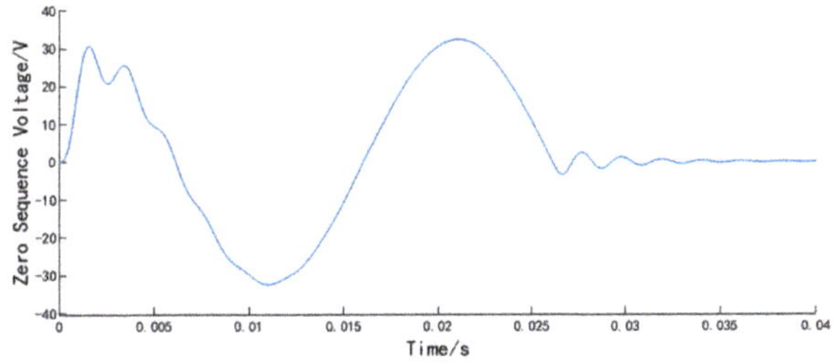

Figure 9. Zero-sequence voltage under load switching.

Figure 10 presents the two-dimensional feature images obtained through the Gramian Angular Summation Field (GASF) transformation of zero-sequence voltage signals under three operating conditions: high-impedance ground fault, capacitor switching operation, and load connection.

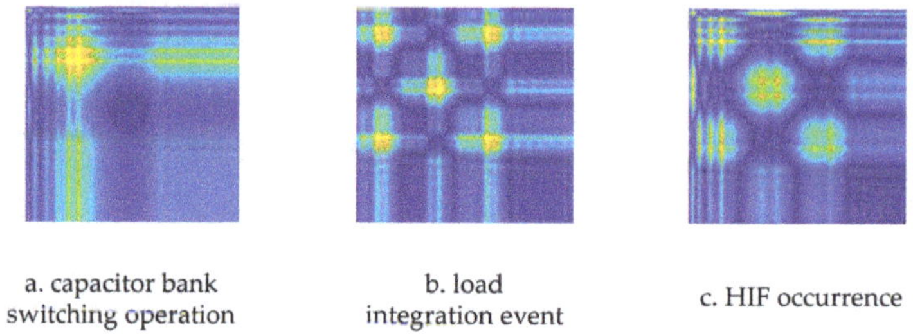

Figure 10. 2D image representations after GASF transformation.

4.2. Model Performance Evaluation and Comparative Analysis

The dataset comprises three types of samples: high-impedance fault, capacitor switching operation, and load connection, split into training and test sets. The model achieved 99.70% accuracy on the test set, demonstrating excellent performance in both fault identification and normal event classification (capacitor switching and load connections). All simulations were performed on a system with Intel(R) Core(TM) i5-10400 CPU @ 2.90 GHz and 16 GB RAM. The model was tested 10 times, and the average testing time per sample was 8.32 ms, making it highly suitable for deployment in large-scale distribution network monitoring systems where real-time performance is crucial.

To demonstrate the effectiveness of feature extraction, we used t-distributed Stochastic Neighbor Embedding (t-SNE) to reduce the high-dimensional features from the fully connected layer to a two-dimensional representation. Figure 11 shows the three event categories (yellow dots, red circles, and blue squares) forming distinct clusters with clear boundaries and tight internal groupings. This visualization confirms the model's ability to extract discriminative features and effectively differentiate between event types.

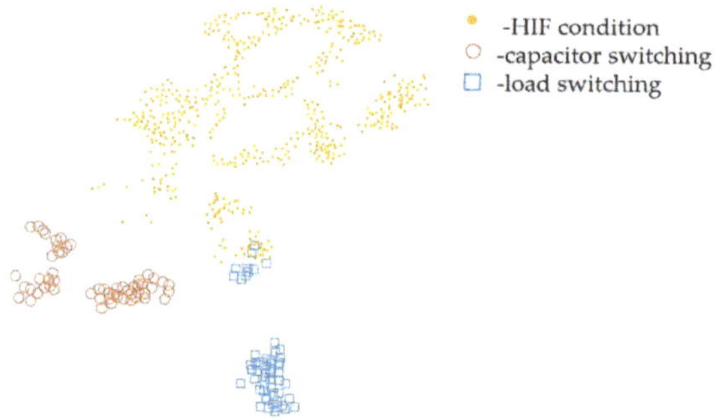

Figure 11. The t-SNE visualization of FC layer features.

Figure 12 shows a radar chart comparing three key performance metrics—Precision, Recall, and F1-score—across all categories. The metrics are plotted on radial axes, where values closer to the perimeter represent better performance. All metrics reach nearly 100%, creating an almost perfect equilateral triangle. This balanced distribution indicates the model's strong performance in both fault identification and normal condition classification, without compromising either task.

Figure 13 shows the confusion matrix illustrating the model's classification performance on the test set. In the matrix, rows indicate true classes while columns represent predicted classes, with each cell showing the number of samples in that category. With only two misclassified samples across the entire test set, these results demonstrate the model's outstanding capability in identifying high-impedance faults.

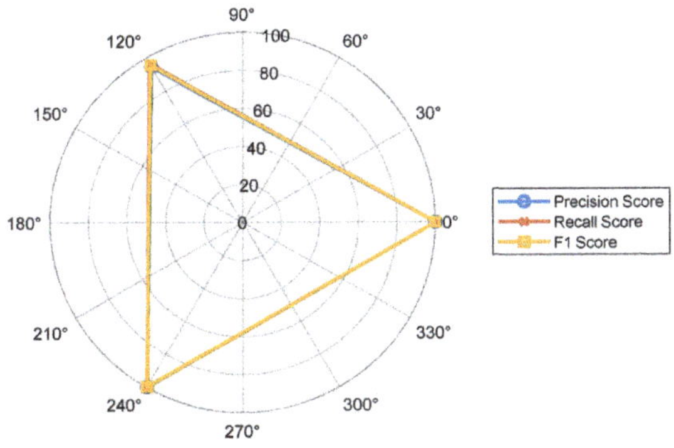

Figure 12. Multi-class performance radar chart.

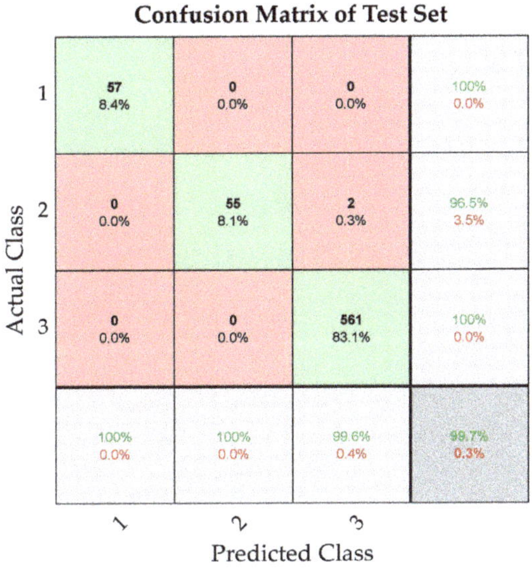

Figure 13. Test set confusion matrix.

4.3. Comparative Analysis of Model Performance Under Noisy Conditions

We evaluated our method against three baseline models using the test dataset, as shown in Table 5. Under noise-free conditions, our method achieved 99.70% accuracy, surpassing GASF-CNN (99.26%), GRU-GASF-CNN (98.81%), and GRU-ATTENTION (97.93%) models, demonstrating its effectiveness in identifying high-impedance faults.

Table 5. Test accuracy of different models under noise interference (%).

Models	Accuracy Without Noise	Accuracy at 20 dB	Accuracy at 30 dB	Accuracy at 40 dB
Proposed method	99.70	96.74	99.41	99.41
GASF-CNN	99.26	95.70	98.52	98.81
GRU-ATTENTION	97.93	94.37	96.00	97.04
GRU-GASF-CNN	98.81	95.11	97.33	98.80

To evaluate the model's resilience to noise, we tested its performance under various noise conditions. We added Gaussian white noise at three SNR levels (20 dB, 30 dB, and

40 dB) to the zero-sequence voltage signals in the test set, with lower SNR values representing stronger noise interference. Our method demonstrated strong noise immunity, achieving accuracies of 96.74%, 99.41%, and 99.41% at 20 dB, 30 dB, and 40 dB, respectively, consistently outperforming the baseline models. These results confirm the model's robustness in real-world power system environments.

4.4. Model Adaptability Analysis Under Different Topological Configurations

To evaluate the model's practical applicability and generalization ability, we tested it on a more complex distribution network topology (Figure 14). Considering practical maintenance needs, we simplified the task to binary classification between HIFs and normal operations, as fault detection is the primary concern for maintenance personnel. For validation, we kept the model's pre-trained parameters unchanged and created a balanced test set by randomly sampling equal numbers of fault and normal operation cases from the new topology. The results show that our model maintains robust performance even under the complex topology, achieving 94% overall accuracy and 96% accuracy in identifying high-impedance faults.

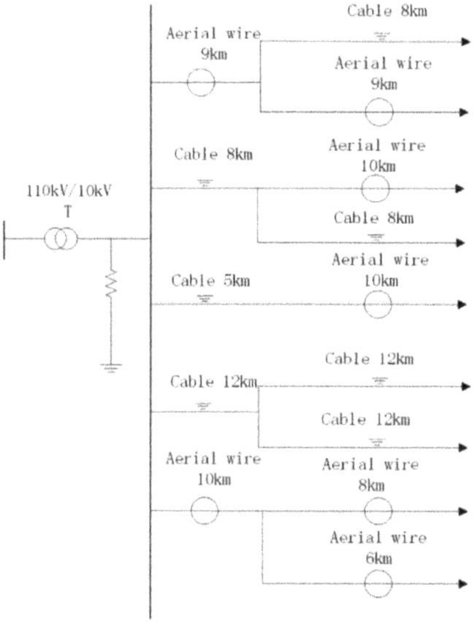

Figure 14. Complex distribution network topology.

The model's performance was further evaluated through ROC curve analysis and multiple classification metrics. As shown in Figure 15, the ROC curve demonstrates strong classification performance with an AUC value of 0.940. The curve's significant deviation from the diagonal line (random classification) indicates the model's strong discriminative ability.

Figure 16 illustrates the model's performance metrics for normal operation (Class 1) and high-impedance faults (Class 2). In fault detection, the model achieved 96.0% precision, with the recall, F1-score, and specificity all maintaining values above 90%. These comprehensive metrics demonstrate the model's robust capability for fault identification in real-world distribution networks.

By contrast, as shown in Figure 17, the single-channel GRU-ATTENTION model shows limited performance, achieving only 89% overall accuracy and 86% accuracy in HIF identification.

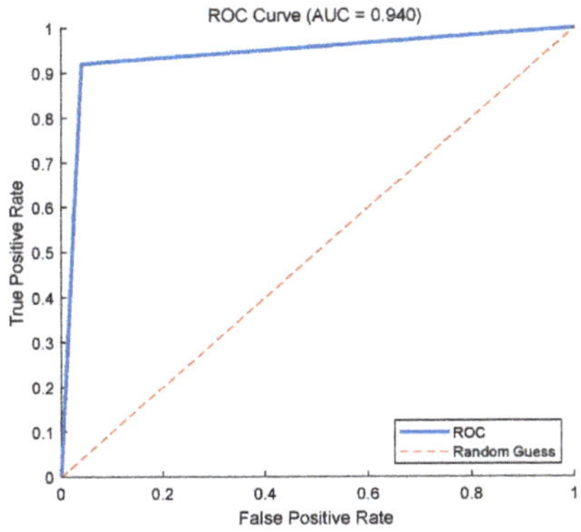

Figure 15. ROC curve of model.

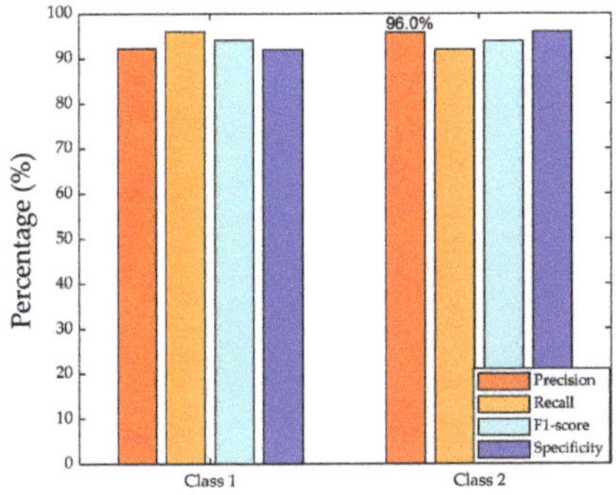

Figure 16. Binary Classification Performance of the Proposed Model.

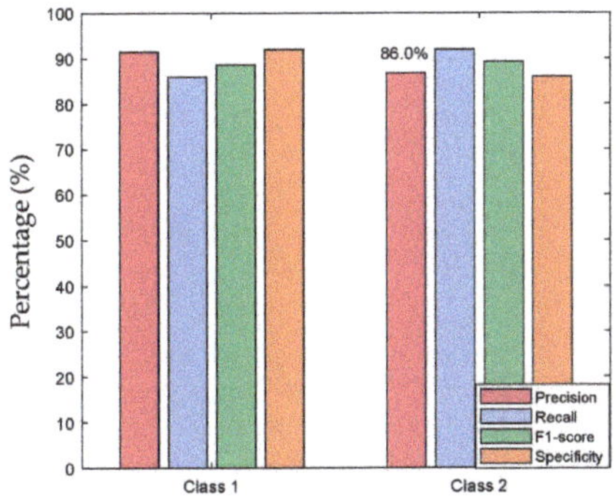

Figure 17. Classification performance metrics of comparative models.

The experimental results demonstrate the method's robustness and accuracy across various network topologies, validating its practical applicability.

4.5. Validation on Real-Time Simulation Platform

We validated the proposed method on the Hardware-in-the-Loop (HIL) experimental platform, as shown in Figure 18. First, we constructed a distribution network model containing five feeders in MATLAB/SIMULINK. In this model, we set up five fault points, labeled as F1 to F5, for fault simulation. Subsequently, using the HIL platform, we performed experiments to collect fault waveform data and imported them into MATLAB for subsequent analysis. To validate the effectiveness of the proposed method, we tested it using 675 samples without retraining the diagnostic model. The fault diagnosis results are shown in Table 6. As indicated in Table 6, the proposed method only resulted in two misclassifications, demonstrating its robust capability in detecting high-impedance faults on the real-time simulation platform.

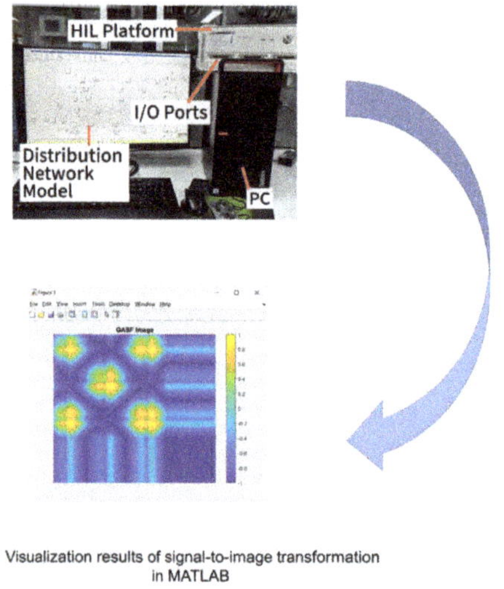

Figure 18. Real-time digital simulator test platform.

Table 6. Detection results on HIL Platform.

Actual Class	Predicted Class		
	HIF	**Capacitor Switching**	**Load Switching**
HIF	561	0	0
Capacitor Switching	0	57	0
Load Switching	2	0	55

5. Conclusions

This paper proposes a dual-path neural network for high-impedance fault detection. The model employs a dual-branch architecture that processes both raw zero-sequence voltage signals and their Gramian Angular Field transformations, effectively combining temporal and spatial features to outperform single-modality methods. The Crested Porcupine Optimizer enhances hyperparameter optimization, improving model adaptability and generalization across various noise levels and network conditions. The Hardware-in-the-Loop validation achieved 99.70% accuracy in distinguishing faults from normal operations, demonstrating the method's practicality. Future work will focus on reducing computational complexity for real-time applications and extending to more complex networks.

However, the model's performance under diverse environmental conditions (such as lightning and snow) and its capability to identify emerging load characteristics require further validation. Future research will focus on model generalization in diverse operating environments and the exploration of adaptive optimization strategies for different fault types and network topologies, aiming to enhance the method's practical value in real distribution networks.

Author Contributions: Data curation, G.L., X.Y. and M.Z.; Writing—original draft, L.Y.; Writing—review & editing, K.N. and W.G.; Super-vision, W.S. All authors have read and agreed to the published version of the manuscript.

Funding: This research was funded by the Yuxiu Innovation Project of NCUT, grant number 2024NCUTYXCX203.

Data Availability Statement: The code, models, and datasets used in this study are available from the author upon request.

Conflicts of Interest: The authors declare no conflicts of interest.

Nomenclature

x_i	the i-th data point in the original time series
X	the complete time-series dataset
t_i	the position of the data point in the sequence
M	the normalization factor
ϕ_i	the angular values at time points i
ϕ_j	the angular values at time points j
$\widetilde{X}$	the normalized time-series matrix
$\widetilde{X}'$	the transpose of $\widetilde{X}$
I	the identity matrix
N	the current population size
N'	the initial population size
$N_{\min}$	the minimum population size
t	the current number of iterations
T	a variable to determine the number of cycles
$T_{\max}$	the maximum number of iterations
$\overrightarrow{x_i^t}$	the i-th individual position
$\overrightarrow{x_{best}^t}$	the global best solution
τ_1	step-size control parameters
τ_2	step-size control parameters
$\overrightarrow{y_i^t}$	the candidate solution
$\overrightarrow{U_1}$	random numbers
τ_3	random numbers
$\overrightarrow{y}$	the target position of the predator after disturbance
$\overrightarrow{x_{r1}^t}$	randomly selected individual positions
$\overrightarrow{x_{r2}^t}$	randomly selected individual positions
$\overrightarrow{x_{r3}^t}$	the position of a randomly selected individual
$\overrightarrow{\delta}$	the parameter controlling the search direction
γ_t	the defense factor
S_i^t	the scent diffusion coefficient
α	the convergence rate control factor
τ_4	random numbers
τ_5	random numbers
$\overrightarrow{F_i^t}$	the force acting on the current individual

References

1. Allawi, M.N.; Hussain, A.N.; Wali, M.K. A new approach to detecting high impedance fault in power distribution feeder based on signal processing hybrid technique and ANNs. *Int. J. Intell. Eng. Syst.* **2023**, *16*.
2. Yang, D.; Lu, B.; Lu, H. High-Resistance Grounding Fault Detection and Line Selection in Resonant Grounding Distribution Network. *Electronics* **2023**, *12*, 4066. [CrossRef]
3. Dashti, R.; Ghasemi, M.; Daisy, M. Fault location in power distribution network with presence of distributed generation resources using impedance based method and applying π line model. *Energy* **2018**, *159*, 344–360. [CrossRef]
4. Li, B. Technology of fault line selection for single-phase-to-earth fault in small current grounding system. *Nonlinear Dyn.* **2012**, *67*, 2111–2122. [CrossRef]
5. Baldwin, T.; Renovich, F. Analysis of Fault Locating Signals for High-Impedance Grounded Systems. In Proceedings of the Conference Record of the 2001 IEEE Industry Applications Conference, 36th IAS Annual Meeting (Cat. No.01CH37248), Chicago, IL, USA, 30 September–4 October 2001; Volume 3, pp. 1823–1830. [CrossRef]
6. Hu, J.; Wei, L.; McGuire, J.; Liu, Z. Flux linkage detection based ground fault identification and system diagnosis in high-resistance grounding systems. *IEEE Trans. Ind. Appl.* **2016**, *53*, 2967–2975. [CrossRef]
7. Xu, H.; Zhang, X.; Sun, H.; Wu, W.; Zhu, J.; Wang, F. Faulty section location method for high impedance grounding fault in resonant grounding system based on discrete Fréchet distance. *Electr. Power Syst. Res.* **2025**, *238*, 111147. [CrossRef]
8. Wang, C.; Feng, L.; Hou, S.; Ren, G.; Lu, T. A High-Impedance Fault Detection Method for Active Distribution Networks Based on Time–Frequency–Space Domain Fusion Features and Hybrid Convolutional Neural Network. *Processes* **2024**, *12*, 2712. [CrossRef]
9. Chandra, A.; Singh, G.K.; Pant, V. A novel high impedance fault detection strategy for microgrid based on differential energy signal of current signatures and entropy estimation. *Electr. Power Compon. Syst.* **2024**, *52*, 532–554. [CrossRef]
10. Liu, H.; Zhang, L.; Hang, M.; Li, L. Fault line selection algorithm for single-phase high-impedance ground faults in distribution networks based on the hilbert-huang transform. *J. Phys. Conf. Ser.* **2024**, *2803*, 012037. [CrossRef]
11. Albanna, E.; Al-Rifaie, A.H.; Al-Karakchi, A.A.A. High impedance fault detection in low voltage overhead distribution based wavelet and harmonic indices. *Prz. Elektrotech.* **2023**, *99*, 243–246. [CrossRef]
12. Gogula, V.; Edward, B. Advanced signal analysis for high-impedance fault detection in distribution systems: A dynamic Hilbert transform method. *Front. Energy Res.* **2024**, *12*, 1365538. [CrossRef]
13. Yao, Z.; Liu, Y.; Chen, J.; Ji, J.; Zhang, M.; Gong, Y. Active High-impedance Fault Detection Method for Resonant Grounding Distribution Networks. *IEEE Access* **2024**, *12*, 10932–10945. [CrossRef]
14. Satea, M.; Elsadd, M.; Zaky, M.; Elgamasy, M. Reliable High Impedance Fault Detection with Experimental Investigation in Distribution Systems. *Eng. Technol. Appl. Sci. Res.* **2024**, *14*, 17248–17255. [CrossRef]
15. Wang, J.; Zhang, B.; Yin, D.; Ouyang, J. Distribution network fault identification method based on multimodal ResNet with recorded waveform-driven feature extraction. *Energy Rep.* **2025**, *13*, 90–104. [CrossRef]
16. Lian, Q.; Luo, X.; Lin, D.; Lin, C.; Chen, B.; Guo, Z. ResNest-SVM-based method for identifying single-phase ground faults in active distribution networks. *Front. Energy Res.* **2024**, *12*, 1501737. [CrossRef]
17. Baharozu, E.; Ilhan, S.; Soykan, G. A Data-Driven Based High Impedance Fault Location Method Considering Traveling Waves in Branched Distribution Networks. *IEEE Access* **2024**, *12*, 186535–186546. [CrossRef]
18. Mohammadi, A.; Jannati, M.; Shams, M. Deep SqueezeNet Based Technique for Detection of High Impedance Arcing Faults in Electric Power Distribution Networks. In Proceedings of the 2024 32nd International Conference on Electrical Engineering (ICEE), Tehran, Iran, 14–16 May 2024; pp. 1–6.
19. Jana, C.; Banerjee, S.; Maur, S.; Dalai, S. Power System Disturbance Classification using CWT Guided Customized AlexNet CNN. *IEEE Sens. Lett.* **2024**, *8*, 6006204. [CrossRef]
20. Zheng, F.; Peng, Y.; Jiang, C.; Lin, Y.; Liang, N. Research on the identification of high-resistance ground faults in the flexible DC distribution network based on VMD–inception–CNN. *Front. Energy Res.* **2023**, *11*, 1258619. [CrossRef]
21. Zhang, Y.; Wang, X.; Luo, Y.; Zhang, D.; Mirsaeidi, S.; He, J. High Impedance Fault Detection Based on Attention Mechanism and Object Identification. *CSEE J. Power Energy Syst.* **2021**, *10*, 197–207.
22. Gogula, V.; Edward, B. Fault detection in a distribution network using a combination of a discrete wavelet transform and a neural Network's radial basis function algorithm to detect high-impedance faults. *Front. Energy Res.* **2023**, *11*, 1101049. [CrossRef]
23. Guo, M.F.; Guo, Z.Y.; Gao, J.H.; Chen, D.Y. High-impedance fault detection methodology using time–frequency spectrum and transfer convolutional neural network in distribution networks. *IEEE Syst. J.* **2023**, *17*, 4002–4013. [CrossRef]
24. Liang, H.; Li, H.; Wang, G. A single-phase-to-ground fault detection method based on the ratio fluctuation coefficient of the zero-sequence current and voltage differential in a distribution network. *IEEE Access* **2023**, *11*, 7297–7308. [CrossRef]
25. Bhatnagar, M.; Yadav, A.; Swetapadma, A.; Abdelaziz, A.Y. LSTM-based low-impedance fault and high-impedance fault detection and classification. *Electr. Eng.* **2024**, *106*, 6589–6613. [CrossRef]
26. Odion, J.; Ekpa, A.K. Detection and Location of High Impedance Fault on the Nigerian 330 kV Transmission System Using Artificial Neural Network. *Int. J. Multidiscip. Res. Anal.* **2024**, *7*, 2092–2101.

27. Wu, H.; Wang, J.; Nan, D.; Cui, Q.; Li, W. Fault Location and Fault Cause Identification Method for Transmission Lines Based on Pose Normalized Multi-Output Convolutional Nets. *IEEE Trans. Instrum. Meas.* **2024**, *74*, 3500412.
28. Ding, C.; Ma, P.; Jiang, C.; Wang, F. Fast Fault Line Selection Technology of Distribution Network Based on MCECA-CloFormer. *Appl. Sci.* **2024**, *14*, 8270. [CrossRef]
29. Zeng, Z.; Li, J.; Wei, Y.; Wang, X.; Zheng, Y.; Zhang, Y. Flexible DC distribution network fault detection method based on MTF-EfficientNetV2 algorithm. *Res. Sq.* **2024**. [CrossRef]
30. Mishra, S.; Giri, N.; Mallick, R.K.; Nayak, P.; Sharma, R.; Gadanayak, D.A. High Impedance Fault Identification Using STransform and 2D-CNN Approach for PV Integrated Micro-grid. In Proceedings of the 2024 IEEE 4th International Conference on Sustainable Energy and Future Electric Transportation (SEFET), Hyderabad, India, 31 July–3 August 2024; pp. 1–5.
31. Wang, Z.; Oates, T. Imaging time-series to improve classification and imputation. *arXiv* **2015**, arXiv:1506.00327.
32. Abdel-Basset, M.; Mohamed, R.; Abouhawwash, M. Crested Porcupine Optimizer: A new nature-inspired metaheuristic. *Knowl.-Based Syst.* **2024**, *284*, 111257. [CrossRef]
33. Li, Z.; Chen, Q.; Qian, B.; Niu, Y.; Zhang, Z. Health Diagnosis of Grid-Connected Inverter Switching Devices Based on Gramian Angular Field and Parallel CNN. *Electr. Power Autom. Equip.* **2024**, *44*, 153–159. [CrossRef]
34. Emanuel, A.E.; Cyganski, D.; Orr, J.A.; Shiller, S.; Gulachenski, E.M. High impedance fault arcing on sandy soil in 15 kV distribution feeders: Contributions to the evaluation of the low frequency spectrum. *IEEE Trans. Power Deliv.* **1990**, *5*, 676–686. [CrossRef]
35. Gautam, S.; Brahma, S.M. Detection of high impedance fault in power distribution systems using mathematical morphology. *IEEE Trans. Power Syst.* **2012**, *28*, 1226–1234. [CrossRef]
36. Abasi-obot, I.; Shehu, G.; Kunya, A.; Jibril, Y. High Impedance Fault Modelling and Simulation of 33kV/11kV Distribution Network Using MATLAB. In Proceedings of the 2022 IEEE Nigeria 4th International Conference on Disruptive Technologies for Sustainable Development (NIGERCON), Lagos, Nigeria, 5–7 April 2022; pp. 1–4. [CrossRef]

mathematics

MDPI

Article

Start Time Planning for Cyclic Queuing and Forwarding in Time-Sensitive Networks

Daqian Liu, Zhewei Zhang, Yuntao Shi *, Yingying Wang, Jingcheng Guo and Zhenwu Lei

School of Electrical and Control Engineering, North China University of Technology, Beijing 100144, China; liudaqian@ncut.edu.cn (D.L.); zzw159@mail.ncut.edu.cn (Z.Z.); wyy@ncut.edu.cn (Y.W.); guojingcheng@ncut.edu.cn (J.G.); leizhenwu@ncut.edu.cn (Z.L.)

* Correspondence: shiyuntao@ncut.edu.cn

Abstract: Time-sensitive networking (TSN) is a kind of network communication technology applied in fields such as industrial internet and intelligent transportation, capable of meeting the application requirements for precise time synchronization and low-latency deterministic forwarding. In TSN, cyclic queuing and forwarding (CQF) is a traffic shaping mechanism that has been extensively discussed in the recent literature, which allows the delay of time-triggered (TT) flow to be definite and easily calculable. In this paper, two algorithms are designed to tackle the start time planning issue with the CQF mechanism, namely the flow–path–offset joint scheduling (FPOJS) algorithm and congestion-aware scheduling algorithm, to improve the scheduling success ratio of TT flows. The FPOJS algorithm, which adopts a novel scheduling object—a combination of flow, path, and offset—implements scheduling in descending order of a well-designed priority that considers the resource capacity and resource requirements of ports. The congestion-aware scheduling algorithm identifies and optimizes congested ports during scheduling and substantially improves the scheduling success ratio by dynamically configuring port resources. The experimental results demonstrate that the FPOJS algorithm achieves a 39% improvement in the scheduling success ratio over the naive algorithm, 13% over the Tabu-ITP algorithm, and 10% over the MSS algorithm. Moreover, the algorithm exhibits a higher scheduling success ratio under large-scale TSN.

Keywords: industrial internet; time-sensitive networking; cyclic queuing and forwarding; joint routing scheduling; start time planning

MSC: 68T20; 68U07; 94A40; 49M05

1. Introduction

With the development of real-time critical systems such as automobiles, aerospace, industrial automation, and industrial control, the ever-increasing communication data traffic puts forward high-bandwidth and low-delay requirements for communication networks [1]. Traditional Ethernet is limited to addressing non-real-time, best-effort data transmission, which poses challenges in fulfilling the diverse and hybrid traffic service transmission requirements demanded by the emerging industry for communication networks. While industrial networks like PROFINET, POWERLINK, and EtherCAT achieve different levels of real-time transmission performance, their compatibility and interoperability are limited by the proprietary nature of their mechanisms [2].

To address the aforementioned issues with Ethernet, TSN, a set of standards specified by IEEE 802 [3], emerged at a historic moment. The IEEE 802.1 TSN Task Group is actively working on the standardization of time-sensitive capabilities across 802 networks. This involves the development of a comprehensive suite of 802.1 sub-standards, which address various aspects including clock synchronization, frame preemption, redundancy management, and enhancements for scheduled traffic [4]. Specifically, the IEEE 802.1Qbv standard outlines a gate mechanism known as the time-aware shaper (TAS), which regulates the selection of queues for connection to the corresponding egress port. This is achieved through a statically generated periodic schedule, referred to as the gate control list (GCL) [5]. GCL allows TT flow and unscheduled flows to be temporally isolated. There is an inherent complexity in generating the GCLs, i.e., finding the right points in time to open and close the gates [6], and demanding dynamic and complex configuration [7]. Consequently, the IEEE 802.1 Qch standard proposed an easy-to-use model named CQF. The principle underlying CQF is that TT flows are periodically queued and transmitted in TSN [8].

Even though CQF simplifies the gate control mechanism, constructing and optimizing data flow schedules to enhance scheduling performance remains a challenge [9]. Data flow scheduling strategies are an active field of research, often adopting a serialized scheduling algorithm. The general step of serialization scheduling is to first sort the flows based on a certain flow attribute (such as packet size, period, deadline, etc.). Then, the algorithm sequentially searches for the initial sending time (also called the offset) for each flow. Finally, the scheduling success is judged by the resource availability of each node through which the target flow passes. By precisely planning the sending times, scheduling failures caused by queue congestion can be effectively avoided, and scheduling performance can be improved. Most scheduling strategies tend to consider only the attributes of flow and do not adequately take into account the remaining capacity of all the port queues along the flow paths, which means that the resource allowance for the scheduling period is ignored. This often leads to congestion in port queues, which limits the flexibility of subsequent scheduling efforts. The resource margin of flow is determined by both path and offset. Only by establishing the path and offset of flow can the scheduling strategy calculate the resource consumption of the flow and determine the resource margin. The serialized scheduling cannot calculate flow offset until flow sorting is determined. Therefore, flow sorting, path planning, and offset search should not be isolated but should be considered comprehensively. To address the aforementioned issues, this study presents a FPOJS algorithm based on load balancing. The primary innovation of this algorithm lies in its comprehensive consideration of the interactions between flow sorting, path planning, and offset search. It integrates these three previously isolated steps into a unified combination, guided by a priority scoring mechanism, to achieve the objective of finding the optimal solution. Furthermore, the superiority of this method has been validated through experimental verification. The significant contributions of this paper can be summarized as follows.

1. The traditional incremental scheduling is improved by shifting from scheduling flow independently to scheduling a novel scheduling object: a combination of (*flow, path, offset*). The scheduling objects can integrate the independent scheduling processes of flow sorting, path planning, and offset search into a cohesive whole.
2. A flow–path–offset joint scheduling algorithm is proposed to schedule based on a novel multi-index priority scoring mechanism, which enhances the load balancing degree and increases the scheduling success ratio. The scoring mechanism depends on the total resources occupied by the scheduling object and the remaining port capacity. The scoring mechanism can accurately reflect the impact of each scheduling object on the scheduling process.
3. A congestion-aware scheduling algorithm is presented that can identify and optimize congested ports during scheduling. The reason for scheduling failure is not that the overall link load ratio is too high, but that the resources of a few ports along the path are congested. This method can detect congested ports early in the scheduling process and reduce scheduling failures caused by small amounts of port congestion.

The rest of this article is organized as follows. In Section 2, the related work is reviewed. Section 3 introduces the network model and CQF mechanism. The target optimization problem with CQF in TSN is presented in Section 4. Section 5 introduces the method for calculating the priority of combination and proposes the FPOJS algorithm. Section 6 presents the evaluation results. Finally, the conclusion is given in Section 7.

2. Related Work

In recent years, research on TSN has primarily encompassed time synchronization, traffic scheduling, reliability analysis, and routing planning. The study of TAS mainly focuses on the configuration of GCL and the planning of time slots. In early research, researchers attempted to address this NP-hard problem using solvers. Steiner et al. [10] proposed a strategy for solving the scheduling problem for time-triggered systems using SMT solvers and defined the formal scheduling constraints that apply in a time-triggered network. Drr et al. [11] modeled the traffic scheduling problem in TSN through the well-known no-wait job shop scheduling problem, proposing an integer linear programming (ILP) model along with a meta-heuristic optimization algorithm. These strategies ensured deterministic transmission while incurring a high time cost. Hence, based on the constraint framework proposed by [10], Nayak et al. [12] synthesized the GCL scheduling as a constrained system through first-order array theory and proved that this method had a universal SMT/OMT solver, which significantly reduced the required run time and improved the scalability. To meet the requirements in large-scale networks, Nayak et al. [13] designed a network architecture based on software-defined networking (SDN). It dynamically computed the routing and scheduling of TT flows through the logical centralization of the control plane, and on this basis, proposed multiple ILP formulations to compute incremental schedules [14] approximating the optimal solutions of their corresponding static scheduling problems.

As previously mentioned, CQF is a simplified model of TAS. Quan et al. [15], building upon the queue model and workflow of CQF, introduced the injection time planning (ITP) mechanism, which mapped TT flows onto the underlying resources both temporally and spatially. The research highlighted a critical issue within CQF, start time planning, and attempted to address it using a Tabu algorithm. This heuristic approach, while effective, incurred a high time cost and was not suitable for large-scale networks. Cheng et al. [16] proposed a deep reinforcement learning-assisted two-stage scheduling algorithm to solve the temporal scheduling problem based on the CQF model, which can be adopted in the off-line and on-line scenarios. Nie et al. [17] designed a method that adaptively adjusts the queue length and slot length according to the flow properties and proposed a start time planning method based on ILP. Zhang et al. [18] proposed a flow sequence analysis method based on divisibility theory after analyzing the mechanism of CQF and designed an incremental scheduling algorithm with flow judgment conditions and variable search boundaries. The aforementioned approaches represent various solutions to the NP-hard problem of initial send time planning within the ITP framework [15].

In the area of route planning, Chang et al. [19] designed an online scheduling framework and proposed a real-time routing scheduling algorithm based on end-to-end maximum delay, which aimed to assign priority according to the time period and determine the order of route processing by the algorithm. To address the issue of fault tolerance against permanent and transient faults for TT flows in TSN, Feng et al. [20] introduced a route scheduling algorithm based on redundant paths and offset allocation for online incremental rerouting and rescheduling of disrupted flows. Nie et al. [21] classified the periodicity of flows and designed an adaptive periodic compensation route scheduling algorithm, which improved the scheduling performance and reduced the execution time of the algorithm. Guo et al. [22] proposed a scheduling method that utilizes the interaction between flow and offsets. However, the research ignores the impact of path selection on overall scheduling. Wang et al. [23] proposed a load-balanced joint route scheduling algorithm based on the scheduling priority of each TT flow. Although this literature takes into account factors such as sorting, path selection, and offset search, it still adheres to the traditional approach of sorting first and then scheduling.

However, the above methods still adopt the serialized scheduling concept, which separates flow sorting, path planning, and offset search from each other, and proposes improvements from one aspect. In this paper, we design a parallel scheduling strategy that transforms the scheduling subject from a single flow to a combination of flow, path, and offset. Meanwhile, a multi-index scoring mechanism based on the total amount of resources occupied by scheduling objects and the remaining port capacity is proposed. Moreover, based on the unique resource occupancy determinism of the scoring mechanism, the scheduling success ratio is enhanced through the optimization of congested resource blocks.

3. System Model

In this section, a comprehensive network model is built, which includes switches, topology, and data flow models. On this basis, a systematic CQF model is designed, which provides a detailed description of the basic principles and guidelines of CQF.

3.1. Network Model

The TSN network can be represented as a directed graph $N =< V, E >$, where V is the set of nodes which include terminal and switch nodes $v_i \in V$ and E is the set of directed links connecting nodes. The notation $(v_a, v_b) \in E$ denotes the actual physical link from node v_a to node v_b. In the model, each node is comprised of multiple ports, with each port encompassing eight priority queues ranging from Q_0 to Q_7. Assuming each queue has the same length, the two highest-priority queues, Q_6 and Q_7, are designated as the transmit and receive queues in the CQF mechanism [3]. The set of flows is denoted by F, with the attributes defined as follows:

$$f_k = \{f_k.src, f_k.dst, f_k.ddl, f_k.period, \\ f_k.size, f_k.path, f_k.offset\} \tag{1}$$

where $f_k.src$ refers to the source node of the flow, $f_k.dst$ is the destination node of the flow, $f_k.ddl$ is the deadline of the flow, $f_k.period$ is the period of the flow, and $f_k.size$ is the size of the flow. It is assumed that each flow is considered to be a unicast flow, since multicast flows can be treated as a set of unicast flows. The path number of the flow f_k in scheduling is $f_k.path$, and $f_k.offset$ is the offset, or the send time when the first frame of flow f_k is transmitted from the source host. The set of shortest paths for a flow, represented by $path_j \in P$, is determined by the shortest path algorithm. The path is represented by the port numbers through which flow f_i is transmitted, typically denoted as a set of ports. The expression is as follows:

$$f_k.path = \{H_x, SW_i^m, SW_{i+1}^n, \cdots, H_y\} \tag{2}$$

where H_x and H_y represent the address of the source host and destination host, respectively. SW_i^m represents port m on node SW_i. Due to different flow periods and multiple repeats in the scheduling period, in order to avoid potential interference, the scheduling period is set to the hyper-period of the least common multiple of all flow periods. T_{sched} represents the hyper-period, which can be calculated based on the following:

$$T_{sched} = LCM(f_k.period). \tag{3}$$

The notations for this paper are listed in Table 1.

Table 1. List of main notations.

Parameters	Connotations
L_{slot}	Time slot length
T_{sched}	Hyper-period
SW_i	TSN switches

Table 1. *Cont.*

Parameters	Connotations
$f_k.offset$	Injection time slot of f_k
D_{proc}	Processing delay
D_{prop}	Propagation delay
BW	Link bandwidth
L_{Queue}	Queue length
h_k	Number of hops for flow f_k
$SQR(i,m,j)$	Slot queue resource of port m on node SW_i during $slot_j$
$O(f_k, SQR(i,m,j))$	Occupancy status of flow f_k at $SQR(i,m,j)$

3.2. CQF Scheduling Model

In the CQF model, the scheduling time is divided into equal time slots. The length of a slot is L_{slot}. The model is defined based on two principles:

1. The packet must be transmitted from the current node to the next node in the same slot.
2. Packets received by a node within $slot_k$ will be forwarded in $slot_{k+1}$.

Combining the above two principles and the goal of maximizing the number of schedulable flows, the following constraints can be derived. It is assumed that node SW_i transmits packets to its downflow neighbor node SW_{i+1}. In the worst case, if SW_j starts transmitting a packet to SW_{j+1} at the beginning of $slot_j$ and SW_{j+1} forwards it at the end of slot $slot_{j+1}$, i.e., transmission and reception occur at the farthest points of two adjacent slots, the delay between these two nodes is $2d$. In the best case, if SW_i transmits a packet to SW_{i+1} at the end of $slot_j$ and SW_{i+1} forwards it at the beginning of $slot_{j+1}$, i.e., transmission and reception occur at the adjacent ends of two slots, the delay between these two nodes is 0. In summary, assuming h is the number of hops, the maximum and minimum delays of a frame are as follows:

$$\begin{aligned} \text{maxDelay} &= (h+1)L_{slot} \\ \text{minDelay} &= (h-1)L_{slot} \end{aligned}. \quad (4)$$

Thus, it is evident that the end-to-end delay range of a frame is determined by the slot length and the number of hops, independent of the network topology. The node model that supports CQF is shown in Figure 1, where Q_6 and Q_7 are responsible for receiving and forwarding TT flows from each port. In a slot, one queue is in receive mode, while the other is in send mode, and the mode of each queue flips between adjacent slots to avoid additional computation and configuration overhead.

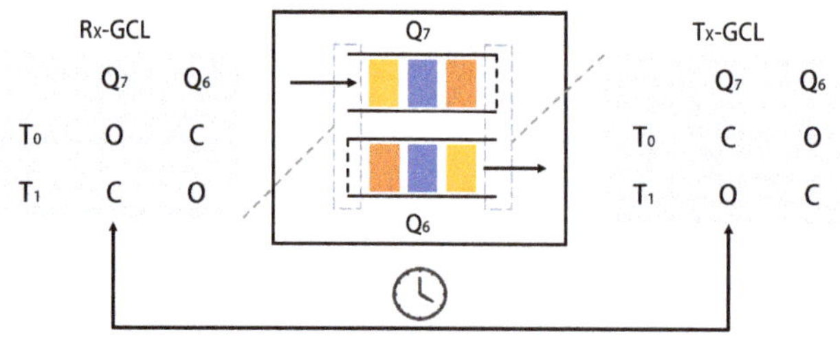

Figure 1. Framework of the CQF mechanism.

4. Problem Statement

In the CQF model, the transmission time planning of flow is the focus of this research. When scheduling resources are improperly allocated, TT flows tend to accumulate in queues at specific slots, which will cause TSN congestion. Therefore, a slot offset method that allocates initial sending time for each flow to avoid congestion is introduced. This method needs to meet the following constraints.

4.1. Slot Length Constraint

According to principle (2) mentioned in Section 3 , the transfer of all data flows in the queue between two adjacent nodes must be completed within a slot. Therefore, the lower bound of the slot length is constrained by the following:

$$\mathrm{Min}(L_{slot}) = \frac{L_{Queue}}{BW} + D_{proc} + D_{prop} + D_{sync} \tag{5}$$

where L_{Queue} denotes the queue length; that is, the maximum byte capacity of each queue, BW represents the bandwidth of the link, D_{proc} and D_{prop} represent the internal processing delay and propagation delay, respectively, and D_{sync} refers to the delay induced by timing synchronization errors. To ensure that the repetition count of all flows within the scheduling period is an integer, the greatest common divisor (GCD) of the periods of all flows is utilized as the scheduling period. The upper bound on the slot length is defined as follows:

$$\mathrm{Max}(L_{slot}) = GCD(f_k.period). \tag{6}$$

In the scheduling process, the slot duration is typically set as a constant value in accordance with the requirements of TSN.

In the CQF model, the arrival time of the flows depends solely on the number of hops and the slot offset. To ensure the QoS of TSN, flows must arrive before the deadline. The constraint on the offset is as follows:

$$f_k.offset + h_k + 1 \le \frac{f_k.deadline}{L_{slot}} \tag{7}$$

where h_k represents the number of hops for flow f_k. Additionally, in the model of data flow, every flow is associated with a deadline. Delays in initiating a flow may result in failure to reach its intended destination by the deadline. To prevent such occurrences, a constraint is applied to guarantee that all flows arrive punctually, adhering to their specified deadlines. The offset constraint stipulates that the starting time of a data flow must fall within its designated period. Failure to comply with this constraint can result in the accumulation of multiple frames of the same flow in the host, thereby consuming valuable and limited buffer space. The constrains can be represented as follows:

$$f_k.offset < \frac{f_k.period}{L_{slot}}. \tag{8}$$

In addition, a single flow will have multiple frames, which requires a significant amount of terminal storage capacity.

4.2. Queue Resource Constraints

Each port of a node has fixed Slot Queue Resources (SQR) for each slot, where the size of SQR equals the length of the port queue L_{Queue}. $SQR(i,m,j)$ denotes the slot queue resource of port m on node SW_i during $slot_j$. A binary decision variable $O(f_k, SQR(i,m,j))$ represents the occupancy status of flow f_k at $SQR(i,m,j)$, and based on this occupancy, queue resource constraints are proposed as follows:

$$\begin{aligned}
&\forall f_k \in F, k \in [0, n-1], i \in [0, x-1] \\
&\forall m \in [0, SW_i.P - 1], j \in [0, \frac{T_{sched}}{L_{slot}} - 1] \\
&O(f_k, SQR(i,m,j)) = \begin{cases} 0, SW_i^m \neq f_k.path[j] \\ 1, SW_i^m = f_k.path[j] \end{cases}
\end{aligned} \tag{9}$$

$$\sum_{k=0}^{n-1} O(f_k, SQR(i,m,j)) \times f_k.size \leq L_{Queue} \tag{10}$$

where n is the total number of flows, x is the number of nodes, and $SW_i.P$ is the total number of ports of node SW_i. When $O(f_k, SQR(i,m,j))$ is equal to 1, it indicates that flow f_k occupies the $SQR(i,m,j)$; otherwise, it is 0. Formula (9) represents the occupancy status of various flows within the system. Specifically, it indicates whether each flow is currently occupying buffer space or not. On the other hand, the queue resource constraint of a port is represented by Formula (10). This constraint stipulates that the total frame length of all frames currently stored in the Shared Queue Region (SQR) of the port cannot exceed the maximum queue length that the port can accommodate. In this article, the optimization objective is maximizing the number of successfully scheduled time-sensitive flows. This involves ensuring that each time-sensitive flow is allocated sufficient SQR resources to meet its transmission requirements within the given scheduling period.

5. Algorithm Design

As previously mentioned, the scheduling priority of flow is influenced by both the resource margin and requirements. The load balancing degree can be improved by transitioning the scheduling object from independent flow to a combination of flow, path, and offset . The multi-index priority scoring mechanism based on resource margin and requirements is introduced using a comprehensive example. The advantages of the novel scheduling object and scoring mechanism over the fixed order and fixed path methods are analyzed. The FPOJS algorithm based on the combinatorial scheduling object and multi-index priority scoring mechanism is proposed. Furthermore, the congestion-aware scheduling algorithm is proposed by calculating resource occupancy in real time during scheduling.

5.1. Scheduling Object and Priority Sorting Mechanism

The novel scheduling object, a combination of flow, path, and offset, and the multi-index priority sorting mechanism are the core of the FPOJS algorithm. In this section, the calculation method of the multi-index priority sorting mechanism is proposed, and the advantages of combinatorial scheduling objects are illustrated using an example.

The TSN topology and port information are shown in Figure 2. It is assumed that this topology is part of a TSN scenario. The attributes of flow are shown in Table 2. The resource requirements that affect the calculated load include packet size, hop count, and period. The total SQR occupied by a flow in a scheduling period can be calculated as follows:

$$O_{Total} = f_k.size \times f_k.hop \times \frac{T_{sched}}{f_k.period}. \tag{11}$$

The greater the resource requirements, the greater the impact on subsequent scheduling.

Assuming that all ports have an initial capacity of 100 and the remaining capacity of ports 2, 3, and 4 at each time slot remains at 100, the remaining capacity of the other ports is shown in Table 3. The numbers in the table indicate the remaining capacity of the ports for the corresponding time slots.

Given that the scheduling object is a combination of flow and offset, which occupies a specific amount of SRQs, congestion of any SRQ along the path can cause scheduling failures. Therefore, the resource margin is defined as the minimum remaining capacity of all SRQs occupied along the path. In Section 4, if flow f_k occupies $SQR(i,m,j)$, then $O(f_k, SQR(i,m,j))$ is equal to 1; otherwise, it is 0. Here, a set of flows $F_{SQR(i,m,j)} = \{f \mid O(f, SQR(i,m,j)) = 1\}$ represent all the flows that occupy the same SQR. The remaining capacity of the SQR is calculated as follows:

$$R_{SQR(i,m,j)} = L_{queue} - \sum_{f \in F_{SQR(i,m,j)}} f.size. \tag{12}$$

Then, the resource capacity is represented as $(MinR_{SQR(i,m,j)} - f_k.size)$.

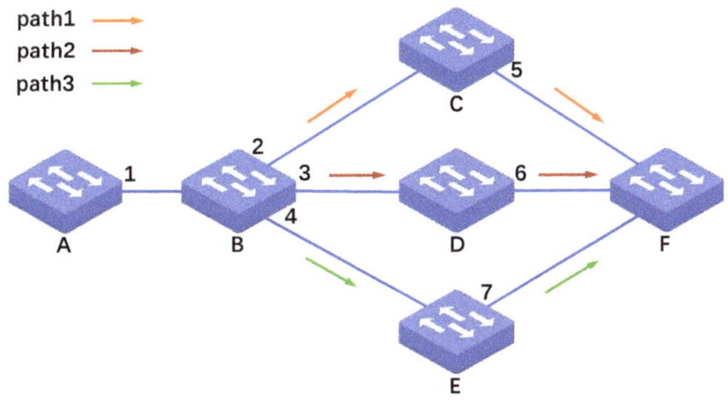

Figure 2. Port resources.

Table 2. Resource requirements.

Flow	Size	Route	Period	O_{total}
f_1	30	B→F	3	120
f_2	40	B→F	3	160
f_3	50	B→F	2	300
f_4	10	A→F	3	90

Table 3. Port capacity.

	Slot0	Slot1	Slot2	Slot3	Slot4	Slot5
Port1	15	15	15	15	15	15
Port5	80	60	50	80	60	50
Port6	40	30	70	40	30	70
Port7	50	90	40	50	90	40

In this example, when selecting path 1 for any flow in Table 1, it must pass through port 5. At this time, the resource margins of port 5 for selecting slot 0, slot 1, slot 2, slot 3, slot 4, and slot 5 are 80, 60, 50, 80, 60, and 50, respectively. As for f_4, since the remaining capacity of port 1 is 15 at all three time slots, which is less than the remaining capacity of any other port at any three time slots, the initial resource margin of f_4, regardless of the chosen path and time slot, is fixed at 15.

The scheduling success ratio is improved by reasonable planning of the link load; that is, each round of scheduling selects the scheduling object that has the lowest impact on the link load. Therefore, scheduling objects with high resource margins and low resource requirements should be prioritized. The formula for calculating the priority of scheduling objects through weight allocation is as follows:

$$Pr = \frac{\alpha \times (MinR_{SQR(i,m,j)} - f_k.size)}{\beta \times O_{Total}}. \tag{13}$$

The weight factors α and β can be adjusted according to the importance of the resource margin and requirements in actual applications. In this example, both α and β are equal to 1. The higher the value of Pr, the smaller the impact on the overall scheduling; hence, the scheduling object with the highest Pr is always chosen in scheduling.

In the first scheduling, the priority Pr of each combination is calculated, among which the combination $(f_4, path3, slot2)$ has a resource demand of 160 and a resource margin of 50; thus, $Pr = 50/160$. After calculation, this combination has the highest Pr among all combinations. Hence, in the first scheduling, the third path of f_2 is chosen and sent after a delay of one slot. In the second scheduling, since the remaining capacity of slot1 with port 7 has changed, the priority of other paths will be elevated.

It can be seen that although f_4 has the lowest resource occupancy, its lower resource margin implies a higher likelihood of causing port congestion; hence, a lower scheduling priority is given. For flow with multiple possible paths, the algorithm selects the path with the highest resource margin, which can enhance the flexibility of the scheduling. Based on the scheduling results of this example, when the proposed priority sorting mechanism is adopted, flows f_1, f_2, f_3, and f_4 can all be successfully scheduled. In contrast, when using the fixed-path scheduling algorithms such as MSS or ITP, no matter which of the three paths is selected, the third flow will fail to schedule; that is, only the first two flows can be scheduled successfully.

5.2. FPOJS Algorithm

The calculation method of scheduling object priority is given in section A, and the following Algorithm 1 utilizes this method for scheduling. Initially, Algorithm 1 calculates all the shortest paths for each flow based on the network topology, along with their possible offsets, to construct a combination of flow, path, and offset . Subsequently, it computes the priority for each scheduling object. Finally, it performs scheduling in descending order of these priorities, and the scheduling object in each iteration is a combination of flow, path, and offset.

Algorithm 1 Flow–Path–Offset Joint Scheduling (FPOJS) Algorithm

Input: Flow Set F, Topology G
Output: Set of successfully scheduled flows F_suc
1: Initialization $SQR[port, t]$, F_{suc}, P, $Pr[f, path, offset]$
2: **for** $i = 1$ to $F.num$ **do**
3:   **for** each flow $f_k \in F$ **do**
4:     $P = computeAllShortestPaths(f_k, G)$
5:     **for** each $p_i \in P$ **do**
6:       **for** each offset $o \in [0, f_k.period - 1]$ **do**
7:         **if** $checkSQR(f_k, p_i, o, SQR) ==$ true **then**
8:           $Pr[f_k, p_i, o] =$
9:           $computePriority(f_k, p_i, o, SQR)$
10:         **else**
11:           $Pr[f_k, p_i, o] = -1$
12:         **end if**
13:       **end for**
14:     **end for**
15:     $[f, p, o] = selectMaxPriority(Pr)$
16:     $f.offset = o, f.path = p$
17:     $updateSQR(f, p, o, SQR)$
18:     Add f to F_{suc}
19:     Invalidate priorities for f and update Pr for unscheduled flows
20:   **end for**
21: **end for**

Lines 1–4 calculate the shortest paths of all flows. Lines 5-6 construct the combinations of flow, path, and offset. In line 7, the function $checkSQR(f_k, p_i, o, SQR)$ checks if all ports along the flow path at the given time slot meet the queue resource constraints. If the constraints are satisfied, the scheduling object priority will be calculated; otherwise, the scheduling object is considered as a scheduling failure (lines 7–9). All scheduling objects are then sorted in order of priority from highest to lowest, and the scheduling object with the highest priority is selected as the scheduling target for this round (lines 14–15). Next, the time slots and ports occupied by this scheduling object are updated, and the scheduling object is considered to be successfully scheduled and deleted from the set of flows waiting for scheduling. The algorithm recalculates other scheduled object priorities and proceeds to the next round of scheduling until there is no flow to schedule (lines 16–18).The original scheduling procedure for this issue initially involved sorting, followed by searching for offsets while treating the routing planning problem as a distinct step. In contrast, the combined routing and scheduling methodology proposed in this paper amalgamates these three steps, utilizing a scoring mechanism based on balanced resource occupancy for selection. This approach achieves a certain reduction in computational complexity, with a time complexity of $O(n^2)$.

5.3. Congestion-Aware Scheduling Algorithm

During scheduling, TSN congestion can be discovered as early as possible by calculating the occupation of resources by flows in real time. Specifically, this involves monitoring the usage of both buffer space and transmission slots in real-time to detect potential bottlenecks. Finding congested nodes and adjusting them properly can improve the scheduling success ratio. Therefore, the congestion-aware scheduling algorithm, Algorithm 2, is proposed. The algorithm is divided into two parts. The first half of the algorithm filters out some ports that may cause congestion, and these ports are often key nodes in the network.This is achieved by utilizing historical data and predictive models to forecast which ports are likely to become congested based on the current flowset and network topology. The algorithm tries to avoid these ports by using other paths of the flows. The second part of the algorithm analyzes the utilization of slot resources of ports after the end of scheduling and selects the ports that are congested in each slot. This involves checking the Shared Queue Region (SQR) of each port for each scheduling slot to determine if the frame length exceeds the maximum transmission unit (MTU). By cross-comparing these ports with those identified as potentially congested, we can determine the transport hub ports that are actually congested.

Algorithm 2 Congestion-Aware Scheduling Optimization

Input: Current flowset F_c, Current topology G_c, Current SQR
Output: Set of rescheduled flows F_r
1: Initialize a list of potential congested ports (PCP)
2: Initialize a list of actual congested ports (ACP)
3: $PCP = ForecastPortUsage(F_c, G_c)$
4: **for** each $f_k \in F_c$ **do**
5:    **for** each $pc \in f_k.path$ **do**
6:       **if** $pc \in PCP$ **then**
7:          Prioritize paths not including ports pc
8:       **end if**
9:    **end for**
10: **end for**
11: **for** each port $\in G_c$ **do**
12:    **for** each slot $\in T_{sched}$ **do**
13:       **if** $SQR[port, slot] < MTU$ **then**
14:          add $port$ to ACP
15:       **end if**
16:    **end for**
17:    **if** $port \in PCP$ and $port \in ACP$ **then**
18:       $SQR[port, :] = 2L_{queue}$
19:    **end if**
20: **end for**

In this algorithm, the function $ForecastPortUsage(F_c, G_c)$ in line 3 is used to collect statistics on all ports. Lines 4–9 represent the pre-scheduling phase, which reduces the priority of flows that may pass through congested ports. Lines 11–16 are used to identify ports where congestion actually occurs. Lines 17–18 are part of the re-scheduling phase, where resources of the congested hub ports are temporarily expanded to twice their original capacity. The expansion method can be either dynamic, where resources are allocated based on real-time congestion levels, or static, where resources are pre-allocated based on predicted congestion patterns.

6. Evaluation

The simulation is conducted within a Python framework, with hardware configurations including an i7-11800H CPU running at 2.3 GHz and 16 GB of RAM. The Python version used in the simulation is 3.9,and the NumPy version is 1.22.0. To validate the performance of the FPOJS algorithm, it is compared against the naive algorithm, the Tabu-ITP algorithm [15], and the MSS algorithm [22]. The naive algorithm sorts flows based on packet size and uses a greedy strategy for offsets. The Tabu list size is set to 20, with a maximum of 300 iterations and 20 repetitions. For the MSS algorithm, the scoring criterion is the ratio of remaining capacity to packet size.

6.1. Simulation Setup

1. Network parameters: In the simulations, the scheduling of CQF is tested using bus, ring, and hybrid network topologies, covering the typical TSN application types. Figure 3 illustrates the bus, ring, and hybrid topology. In the experiments, different TSNs all contains 21 nodes, each with 8 ports. One to three ports of each node connect to the host, and the remaining ports are used for interconnection between nodes. The queue capacity of each port is 8k, the network bandwidth is 1 Gb/s, and the slot length is 125 µs.
2. Flow parameters: The flow period is set between 2 to 9 slots, which is consistent with the properties of flows observed in the real world, and a total of 500 flows are scheduled. Packet sizes are randomly selected within the range of 64 to 1500 bytes. The deadline of flows is set between 2 to 7 milliseconds. The simulation focuses exclusively on unicast flows, while multicast flows can be decomposed into multiple unicast flows.

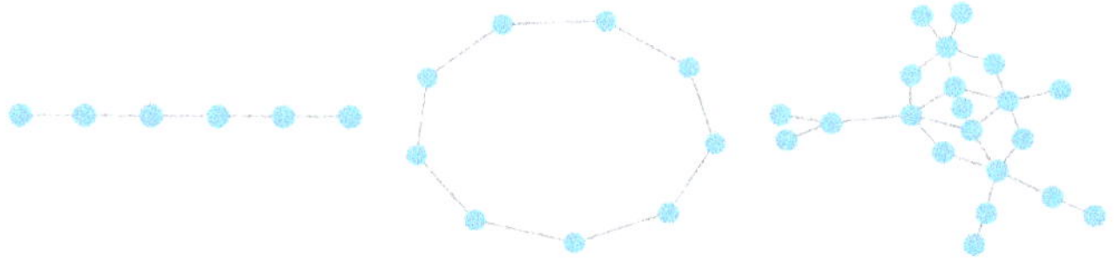

(a) (b) (c)

Figure 3. Topology structure: (**a**) bus, (**b**) ring, (**c**) hybrid.

6.2. Simulation Results

6.2.1. Algorithm Performance Under Different Topology Structures

To comprehensively evaluate the performance of our algorithm, it is compared with the naive algorithm, greedy algorithm, Tabu-ITP algorithm, and MSS algorithm across three metrics: scheduling success ratio, execution time, and resource utilization. Figures 4 and 5 show the scheduling success ratios of each algorithm under bus, ring, and hybrid network topologies without considering path constraints, under the conditions of 500 and 800 flows, respectively. The FPOJS algorithm achieves higher scheduling success ratios compared to other algorithms in different topologies and scheduling scales.

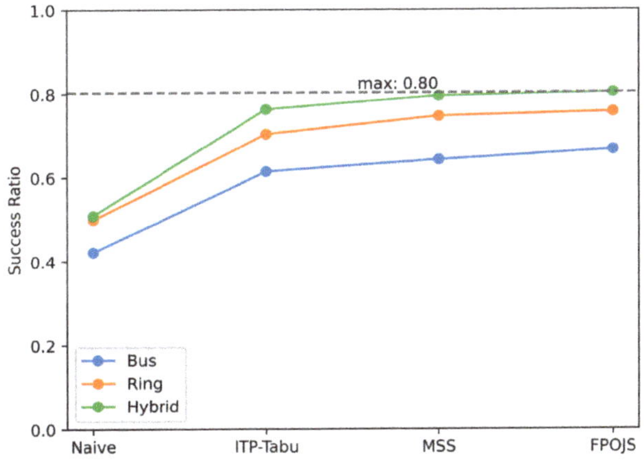

Figure 4. Scheduling success ratio in different topologies with 500 flows.

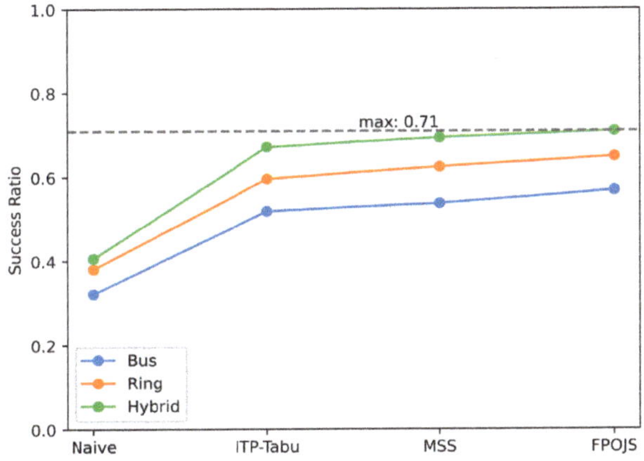

Figure 5. Scheduling success ratio in different topologies with 800 flows.

In the aforementioned experiments, path selection was not incorporated into the scheduling process. The purpose is to demonstrate the success ratio improvement created by the modifications to the priority calculation in the FPOJS algorithm. Across 100 experimental runs, the FPOJS algorithm achieved an average scheduling success ratio that was 1.4% higher than the MSS algorithm and 4% higher than the Tabu-ITP algorithm, with both computation speed and resource utilization surpassing MSS. In subsequent experiments, to demonstrate the validity of incorporating path selection, tests will be conducted in the more complex hybrid topology illustrated in Figure 3. In the hybrid topology, we first test the FPOJS algorithm without using the port resource optimization function. The results are shown in Figure 6. After adding path options, the number of available flows increased by 26%, indicating greater flexibility in scheduling. The scheduling results show that the scheduling success ratio of the FPOJS algorithm is 4% higher than that of MSS without changing the total amount of resources. In large-scale hybrid network scenarios, the FPOJS algorithm has a higher scheduling success ratio. Figure 7 presents a comparison of the scheduling success ratios under varying numbers of nodes. The aforementioned experiments prove that the FPOJS algorithm can be effectively applied to both simple and complex scenarios. Notably, the improvement in scheduling success rate brought about by the FPOJS algorithm is more significant in complex topologies than in simple ones.The overflow of queue resources caused by traffic accumulation is one of the important reasons for the scheduling success rate. Improving the load balancing level can alleviate this phenomenon. Resource utilization can reflect the load balancing level to a certain extent and is positively correlated with the scheduling success rate on the whole. As shown in Figure 8, based on the resource utilization rate of each algorithm with different numbers of nodes in the complex topology, the FPOJS algorithm has better load balancing levels in the complex topology environment. However, due to the inclusion of path selection and an additional step for port resource optimization, it does not exhibit a superior performance in overall computational speed, with an average computation duration of approximately 20% longer than that of the MSS algorithm. Although this has increased the execution time to a certain extent, it is accompanied by significant improvements in scheduling success rate and resource utilization. The comparison of execution time is presented in Figure 9.

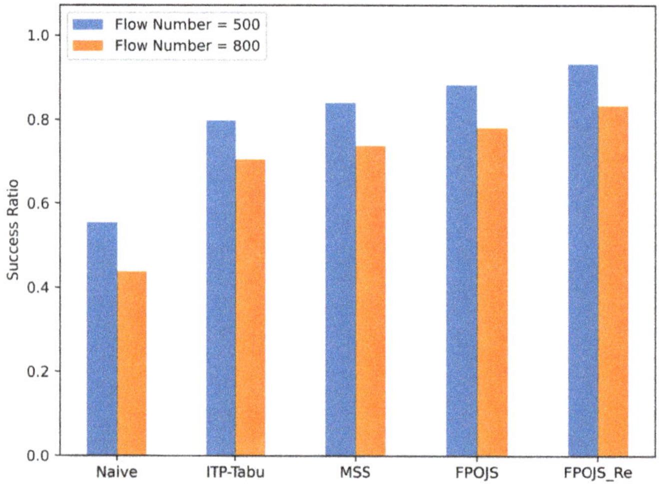

Figure 6. Scheduling success ratios of various algorithms under different loads.

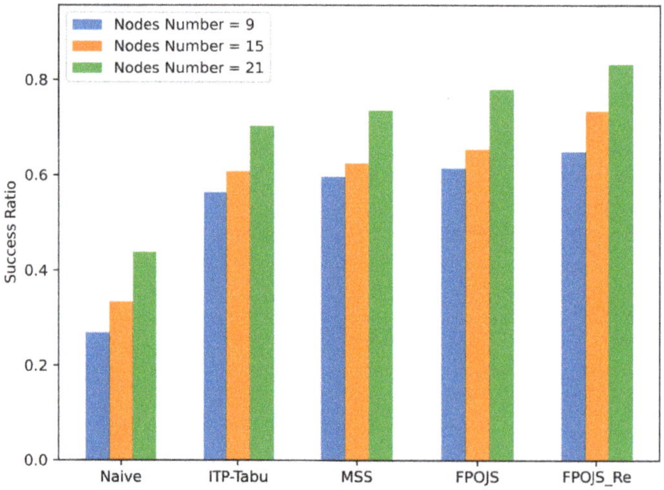

Figure 7. Scheduling success ratios of various algorithms under different node numbers.

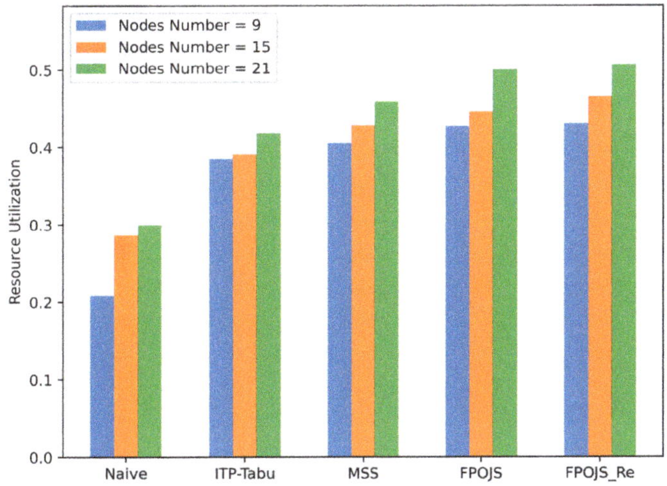

Figure 8. Resource utilization of various algorithms.

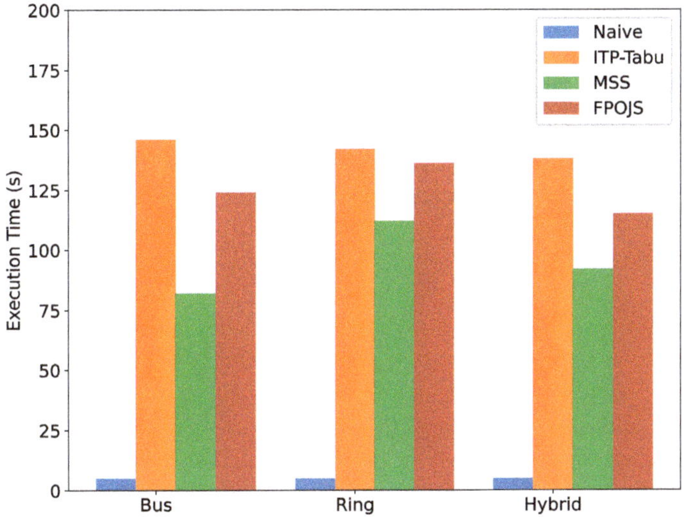

Figure 9. Execution time comparisons of algorithms in different topologies (500 flows).

6.2.2. The Impact of Slot Length and Queue Length on Scheduling

The slot length is related to several factors, including flow period, deadline, link speed, node cache queue length, and network scale. An increase in the node cache queue length can increase the lower bound of the slot length to some extent. Bello et al. [6] and Steiner et al. [7] indicate that an increase in slot length allows nodes to accommodate more packets, thereby increasing the number of flows that can be scheduled. However, the constraint that packets cached from the previous time slot must be entirely transmitted in the next time slot increases the single-hop delay. When single-hop delays accumulate on the path, the total end-to-end delay of the flow increases, resulting in a flow that cannot be scheduled. Additionally, due to the limitations of node hardware resources, the increase in time slot length requires higher memory requirements on the nodes, which in turn increases the complexity and cost of node implementation. More importantly, the precision of gated control is inversely proportional to the slot length. In a certain traffic period, the range of injection offsets that can be selected by the source system increases with the decrease in the slot length, which not only improves the control accuracy but also increases the search range. The size of the slot length is limited by the bandwidth of the link, and if the time reserved is much longer than the time required to send the queue cache, no data will be transferred to the remaining slots. Figure 10 compares the scheduling success rates among various algorithms for queue lengths of 6000, 8000, 12,000, and 15,000. The comparison reveals that as the queue length increases, more flows can be accommodated in a single scheduling instance, thereby reducing the probability of congestion. This leads to an increase in the number of flows that can be successfully scheduled. Specifically, when the queue length reaches 15,000, the scheduling success ratio of Algorithm FPOJS_RE approaches 100%. This observation underscores the importance of queue length in optimizing scheduling performance and highlights the efficacy of Algorithm FPOJS_RE in managing large-scale flow scheduling with minimal congestion.

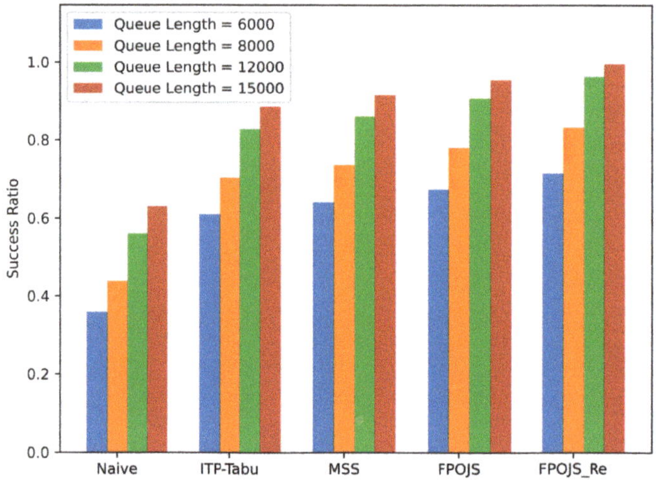

Figure 10. Scheduling success ratios of various algorithms under different queue lengths.

6.2.3. Impact Analysis of Port Resource Expansion on Scheduling Success Ratio

The congestion-aware scheduling algorithm, also known as FPOJS_Re, is an enhanced version of the FPOJS algorithm, which adopts the method of dynamically configuring port resources. In this experiment, the total number of ports is related to the number of access hosts and the topology of TSNs. During scheduling, the algorithm can calculate the congestion degree of the port and sort it. According to the pre-configuration, some ports with high congestion will be expanded by a certain amount. Figure 11 shows the relationship between the number of expanded ports and the scheduling success ratio under the configuration of doubling the capacity of some congested ports. It shows that when the number of expanded ports is 5, the scheduling success ratio increases by approximately 4%; with 10 expanded ports, the scheduling success ratio improves by approximately 8%; and when the number of expanded ports exceeds 20, the increment of the scheduling success ratio becomes more gradual, peaking at around 96%. The experimental results show that selecting the number of expanded ports to be between 5 and 15 can achieve a better balance between scheduling success ratio and resource utilization. Searching for congested ports can lead to an increase in computation time, but in a fixed offline scheduling scenario, the first calculated congested port remains applicable in subsequent scheduling and does not increase the subsequent scheduling time.

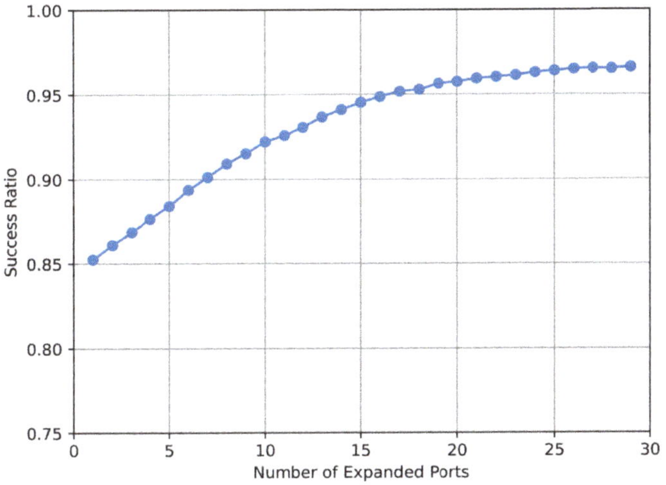

Figure 11. Relationship between the number of expanded ports and the scheduling success ratio.

7. Conclusions and Future Work

In this paper, we presented a novel scheduling object, a combination of flow, path, and offset , and analyzed its importance using an example. We proposed two algorithms to tackle the start time planning issue with the CQF mechanism, namely the FPOJS algorithm and the congestion-aware scheduling algorithm. The FPOJS algorithm performed scheduling in descending order of a well-designed priority, which considered the resource margin and resource requirements of the ports. The congestion-aware scheduling algorithm enhanced the FPOJS algorithm by dynamically configuring port resources. Finally, the experimental results showed that the FPOJS algorithm achieved a 39% improvement in scheduling success ratio over the naive algorithm, a 13% improvement over the Tabu-ITP algorithm, and a 10% improvement over the MSS algorithm. The results also showed that the scheduling success ratio was higher in large-scale heterogeneous network topology. The congestion-aware scheduling algorithm can filter congested resources, and by dynamically expanding only 10% to 20% of the total number of ports in real-time, it can increase the scheduling success ratio by 5% to 10%. It showed great practicability in CQF scheduling applications, which can dynamically allocate port resources.

This study focuses on improving the success ratio in the context of offline scheduling. The online scheduling of CQF mechanisms has higher requirements for computing speed. In future work, we will explore scheduling algorithms that reduce the scheduling computation time.

Author Contributions: Data curation, D.L.; formal analysis, D.L. and Z.Z.; methodology, Z.Z.; writing—original draft, D.L. and Z.Z.; Validation, Z.L.; Formal analysis, Y.W.; Investigation, Z.Z.; Resources, Y.S.; Data curation, J.G.; writing—review and editing, Y.S.; Project administration, Y.S.; Funding acquisition, Y.S. All authors have read and agreed to the published version of the manuscript.

Funding: This research received no external funding.

Data Availability Statement: The data are not publicly available, as this is ongoing research.

Conflicts of Interest: The authors declare no conflicts of interest.

References

1. Deng, L.; Xie, G.; Liu, H.; Han, Y.; Li, R.; Li, K. A Survey of Real-Time Ethernet Modeling and Design Methodologies: From AVB to TSN. *ACM Comput. Surv.* **2023**, *55*, 1–36. [CrossRef]
2. Pei, J.; Hu, Y.; Tian, L.; Li, M.; Li, Z. A Hybrid Traffic Scheduling Strategy for Time-Sensitive Networking. *Electronics* **2022**, *11*, 3762. [CrossRef]
3. Farkas, J.; Bello, L.L.; Gunther, C. Time-Sensitive Networking Standards. *IEEE Commun. Stand. Mag.* **2018**, *2*, 20–21. [CrossRef]
4. Craciunas, S.S.; Oliver, R.S.; Chmelík, M.; Steiner, W. Scheduling Real-Time Communication in IEEE 802.1Qbv Time Sensitive Networks. In Proceedings of the 24th International Conference on Real-Time Networks and Systems, Brest France, 19–21 October 2016; ACM: New York, NY, USA , 2016; pp. 183–192.
5. Vlk, M.; Hanzalek, Z.; Brejchova, K.; Tang, S.; Bhattacharjee, S.; Fu, S. Enhancing Schedulability and Throughput of Time-Triggered Traffic in IEEE 802.1Qbv Time-Sensitive Networks. *IEEE Trans. Commun.* **2020**, *68*, 7023–7038. [CrossRef]
6. Bello, L.L.; Steiner, W. A Perspective on IEEE Time-Sensitive Networking for Industrial Communication and Automation Systems. *Proc. IEEE* **2019**, *107*, 1094–1120. [CrossRef]
7. Steiner, W.; Craciunas, S.S.; Oliver, R.S. Traffic Planning for Time-Sensitive Communication. *IEEE Commun. Stand. Mag.* **2018**, *2*, 42–47. [CrossRef]
8. Quan, W.; Yan, J.; Jiang, X.; Sun, Z. On-line Traffic Scheduling optimization in IEEE 802.1Qch based Time-Sensitive Networks. In Proceedings of the 2020 IEEE 22nd International Conference on High Performance Computing and Communications; IEEE 18th International Conference on Smart City; IEEE 6th International Conference on Data Science and Systems (HPCC/SmartCity/DSS), Yanuca Island, Cuvu, Fiji, 14–16 December 2020; IEEE: New York, NY, USA, 2020; pp. 369–376.
9. Huang, Y.; Wang, S.; Wu, B.; Huang, T.; Liu, Y. TACQ: Enabling Zero-jitter for Cyclic-Queuing and Forwarding in Time-Sensitive Networks. In Proceedings of the IEEE International Conference on Communications, Montreal, QC, Canada, 14–23 June 2021 ; pp. 1–6.
10. Steiner, W. An Evaluation of SMT-Based Schedule Synthesis for Time-Triggered Multi-hop Networks. In Proceedings of the 2010 31st IEEE Real-Time Systems Symposium, San Diego, CA, USA, 30 November–3 December 2010; IEEE: New York, NY, USA, 2010; pp. 375–384.
11. Dürr, F.; Nayak, N.G. No-wait Packet Scheduling for IEEE Time-sensitive Networks (TSN). In Proceedings of the 24th International Conference on Real-Time Networks and Systems, Brest, France, 19–21 October 2016; ACM: New York, NY, USA, 2016; pp. 203–212.
12. Oliver, R.S.; Craciunas, S.S.; Steiner, W. IEEE 802.1Qbv Gate Control List Synthesis Using Array Theory Encoding. In Proceedings of the 2018 IEEE Real-Time and Embedded Technology and Applications Symposium (RTAS), Porto, Portugal, 11–13 April 2018; IEEE: New York, NY, USA, 2018; pp. 13–24.
13. Nayak, N.G.; Dürr, F.; Rothermel, K. Time-sensitive Software-defined Network (TSSDN) for Real-time Applications. In Proceedings of the 24th International Conference on Real-Time Networks and Systems, Brest, France, 19–21 October 2016; ACM: New York, NY, USA, 2016; pp. 193–202.
14. Alnajim, A.; Salehi, S.; Shen, C.-C. Incremental Path-Selection and Scheduling for Time-Sensitive Networks. In Proceedings of the 2019 IEEE Global Communications Conference (GLOBECOM), Waikoloa, HI, USA, 9–13 December 2019; IEEE: New York, NY, USA, 2019; pp. 1–6.
15. Yan, J.; Quan, W.; Jiang, X.; Sun, Z. Injection Time Planning: Making CQF Practical in Time-Sensitive Networking. In Proceedings of the IEEE INFOCOM 2020—IEEE Conference on Computer Communications, Toronto, ON, Canada, 6–9 July 2020; IEEE: New York, NY, USA, 2020; pp. 616–625.
16. Cheng, Z.; Yang, D.; Zhang, W.; Ren, J.; Wang, H.; Zhang, H. DeepCQF: Making CQF Scheduling More Intelligent and Practicable. In Proceedings of the IEEE International Conference on Communications, Seoul, Republic of Korea, 16–20 May 2022; IEEE: New York, NY, USA, 2022; pp. 1–6.
17. Nie, H.; Li, S.; Liu, Y. Optimized scheduling mechanism based on IEEE 802.1Qch standard in time-sensitive networking. *J. Commun.* **2022**, *43*, 12–26.
18. Zhang, Y.; Xu, Q.; Xu, L.; Chen, C.; Guan, X. Efficient Flow Scheduling for Industrial Time-Sensitive Networking: A Divisibility Theory-Based Method. *IEEE Trans. Ind. Inf.* **2022**, *18*, 9312–9323. [CrossRef]
19. Chang, S.-H.; Chen, H.; Cheng, B.-C. Time-predictable routing algorithm for Time-Sensitive Networking: Schedulable guarantee of Time-Triggered streams. Comput. Commun. **2021**, *172*, 183–195. [CrossRef]
20. Feng, Z.; Gu, Z.; Yu, H.; Deng, Q.; Niu, L. Online Rerouting and Rescheduling of Time-Triggered Flows for Fault Tolerance in Time-Sensitive Networking. *IEEE Trans. Comput. Aided Des. Integr. Circuits Syst.* **2022**, *41*, 4253–4264. [CrossRef]
21. Nie, H.; Li, S.; Liu, Y. An Enhanced Routing and Scheduling Mechanism for Time-Triggered Traffic with Large Period Differences in Time-Sensitive Networking. *Appl. Sci.* **2022**, *12*, 4448. [CrossRef]

22. Guo, M.; Gu, C.; He, S.; Shi, Z.; Chen, J. MSS: Exploiting Mapping Score for CQF Start Time Planning in Time-Sensitive Networking. *IEEE Trans. Ind. Inf.* **2023**, *19*, 2140–2150. [CrossRef]
23. Wang, X.; Yao, H.; Mai, T.; Xiong, Z.; Wang, F.; Liu, Y. Joint Routing and Scheduling with Cyclic Queuing and Forwarding for Time-Sensitive Networks. *IEEE Trans. Veh. Technol.* **2023**, *72*, 3793–3804. [CrossRef]

mathematics

MDPI

Article

Improved Real-Time Detection Transformer-Based Rail Fastener Defect Detection Algorithm

Wei Song, Bin Liao, Keqing Ning * and Xiaoyu Yan

School of Information, North China University of Technology, Beijing 100144, China; songwei@ncut.edu.cn (W.S.); 13558214391@163.com (B.L.); 18342990783@163.com (X.Y.)
* Correspondence: ningkq@ncut.edu.cn

Abstract: To address the issues of the Real-Time DEtection TRansformer (RT-DETR) object detection model, including poor defect feature extraction in the task of rail fastener defect detection, inefficient use of computational resources, and suboptimal channel attention in the self-attention mechanism, the following improvements were made. Firstly, a Super-Resolution Convolutional Module (SRConv) was designed as a separate component and integrated into the Backbone network, which enhances the image details and clarity while preserving the original image structure and semantic content. This integration improves the model's ability to extract defect features. Secondly, a channel attention mechanism was integrated into the self-attention module of RT-DETR to enhance the focus on feature map channels, addressing the problem of sparse attention maps caused by the lack of channel attention while saving computational resources. Finally, the experimental results show that compared to the original model, the improved RT-DETR-based rail fastener defect detection algorithm, with an additional 0.4 MB of parameters, achieved a higher accuracy, with a 2.8 percentage point increase in the Mean Average Precision (mAP) across IoU thresholds from 0.5 to 0.9 and a 1.7 percentage point increase in the Average Recall (AR) across the same thresholds.

Keywords: transformer; super-resolution; fastener; track; defect detection

MSC: 68U10

1. Introduction

As of early 2023, the total mileage of China's railroads in operation has exceeded 155,000 km, and according to China's medium- and long-term railroad development plan, the total mileage of China's railroads is expected to reach 175,000 km by 2025 and 200,000 km by 2030 [1]. With the continuous improvement in China's railroad transportation network, the safety and reliability requirements of railroad operations have become higher. Track fasteners are an essential part of fixed rails. Rails are primarily composed of three parts: the rails themselves, sleepers, and fasteners. Among these, the rail fasteners are crucial components that connect the rails and sleepers, enabling the stable operation of the railway lines. However, due to factors such as the movement of trains or other external influences, issues like the displacement, loss, and incorrect installation of rail fasteners may arise, affecting the safe operation of trains. Therefore, detecting defects in rail fasteners is crucial for ensuring the safe and smooth operation of trains.

Existing deep learning-based defect detection algorithms for rail fasteners primarily use the You Only Look Once (YOLO) series [2–4] algorithms. The advantages of the YOLO series algorithms include their fast detection rates, small model sizes, and high accuracy. However, with the rise of Transformer-based object detection methods, they can directly predict the final detection results, simplifying the complex steps in traditional object detection methods, such as post-processing steps like Non-Maximum Suppression (NMS). This simplified architecture not only reduces the need for heuristic methods but also improves the overall detection efficiency. Its powerful self-attention mechanism can better capture long-range dependencies in images, leading to improved performance in object detection tasks. Typical Transformer-based object detection models include end-to-end object detection with Transformers (DETR) [5], Deformable Transformers for end-to-end object detection (Deformable DETR) [6], and DETR with improved denoising anchor boxes for end-to-end object detection (DINO) [7]. Although its performance is better than that of the traditional YOLO series algorithms, it is far more inferior in real-time detection. In 2023, Wenyu Lv and colleagues proposed the DETRs Beat YOLOs on Real-time Object Detection (RT-DETR) [8] network, which optimizes the detection rate, accuracy, and model parameter size, and it is better than the YOLO series of algorithms in real-time detection. Consequently, we propose using the powerful detection capabilities of the RT-DETR network for fastener defect detection tasks and improving it to better suit these tasks.

Through experimental validation, we have found that the original network performs poorly in extracting the defect features of rail fasteners. Additionally, its self-attention mechanism, due to the use of Deformable Attention, exhibits insufficient spatial channel focus on feature maps. Deformable Attention's need to flexibly select regions of interest in the feature maps may lead to the underutilization of padding areas and possible sparsity in attention maps, affecting the overall performance of the model. Therefore, the main focus of this paper is to improve the original network model to better adapt to rail fastener defect detection tasks. The primary contributions of this paper are as follows: (1) The design of a Super-Resolution Convolution Module (SRConv) as a separate component and integrating it into the Backbone network. This module enhances image details and clarity while preserving the original image structure and semantic content, thereby improving defect feature extraction capabilities. (2) The incorporation of channel attention (CA) into the self-attention mechanism of RT-DETR to enhance the model's spatial focus on feature maps, to address the issue of attention map sparsity, and to save computational resources.

2. Related Work

Traditional image processing detection methods require the manual design and extraction of fastener features, followed by the use of a trained classifier for defect identification and classification [9]. This is largely constrained by subjective feature design and extraction, with limited capabilities for feature extraction from images. As a result, the detection accuracy and speed are relatively low. Additionally, in practical detection scenarios, it is easily affected by factors such as lighting conditions, image noise, and environmental tracking, requiring a better generalization ability and robustness. Ma et al. [10] used a median filter to extract fastener edge features, improved the Canny edge detection method, and matched the feature templates of defective fasteners for real-time detection. Gibert et al. [11,12] proposed a fastener detection algorithm based on a multi-task learning framework, which combines multiple detectors. It uses the Histogram of Oriented Gradients (HOG) from images to extract fastener features and uses an SVM classifier to classify and identify damaged or missing fasteners. Ou et al. [13] developed a Bayesian hierarchical model for fastener features and structural labels and used a Support Vector Machine (SVM) classifier to classify defective fasteners. To address the lack of defective fastener samples, Dai et al. [14] proposed a method for generating images of broken fasteners. After obtaining a large number of virtual samples of broken fasteners, they used HOG feature extraction to compute gradient features from images and applied a principal component analysis for dimensionality reduction. Finally, a trained SVM classifier was used to detect defective fasteners. Although the aforementioned traditional image processing detection methods have improved the detection accuracy to some extent, their complex image processing and feature extraction processes still fail to improve the detection efficiency of fasteners.

Deep learning-based detection methods primarily use Convolutional Neural Networks (CNNs) to learn the feature information of detection targets from large amounts of image data, enabling fast and accurate target identification. Compared to traditional image processing methods, they avoid the drawbacks of manually designing feature information, thus offering good generalization ability and robustness. Deep learning-based object detection algorithms are mainly categorized into two types: two-stage and one-stage. Two-stage algorithms include Region-CNN (R-CNN) [15], Fast-R-CNN [15], Faster R-CNN: Real-time object detection with region proposal networks (Faster-R-CNN) [16] and Mask r-cnn [17] require two steps for target identification based on candidate frames. One study [18] used Faster-R-CNN to detect rail fasteners. Although the detection accuracy improved, the model has a large number of parameters, and the detection speed could be more satisfactory. One-stage algorithms, such as SSD [19] and the YOLO series [2–4], can directly predict the location and category of objects without generating candidate regions. Compared to other object detection algorithms, the YOLO series proposed by Redmon et al. has significant advantages in terms of detection speed and accuracy, making it widely applied in rail fastener defect detection [20–22]. Guo et al. [23] proposed a real-time fastener tracking detection model based on an improved Yolov4: It combines the optimal speed and accuracy of object detection (YOLOv4) [2], with experimental results showing a 94.4% mAP for fastener detection. Subsequently, Jocher et al. introduced YOLOv5 [24], an improvement over YOLOv4 [23], which incorporated deep separable convolutions [25] and fine-grained feature pyramid networks [26], among other deep learning techniques, to further enhance the detection accuracy and speed. While these methods accurately detect fastener defects, they may be more effective in detecting shifted, missing, and broken fasteners. The poor generalization and robustness of the model make it difficult to apply to engineering practice [27]. The aforementioned traditional methods and deep learning-based methods have significantly improved defect detection in rail fasteners. But they need to generate a large number of candidate boxes and then use the Non-Maximum Suppression (NMS) algorithm to filter out suitable candidates, which consumes a significant amount of computational resources, and neither single-stage nor two-stage object detection algorithms are as straightforward and efficient as Transformer-based methods. Its powerful self-attention mechanism can more accurately identify the categories of fastener defects in complex scenes. However, the powerful self-attention mechanism of Transformer requires a lot of computational cost, which leads to the real-time detection ability of Transformer-based target detection algorithms being inferior to other deep learning algorithms. Wenyu Lv et al. proposed the RT-DETR network, which is the first Transformer-based target detection network to surpass the YOLO series in real-time detection performance [8]. This provides the possibility to apply the Transformer-based target valence detection network in the field of fastener defect detection. This study is mainly optimized through the feature extraction ability and computational efficiency of the RT-DETR network.

3. Improved RT-DETR-Based Algorithm for Rail Fastener Defect Detection

Transformer-based object detection network models generally consist of three main components: the Backbone, Encoder, and Decoder. In the Backbone section, the input image is first processed by a CNN network (e.g., ResNet) for feature extraction. To enable the Transformer to handle 2D image data, the feature maps are flattened and combined with positional encoding. Positional encoding preserves the spatial information, which allows the Transformer to recognize the positional relationships. The feature maps and positional encodings are then input into the Transformer's Encoder, with the Encoder's output serving as the input for the Decoder. The Decoder also receives a set of learnable object query vectors, which are used to generate the final detection results. The output of the Decoder is used to produce the final bounding boxes and class predictions. The output object vectors are transformed into specific detection results, including the bounding box regression and classification results, through a linear layer.

The implementation process of the original network model is generally similar to that of other Transformer-based object detection models, but the encoding part is significantly different. As shown in the output results of the Backbone network in Figure 1, we obtain three scales of feature maps (S3, S4, and S5) after processing. Among these, S3 contains rich high-level feature information. The original network fuses the feature maps S4 and

S5 with S3 using a feature pyramid approach, so that S3 contains both high-level and low-level feature information, requiring only S3 to be encoded, which greatly enhances the model's efficiency.

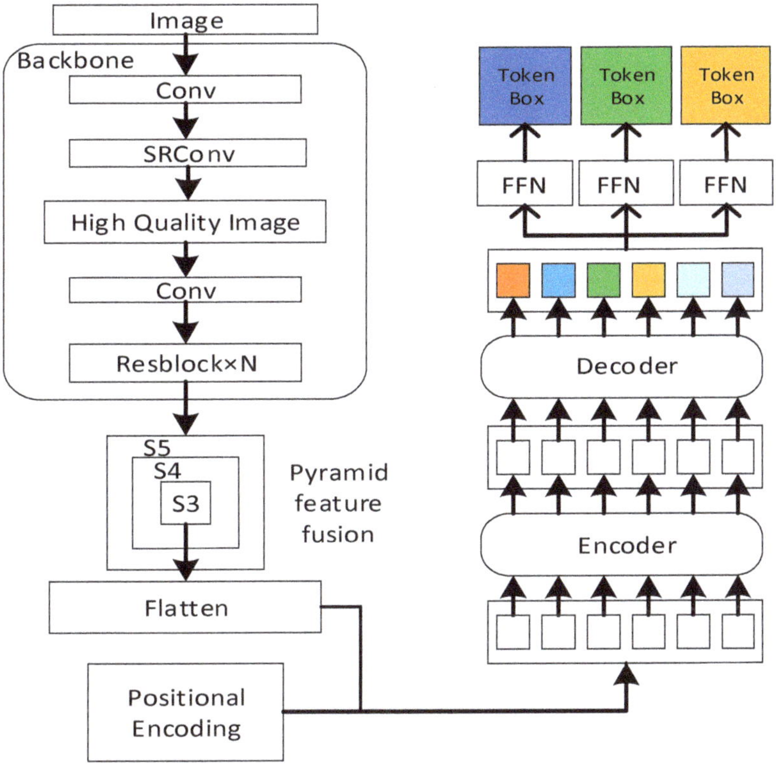

Figure 1. Algorithm flow chart.

The improved model builds on this foundation by incorporating an SRConv convolution module into the Backbone network to enhance the quality of the input images. In the Encoder–Decoder section, the original Deformable Attention is integrated with the channel attention mechanism (as shown in Figure 2). The overall algorithm process is illustrated in Figure 1, where the input images undergo quality enhancement to improve their quality while preserving the original information. The residual blocks in the Backbone network perform deep feature extraction, resulting in three feature maps (S3, S4, and S5) of different scales. These feature maps are then fused using a pyramid feature fusion approach, followed by flattening the fused feature map and adding positional encoding as the input to the Encoder. The Encoder utilizes powerful self-attention computations to obtain contextual information, and then the Decoder decodes this information and predicts the object locations, categories, and other details using a simple convolutional network (FFN). The overall structure of the improved network model is shown in Figure 3.

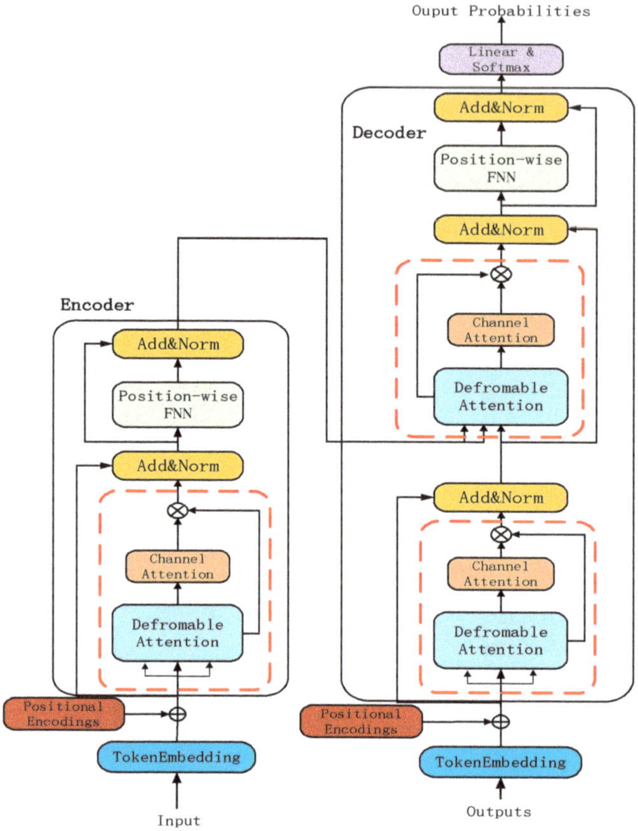

Figure 2. The Encoder–Decoder structure of the improved RT-DETR.

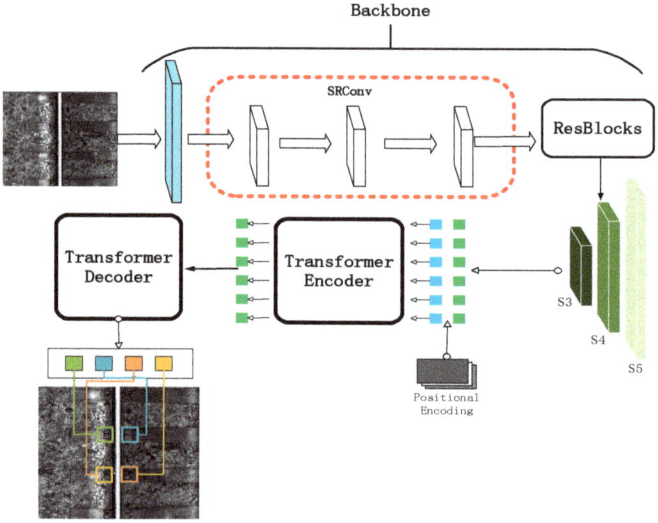

Figure 3. The improved RT-DETR network model (S3, S4, and S5 represent feature maps extracted at different scales).

3.1. Backbone Network Integrated with Super-Resolution Convolution Module

The original Backbone network often leads to the loss of important details and information during feature extraction. To address this issue, this paper is inspired by super-resolution techniques and designs a Super-Resolution Convolution (SRConv) [28] module. This module enhances the resolution of input images, improving the image quality so that the defect details in the railway fastener images become clearer and more prominent, thereby enhancing the network's ability to extract defect features.

For object detection tasks, the Backbone network typically adopts the ResNet 50 (ResNet-50) [29] architecture, which stacks multiple residual blocks to perform deep feature extraction. As the image propagates through the network, each residual block progressively extracts more abstract and higher-level features. The deeper residual blocks can capture more complex information about the image, such as textures, shapes, and object parts. The goal of super-resolution processing is to enhance the image quality by recovering lost details and information. This process is typically achieved by using deep learning models to predict a higher-resolution image from a low-resolution input. Although super-resolution techniques can significantly improve the visual quality, they are essentially a reconstruction process aimed at restoring as much of the original image's detail and structure as possible. After super-resolution processing, the image's detail and clarity are improved while preserving its original structure and semantic content. Using these enhanced images for feature extraction improves the model's ability to capture detailed defect features. In this paper, an SRConv module (as shown in Figure 4) is integrated into the Backbone network to apply super-resolution processing to the input images before they are passed into the subsequent residual blocks. This approach enhances the extraction of defect-related features. The SRConv module primarily consists of three convolutional layers:

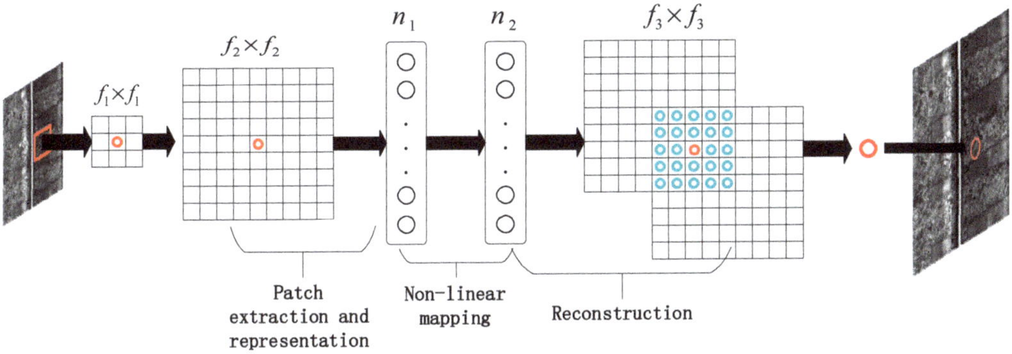

Figure 4. Schematic diagram of SRConv.

The first convolutional layer is used to extract features from the upsampled low-resolution image. It is responsible for extracting features from low-resolution images, typically using smaller convolution kernels (e.g., 9 × 9) to capture information such as edges and textures. By increasing the number of channels, the model can learn more feature representations. This process can be expressed as

$$F_1(Y) = \max(0, W_1 \times Y + B_1) \tag{1}$$

W_1 and B_1 represent the filters and biases, respectively, with × denoting the convolution operation. Here, W_1 corresponds to n_1 convolution kernels of size $c \times f_1 \times f_1$, where c is the number of channels in the input image and f_1 is the spatial scale of the kernels. Conceptually, n_1 convolutions are applied to the image, each with a kernel size of

$c \times f_1 \times f_1$. The output consists of n1 feature maps. B_1 is an n-dimensional vector, with each element being associated with the filters and RELU serving as the activation function.

The second convolutional layer is used to perform nonlinear mapping of the extracted feature maps, transforming low-level features into high-dimensional ones. It performs nonlinear mapping of the features extracted from the first layer, typically using smaller convolution kernels (e.g., 5 × 5). This step helps the model better understand complex image patterns and enhances the reconstruction quality. This process can be represented as

$$F_2(Y) = \max(0, W_2 \times F_1(Y) + B_2) \tag{2}$$

W_2 contains n filters, each of size $n_1 \times f_2 \times f_2$, and B_2 is an n_2-dimensional vector. Each output n_2-dimensional vector can conceptually be seen as being applied to reconstruct high-resolution image patches.

The third convolutional layer is used to convert the processed features back into a high-resolution image. It employs smaller convolution kernels (e.g., 5 × 5) and outputs the channels of the target image. The key to this layer is to integrate all extracted features to generate the final high-quality image. This process can be represented as

$$F_3(Y) = W_3 \times F_2(Y) + B_3 \tag{3}$$

W_3 corresponds to c filters, each of size $n_2 \times f_3 \times f_3$, and B_3 is a c-dimensional vector. F_3 represents the final generated high-resolution image.

Images processed by the SRConv module exhibit the following features:

(1) More details and higher clarity: super-resolution processing typically provides clearer and sharper edges, making the image appear more detailed and realistic.
(2) Richer textures: by restoring more detail information, super-resolution processing can reveal richer texture effects, making surface materials appear more realistic.
(3) Preservation of the original image's structure and semantic content: Super-resolution technology generally aims to retain the original image's structure and semantic content, rather than making substantial changes or modifications to the image. Overall, super-resolution processing can be seen as an enhancement of the image quality rather than a modification of the image content itself.

Therefore, while the content of the image remains essentially unchanged after super-resolution, the visual clarity and realism are improved. The size of the original image, the location of the defects, and the bounding boxes for the defects are not altered; only the details of the defects are made more apparent, with no need for the additional processing of the high-quality output image. The image processed by SRConv is shown in Figure 5, where it is evident that the image quality of the processed image in Figure 5b has significantly improved compared to that in Figure 5a.

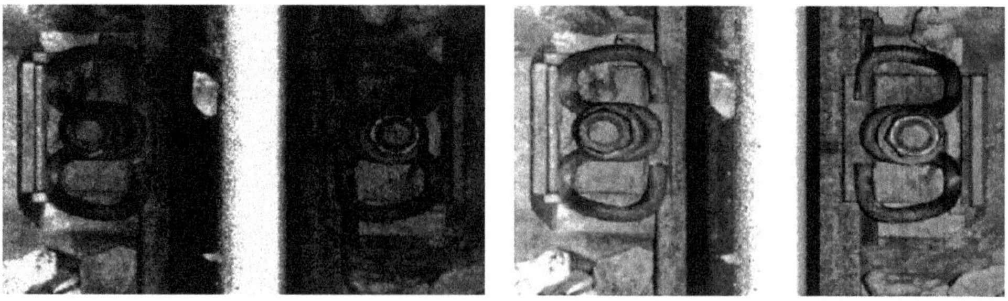

(a) (b)

Figure 5. (**a**) Original image; (**b**) image processed by the SRConv module.

Applying the SRConv module in the RT-DETR network model yields better results. This is because, unlike other Transformer-based object detection models, RT-DETR's Encoder section encodes only feature maps rich in high-level semantic information. It uses the PAN pyramid to facilitate feature interaction between the encoded high-level semantic feature maps and low-level semantic feature maps. The SRConv module enhances the high-level semantic feature maps, thereby improving the encoding performance and resulting in better outcomes during the decoding phase. The experimental results will demonstrate that our SRConv module improves the performance of the RT-DETR network model and is also effective for other Transformer-based object detection models.

3.2. Self-Attention Mechanism Integrated with CA

Transformer-based object detection models use Multi-Head Self-Attention (MultiHeadAttn) mechanisms to allow the model to focus more on critical regions, adaptively learning important features. This improves the detection accuracy in cases of deformation, rotation, and occlusion, and effectively captures contextual relationships. This significantly enhances the expressive capability, generalization ability, and computational efficiency of deep learning models when handling complex tasks and data. Multi-Head Attention can be considered one of the core components of the DETR [5] model, enabling the effective completion of object detection tasks. The basic principle of Multi-Head Attention is illustrated in Formula (4):

$$\mathrm{MultiHeadAttn}(z_q, x_k) = \sum_{m=1}^{M} \mathrm{W}_m[\sum_{k\in\Omega_k} A_{mqk}\cdot \mathrm{W}\prime_{m x_k}] \tag{4}$$

m denotes the m-th attention head in the Multi-Head Attention mechanism, x represents the Key and Value input features, z represents the Query input feature, and W_m is the transformation matrix from the features input to Value, used to transform x_k into Value. W_m performs a linear transformation on the result of applying attention to the Value to obtain outputs from different heads, and the scalar A_{mqk} represents the attention weights.

However, in object detection tasks, the need to compute extensive attention mechanisms often requires many epochs to train the model, significantly reducing the training efficiency. In 2023, Deformable Attention was introduced based on deformable convolutions. Deformable Attention is a module designed to enhance the neural network's ability to adapt to spatial transformations by adding offsets to the current sampling points. This allows the model to focus more quickly on the most critical features, thus accelerating convergence. In traditional attention mechanisms, weights are computed using a fixed-position attention model. In contrast, Deformable Attention can dynamically adjust the shape and size of the attention model to better adapt to different tasks and input data characteristics. The main process of the Deformable Attention module involves converting the input vectors into feature maps, generating query vectors while considering the coordinates of the reference points, and then inputting these feature maps and query vectors into the offset module. The results from the offset module are combined with the query vectors and input into the attention module to obtain the final result. The basic principle is illustrated by the following formula:

$$\mathrm{DeformAttn}\ (z_q, p_q, x) = \sum_{m=1}^{M} \mathrm{W}_\mathrm{m}[\sum_{k=1}^{K} A_{mqk}\cdot \mathrm{W}'_{m x_k}(p_q + \Delta p_{mqk})] \tag{5}$$

A_{mqk} is not obtained by the dot product of the Query and Key matrices, but directly derived from the input feature z_q through a fully connected layer. p_q represents the position (i.e., coordinates) of z_q, which is a 2D vector and referred to as the reference point by the authors. Δp_{mqk} denotes the positional offset of the k-th sampling point of the m-th attention head relative to the reference point. K is the total number of sampled keys.

Currently, most Transformer-based object detection models use Deformable Attention to replace the original Multi-Head Attention mechanism. Deformable Attention improves the network's adaptability to spatial transformations by converting the encoding into feature maps and adding offsets to the sampling points. This allows the model to focus more quickly on critical features and speeds up convergence.

However, because Deformable Self-Attention needs to flexibly select regions of focus within the feature maps, it may lead to underutilized regions and sparse attention maps in some cases, affecting the overall model performance. Inspired by the work on HAT (Activating More Pixels in Image Super-Resolution Transformer) [30], where convolution helps Transformers achieve better visual representation or easier optimization, incorporating channel attention [29] into the Transformer's self-attention mechanism significantly enhances the model performance. The sparsity problem of the Deformable Attention mechanism mainly manifests as sparse sampling in the spatial dimension, while channel attention adjusts features in the channel dimension, making the two approaches complementary. Thus, channel attention is proposed to be integrated into Deformable Attention.

As shown in Figure 6, channel attention involves applying global max pooling to each channel's feature map to obtain global features for each channel. These global features are then mapped to attention weights through fully connected layers or similar operations, indicating the importance of each channel for the current task. Using channel attention can improve the model's representational ability, allowing it to better capture the correlations between channels in the input data, thereby enhancing generalization and performance. Channel attention has widespread applications in image, speech, and natural language processing and has been proven to significantly improve the model performance.

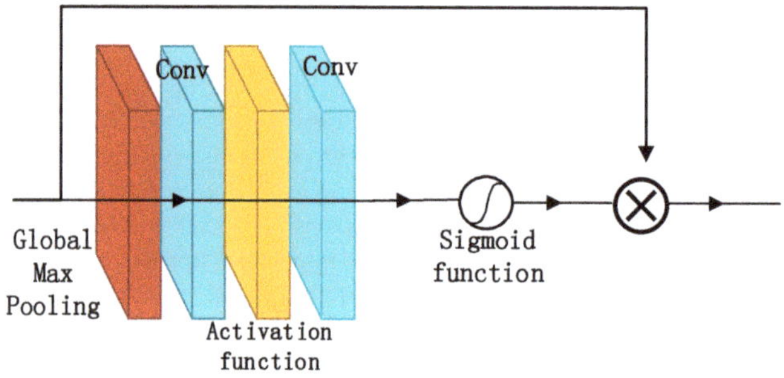

Figure 6. Schematic diagram of the channel attention mechanism.

Transformer-based structures often require a large number of channels for token embedding, making direct use of fixed-width convolutions that are computationally expensive. Therefore, HAT and others have reduced the number of channels in two convolutional layers to a constant B. For input features with C channels, the number of channels in the output feature after the first convolution layer is reduced to C/B, and then expanded back to C channels through the second convolution layer. Subsequently, a standard channel attention (CA) module is used to adaptively readjust the channel features. Unlike HAT [30] networks, in Transformer-based object detection models, Deformable Attention operates directly on feature maps obtained by converting the input vectors. Therefore, integrating channel attention [29] into this framework is less complex than in HAT networks. The process of integrating channel attention [29] is as follows:

(1) Input Feature Map: assume the input feature map is F, with dimensions $C \times H \times W$, where C is the number of channels, and H and W are the height and width of the feature map, respectively.

(2) Channel Description: global max pooling reduces the dimensionality of the feature map, generating a channel descriptor vector z.

$$z = F_{\max} = \max_{i,j} F(:, i, j) \tag{6}$$

(3) Channel Attention Weight Calculation: a simple feedforward neural network (e.g., consisting of two fully connected layers and an activation function) maps the channel descriptor vector z to compute the channel attention weight α:

$$\alpha = \sigma(W_2\delta(W_1 z + b_1) + b_2) \tag{7}$$

W_1 and W_2 are weights, b_1 and b_2 are biases, σ is the activation function (e.g., sigmoid) applied.

(4) Feature Map Recalibration: the computed attention weights α are used to rescale the original feature map F:

$$F' = \alpha \odot F \tag{8}$$

$\odot$ denotes element-wise multiplication.

This channel attention mechanism helps the model automatically learn important features, enhancing its feature representation capability. By using this mechanism, the model can increase sensitivity to specific features. Experiments have shown that integrating channel attention (CA) into the self-attention mechanism can improve model performance while adding only a minimal number of model parameters.

4. Experiments

4.1. Dataset Description and Evaluation Metrics

The experimental dataset consists of images of rail fasteners from several railway sections in China. By applying preprocessing methods such as scaling, rotation, cropping, and random color adjustments, the dataset was expanded to 6300 images, including 38,000 rail fasteners. The dataset is divided into training and validation sets at a 90:10 ratio. It includes rail fastener defect samples categorized into four classes: Normal, Lost, Reversed, and Displaced.

To validate the effectiveness of the proposed algorithm, metrics such as Precision (P), Recall (R), Average Precision (AP), and Mean Average Precision (mAP) are used to evaluate the model performance. The model complexity is assessed based on the number of parameters and model size. Since the dataset used is in the COCO format, mAP@0.5:0.9 is the primary evaluation criterion, indicating the average AP at IoU thresholds of 0.5 to 0.9, which directly reflects the model's detection capability. The calculation formulas for these parameters are as follows:

$$\mathrm{P} = \frac{\mathrm{TP}}{\mathrm{TP} + \mathrm{FP}} \times 100\% \tag{9}$$

$$\mathrm{R} = \frac{\mathrm{TP}}{\mathrm{TP} + \mathrm{FN}} \times 100\% \tag{10}$$

$$\mathrm{AP} = \int_0^1 \mathrm{P(R)dR} \tag{11}$$

$$\mathrm{mAP} = \frac{1}{\mathrm{K}} \sum_{i=1}^{\mathrm{K}} \mathrm{AP}(i) \tag{12}$$

$$\mathrm{IoU} = \frac{\mathrm{A} \cap \mathrm{B}}{\mathrm{A} \cup \mathrm{B}} \tag{13}$$

In the formula, TP denotes the number of correctly detected defects; FP denotes the number of false positives; FN denotes the number of missed defects; and K represents the number of defect categories in the dataset.

4.2. Experimental Environment and Parameter Setting

The experimental environment was configured with Windows 10 as the operating system, NVIDIA TITAN XP as the GPU model with 12 G of video memory, Python 3.8

as the compilation language, Pytorch 1.7.0 as the deep learning framework, and CUDA 12.0 as the CUDA version. The training parameters were set as follows: the initial learning rate is 0.01, the momentum parameter is 0.937, the weight decay factor is 0.0005, and the Batch_Size is 8. A total of 72 epochs were trained by stochastic gradient descent (SGD) for the whole training process.

4.3. Experimental Results and Analysis

By training existing Transformer-based object detection methods on the railway fastener defect dataset, it was found that the RT-DETR model had the best performance and model parameter efficiency compared to the other models. Therefore, RT-DETR was chosen as the baseline for further improvements. As shown in Table 1, the improved RT-DETR model achieved a 2.8 percentage point increase in mAP@0.5:0.9, a 1.7 percentage point increase in AR, with only a 0.4 MB increase in model parameters. Compared to other Transformer-based object detection models, mAP@0.5:0.9 increased by 8.0, 7.7, and 2.3 percentage points, and AR increased by 7.8, 5.9, and 2.2 percentage points, achieving optimal results in these three key metrics. This indicates that the improvements to the model were successful.

Table 1. Main results.

Model	AR/%	mAP@0.5:0.9/%	Params/MB
DETR	84.5	80.2	158
Deformable DETR	86.4	80.5	153
Dino	90.1	85.9	181
RT-DETR (baseline)	90.6	85.4	77
The proposed model	92.3	88.2	77.4

5. Ablation Study

To evaluate the impact of each improvement module of the enhanced RT-DETR model on the detection performance of railway fastener defects, an ablation study was conducted under a consistent experimental environment and parameter settings. The ablation study comprised 12 configurations, using three base object detection models with Deformable Attention as the self-attention mechanism: DINO, Deformable DETR, and RT-DETR. These base models served as the baseline, and the proposed SRConv and channel attention-integrated self-attention modules were added. The experimental results are shown in Table 2, where "√" indicates the use of the respective module.

Table 2. Experimental results of adding different modules with different models.

Model	SRConv	CA	mAP@0.5:0.9/%	Params/MB
DINO			85.9	181
DINO	√		87.1	183
DINO		√	88.2	181
DINO	√	√	89	183
Deformable DETR			80.1	153
Deformable DETR	√		81.6	154
Deformable DETR		√	83	153
Deformable DETR	√	√	83.4	154
RT-DETR			85.4	77
RT-DETR	√		86.9	77.4
RT-DETR		√	87	77
RT-DETR	√	√	87.6	77.4

An ablation study was conducted by adding the proposed SRConv module and the channel attention (CA) integrated self-attention module to the original object detection models. Initially, the SRConv module was added to each model, resulting in increases in mAP@0.5:0.9 of 1.2, 1.5, and 1.5 percentage points, respectively, with model parameter increases of 2 MB, 1 MB, and 0.4 MB; the increase in these parameters is minor relative to the performance gains. Next, the CA-integrated self-attention module was added to the original models, resulting in mAP@0.5:0.9 increases of 2.3, 2.9, and 1.6 percentage points, respectively, with no change in the model parameters. This result is due to the CA module being applied directly to feature maps; it operates on the aggregated information of each channel rather than on individual spatial locations. This means that the computational burden is focused on fewer dimensions, as the attention mechanism condenses the spatial information into a single value per channel. The CA module typically uses a lightweight architecture, often comprising fully connected layers after global pooling. This structure has significantly fewer parameters than a full convolutional layer applied to the entire feature map. Fewer parameters translate to lower memory usage and faster computations, which is why it requires minimal additional computational resources while showing significant improvements. Finally, incorporating both modules resulted in mAP@0.5:0.9 increases of 3.1, 3.3, and 2.2 percentage points, with the model parameter changes consistent with those of models that only include the SRConv module. The ablation study results demonstrate that both the SRConv module and the CA-integrated self-attention module significantly improve the mAP@0.5:0.9 metric for the railway fastener defect dataset while only minimally increasing the model parameters.

6. Conclusions

This paper focuses on the application of Transformer-based object detection models in rail track fastener defect detection tasks. The improved RT-DETR network model better adapts to rail track fastener defect detection, achieving a higher model accuracy with only a minimal increase in the model parameters. Specifically, the Backbone network was enhanced by incorporating the SRConv module to improve its ability to extract rail track fastener defect features. Additionally, the channel attention was integrated into the self-attention mechanisms of the Encoder and Decoder to address the issue of underutilized padding areas and sparse attention maps caused by the deformable self-attention mechanism. The experimental results indicate that, using the proposed method, the original RT-DETR network model achieved optimal performance on the rail track fastener defect dataset. The mAP@0.5:0.9 reached 88.2%, an increase of 2.8 percentage points over the original model, and the AR@0.5:0.9 improved by 1.7 percentage points, with only a 0.4 MB increase in model parameters. Finally, through conducting ablation experiments, we validated the effectiveness of the proposed improvement strategies on other Transformer-based object detection models for rail track fastener defect detection. The results of the ablation experiments demonstrated that the proposed strategies are effective for object detection models utilizing Deformable Attention as the self-attention mechanism. Due to the variability in the shapes of rail track fastener defects, future defect types may become more diverse. Therefore, we will continue to enhance the model's accuracy in detecting complex and diverse rail track fastener defects in future research efforts.

Author Contributions: Data curation, X.Y.; writing—original draft, B.L.; writing—review and editing, W.S. and K.N. All authors have read and agreed to the published version of the manuscript.

Funding: This research received no external funding.

Data Availability Statement: No new data were created or analyzed in this study.

Conflicts of Interest: The authors declare no conflict of interest.

References

1. Fei, Y.; Tu, W.-J.; Wei, Z.-L.; Ke, Z.-T.; Liu, X.-B.; Yang, A.-H.; Wang, S.-L. Review on Development Status of Inspection Equipment for Track Maintenance. *Commun. Signal. Power Supply Railw.* **2023**, *23*, 47–69.
2. Bochkovskiy, A.; Wang, C.-Y.; Liao, H.-Y.M. Yolov4: Optimal speed and accuracy of object detection. *arXiv* **2020**, arXiv:2004.10934.
3. Li, C.; Li, L.; Jiang, H.; Weng, K.; Geng, Y.; Li, L.; Ke, Z. YOLOv6: A single-stage object detection framework for industrial applications. *arXiv* **2022**, arXiv:2209.02976.
4. Wang, C.-Y.; Bochkovskiy, A.; Liao, H.-Y.M. YOLOv7: Trainable bag-of-freebies sets new state-of-the-art for real-time object detectors. In Proceedings of the IEEE/CVF Conference on Computer Vision and Pattern Recognition, Vancouver, BC, Canada, 17–24 June 2023; pp. 7464–7475.
5. Carion, N.; Massa, F.; Synnaeve, G.; Usunier, N.; Kirillov, A.; Zagoruyko, S. End-to-end object detection with transformers. In *European Conference on Computer Vision*; Springer International Publishing: Cham, Switzerland, 2020; pp. 213–229.
6. Zhu, X.; Su, W.; Lu, L.; Li, B.; Wang, X.; Dai, J. Deformable detr: Deformable transformers for end-to-end object detection. *arXiv* **2020**, arXiv:2010.04159.
7. Zhang, H.; Li, F.; Liu, S.; Zhang, L.; Su, H.; Zhu, J.; Ni, L.M.; Shum, H.-Y. Dino: Detr with improved denoising anchor boxes for end-to-end object detection. *arXiv* **2022**, arXiv:2203.03605.
8. Zhao, Y.; Lv, W.; Xu, S.; Wei, J.; Wang, G.; Dang, Q.; Liu, Y.; Chen, J. Detrs beat yolos on real-time object detection. In Proceedings of the IEEE/CVF Conference on Computer Vision and Pattern Recognition, Seattle, WA, USA, 16–22 June 2024; pp. 16965–16974.
9. Viola, P.; Jones, M. Rapid object detection using a boosted cascade of simple features. In Proceedings of the 2001 IEEE Computer Society Conference on Computer Vision and Pattern Recognition. CVPR 2001, Kauai, HI, USA, 8–14 December 2001; IEEE: Piscataway, NJ, USA, 2001; Volume 1, p. I-I.
10. Ma, H.; Min, Y.; Yin, C.; Cheng, T.; Xiao, B.; Yue, B.; Li, X. A real time detection method of track fasteners missing of railway based on machine vision. *Int. J. Perform. Eng.* **2018**, *14*, 1190. [CrossRef]
11. Gibert, X.; Patel, V.M.; Chellappa, R. Sequential score adaptation with extreme value theory for robust railway track inspection. In Proceedings of the IEEE International Conference on Computer Vision Workshops, Boston, MA, USA, 7–12 June 2015; pp. 42–49.
12. Gibert, X.; Patel, V.M.; Chellappa, R. Deep multitask learning for railway track inspection. *IEEE Trans. Intell. Transp. Syst.* **2016**, *18*, 153–164. [CrossRef]
13. Ou, Y.; Luo, J.; Li, B.; He, B. A classification model of railway fasteners based on computer vision. *Neural Comput. Appl.* **2019**, *31*, 9307–9319. [CrossRef]
14. Dai, X.X.; Ding, S.H.; Yang, E.H. Development and verification of automatic inspection system for high-speed railway fastener. *J. Railw. Sci. Eng.* **2018**, *15*, 2478–2486.
15. Girshick, R.; Donahue, J.; Darrell, T.; Malik, J. Rich feature hierarchies for accurate object detection and semantic segmentation. In Proceedings of the IEEE Conference on Computer Vision and Pattern Recognition, Columbus, OH, USA, 23–28 June 2014; pp. 580–587.
16. Girshick, R. Fast r-cnn. In Proceedings of the IEEE International Conference on Computer Vision, Santiago, Chile, 7–13 December 2015; pp. 1440–1448.
17. He, K.; Gkioxari, G.; Dollár, P.; Girshick, R. Mask r-cnn. In Proceedings of the IEEE International Conference on Computer Vision, Venice, Italy, 22–29 October 2017; pp. 2961–2969.
18. Ren, S.; He, K.; Girshick, R.; Sun, J. Faster R-CNN: Towards real-time object detection with region proposal networks. *IEEE Trans. Pattern Anal. Mach. Intell.* **2016**, *39*, 1137–1149. [CrossRef] [PubMed]
19. Wei, X.; Yang, Z.; Liu, Y.; Wei, D.; Jia, L.; Li, Y. Railway track fastener defect detection based on image processing and deep learning techniques: A comparative study. *Eng. Appl. Artif. Intell.* **2019**, *80*, 66–81. [CrossRef]
20. Redmon, J. You only look once: Unified, real-time object detection. In Proceedings of the IEEE Conference on Computer Vision and Pattern Recognition, Las Vegas, NV, USA, 27–30 June 2016.
21. Redmon, J.; Farhadi, A. YOLO9000: Better, faster, stronger. In Proceedings of the IEEE Conference on Computer Vision and Pattern Recognition, Honolulu, HI, USA, 21–26 July 2017; pp. 7263–7271.
22. Redmon, J. Yolov3: An incremental improvement. *arXiv* **2018**, arXiv:1804.02767.
23. Guo, F.; Qian, Y.; Shi, Y. Real-time railroad track components inspection based on the improved YOLOv4 framework. *Autom. Constr.* **2021**, *125*, 103596. [CrossRef]
24. Jocher, G.; Chaurasia, A.; Stoken, A.; Borovec, J.; Kwon, Y.; Michael, K.; Fang, J.; Wong, C.; Yifu, Z.; Montes, D.; et al. v6.2-YOLOv5 Classification Models, Apple M1, Reproducibility, ClearML and Deci.ai Integrations. Zenodo (2022). Available online: https://github.com/ultralytics/yolov5/discussions/8996 (accessed on 26 September 2024).
25. Chollet, F. Xception: Deep learning with depthwise separable convolutions. In Proceedings of the IEEE Conference on Computer Vision and Pattern Recognition, Honolulu, HI, USA, 21–26 July 2017; pp. 1251–1258.
26. Lin, T.Y.; Dollár, P.; Girshick, R.; He, K.; Hariharan, B.; Belongie, S. Feature pyramid networks for object detection. In Proceedings of the IEEE Conference on Computer Vision and Pattern Recognition, Honolulu, HI, USA, 21–26 July 2017; pp. 2117–2125.
27. Li, X.; Wang, Q.; Yang, X.; Wang, K.; Zhang, H. Track fastener defect detection model based on improved YOLOv5s. *Sensors* **2023**, *23*, 6457. [CrossRef] [PubMed]

28. Ward, C.M.; Harguess, J.; Crabb, B.; Parameswaran, S. Image quality assessment for determining efficacy and limitations of Super-Resolution Convolutional Neural Network (SRCNN). In *Applications of Digital Image Processing XL*; SPIE: San Diego, CA, USA, 2017; Volume 10396, pp. 19–30.
29. Koonce, B.; Koonce, B. ResNet 50. In *Convolutional Neural Networks with Swift for Tensorflow: Image Recognition and Dataset Categorization*; Apress: Berkeley, CA, USA, 2021; pp. 63–72.
30. Chen, X.; Wang, X.; Zhou, J.; Qiao, Y.; Dong, C. Activating more pixels in image super-resolution transformer. In Proceedings of the IEEE/CVF Conference on Computer Vision and Pattern Recognition, Vancouver, BC, Canada, 17–24 June 2023; pp. 22367–22377.

mathematics

MDPI

Article

Anti-Disturbance Bumpless Transfer Control for a Switched Systems via a Switched Equivalent-Input-Disturbance Approach

Jiawen Wu [1], Qian Liu [2,*] and Pan Yu [2]

[1] School of Information Science and Technology, Beijing University of Technology, Beijing 100124, China; wujiawen@emails.bjut.edu.cn
[2] Beijing Institute of Artificial Intelligence, and School of Information Science and Technology, Beijing University of Technology, Beijing 100124, China; panyu@bjut.edu.cn
* Correspondence: liuqian02@bjut.edu.cn

Abstract: This paper concentrates on the issue of anti-disturbance bumpless transfer (ADBT) control design for switched systems. The ADBT control design problem refers to designing a continuous controller and a switching rule to ensure the switched system satisfies the ADBT property. First, the concept of the ADBT property is introduced. Then, via a switched equivalent-input-disturbance (EID) methodology, a switched EID estimator is formulated to estimate the impact of external disturbances within the switched system. Second, a bumpless transfer control is then constructed via a compensator integrating an EID estimation. Finally, the effectiveness of the presented control scheme is verified by controlling a switching resistor–inductor–capacitor circuit on the Matlab platform. Above all, a new configuration for ADBT control of switched systems is established via a switched EID methodology.

Keywords: bumpless transfer control; switched equivalent-input-disturbance estimator; compensator; switched systems; average dwell time

MSC: 93B52

1. Introduction

With the advancement in control technologies, switching control is extensively utilized across engineering practices to meet various control requirements [1,2]. However, the sudden change in the control input signal during switching can occasionally adversely affect the dynamic behaviour of a practical system [3,4]. Meanwhile, external and internal disturbances are unavoidable during the operation of automated systems, which can potentially cause decreased efficiency or even instability [5,6]. Thereby, the ADBT control technique is significant for effectively suppressing disturbances, ensuring smooth transitions during control system switching, and guaranteeing stable system operation.

Anti-disturbance (AD) control techniques effectively attenuate unpredictable disturbances [7–9]. Many existing AD control methods have been proposed so far to achieve efficient disturbance suppression, such as output regulation theory [10,11], adaptive robust control theory [12,13] and active disturbance rejection control [14–16]. The EID approach, as an effectively active disturbance rejection method, is introduced to counteract both anticipated and unanticipated disruptions [17,18]. Utilizing a signal within the channel of the control input, this approach creates an equivalent effect on the output which is induced by actual disturbances. However, most of the existing results via the EID approach are for nonswitched systems, and these results cannot be applied to switched systems directly. In fact, differing from nonswitched systems, the EID estimator design and AD analysis for switched systems possess greater complexity and difficulty.

For switched systems, transient behaviours are inevitable when switching between different subsystems [19–21]. At the switching instant, the control input signal undergoes abrupt changes, which often results in undesirable transient performance between different controllers. BT control effectively mitigates bumps during switching transitions. Recently, based on different definitions of the BT level, many controller designing strategies are introduced to guarantee the BT performance for switched systems, such as event-triggered controller designs [22,23], state-dependent switching methods [24,25], time-dependent switching methods [26,27] and compensation-based BT controllers [28,29]. The concept of compensation is often employed to address the BT problem [29]. Yan Shi et al. introduce a straightforward bumpless transfer control framework that includes components such as a differentiator and an integrator for maintaining the smoothness of control [29]. Additionally, a compensator is implemented to address deviations from the original switching control input signal, aiming to eliminate steady-state errors. Further, it is essential to preserve switching transient performance when handling both matched and unmatched disturbances.

In this work, a switching methodology based on average dwell time (ADT) and a switched EID estimator are presented for the control of switched linear systems to suppress unknown disturbances via ADBT control. To summarize, the following contributions are proposed:

1. Although there exist many works on the ADBT control design problem, such as [10,30,31], the definitions of the ADBT control problem are different. In all these works, the BT performance is described by limiting the jump amplitude at switching instants or the amplitude difference between the actual control law $u(t)$ and the auxiliary control signal $v(t)$ rather than requiring the controller to operate continuously. In our work, a continuous controller is obtained. Moreover, in these existing works, H_∞ reliable controller design (as in [30]) and disturbance observer design (as in [10,31]) are always provided to achieve the AD performance. However, a switched EID methodology is introduced in our paper to achieve the AD performance. In fact, rare results are provided on the design of the switched EID estimator for switched systems.
2. We extend the EID estimator design issue from its original nonswitched version. The switched EID estimator, which relies on switching signals, indicates that each subsystem possesses its own EID estimator. To reduce the conservativeness that arises from using a common EID estimator for all subsystems, distinct EID estimators are designed for each subsystem.
3. Based on the switched EID estimator, through the construction of an additional compensator, a new formulation for the ADBT controller is devised for switched systems. Through an ADT switching methodology, sufficient conditions are derived for the ADBT control of switched systems. A continuous controller and an ADT switching strategy are jointly developed to address the ADBT control design problem for switched systems.

Below, we outline the organization of our work. It begins with the configuration of switched EID-based ADBT control and problem formulation in Section 2. The ADBT control designing analysis is put forward in Section 3. The effectiveness is demonstrated using a model of a switching RLC circuit, discussed in Section 4. A discussion is provided in Section 5. Lastly, our study is concluded in Section 6.

Notations	**Meaning**
R^n	n-dimensional real vector space
$\|x\|$	2-norm of x
$\lambda_{max}(P)(\lambda_{min}(P))$	Greatest (least) eigenvalue of the matrix P
N	Set of natural numbers
LMI	Linear matrix inequality

2. Configuration of Switched EID-Based ADBT Control and Problem Formulation

Take into account a switched linear system (SLS) affected by an external disturbance:

$$\dot{x}(t) = \hat{A}_{\sigma(t)}x(t) + \hat{B}_{\sigma(t)}u(t) + \hat{B}_d^{\sigma(t)}d(t), \quad (1a)$$
$$y(t) = \hat{C}x(t), \quad (1b)$$

where $\sigma(t) \in M = \{1, \cdots, m\}$. The state $x(t)$ maintains its continuity at every point; the control is denoted by $u(t) \in R^{n_u}$; the unknown disturbance is represented by $d(t) \in R^{n_d}$; the performance output is indicated by $y(t) \in R^{n_y}$; real constant matrices $\hat{A}_i$, $\hat{B}_i$, $\hat{B}_d^i$, and $\hat{C}$ are of suitable dimensions, $i \in M$. We denote the switching instants as $t_0 < t_1 < \cdots < t_l < \cdots$. For $\forall t \in [t_l, t_{l+1}), \sigma(t) = i_l, l \in N$.

Assumption 1 ([32]). *The controllability of $(\hat{A}_i, \hat{B}_i)$ and the observability of $(\hat{A}_i, \hat{C})$ are assumed.*

In many cases, obtaining all state information is difficult or expensive. In that case, it is necessary to formulate a switched state observer as

$$\dot{\hat{x}}(t) = \hat{A}_{\sigma(t)}\hat{x}(t) + \hat{B}_{\sigma(t)}u_f(t) + L_{\sigma(t)}(y(t) - \hat{y}(t)), \quad (2a)$$
$$\hat{y}(t) = \hat{C}\hat{x}(t), \quad (2b)$$

where $\hat{x}(t) \in R^n$ is the estimation of the system state; the input is denoted as $u_f(t)$, the measured output is represented by $\hat{y}(t)$; and the switched observer gain, denoted as $L_{\sigma(t)}$, is required to be determined.

Firstly, we denote the estimation error

$$\tilde{x}(t) = x(t) - \hat{x}(t), \quad (3a)$$
$$\tilde{y}(t) = y(t) - \hat{y}(t). \quad (3b)$$

Additionally, a switched EID estimator from a general switched filter and a switched controller gain is utilized to estimate the EID $d_e(t)$ associated with the disturbance $d(t)$. The EID is estimated as

$$\hat{d}_e(t) = -u(t) + u_f(t) + K_{e\sigma(t)}\tilde{y}(t), \quad (4)$$

where $K_{e\sigma(t)}$ is the switched estimator gain. In the meantime, the switched filter's state-space representation is

$$\dot{x}_F(t) = \hat{A}_{F\sigma(t)}x_F(t) + \hat{B}_{F\sigma(t)}\hat{d}_e(t), \quad (5a)$$
$$\tilde{d}_e(t) = \hat{C}_F x_F(t), \quad (5b)$$

where $x_F(t) \in R^{n_f}$ is the state and $\tilde{d}_e(t)$ represents the filtered estimate of $d_e(t)$. For $i \in M$, define

$$\hat{A}_{ei} = \hat{A}_{Fi},\ \hat{B}_{ei} = \hat{B}_{Fi}K_{ei},\ \hat{C}_e = \hat{C}_F. \quad (6)$$

One has

$$\dot{x}_e(t) = \hat{A}_{e\sigma(t)}x_e(t) + \hat{B}_{e\sigma(t)}\tilde{y}(t) + \hat{B}_{F\sigma(t)}(u_f(t) - u(t)), \quad (7a)$$
$$\tilde{d}_e(t) = \hat{C}_e x_e(t), \quad (7b)$$

where $x_e(t) = x_F(t) \in R^{n_f}$ represents the state variable for the switched EID estimator.

Further, to ensure the continuity of the input signal, based on the idea of [29] on the BT controller design, a compensator takes the form

$$\dot{x}_c(t) = -k_c\big(x_c(t) - K_{p\sigma(t)}\hat{x}(t) + \textstyle\int_{t_0}^{t} K_{p\sigma(\tau)}\dot{\hat{x}}(\tau)d\tau + K_{p\sigma(t_0)}\hat{x}(t_0)\big), \tag{8}$$

where $x_c(t) \in R^l$ represents the compensator's state, $k_c > 0$ represents an adjustable coefficient, initialized with $x_c(t_0) = 0$. The BT controller is designed as

$$u(t) = -\tilde{d}_e(t) + x_c(t) + u_f(t) - \Delta_{\sigma(t)}(\hat{x}(t)), \tag{9}$$

where $u_f(t)$ and $\Delta_{\sigma(t)}(\hat{x}(t))$ are taken as

$$u_f(t) = K_{p\sigma(t)}\hat{x}(t), \tag{10a}$$

$$\begin{aligned}\Delta_{\sigma(t)}(\hat{x}(t)) &= K_{p\sigma(t)}\hat{x}(t) - \big(\textstyle\int_{t_0}^{t} K_{p\sigma(\tau)}\dot{\hat{x}}(\tau)d\tau + K_{p\sigma(t_0)}\hat{x}(t_0)\big)\\ &= \sum_{k=1}^{N_\sigma(t,t_0)} \big(K_{p\sigma(t_k)} - K_{p\sigma(t_{k-1})}\big)\hat{x}(t_k).\end{aligned} \tag{10b}$$

Then, with setting $\bar{x}_c(t) = x_c(t) - \Delta_{\sigma(t)}(\hat{x}(t))$, the complete closed-loop representation of the SLS is inferred by

$$\begin{aligned}\dot{x}(t) &= (\hat{A}_{\sigma(t)} + \hat{B}_{\sigma(t)}K_{p\sigma(t)})x(t) - \hat{B}_{\sigma(t)}K_{p\sigma(t)}\tilde{x}(t)\\ &-\hat{B}_{\sigma(t)}\hat{C}_e x_e(t) + \hat{B}_{\sigma(t)}\bar{x}_c(t) + \hat{B}_d^{\sigma(t)}d(t),\end{aligned} \tag{11a}$$

$$\dot{\tilde{x}}(t) = (\hat{A}_{\sigma(t)} - L_{\sigma(t)}\hat{C})\tilde{x}(t) - \hat{B}_{\sigma(t)}\hat{C}_e x_e(t) + \hat{B}_{\sigma(t)}\bar{x}_c(t) + \hat{B}_d^{\sigma(t)}d(t), \tag{11b}$$

$$\dot{x}_e(t) = (\hat{A}_{e\sigma(t)} + \hat{B}_{F\sigma(t)}\hat{C}_e)x_e(t) + \hat{B}_{e\sigma(t)}\hat{C}\tilde{x}(t) - \hat{B}_{F\sigma(t)}\bar{x}_c(t), \tag{11c}$$

$$\dot{\bar{x}}_c(t) = -k_c I_{l\times l}\bar{x}_c(t). \tag{11d}$$

Therefore, the augmented system described above is formulated as

$$\dot{\xi}(t) = \bar{A}_{\sigma(t)}\xi(t) + \bar{B}_d^{\sigma(t)}d(t), \tag{12}$$

where $\xi(t) = \begin{bmatrix} x^T(t) & \tilde{x}^T(t) & x_e^T(t) & \bar{x}_c^T(t) \end{bmatrix}^T$,

$$\bar{A}_i = \begin{bmatrix} \hat{A}_i + \hat{B}_i K_{pi} & -\hat{B}_i K_{pi} & -\hat{B}_i\hat{C}_e & \hat{B}_i \\ 0 & \hat{A}_i - L_i\hat{C} & -\hat{B}_i\hat{C}_e & \hat{B}_i \\ 0 & \hat{B}_{ei}\hat{C} & \hat{A}_{ei} + \hat{B}_{Fi}\hat{C}_e & -\hat{B}_{Fi} \\ 0 & 0 & 0 & -k_c I_{l\times l} \end{bmatrix},\ \bar{B}_d^i = \begin{bmatrix} \hat{B}_d^i \\ \hat{B}_d^i \\ 0 \\ 0 \end{bmatrix},\ i \in M.$$

To this end, let us illustrate the issue of the ADBT control design problem.

Problem 1. *Considering the SLS (1), the issue of ADBT control design problem involves the constructions of a continuous controller $u(t)$ and the switching law $\sigma(t)$ satisfying the AD property as described below:*

(i) (Asymptotic stability) Assuming the perturbation signal $d(t) \equiv 0$, the system (12) is of asymptotic stability.

(ii) (L_2-gain property) Assuming the perturbation signal $d(t) \neq 0$, the system (12) meets the L_2-gain property:

$$\textstyle\int_0^\infty y^T(\tau)y(\tau)d\tau \le \frac{1}{\varepsilon}\int_0^\infty d^T(\tau)d(\tau)d\tau + \delta(x_0) \tag{13}$$

for any $d(t) \in L_2[0,\infty)$ with an initial condition of zero, where $\varepsilon > 0$ and the function $\delta(x_0)$ is a real value function and satisfies the condition $\delta(0) = 0$.

3. Anti-Disturbance Bumpless Transfer Control

In this section, the main results about the ADBT control of the system (12) can be encapsulated in the subsequent theorem. With the continuous controller designed in (9), a switching law characterized by ADT is constructed to solve the ADBT control design issue for the SLS (1).

Theorem 1. *Suppose there are symmetric positive definite matrices P_{0i}, P_{1i}, P_{2i}, and P_{3i}, constants $\alpha > 0$, $k_c > 0$, $\mu > 0$ and appropriate matrices L_i, K_{pi}, $\hat{A}_{ei}$, $\hat{B}_{ei}$, $\hat{C}_e$ and K_{ei}, such that for $\forall i, j \in M$,*

$$\begin{bmatrix} G_i + G_d^i + \hat{C}^T\hat{C} + \alpha P_{0i} & -P_{0i}\hat{B}_iK_{pi} + D_i & -P_{0i}\hat{B}_i\hat{C}_e & P_{0i}\hat{B}_i \\ * & W_i + T_i + \alpha P_{1i} & S_i & P_{1i}\hat{B}_i \\ * & * & Q_i + \alpha P_{2i} & -P_{2i}\hat{B}_{Fi} \\ * & * & * & -2k_cP_{3i} + \alpha P_{3i} \end{bmatrix} \leq 0, \tag{14a}$$

$$P_{0i} \leq \mu P_{0j}, \quad P_{1i} \leq \mu P_{1j}, \quad P_{2i} \leq \mu P_{2j}, \quad P_{3i} \leq \mu P_{3j}, \tag{14b}$$

where $G_i = (\hat{A}_i + \hat{B}_iK_{pi})^TP_{0i} + P_{0i}(\hat{A}_i + \hat{B}_iK_{pi})$, $G_d^i = P_{0i}\hat{B}_d^i(\hat{B}_d^i)^TP_{0i}$, $D_i = P_{0i}\hat{B}_d^i(\hat{B}_d^i)^TP_{1i}$, $W_i = P_{1i}\hat{B}_d^i(\hat{B}_d^i)^TP_{1i}$, $T_i = (\hat{A}_i - L_i\hat{C})^TP_{1i} + P_{1i}(\hat{A}_i - L_i\hat{C})$, $S_i = (\hat{B}_{ei}\hat{C})^TP_{2i} - P_{1i}\hat{B}_i\hat{C}_e$, $Q_i = (\hat{A}_{ei} + \hat{B}_{Fi}\hat{C}_e)^TP_{2i} + P_{2i}(\hat{A}_{ei} + \hat{B}_{Fi}\hat{C}_e)$. The problem of ADBT control is resolved utilizing controller (9) while ensuring each switching signal is characterized by ADT τ_d satisfying

$$\tau_d \geq \frac{ln(\mu\gamma)}{\alpha - \hat{\alpha}}, \tag{15}$$

where $0 < \hat{\alpha} < \alpha$ and $\gamma = 1 + \max\{\sup_{i,j} \frac{2(1+\epsilon_i)\lambda_{max}(K_{pji}^TP_{3i}K_{pji})}{\min\{\lambda_{min}(P_{0i}),\lambda_{min}(P_{1i}),\lambda_{min}(P_{2i})\}}, \sup_i \frac{1}{\epsilon_i}\}$ with $K_{pji} = K_{pj} - K_{pi}$ and $\epsilon_i > 0$ for $i, j \in M$.

Proof. Firstly, for $i \in M$, we choose the multiple Lyapunov function as

$$V_i(\xi) = \xi^TP_i\xi, \tag{16}$$

where $P_i = \text{diag}\{P_{0i}, P_{1i}, P_{2i}, P_{3i}\}$. □

When $\sigma(t) = i$, we calculate the derivative with respect to time of $V_i(\xi(t))$ as

$$\begin{aligned} \dot{V}_i(\xi(t)) &= \dot{\xi}^T(t)P_i\xi(t) + \xi^T(t)P_i\dot{\xi}(t) \\ &= \xi^T(t)\begin{bmatrix} G_i & -P_{0i}\hat{B}_iK_{pi} & -P_{0i}\hat{B}_i\hat{C}_e & P_{0i}\hat{B}_i \\ * & T_i & S_i & P_{1i}\hat{B}_i \\ * & * & Q_i & -P_{2i}\hat{B}_{Fi} \\ * & * & * & -2k_cP_{3i} \end{bmatrix}\xi(t) \\ &\quad + d^T(t)\begin{bmatrix} (\hat{B}_d^i)^TP_{0i} & (\hat{B}_d^i)^TP_{1i} & 0 & 0 \end{bmatrix}\xi(t) + \xi^T(t)\begin{bmatrix} P_{0i}\hat{B}_d^i \\ P_{1i}\hat{B}_d^i \\ 0 \\ 0 \end{bmatrix}d(t), \\ &\leq \xi^T(t)\left(\begin{bmatrix} G_i & -P_{0i}\hat{B}_iK_{pi} & -P_{0i}\hat{B}_iC_e & P_{0i}\hat{B}_i \\ * & T_i & S_i & P_{1i}\hat{B}_i \\ * & * & Q_i & -P_{2i}\hat{B}_{Fi} \\ * & * & * & -2k_cP_{3i} \end{bmatrix} + \varepsilon\begin{bmatrix} P_{0i}\hat{B}_d^i \\ P_{1i}\hat{B}_d^i \\ 0 \\ 0 \end{bmatrix}\begin{bmatrix} P_{0i}\hat{B}_d^i \\ P_{1i}\hat{B}_d^i \\ 0 \\ 0 \end{bmatrix}^T\right)\xi(t) \\ &\quad + \frac{1}{\varepsilon}d^T(t)d(t). \end{aligned} \tag{17}$$

Set $\Xi(t) = y^T(t)y(t) - \frac{1}{\varepsilon}d^T(t)d(t)$. It generates

$$\begin{aligned}
&\dot{V}_i(\xi(t)) + \Xi(t) = \dot{\xi}^T(t)P_i\xi(t) + \xi^T(t)P_i\dot{\xi}(t) + \Xi(t) \\
&\leq \xi^T(t)\left(\begin{bmatrix} G_i & -P_{0i}\hat{B}_iK_{pi} & -P_{0i}\hat{B}_i\hat{C}_e & P_{0i}\hat{B}_i \\ * & T_i & S_i & P_{1i}\hat{B}_i \\ * & * & Q_i & -P_{2i}\hat{B}_{Fi} \\ * & * & * & -2k_cP_{3i} \end{bmatrix} + \varepsilon \begin{bmatrix} P_{0i}\hat{B}_d^i \\ P_{1i}\hat{B}_d^i \\ 0 \\ 0 \end{bmatrix}\begin{bmatrix} P_{0i}\hat{B}_d^i \\ P_{1i}\hat{B}_d^i \\ 0 \\ 0 \end{bmatrix}^T\right)\xi(t) \\
&+\tfrac{1}{\varepsilon}d^T(t)d(t) + \xi^T(t)\begin{bmatrix} \hat{C}^T\hat{C} & 0 & 0 & 0 \\ 0 & 0 & 0 & 0 \\ 0 & 0 & 0 & 0 \\ 0 & 0 & 0 & 0 \end{bmatrix}\xi(t) - \tfrac{1}{\varepsilon}d^T(t)d(t).
\end{aligned} \tag{18}$$

When $d(t) \equiv 0$, if the ith subsystem is activated, via (14a), one deduces

$$\dot{V}_i(\xi(t)) \leq -\alpha V_i(\xi(t)). \tag{19}$$

Without loss of generality, assuming at t_l, the SLS transitions from ith subsystem to jth subsystem. Then, the state $\bar{x}_c(t)$ exhibits discontinuity and jumps from $\bar{x}_c(t_l^-) = \left(x_c(t_l^-) - \Delta_{\sigma(t_{l-1})}(\hat{x}(t_l^-))\right)^T$ to $\bar{x}_c(t_l) = \left(x_c(t_l) - \Delta_{\sigma(t_l)}(\hat{x}(t_l))\right)^T$ at t_l. Let $\Phi = \sum_{n=1}^{l-1}(K_{p\sigma(t_n)} - K_{p\sigma(t_{n-1})})\hat{x}(t_n)$, $K_{pji} = K_{pj} - K_{pi}$ and $\Psi = x_c(t_l) - \Phi$. Employing Lemma 1 in [29], for any $\epsilon_i > 0$, one obtains

$$\begin{aligned}
\frac{V_i(\xi(t_l))}{V_i(\xi(t_l^-))} &\leq \frac{x^T(t_l)P_{0i}x(t_l) + \tilde{x}^T(t_l)P_{1i}\tilde{x}(t_l) + x_e^T(t_l)P_{2i}x_e(t_l)}{x^T(t_l)P_{0i}x(t_l) + \tilde{x}^T(t_l)P_{1i}\tilde{x}(t_l) + x_e^T(t_l)P_{2i}x_e(t_l) + \Psi^TP_{3i}\Psi} \\
&+ \frac{(\Psi - K_{pji}\hat{x}(t_l))^TP_{3i}(\Psi - K_{pji}\hat{x}(t_l))}{x^T(t_l)P_{0i}x(t_l) + \tilde{x}^T(t_l)P_{1i}\tilde{x}(t_l) + x_e^T(t_l)P_{2i}x_e(t_l) + \Psi^TP_{3i}\Psi} \\
&\leq 1 + \frac{\hat{x}^T(t_l)K_{pji}^TP_{3i}K_{pji}\hat{x}(t_l) - 2\hat{x}^T(t_l)K_{pji}^TP_{3i}\Psi}{x^T(t_l)P_{0i}x(t_l) + \tilde{x}^T(t_l)P_{1i}\tilde{x}(t_l) + x_e^T(t_l)P_{2i}x_e(t_l) + \Psi^TP_{3i}\Psi}.
\end{aligned} \tag{20}$$

Denote $\Gamma_{ji} = K_{pji}^TP_{3i}K_{pji}$ and $\lambda_i = \min\{\lambda_{min}(P_{0i}), \lambda_{min}(P_{1i}), \lambda_{min}(P_{2i})\}$,

$$\begin{aligned}
\frac{V_i(\xi(t_l))}{V_i(\xi(t_l^-))} &\leq 1 + \frac{(1+\epsilon_i)\lambda_{max}(\Gamma_{ji})\|\hat{x}(t_l)\|^2 + \frac{1}{\epsilon_i}\Psi^TP_{3i}\Psi}{\lambda_{min}(P_{0i})\|x(t_l)\|^2 + \lambda_{min}(P_{1i})\|\tilde{x}(t_l)\|^2 + \lambda_{min}(P_{2i})\|x_e(t_l)\|^2 + \Psi^TP_{3i}\Psi} \\
&\leq 1 + \frac{2(1+\epsilon_i)\lambda_{max}(\Gamma_{ji})(\|x(t_l)\|^2 + \|\tilde{x}(t_l)\|^2) + \frac{1}{\epsilon_i}\Psi^TP_{3i}\Psi}{\lambda_{min}(P_{0i})\|x(t_l)\|^2 + \lambda_{min}(P_{1i})\|\tilde{x}(t_l)\|^2 + \lambda_{min}(P_{2i})\|x_e(t_l)\|^2 + \Psi^TP_{3i}\Psi} \\
&\leq 1 + \frac{2(1+\epsilon_i)\lambda_{max}(\Gamma_{ji})(\|x(t_l)\|^2 + \|\tilde{x}(t_l)\|^2 + \|x_e(t_l)\|^2) + \frac{1}{\epsilon_i}\Psi^TP_{3i}\Psi}{\lambda_i(\|x(t_l)\|^2 + \|\tilde{x}(t_l)\|^2 + \|x_e(t_l)\|^2) + \Psi^TP_{3i}\Psi}.
\end{aligned} \tag{21}$$

Hence, there is a constant

$$\gamma = 1 + \max\{\sup_{i,j}\frac{2(1+\epsilon_i)\lambda_{max}(\Gamma_{ji})}{\lambda_i}, \sup_i \frac{1}{\epsilon_i}\} > 1$$

such that

$$V_i(\xi(t_l)) \leq \gamma V_i(\xi(t_l^-)). \tag{22}$$

In addition, taking into account the variation in adjacent Lyapunov functions during switching instants, with condition (14b), one has

$$V_j(\xi(t_l)) \leq \mu\gamma V_i(\xi(t_l^-)). \tag{23}$$

Thereby, following a similar proving procedure in [33], via the ADT method, when we denote $\tau_a \geq \frac{ln(\mu\gamma)}{\alpha}$, the SLS (12) has asymptotic stability when $d(t) \equiv 0$.

Under a zero initial condition, when $d(t) \neq 0$, for $\forall d(t) \in L_2[0,\infty)$, we compute the integral of $\dot{V}_i(\xi(t)) + \Xi(t) \leq 0$ over the variable τ, employing a similar induction procedure as the one described in [33], by defining $V(t) = V_{\sigma(t)}(x(t))$, for $t \in [t_l, t_{l+1})$, one obtains

$$\begin{aligned} V(t) &\leq V(t_l)e^{-\alpha(t-t_l)} - \int_{t_l}^{t} e^{-\alpha(t-\tau)}\Xi(\tau)d\tau \\ &\leq \mu\gamma V(t_l^-)e^{-\alpha(t-t_l)} - \int_{t_l}^{t} e^{-\alpha(t-\tau)}\Xi(\tau)d\tau \\ &\leq \cdots \\ &\leq e^{-\alpha(t-t_0)+N_\sigma(t_0,t)ln(\mu\gamma)}V(t_0) - \int_{t_0}^{t} e^{-\alpha(t-\tau)+N_\sigma(\tau,t)ln(\mu\gamma)}\Xi(\tau)d\tau. \end{aligned} \tag{24}$$

Further, due to $\mu\gamma > 1$, by setting other positive constants $\lambda > 0$ and $\hat{\alpha} < \alpha$, combined with the ADT condition:

$$N_\sigma(\tau,t) \leq N_0 + \frac{t-\tau}{\tau_d}, \; N_0 = \frac{\lambda}{ln(\mu\gamma)}, \; \tau_d = \frac{ln(\mu\gamma)}{\alpha - \hat{\alpha}}. \tag{25}$$

Then, from (24) and $V(t) \geq 0$, one obtains

$$\begin{aligned} &\int_{t_0}^{t} e^{-\alpha(t-\tau)}y^T(\tau)y(\tau)d\tau \leq V(t) + \int_{t_0}^{t} e^{-\alpha(t-\tau)+N_\sigma(\tau,t)ln(\mu\gamma)}y^T(\tau)y(\tau)d\tau \\ &\leq e^{-\alpha(t-t_0)+N_\sigma(t_0,t)ln(\mu\gamma)}V(t_0) + \frac{1}{\varepsilon}\int_{t_0}^{t} e^{-\alpha(t-\tau)+N_\sigma(\tau,t)ln(\mu\gamma)}d^T(\tau)d(\tau)d\tau \\ &= e^{\lambda-\hat{\alpha}(t-t_0)}V(t_0) + \frac{1}{\varepsilon}\int_{t_0}^{t} e^{\lambda-\hat{\alpha}(t-\tau)}d^T(\tau)d(\tau)d\tau. \end{aligned} \tag{26}$$

By integrating the above inequality from t_0 to ∞, one obtains

$$\frac{1}{\alpha}\int_{t_0}^{\infty} y^T(\tau)y(\tau)d\tau \leq \frac{e^\lambda}{\hat{\alpha}}V(t_0) + \frac{e^\lambda}{\varepsilon\hat{\alpha}}\int_{t_0}^{\infty} d^T(\tau)d(\tau)d\tau. \tag{27}$$

Thus, addressing the ADBT control problem for the system (12) involves selecting the L_2 gain as $\frac{\alpha e^\lambda}{\varepsilon\hat{\alpha}}$ and $\delta(x_0) = \frac{\alpha e^\lambda}{\hat{\alpha}}V(x_0)$.

In the given scenario, Theorem 1 provides a collection of sufficient conditions for resolving the ADBT control design issue. In fact, condition (14) is formulated nonlinearly through a matrix inequality. Then, it becomes apparent that solving (14a) and (14b) simultaneously presents challenges. By setting $\mu = \frac{\max_{\kappa\in\{0,1,2,3\},i\in M}\{\lambda_{max}\{P_{\kappa i}\}\}}{\min_{\kappa\in\{0,1,2,3\},i\in M}\{\lambda_{min}\{P_{\kappa i}\}\}}$, condition (14b) is satisfied, directly. In the following, we illustrate how to solve the condition (14a).

Corollary 1. *With given constants $\alpha > 0$, $k_c > 0$, assume there are symmetric positive definite matrices P_{0i}, P_{1i}, P_{2i}, P_{3i} and appropriate matrices L_i, K_{pi}, $\hat{A}_{ei}$, $\hat{B}_{ei}$, $\hat{C}_e$ and K_{ei} such that for $\forall i \in M$,*

$$\begin{bmatrix} \Gamma_{0i} & -\hat{B}_i W_{1i} + \hat{B}_d^i(\hat{B}_d^i)^T \\ * & \Gamma_{1i} \end{bmatrix} < 0, \tag{28a}$$

$$\begin{bmatrix} \tilde{A}_{2i}^T + \tilde{A}_{2i} + \alpha P_{2i} + \check{\Gamma}_{11}^i - \check{\Gamma}_{12}^i & \tilde{B}_{2i} - \Gamma_{11}^i P_{0i}\hat{B}_i - \Gamma_{12}^i P_{1i}\hat{B}_i \\ \tilde{B}_{2i}^T + \Gamma_{21}^i P_{0i}\hat{B}_i\hat{C}_e - \Gamma_{22}^i(\hat{C}^T\tilde{B}_{2ei} - P_{1i}\hat{B}_i\hat{C}_e) & (\alpha - 2k_c)P_{3i} - \Gamma_{21}^i P_{0i}\hat{B}_i - \Gamma_{22}^i P_{1i}\hat{B}_i \end{bmatrix} < 0, \tag{28b}$$

where

$$\Gamma_{0i} = (\hat{A}_i X_{0i} + \hat{B}_i W_{0i}) + (\hat{A}_i X_{0i} + \hat{B}_i W_{0i})^T + \hat{B}_d^i (\hat{B}_d^i)^T + X_{0i}\hat{C}^T\hat{C}X_{0i} + \alpha X_{0i},$$
$$\Gamma_{1i} = \hat{B}_d^i(\hat{B}_d^i)^T + (\hat{A}_i X_{1i} - \Theta_i) + (\hat{A}_i X_{1i} - \Theta_i)^T,$$
$$X_{0i} = P_{0i}^{-1},\ W_{0i} = K_{pi}X_{0i},\ X_{1i} = P_{1i}^{-1},\ W_{1i} = K_{pi}X_{1i},\ \Theta_i = L_i\hat{C}X_{1i},$$
$$\begin{bmatrix} G_i + G_d^i + \hat{C}^T\hat{C} + \alpha P_{0i} & -P_{0i}\hat{B}_iK_{pi} + D_i \\ * & W_i + T_i + \alpha P_{1i} \end{bmatrix}^{-1} = \begin{bmatrix} \Xi_{11}^i & \Xi_{12}^i \\ \Xi_{21}^i & \Xi_{22}^i \end{bmatrix},$$
$$\Gamma_{11}^i = -\hat{C}_e^T\hat{B}_i^TP_{0i}\Xi_{11}^i + (\tilde{B}_{2ei}^T\hat{C} - \hat{C}_e^T\hat{B}_i^TP_{1i})\Xi_{21}^i,\ \check{\Gamma}_{11}^i = \Gamma_{11}^iP_{0i}\hat{B}_i\hat{C}_e,$$
$$\Gamma_{12}^i = -\hat{C}_e^T\hat{B}_i^TP_{0i}\Xi_{12}^i + (\tilde{B}_{2ei}^T\hat{C} - \hat{C}_e^T\hat{B}_i^TP_{1i})\Xi_{22}^i,\ \check{\Gamma}_{12}^i = \Gamma_{12}^i(\hat{C}^T\tilde{B}_{2ei} - P_{1i}\hat{B}_i\hat{C}_e),$$
$$\Gamma_{21}^i = \hat{B}_i^TP_{0i}\Xi_{11}^i + \hat{B}_i^TP_{1i}\Xi_{21}^i,\ \Gamma_{22}^i = \hat{B}_i^TP_{0i}\Xi_{12}^i + \hat{B}_i^TP_{1i}\Xi_{22}^i,$$
$$\tilde{A}_{2i} = P_{2i}\hat{A}_{ei} + \tilde{B}_{2i}\hat{C}_e,\ \tilde{B}_{2i} = P_{2i}\hat{B}_{Fi},\ \tilde{B}_{2ei} = \hat{B}_{ei}^TP_{2i},\ \hat{B}_{ei} = \hat{B}_{Fi}K_{ei},$$
$$D_i = P_{0i}\hat{B}_d^i(\hat{B}_d^i)^TP_{1i},\ W_i = P_{1i}\hat{B}_d^i(\hat{B}_d^i)^TP_{1i},\ T_i = (\hat{A}_i - L_iC)^TP_{1i} + P_{1i}(\hat{A}_i - L_iC).$$

Then, the condition (14a) is solvable.

Proof. Firstly, set

$$\begin{bmatrix} G_i + G_d^i + \hat{C}^T\hat{C} + \alpha P_{0i} & -P_{0i}\hat{B}_iK_{pi} + D_i & -P_{0i}\hat{B}_i\hat{C}_e & P_{0i}\hat{B}_i \\ * & W_i + T_i + \alpha P_{1i} & S_i & P_{1i}\hat{B}_i \\ * & * & Q_i + \alpha P_{2i} & -P_{2i}\hat{B}_{Fi} \\ * & * & * & -2k_cP_{3i} + \alpha P_{3i} \end{bmatrix} = \begin{bmatrix} S_{11}^i & S_{12}^i \\ S_{21}^i & S_{22}^i \end{bmatrix}.$$

with denoting

$$S_{11}^i = \begin{bmatrix} G_i + G_d^i + \hat{C}^T\hat{C} + \alpha P_{0i} & -P_{0i}\hat{B}_iK_{pi} + D_i \\ * & W_i + T_i + \alpha P_{1i} \end{bmatrix},$$
$$S_{12}^i = \begin{bmatrix} -P_{0i}\hat{B}_i\hat{C}_e & P_{0i}\hat{B}_i \\ S_i & P_{1i}\hat{B}_i \end{bmatrix},\ S_{21}^i = \begin{bmatrix} -\hat{C}_e^T\hat{B}_i^TP_{0i} & S_i^T \\ \hat{B}_i^TP_{0i} & \hat{B}_i^TP_{1i} \end{bmatrix},$$
$$S_{22}^i = \begin{bmatrix} Q_i + \alpha P_{2i} & -P_{2i}\hat{B}_{Fi} \\ * & -2k_cP_{3i} + \alpha P_{3i} \end{bmatrix}.$$

Then, by employing the Schur complement lemma, multiplying S_{11}^i by $\mathrm{diag}\{P_{0i}^{-1}, I\}$ and $\mathrm{diag}\{I, P_{1i}^{-1}\}$ on both sides, the condition (28a) is deduced, where P_{0i}^{-1}, $K_{pi}X_{0i}$, P_{1i}^{-1}, $K_{pi}X_{1i}$ and $L_i\hat{C}X_{1i}$ in S_{11}^i are replaced by their specific expressions X_{0i}, W_{0i}, X_{1i}, W_{1i} and Θ_i. Hence, the condition (28a) is a LMI. Thereby, with the fixed constant α, one can easily compute P_{0i}, P_{1i}. L_i and K_{pi}.

Moreover, with the above chosen matrices, the condition (28b) is deduced by $S_{22}^i - S_{12}^i(S_{11}^i)^{-1}S_{21}^i \leq 0$, where (28b) is also a LMI. Then, with fixed constants α and k_c, one can easily compute $\hat{A}_{ei}$, $\hat{B}_{Fi}$, K_{ei}, $\hat{C}_e$, P_{2i} and P_{3i}. Thus, by fixing constants α and k_c, the computation of the controller gains K_{pi} and the switched EID estimator can be carried out. □

4. Simulation Example

This section is devoted to demonstrating the effectiveness of the developed ADBT control. We consider a switching resistor–inductor–capacitor (RLC) circuit [10] which is shown in Figure 1

$$\dot{z}(t) = \hat{A}_{\sigma(t)}z(t) + \hat{B}_{\sigma(t)}u(t), \tag{29a}$$
$$y(t) = \hat{C}z(t), \tag{29b}$$

where $z(t) = [q_c\ \phi_L]^T$. q_c represents the charge on the capacitor C_j, $j \in \{1,2\}$. ϕ_L indicates the flux through inductor L. The input voltage supply is noted as $u(t)$. $\sigma(t) \in \{1,2\}$ indicates the switching signal. Let us assume that the model (29) is affected by the disturbance $d(t) = e^{-2t}\cos t$.

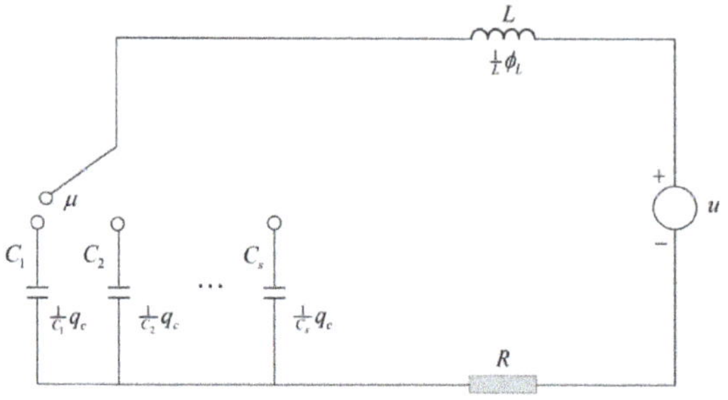

Figure 1. A switching resistor–inductor–capacitor (RLC) circuit.

Below, the model data are presented.

$$\hat{A}_i = \begin{bmatrix} 0 & \frac{1}{L} \\ -\frac{1}{\hat{C}_i} & -\frac{R}{L} \end{bmatrix}, \; \hat{B}_1 = \begin{bmatrix} 0 \\ 1 \end{bmatrix}, \; \hat{B}_2 = \begin{bmatrix} 0.1 \\ 1 \end{bmatrix}, \; \hat{B}_d^1 = \begin{bmatrix} 0.5 \\ -0.3 \end{bmatrix}, \; \hat{B}_d^2 = \begin{bmatrix} 0.2 \\ -0.1 \end{bmatrix},$$
$$\hat{C} = \begin{bmatrix} 1 & 0 \end{bmatrix}, \; R = 3, \; L = 2, \; C_1 = 2, \; C_2 = 4, \; z(t_0) = [3 \; -3]^T.$$

In the ADBT control designing scenario, by computing the conditions of Corollary 1, we set $\alpha = 0.8$, $k_c = 2$, $\hat{A}_{e1} = -31$, $\hat{A}_{e2} = -30$, $\hat{B}_{F1} = 30$, $\hat{B}_{F2} = 30$, $\hat{C}_e = 1$, $K_{e1} = K_{e2} = 1.7 \times 10^{-5}$, $K_{p1} = \begin{bmatrix} 0 & 1 \end{bmatrix}$, $K_{p2} = \begin{bmatrix} 0 & 0.8 \end{bmatrix}$, $L_1 = \begin{bmatrix} -2.3016 & 0.1620 \end{bmatrix}^T$, $L_2 = \begin{bmatrix} -3.1270 & 0.1765 \end{bmatrix}^T$. The results indicate that the ADBT control strategy exhibits continuous behavior. Figure 2 illustrates the switching rule. In Figure 3, the amount of charge $q_c(t)$ stored in the capacitor and the magnetic flux passing through the inductance L are depicted. As shown in Figure 4, the power input source $u(t)$ demonstrates that no bumping occurs.

To verify the effectiveness of the proposed ADBT control designing strategy, we use the sawtooth wave signal as a disturbance signal affecting the system. The sawtooth wave signal is commonly generated in many circuit models and is difficult to describe using general exogenous systems. From Figures 2–4, one can clearly see that the proposed ADBT control strategy can estimate the sawtooth wave disturbance and, at the same time, achieve good BT performance. Hence, it can be concluded that the designed ADBT control strategy is effective.

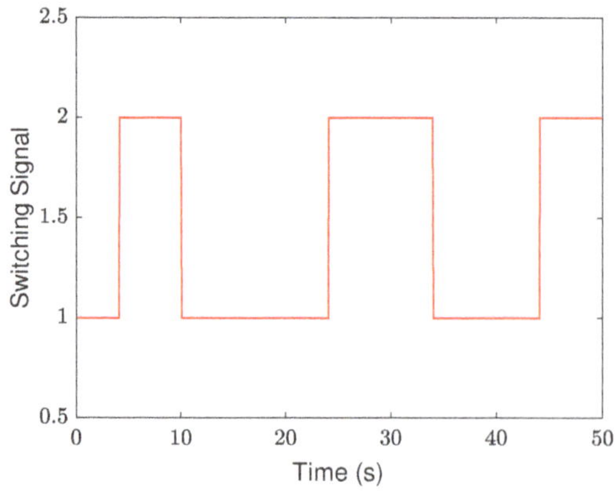

Figure 2. The switching signal $\sigma(t)$ of the switching RLC circuit.

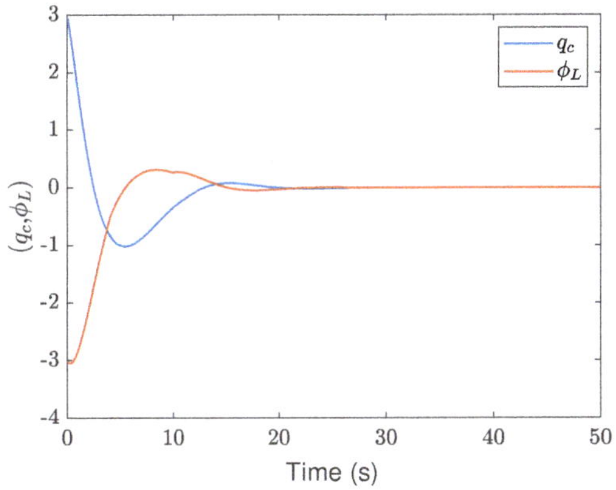

Figure 3. The charge $q_c(t)$ in the switched capacitor $C_{\sigma(t)}$ and the flux $\phi_L(t)$ in the inductance L.

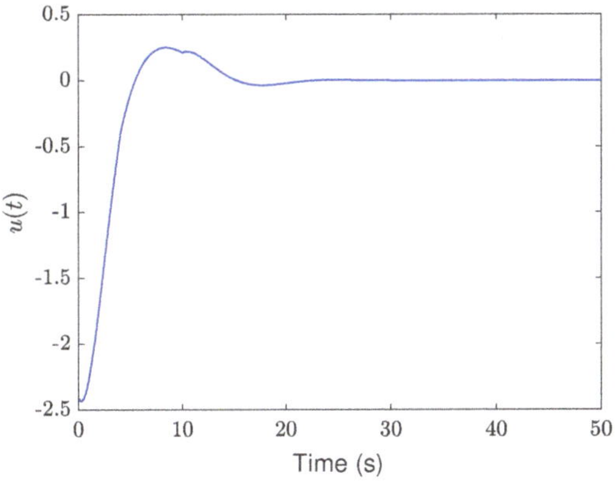

Figure 4. The input power source $u(t)$ of the switching RLC circuit.

5. Discussion

This paper proposes a new configuration for ADBT control via a switched EID methodology for switched linear systems. Although the ADBT control design problem has been solved in this paper, there still exist three aspects worth discussing. First, while our control method achieved good results in AD response, the convergence speed was slow. This is attributable to the choice of adjustable parameters and is worth studying in the future. Second, the ADBT control method in this paper is for switched linear systems; however, nonlinearities appear in most practical systems, such as spacecraft, robots and industrial processes. Therefore, this requires further research and discussion for switched nonlinear systems. A possible solution to the current implementation is to develop a switched nonlinear EID approach. We will leave this problem for future work. Additionally, we will try to apply the proposed control method to switched systems with more general structures and switched multi-agent systems.

6. Conclusions

In this paper, we studied the ADBT control design problem for switched linear systems. Firstly, a new switched EID estimator was established to estimate the impact of external disturbances for switched linear systems. Then, through the collaborative efforts of a switched EID estimator and a compensator, a continuous controller and a switching rule characterized by ADT were dual designed. Finally, by employing a switching RLC circuit model, we successfully demonstrated the effectiveness and practicality of the proposed ADBT control method. Through the simulation result, we showcased the great potential of the switched EID estimator in practical applications, offering valuable insights for future research and development. This research provides a new approach to solve the ADBT control design problem for switched linear systems. Moreover, notice that time delays and faults often occur in the practical systems. As an interesting research topic, the interaction between delays and the BT performance and the interaction between faults and BT performance need to be studied in the future.

Author Contributions: Conceptualization, Q.L.; methodology, Q.L. and J.W.; validation, J.W., Q.L. and P.Y.; formal analysis, Q.L.; investigation, J.W.; writing—original draft preparation, J.W.; writing—review and editing, Q.L.; visualization, Q.L.; supervision, P.Y.; funding acquisition, P.Y. All authors have read and agreed to the published version of the manuscript.

Funding: This research was funded by the National Natural Science Foundation of China grant number 62003010 and the R&D Program of Beijing Municipal Education Commission grant number KM202410005036.

Data Availability Statement: The data are contained within the article.

Conflicts of Interest: The authors declare no conflicts of interest.

References

1. Zhang, J.; Huang, J.; Li, C. Distributed interval observers with switching topology design for cyber-physical systems. *Mathematics* **2024**, *12*, 163. [CrossRef]
2. Ronanki, D.; Dasari, Y.; Williamson, S.S. Power electronics-based switched supercapacitor bank circuits with enhanced power delivery capability for pulsed power applications. In Proceedings of the 2021 IEEE Applied Power Electronics Conference and Exposition (APEC), Phoenix, AZ, USA, 14–17 June 2021; pp. 2271–2276.
3. Shi, Y.; Sun, X. Bumpless transfer control for switched linear systems and its application to aero-engines. *IEEE Trans. Circuits Syst. I Regul. Pap.* **2021**, *68*, 2171–2182. [CrossRef]
4. Zong, G.; Yang, D.; Lam, J.; Song, X. Fault-tolerant control of switched LPV systems: A bumpless transfer approach. *IEEE/ASME Trans. Mechatron.* **2021**, *27*, 1436–1446.
5. Chen, W.; Yang, J.; Guo, L.; Li, S. Disturbance-observer-based control and related methods—An overview. *IEEE Trans. Ind. Electron.* **2015**, *63*, 1083–1095. [CrossRef]
6. Han, J. From PID to active disturbance rejection control. *IEEE Trans. Ind. Electron.* **2009**, *56*, 900–906. [CrossRef]
7. Guo, L.; Cao, S. *Anti-Disturbance Control for Systems with Multiple Disturbances*; CRC Press: Boca Raton, FL, USA, 2013.
8. Guo, L.; Cao, S. Anti-disturbance control theory for systems with multiple disturbances: A survey. *ISA Trans.* **2014**, *53*, 846–849. [CrossRef] [PubMed]
9. Yong, K.; Chen, M.; Wu, Q. Anti-disturbance control for nonlinear systems based on interval observer. *IEEE Trans. Ind. Electron.* **2019**, *67*, 1261–1269. [CrossRef]
10. Zhao, Y.; Wu, D.; Xu, C.; Yu, S.; Liu, T.; Yang, D. Adaptive anti-disturbance bumpless transfer control for switched neural network systems with its application to switched circuit model. *IEEE Trans. Circuits Syst. I Regul. Pap.* **2024**, *71*, 411–420. [CrossRef]
11. Liu, F.; Chen, M.; Shi, S.; Tao, L. Almost output regulation for turbofan switched systems under multi-source disturbances and time delay. *Int. J. Robust Nonlinear Control* **2024**, *34*, 378–396. [CrossRef]
12. Yang, Y.; Zheng, W.; Liu, B. Adaptive anti-disturbance control for systems with saturating input via dynamic neural network disturbance modeling. *IEEE Trans. Cybern.* **2020**, *52*, 5290–5300.
13. Zhang, S.; Zhang, B.; Li, X.; Wang, Z.; Qian, F. A method of enhancing fast steering mirror's ability of anti-disturbance based on adaptive robust control. *Math. Probl. Eng.* **2019**, *2019*, 2152858. [CrossRef]
14. Huang, Y.; Xue, W. Active disturbance rejection control: Methodology and theoretical analysis. *ISA Trans.* **2014**, *53*, 963–976. [CrossRef] [PubMed]
15. Feng, H.; Guo, B. Active disturbance rejection control: Old and new results. *Annu. Rev. Control* **2017**, *44*, 238–248. [CrossRef]
16. Du, Y.; Cao, W.; She, J.; Wu, M.; Fang, M.; Kawata, S. Disturbance rejection and robustness of improved equivalent-input-disturbance-based system. *IEEE Trans. Cybern.* **2021**, *52*, 8537–8546. [CrossRef]
17. Yu, P.; Liu, K.Z.; Wu, M.; She, J. Improved Equivalent-Input-Disturbance Approach Based on H_∞ Control. *IEEE Trans. Ind. Electron.* **2019**, *67*, 8670–8679. [CrossRef]
18. Mei, Q.; She, J.; Wang, F.; Nakanishi, Y.; Hashimoto, H.; Chugo, D. Disturbance rejection and control system design using 1-inverse-based equivalent-input-disturbance approach. *IEEE Trans. Ind. Electron.* **2022**, *70*, 1666–1675. [CrossRef]
19. Zhang, L.; Xu, K.; Yang, J.; Han, M.; Yuan, S. Transition-dependent bumpless transfer control synthesis of switched linear systems. *IEEE Trans. Autom. Control* **2022**, *68*, 1678–1684. [CrossRef]

20. Wu, T.; Zhu, Y.; Zhang, L.; Shi, P. Bumpless transfer model predictive control for Markov jump linear systems. *IEEE Trans. Autom. Control* **2023**. [CrossRef]
21. Yang, Y.; Huang, Z.; Zhang, P. Double-observer-based bumpless transfer control of switched positive systems. *Mathematics* **2024**, *12*, 1724. [CrossRef]
22. Li, J.; Zhao, J. Bumpless transfer control for switched linear systems with bump induced event-triggered mechanism. *J. Frankl. Inst.* **2023**, *360*, 6081–6098. [CrossRef]
23. Wang, Y.; Wang, X.; Zhao, Y.; Chen, Y.; Li, W. Finite-time event-triggered bumpless transfer control for switched systems. *Int. J. Robust Nonlinear Control* **2022**, *32*, 6962–6982. [CrossRef]
24. Zong, G.; Huang, C.; Yang, D. Bumpless transfer fault detection for switched systems: A state-dependent switching approach. *Sci. China Inf. Sci.* **2021**, *64*, 172208. [CrossRef]
25. Shi, J.; Zhao, J. State bumpless transfer control for a class of switched descriptor systems. *IEEE Trans. Circuits Syst. I Regul. Pap.* **2021**, *68*, 3846–3856. [CrossRef]
26. Zhang, S.; Zhao, J. Dwell-Time-Dependent H_∞ Bumpless transfer control for discrete-time switched interval type-2 fuzzy systems. *IEEE Trans. Fuzzy Syst.* **2021**, *30*, 2426–2437. [CrossRef]
27. Wen, S.X.; Shi, Y.; Pan, Z.R.; Sun, X.M. Practical bumpless transfer design for switched linear systems: Application to aeroengines. *IEEE Trans. Ind. Inform.* **2023**, *19*, 11910–11919. [CrossRef]
28. Wu, F.; Wang, D.; Lian, J. Bumpless transfer control for switched systems via a dynamic feedback and a bump-dependent switching law. *IEEE Trans. Cybern.* **2022**, *53*, 5372–5379. [CrossRef]
29. Shi, Y.; Zhao, J.; Sun, X. A bumpless transfer control strategy for switched systems and its application to an aero-engine. *IEEE Trans. Ind. Inform.* **2020**, *17*, 52–62. [CrossRef]
30. Zhao, Y.; Zhao, J. H_∞ reliable bumpless transfer control for switched systems with state and rate constraints. *IEEE Trans. Syst. Man Cybern. Syst.* **2018**, *50*, 3925–3935. [CrossRef]
31. Yang, D.; Zong, G.; Nguang, S.K.; Zhao, X. Bumpless transfer H_∞ anti-disturbance control of switching Markovian LPV systems under the hybrid switching. *IEEE Trans. Cybern.* **2020**, *52*, 2833–2845. [CrossRef]
32. Levine, W.S. *The Control Handbook*; CRC Press: Boca Raton, FL, USA, 1996.
33. Zhai, G.; Hu, B.; Kazunori, Y.; Michel, A. L_2 gain analysis of switched systems with average dwell time. *Trans. Soc. Instrum. Control Eng.* **2000**, *36*, 937–942. [CrossRef]

mathematics

MDPI

Article

Time-Series Prediction of Electricity Load for Charging Piles in a Region of China Based on Broad Learning System

Liansong Yu [1,2,†] and Xiaohu Ge [1,*,†]

[1] School of Electronic Information and Communications, Huazhong University of Science and Technology, Wuhan 430074, China; d202080754@hust.edu.cn

[2] State Grid Electric Power Research Institute Wuhan Nanrui Co., Ltd., Wuhan 430070, China

* Correspondence: xhge@mail.hust.edu.cn

† These authors contributed equally to this work.

Abstract: This paper introduces a novel electricity load time-series prediction model, utilizing a broad learning system to tackle the challenge of low prediction accuracy caused by the unpredictable nature of electricity load sequences in a specific region of China. First, a correlation analysis with mutual information is utilized to identify the key factors affecting the electricity load. Second, variational mode decomposition is employed to obtain different mode information, and then a broad learning system is utilized to build a prediction model with different mode information. Finally, particle swarm optimization is used to fuse the prediction models under different modes. Simulation experiments using real data validate the efficiency of the proposed method, demonstrating that it offers higher accuracy compared to advanced modeling techniques and can assist in optimal electricity-load scheduling decision-making. Additionally, the R^2 of the proposed model is 0.9831, the P_{RMSE} is 21.8502, the P_{MAE} is 17.0097, and the P_{MAPE} is 2.6468.

Keywords: electricity load; time-series prediction; broad learning system; variational mode decomposition; actual data

MSC: 68T20

1. Introduction

Load forecasting plays a critical role in ensuring the reliable operation and efficient management of smart grids. The precise prediction of electricity demand is a crucial step in enhancing the safety and cost-effectiveness of charging stations. Additionally, it serves as a key factor in supporting smart grid security monitoring, cost management, regulatory compliance, and decision-making processes.

Currently, traditional load forecasting methods include wavelet analysis, regression analysis, neural network, support vector machine, and Monte Carlo simulation [1–3]. For example, Buzna et al. [4] proposed a hierarchical probabilistic load prediction method, which utilizes a hierarchical approach to decompose the problem into sub-problems in low-level areas, combines principal component analysis to reduce the dimensionality of the sub-problems, and then solves the problem by standard probabilistic models, such as gradient-enhanced regression tree, quantile regression forest method, and quantile regression neural network, so that the total load of high-level geographic areas can be predicted. Yi et al. [5] employed Monte Carlo modeling and Markov decision making to determine drivers' travel paths, and the results show that changes in the travel chain lead to significant differences in the distribution of charging loads between weekdays and weekends, and that high temperatures and traffic congestion cause an increase in the amplitude of charging loads. Tang et al. [6] introduced a probabilistic model for node charging demand by considering spatiotemporal dynamics within graph-theoretic integrated systems. Zhu et al. [7] proposed a charging load prediction method for electric vehicles based on the long short-term memory method, and the simulation results based on the actual data show that this method has better performance. Rao et al. [8] proposed a new class of nonlinear functional regression models. The above methods are able to achieve an effective prediction of electricity loads to a certain extent, but they still suffer from problems such as underfitting and the tendency to fall into local optimization during training.

In addition, electricity load is subject to randomness and uncertainty due to a variety of random factors such as traffic, weather, etc., which makes it difficult to choose an appropriate method. In recent years, a variety of deep learning algorithms have been utilized in power system forecasting. For example, Wang et al. [9] established a photovoltaic power prediction model based on wavelet transform and convolutional neural network. Chang et al. [10] proposed a prediction model for photovoltaic output day ahead based on deep belief network. Yi et al. [11] proposed a time-series prediction of monthly commercial electric vehicle charging loads based on a deep sequence-to-sequence model. Compared with single-layer networks, deep neural networks show a higher prediction accuracy, but their complex network structure also brings problems such as time-consuming training and difficulty in tuning parameters. For this reason, a new neural network structure, i.e., a broad learning system (BLS), has been proposed [12,13]. And some scholars have applied it to multi-view classification [14], harmonic detection [15], and energy consumption prediction [16], which have all achieved computational results with high accuracy while ensuring computational efficiency. However, no study in the literature has addressed the application of BLS in electricity load prediction. Therefore, the application of BLS to electricity load prediction in this paper is of great research significance.

This paper introduces a new electricity load time-series prediction model based on BLS, with the goal of addressing issues related to redundant, periodic, and stochastic electricity load data, as well as reducing the time spent training deep neural networks as seen in previous research. Initially, the data correlation analysis method is employed to identify the primary factors that have a direct impact on the electricity load. Then, the variational modal decomposition [17] is used to obtain the data under different modes; and the BLS-based electricity load prediction models are established for different modes, respectively. Finally, a multi-model fusion strategy based on particle swarm optimization (PSO) [18,19] is proposed in order to fuse the prediction models in different modes. At the same time, experiments are being carried out using actual electricity load data to confirm the efficacy of the proposed method.

This paper is structured as follows. Section 2 analyzes the electricity load data characteristics. Section 3 shows in detail how to build an electricity load time-series prediction model. Simulation experiments based on actual data are given in Section 4. Section 5 provides a summary of the paper and outlines potential future research directions.

2. Analysis of Electricity Load Characteristics

This section briefly analyzes the characteristics of electricity load.

2.1. Load Characteristics

Load characteristics in power systems include the following:

1. Periodicity: Electricity load can be based on time-divided cycles to complete electricity load prediction. Periodicity shows that the change trend of electricity load is roughly the same in a continuous period of time and is roughly the same as a change law measured in days.
2. Conditionality: The methods of load prediction in the power system all need specific conditions, which need to be satisfied after the conditions in order to minimize the likelihood of distortion of the results.
3. Randomness; Electricity load can reflect randomness in cyclical loads, where the load of electricity used on any given day can change randomly. In real life, such randomly changing loads are more difficult to predict.

These characteristics must be taken into account for an accurate time-series prediction model of electricity load.

2.2. Analysis of Influencing Factors of Electricity Load

The electricity load prediction system is a multivariate input nonlinear system. The electricity load is affected by a variety of variables, and the correlation between the variables and the electricity load in the prediction system of different regions shows different correlations. Therefore, if the system wants to better predict the changes of the electricity load, and to design a high-precision and high-performance electricity load prediction model, it must first comprehend the factors that influence these fluctuations.

1. Climatic factor: Climatic factors include temperature, humidity, and rainfall. Among them, temperature is one of the many influencing factors that have the greatest impact on the change in electricity load. Typically, there is a relationship between temperature and electricity demand, meaning that fluctuations in temperature impact shifts in electricity usage.
2. Date factor: Electricity load is subject to change with time; the normal electricity load change will not jump in a split second and a complete daily load in different moments of the load value is not the same. The selection of date factors will directly affect the effect of electricity load prediction.
3. Random factor: The factors affecting electricity load prediction are not limited to the above, but include the influence of a variety of factors. The main random factors are holidays, policies, etc. Therefore, it is necessary to select appropriate influencing factors according to the actual electricity consumption, and to analyze the selection of influencing factors through a prediction error of electricity load prediction.

3. Time-Series Prediction Model of Electricity Load Using BLS

This section describes how to build a time-series prediction model of electricity load for charging piles using BLS in a region of China.

3.1. Design of Electricity Load Time-Series Modeling Structure

Due to the large number and complexity of influencing factors affecting electricity load, it is essential to take these complex characteristics into account in order to establish an accurate time-series prediction model for electricity load. A novel modeling structure is then proposed, as depicted in Figure 1.

From Figure 1, the correlation analysis of the electricity load data is firstly carried out to determine the main factors affecting the electricity load. Due to the complexity and variability in electricity load data, we consider the use of variational modal decomposition to process the data to obtain different feature components. Based on these feature components, the electricity load prediction models based on the broad learning system are built, respectively. However, the prediction performance of different models varies, so we propose a multi-model fusion strategy based on PSO to improve the performance of the electricity load time-series prediction model.

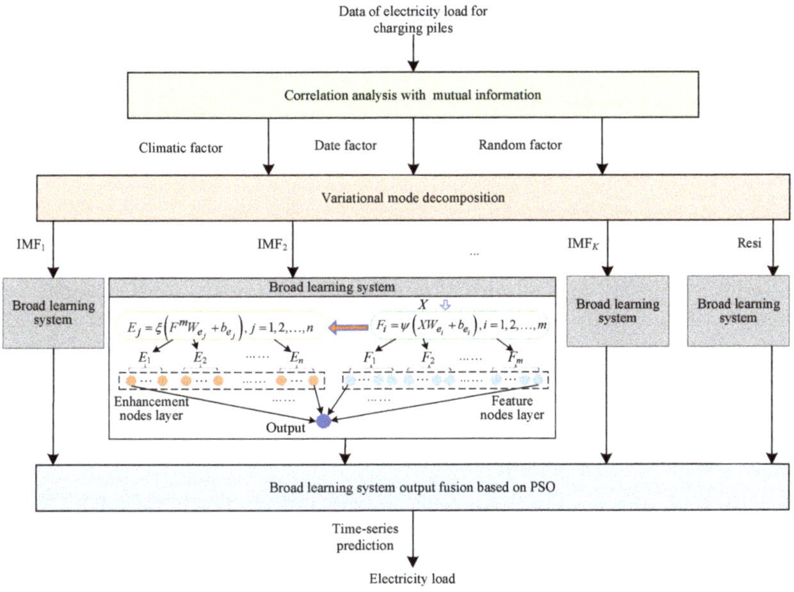

Figure 1. Electricity load time-series modeling structure.

3.2. Correlation Analysis and Modal Decomposition

Based on the analysis of electricity load-related characteristics, it is clear that the factors related to electricity load need to be obtained for modeling. There may be redundancies in these factors, which can affect the accuracy of electricity load prediction. In order to avoid this problem, the mutual information method [20] is adopted in this paper for the selection of the main affecting factors. The mutual information value between the electricity load and related factors is calculated as

$$I(X,Y) = \sum_{x\in X}\sum_{y\in Y} p(x_o,y_o)\log\frac{p(x_o,y_o)}{p(x_o)p(y_o)}, \tag{1}$$

where $X = [x_1, x_2, \ldots, x_o, \ldots, x_N]$ and $Y = [y_1, y_2, \ldots, y_o, \ldots, y_N]$ are related factors and electricity load, respectively. Moreover, a higher value of mutual information indicates a higher degree of correlation between the two parameters.

On this basis, it is also necessary to process the historical information of electricity load to extract its potential cyclical features, which will enhance the model training process. The variational modal decomposition method utilized in this paper is able to separate the original signal into several individual FM–AM signals with varying central frequencies. While the empirical mode decomposition can decompose the signal from high frequency to low frequency, it is plagued by end-point effects and mode overlapping, potentially causing the resulting modes to inadequately capture the intrinsic properties of the original signal. The variational modal decomposition method utilizes Wiener filtering, Hilbert transform, and frequency mixing techniques to convert the signal decomposition challenge into a variational constraint-solving problem. This approach successfully addresses the issues of end-point effects and mode aliasing encountered in empirical modal decomposition.

The variational modal decomposition method breaks down the initial data into a series of eigenmode functions that vary in center frequencies based on a predetermined number of decompositions. The method takes the optimal center frequency and power spectrum center of each eigenmode function as the target, and the sum of the decomposed signals is equal to the original signal as the constraint.

$$\begin{cases} \min_{\{u_k\},\{\omega_k\}} \left\{ \sum_k^K \left\| \partial_t [(\delta(t) + \frac{j}{\pi t}) * u_k(t)] e^{-j\omega_k t} \right\|_2^2 \right\} \\ \text{s.t. } f(t) = \sum_k^K u_k(t) \end{cases} \tag{2}$$

where $u_k(t)$ and ω_k are, respectively, the eigenmode function obtained from the decomposition of electricity load data and the corresponding center frequency, $f(t)$ is the original signal, $\delta(t)$ is the impulse function, and K is the artificially set decomposition quantity.

In order to solve the above constraint equation, it is transformed into an unconstrained problem by introducing the Lagrange multiplier $\lambda(t)$ and the quadratic penalty term α. The unconstrained equations' saddle points are determined through the alternating direction multiplier method, with updates for the intrinsic modal function $u_k(t)$, center frequency ω_k, and the frequency domain of the Lagrange multiplier $\lambda(t)$ as outlined in the following equations.

$$\hat{u}^{n+1}(\omega) = \frac{\hat{f}(\omega) - \sum_{i \neq k} \hat{u}_i(\omega) + \frac{\hat{\lambda}(\omega)}{2}}{1 + 2\alpha(\omega - \omega_k)^2}, \tag{3}$$

$$\omega_k^{n+1} = \frac{\int_0^\infty \omega |\hat{u}_k(\omega)|^2 d\omega}{\int_0^\infty |\hat{u}_k(\omega)|^2 d\omega}, \tag{4}$$

$$\hat{\lambda}^{n+1}(\omega) = \hat{\lambda}^n(\omega) + \tau \left[\hat{f}(\omega) - \sum_k \hat{u}_k^{n+1}(\omega) \right], \tag{5}$$

$$\sum_k \frac{\left\| \hat{u}_k^{n+1} - \hat{u}_k^n \right\|_2^2}{\left\| \hat{u}_k^n \right\|_2^2} \leq \varepsilon. \tag{6}$$

After performing continuous iterations, the inverse Fourier transform of the decomposition results is conducted to obtain K sets of eigenmode functions.

3.3. Electricity Load Time-Series Modeling Based on Broad Learning System

Based on the structure of the BLS in Figure 1, the features extracted from the input data in the BLS are mapped into feature nodes, which are then subject to nonlinear transformation to produce enhancement nodes. These nodes, along with the feature nodes, are connected directly to the output layer. Unlike deep learning, which improves fitting ability by increasing the number of neural network layers, BLS enhances network performance by expanding feature nodes and enhancement nodes in width. This flat network structure is characterized by fast training.

The input data X are first obtained by feature extraction to obtain a series of feature nodes, where the i-th group of feature mapping is obtained by the following equation:

$$F_i = \psi(XW_{e_i} + b_{e_i}), i = 1, 2, \ldots, m, \tag{7}$$

where b_{e_i} and W_{e_i} are the bias and the weight associated with the feature node, respectively, and ψ is the feature mapping incentive function.

The combination of all feature nodes is denoted as

$$F^m = [F_1, F_2, \ldots, F_m]. \tag{8}$$

There is an extension of all feature nodes to the enhancement layer via a nonlinear excitation function. The j-th enhancement node is represented as

$$E_j = \xi\left(F^m W_{e_j} + b_{e_j}\right), j = 1, 2, \ldots, n, \tag{9}$$

where W_{e_j} and b_{e_j} are the weight and bias associated with the enhancement node, respectively, and ξ is the nonlinear excitation function.

$$\xi(x) = \frac{1 - e^{-2x}}{1 + e^{-2x}}. \tag{10}$$

In addition, all augmented nodes are described as

$$E^n = [E_1, E_2, \ldots, E_n]. \tag{11}$$

The feature node layer and the augmentation node layer are connected to each other through a weight matrix, which ultimately forms the mathematical expression of the BLS.

$$\begin{aligned} y &= [F_1, F_2, \ldots, F_m | E_1, E_2, \ldots, E_n] W, \\ &= [F^m | E^n] W, \end{aligned} \tag{12}$$

where W is the weight matrix and y is the output of BLS, i.e., the prediction value of electricity load.

The weight matrix W can be computed by a pseudoinverse algorithm.

$$W = [F^m | E^n]^+ y. \tag{13}$$

Let

$$\Omega = [F^m | E^n]. \tag{14}$$

The weight matrix W can be approximately calculated as

$$W = \left(\Omega\Omega^T + \eta I\right)^{-1} \Omega^T y, \tag{15}$$

$$\Omega^+ = \lim_{\eta \to 0} \left(\Omega\Omega^T + \eta I\right)^{-1} \Omega^T, \tag{16}$$

where η represents the ridge coefficient.

It can be seen that BLS training does not require a learning algorithm based on gradient descent, and it is faster and less likely to fall into local optimization. Using BLS with a single hidden layer structure and expanding the number of nodes in width as a prediction method can fit the historical data better and ensure the computational efficiency of the model.

3.4. PSO-Based Fusion of Independent Output Result

Based on the BLS model established in different modes, the final electricity load prediction model is established:

$$Y(t) = \sum_{o=1}^{K+1} a_o y(t)_o, \tag{17}$$

where a_o $(0 < a_o < 1)$ is the linear fusion parameter.

To choose the most appropriate a_o, the PSO method is used here. The optimization objective is defined as

$$e = \frac{1}{M} \sum_{t=1}^{M} \left| Y_{\text{real}}(t) - \sum_{o=1}^{K+1} a_o y(t)_o \right|, \tag{18}$$

where $Y_{\text{real}}(t)$ is the real value of electricity load data and M is the number of testing data.

The position and velocity update equations for the PSO algorithm are shown below.

$$V_h^{g+1} = \varpi V_h^g + c_1 r_1 (P_h - L_h^g) + c_2 r_2 (G_h - L_h^g), \tag{19}$$

$$L_h^{g+1} = L_h^g + V_h^{g+1}, \tag{20}$$

where $h = 1 \ldots H$; H denotes the total number of particles; V_h^g denotes the velocity of the particle at the gth iteration; c_1 and c_2 are the learning factors; r_1 and r_2 are random numbers between [0, 1]; P_h is the particle's individual extreme value; G_h is the particle's global optimum; L_h^g is the particle's position at the gth iteration; and ϖ is the inertia factor.

4. Experiments and Discussion

In this section, we experimentally verify the effectiveness of the proposed method using actual electricity load data from a region in Wuhan, China.

4.1. Performance Metrics

To assess the performance of the proposed model, we utilize the following performance metrics for testing its effectiveness. Here, we consider the correlation coefficient (R^2), root-mean-squared error (P_{RMSE}), mean absolute error (P_{MAE}), and mean absolute percentage error (P_{MAPE}).

$$R^2 = 1 - \frac{\sum_{t=1}^{M} [Y(t) - \bar{Y}_{\text{real}}(t)]^2}{\sum_{t=1}^{M} [Y_{\text{real}}(t) - \bar{Y}_{\text{real}}(t)]^2}, \tag{21}$$

$$P_{RMSE} = \sqrt{\frac{\sum_{t=1}^{M} [Y(t) - Y_{\text{real}}(t)]^2}{M}}, \tag{22}$$

$$P_{MAE} = \frac{1}{M} \sum_{t=1}^{M} |Y(t) - Y_{\text{real}}(t)|, \tag{23}$$

$$P_{MAPE} = \frac{100}{M} \sum_{t=1}^{M} \left| \frac{Y(t) - Y_{\text{real}}(t)}{Y_{\text{real}}(t)} \right|, \tag{24}$$

where $\bar{Y}_{\text{real}}(t)$ is the mean value for electricity load data in testing data and $Y(t)$ is the prediction value.

4.2. Experiments with Actual Data

A total of 460 sets of actual electricity load data were collected from a region in Wuhan, China. The first 368 datasets were utilized for model training and the remaining 92 datasets were employed for model testing. To validate the proposed model's effectiveness, we compared it with the long short-term memory (LSTM) [21,22] model, nonlinear auto-regressive model with exogenous inputs (NARX) [23], BLS [24], and the extreme learning machine (ELM) [25] model. Model inputs included temperature, humidity, rainfall, charging time, charging power, policy, etc. The model output was electricity load.

The variational mode decomposition of electricity load data requires the determination of the number of decomposed modes. As the value was small, the data complexity could not be fully reduced. When the value is large, however, the signal will be over-decomposed, resulting in frequency aliasing. This paper uses the method proposed in [26] to determine the number of modes. The Figure 2 displays the outcome of the variational mode decomposition.

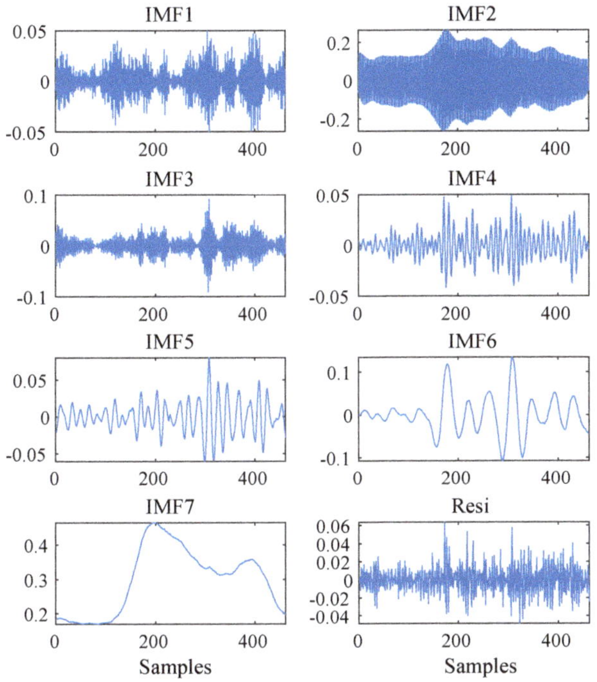

Figure 2. Result of the variational mode decomposition.

Each model is trained using the same electricity load data as well as the same data on factors influencing electricity load. The Figures 3–7 display the outcomes of various models used to forecast electricity load. Here, the solid blue line with circle indicates the actual electricity load value. Among them, it can be deduced that the electricity load curve exhibits both periodic patterns and random variations based on the data. From Figure 3, the LSTM prediction error falls within the range of [−600, 600]. From Figure 4, the NARX has a prediction error between [−400, 300]. From Figure 5, the prediction error of BLS is between [−400, 600]. From Figure 6, the prediction error of ELM is between [−200, 400]. However, as shown in Figure 7, the prediction error of the proposed method is only ±60. These results show that although each prediction model can predict the trend of electricity load, the electricity load prediction model of the proposed method in this paper has a higher fit to the actual electricity load curve, and the proposed method is able to follow the actual electricity load values better.

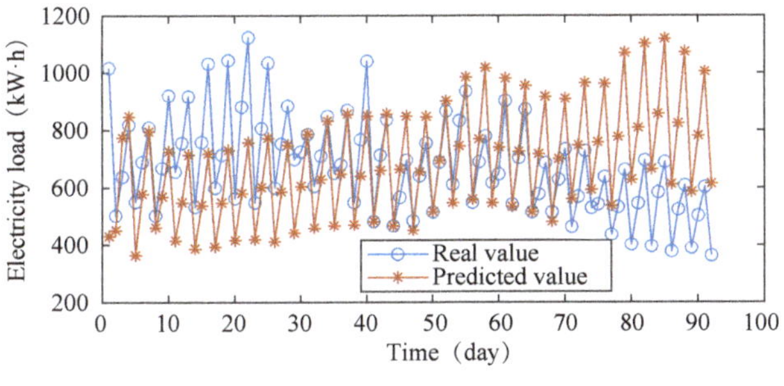

Figure 3. Electricity load prediction results for LSTM.

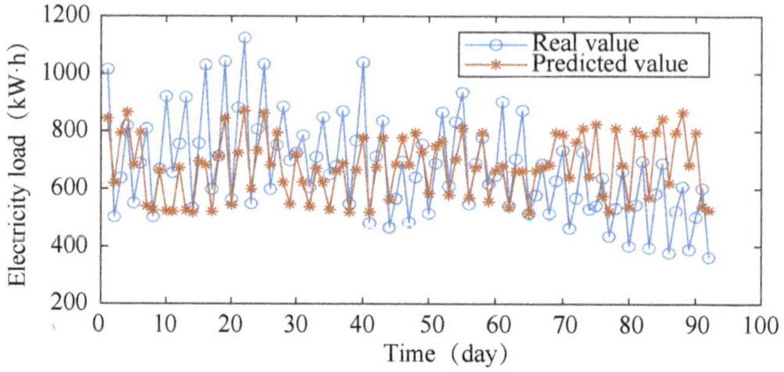

Figure 4. Electricity load prediction results for NARX.

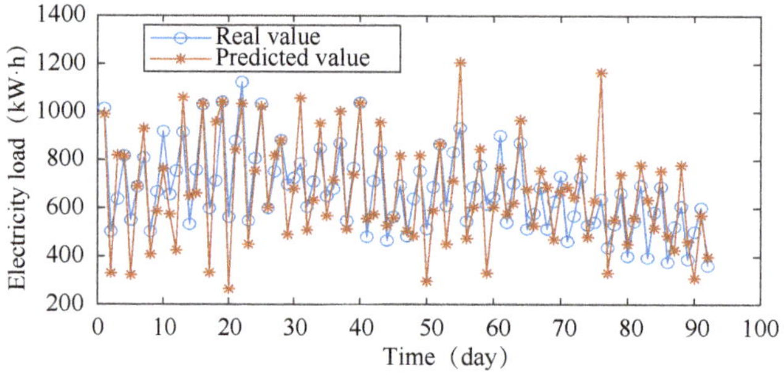

Figure 5. Electricity load prediction results for BLS.

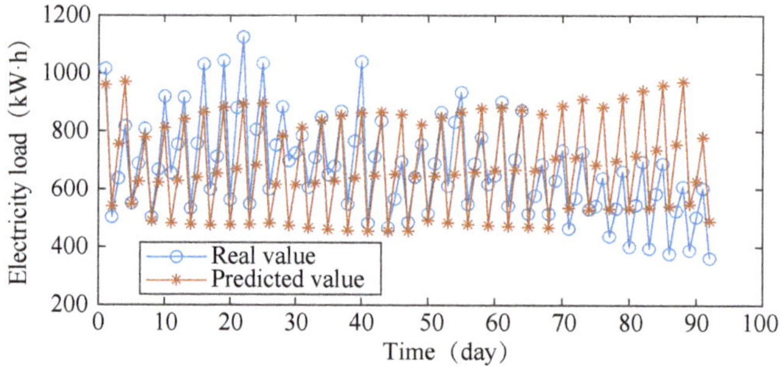

Figure 6. Electricity load prediction results for ELM.

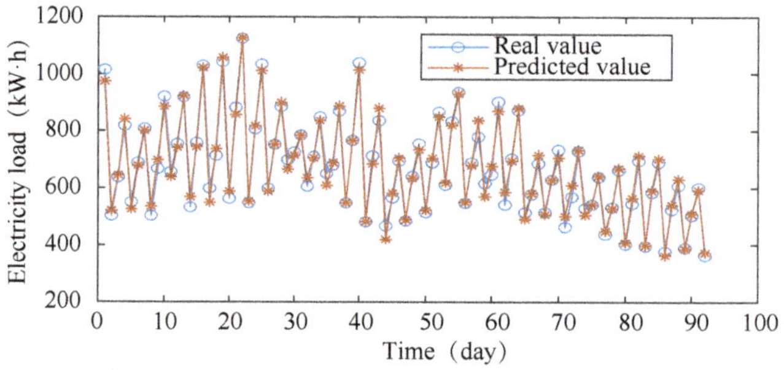

Figure 7. Electricity load prediction results for the proposed method.

The R^2, P_{RMSE}, P_{MAE}, and P_{MAPE} results of the prediction performance of each comparative prediction method for electricity load prediction are shown in Table 1. From the results of these performance metrics, it is clear that LSTM has the worst prediction performance, indicating that LSTM may be suitable for modeling time-series data with many samples. In contrast, our proposed method is able to fully consider the effects of time-series, periodicity, and robustness of electricity load data. Compared with the LSTM model, the proposed method improves by 85.78%, 89.05%, 89.12%, and 89.16% on the R^2, P_{RMSE}, P_{MAE}, and P_{MAPE} metrics, respectively. Compared with the NARX model, the proposed method improves by 82.84%, 86.14%, 86.32%, and 86.43% on the R^2, P_{RMSE}, P_{MAE}, and P_{MAPE} metrics, respectively. Compared with the BLS model, the proposed method improves by 39.23%, 84.28%, 83.94%, and 84.59% on the R^2, P_{RMSE}, P_{MAE}, and P_{MAPE} metrics, respectively. Compared with the ELM model, the proposed method improves by 52.04%, 83.34%, 84.18%, and 84.44% on the R^2, P_{RMSE}, P_{MAE}, and P_{MAPE} metrics, respectively. Among these results, the prediction performance of BLS is better than that of LSTM, NARX, and ELM except for the proposed method. This is because BLS performs feature extraction and is able to fit the relationship between high-dimensional variables more accurately.

Based on the above discussion, the proposed model in this paper demonstrates high prediction accuracy and better prediction performance in electricity load time-series prediction.

Table 1. Prediction performance of different models.

Model	R^2	P_{RMSE}	P_{MAE}	P_{MAPE}
LSTM [21]	0.1398	199.6250	157.7817	24.4203
NARX [23]	0.1687	157.6158	125.4578	19.5021
BLS [24]	0.5974	139.0036	106.8798	17.1711
ELM [25]	0.4715	131.1854	108.5291	17.0097
Proposed	0.9831	21.8502	17.1680	2.6468

5. Conclusions

To tackle the non-stationary nature of electricity load time-series data, which is influenced by various variables, a new modeling structure for electricity load time-series is suggested. Experiments comparing LSTM, NARX, BLS, and ELM methods are also performed. The experimental results based on actual data show that the proposed method can better tap the intrinsic change rule of electricity load sequence from back to front, which improves the prediction accuracy and prediction performance, and verifies the validity of the proposed method, which can be applied to large-scale electricity load prediction and provide a reference for the optimal scheduling of electricity load. In future research, we will consider using classification ideas to cluster the electricity load data and then perform individual modeling for different categories.

Author Contributions: Conceptualization, L.Y.; methodology, L.Y.; software, L.Y.; validation, L.Y. and X.G.; formal analysis, L.Y. and X.G.; investigation, L.Y.; resources, L.Y. and X.G.; data curation, L.Y. and X.G.; writing—original draft preparation, L.Y. and X.G.; writing—review and editing, L.Y. and X.G.; visualization, L.Y. and X.G.; supervision, X.G.; project administration, L.Y. and X.G.; funding acquisition, L.Y. and X.G. All authors have read and agreed to the published version of the manuscript.

Funding: This work was supported in part by the Science and Technology Program of State Grid Electric Power Research Institute under grant 524625220035 and in part by the State Grid Hubei Electric Power Company Science and Technology Program under grant WNJ221-2391/2392.

Data Availability Statement: The results/data/figures in this manuscript have not been published elsewhere, nor are they under consideration by another publisher. The original contributions presented in the study are included in the article, further inquiries can be directed to the corresponding author.

Conflicts of Interest: Author Liansong Yu was employed by the company State Grid Electric Power Research Institute Wuhan Nanrui. The remaining authors declare that the research was conducted in the absence of any commercial or financial relationships that could be construed as a potential conflict of interest.

Abbreviations

BLS	broad learning system
PSO	particle swarm optimization
R^2	correlation coefficient
P_{RMSE}	root mean square error
P_{MAE}	mean absolute error
P_{MAPE}	mean absolute percentage error
LSTM	long short term memory
NARX	nonlinear auto-regressive model with exogenous inputs
ELM	extreme learning machine
Symbols	
$f(t)$	original signal
$\delta(t)$	impulse function
K	artificially set decomposition quantity
ψ	feature mapping incentive function
ξ	nonlinear excitation function
W	weight matrix
η	ridge coefficient
a_o	linear fusion parameter
H	the total number of particles
V_h^g	the velocity of the particle at the gth iteration
V_h^g	the velocity of the particle at the gth iteration
c_1 and c_2	learning factors
r_1 and r_2	random numbers between [0, 1]
P_h	the particle's individual extreme value
G_h	the particle's global optimum
L_h^g	the particle's position at the gth iteration
ϖ	inertia factor

References

1. Zhai, M.Y. A new method for short-term load forecasting based on fractal interpretation and wavelet analysis. *Int. J. Electr. Power Energy Syst.* **2015**, *69*, 241–245. [CrossRef]
2. Urgun, D.; Singh, C. A hybrid Monte Carlo simulation and multi label classification method for composite system reliability evaluation. *IEEE Trans. Power Syst.* **2019**, *34*, 908–917. [CrossRef]
3. Zulfiqar, M.; Kamran, M.; Rasheed, M.B.; Alquthami, T.; Milyani, A.H. Hyperparameter optimization of support vector machine using adaptive differential evolution for electricity load forecasting. *Energy Rep.* **2022**, *8*, 13333–13352. [CrossRef]
4. Buzna, L.; De Falco, P.; Ferruzzi, G.; Khormali, S.; Proto, D.; Refa, N.; Straka, M.; van der Poel, G. An ensemble methodology for hierarchical probabilistic electric vehicle load forecasting at regular charging stations. *Appl. Energy* **2021**, *283*, 116337. [CrossRef]
5. Yi, T.; Zhang, C.; Lin, T.; Liu, J. Research on the spatial-temporal distribution of electric vehicle charging load demand: A case study in China. *J. Clean. Prod.* **2020**, *242*, 118457. [CrossRef]
6. Tang, D.; Wang, P. Probabilistic modeling of nodal charging demand based on spatial-temporal dynamics of moving electric vehicles. *IEEE Trans. Smart Grid* **2016**, *7*, 627–636. [CrossRef]
7. Zhu, J.; Yang, Z.; Mourshed, M.; Guo, Y.; Zhou, Y.; Chang, Y.; Wei, Y.; Feng, S. Electric vehicle charging load forecasting: A comparative study of deep learning approaches. *Energies* **2019**, *12*, 2692. [CrossRef]
8. Rao, A.R.; Reimherr, M. Modern non-linear function-on-function regression. *Stat. Comput.* **2023**, *33*, 130. [CrossRef]
9. Wang, H.; Yi, H.; Peng, J.; Wang, G.; Liu, Y.; Jiang, H.; Liu, W. Deterministic and probabilistic forecasting of photovoltaic power based on deep convolutional neural network. *Energy Convers. Manag.* **2017**, *153*, 409–422. [CrossRef]
10. Chang, G.W.; Lu, H.J. Integrating grey data preprocessor and deep belief network for day-ahead PV power output forecast. *IEEE Trans. Sustain. Energy* **2020**, *11*, 185–194. [CrossRef]
11. Yi, Z.; Liu, X.C.; Wei, R.; Chen, X.; Dai, J. Electric vehicle charging demand forecasting using deep learning model. *J. Intell. Transp. Syst.* **2022**, *26*, 690–703. [CrossRef]
12. Chen, C.L.P.; Liu, Z. Broad learning system: An effective and efficient incremental learning system without the need for deep architecture. *IEEE Trans. Neural Netw. Learn. Syst.* **2018**, *29*, 10–24. [CrossRef]

13. Gong, X.; Zhang, T.; Chen, C.L.P.; Liu, Z. Research review for broad learning system: Algorithms, theory, and applications. *IEEE Trans. Cybern.* **2022**, *52*, 8922–8950. [CrossRef]
14. Shi, Z.; Chen, X.; Zhao, C.; He, H.; Stuphorn, V.; Wu, D. Multi-view broad learning system for pPrimate oculomotor decision decoding. *IEEE Trans. Neural Syst. Rehabil. Eng.* **2020**, *28*, 1908–1920. [CrossRef]
15. Li, C.; Sun, C.; Chen, Z.; Zhang, Y. Broad learning system using rectified adaptive moment estimation for harmonic detection and analysis. *IEEE Trans. Ind. Electron.* **2024**, *71*, 2873–2882. [CrossRef]
16. Shen, H.; Wang, Z.; Zhou, X.; Lamantia, M.; Yang, K.; Chen, P.; Wang, J. Electric vehicle velocity and energy consumption predictions using transformer and markov-chain monte carlo. *IEEE Trans. Transp. Electrif.* **2022**, *8*, 3836–3847. [CrossRef]
17. Wang, S.; Ma, H.; Zhang, Y.; Li, S.; He, W. Remaining useful life prediction method of lithium-ion batteries is based on variational modal decomposition and deep learning integrated approach. *Energy* **2023**, *282*, 128984. [CrossRef]
18. Piotrowski, A.P.; Napiorkowski, J.J.; Piotrowska, A.E. Particle swarm optimization or differential evolution—A comparison. *Eng. Appl. Artif. Intell.* **2023**, *121*, 106008. [CrossRef]
19. Wang, J.; Zhang, F.; Liu, H.; Ding, J.; Gao, C. Interruptible load scheduling model based on an improved chicken swarm optimization algorithm. *CSEE J. Power Energy Syst.* **2021**, *7*, 232–240.
20. Liu, Y.; Wang, P. Partial correlation analysis based identification of distribution network topology. *CSEE J. Power Energy Syst.* **2023**, *9*, 1493–1504.
21. Sarmas, E.; Spiliotis, E.; Stamatopoulos, E.; Marinakis, V.; Doukas, H. Short-term photovoltaic power forecasting using meta-learning and numerical weather prediction independent long short-term memory models. *Renew Energy* **2023**, *216*, 118997. [CrossRef]
22. Wu, W.; Chi, Z. Electric vehicle charging load forecasting method considering the impact of the emergency. *Acad. J. Eng. Technol. Sci.* **2022**, *5*, 1–9.
23. López, G.; Arboleya, P. Short-term wind speed forecasting over complex terrain using linearregression models and multivariable LSTM and NARX networks in theAndes Mountains, Ecuador. *Renew. Energy* **2022**, *183*, 351–368. [CrossRef]
24. Hu, J.; Wu, M.; Chen, L.; Zhou, K.; Zhang, P.; Pedrycz, W. Weighted kernel fuzzy c-means-based broad learning model for time-series prediction of carbon efficiency in iron ore sintering process. *IEEE Trans. Cybern.* **2022**, *52*, 4751–4763. [CrossRef]
25. Anandhakumar, C.; Murugan, N.S.S.; Kumaresan, K. Extreme learning machine model with honey badger algorithm based state-of-charge estimation of lithium-ion battery. *Expert Syst. Appl.* **2024**, *238*, 121609. [CrossRef]
26. Zhang, C.; Zhou, J.; Li, C.; Fu, W.; Peng, T. A compound structure of ELM based on feature selection and parameter optimization using hybrid backtracking search algorithm for wind speed forecasting. *Energy Convers. Manag.* **2017**, *143*, 360–376. [CrossRef]

mathematics

MDPI

Article

Fault Distance Measurement in Distribution Networks Based on Markov Transition Field and Darknet-19

Haozhi Wang †, Wei Guo *,† and Yuntao Shi †

School of Electrical and Control Engineering, North China University of Technology, Shijingshan District, Beijing 100144, China; whz1271@163.com (H.W.); shiyuntao@ncut.edu.cn (Y.S.)

* Correspondence: guowei0903@ncut.edu.cn; Tel.: +86-1513-431-6988

† These authors contributed equally to this work.

Abstract: The modern distribution network system is gradually becoming more complex and diverse, and traditional fault location methods have difficulty in quickly and accurately locating the fault location after a single-phase ground fault occurs. Therefore, this study proposes a new solution based on the Markov transfer field and deep learning to predict the fault location, which can accurately predict the location of a single-phase ground fault in the distribution network. First, a new phase-mode transformation matrix is used to take the fault current of the distribution network as the modulus 1 component, avoiding complex calculations in the complex field; then, the extracted modulus 1 component of the current is transformed into a Markov transfer field and converted into an image using pseudo-color coding, thereby fully exploiting the fault signal characteristics; finally, the Darknet-19 network is used to automatically extract fault features and predict the distance of the fault occurrence. Through simulations on existing models and training and testing with a large amount of data, the experimental results show that this method has good stability, high accuracy, and strong anti-interference ability. This solution can effectively predict the distance of ground faults in distribution networks.

Keywords: distribution network; fault distance measurement; Markov transition field; deep learning

MSC: 68T20

1. Introduction

The distribution network plays a crucial role in the electrical grid by ensuring the safe, efficient, and reliable delivery of electricity to end users. With an increasingly complex network structure and diverse operational conditions, the system is more susceptible to faults, particularly single-phase grounding faults [1,2]. If single-phase grounding faults are not rectified for a long time, they can easily escalate into two-point or multiple-point grounding short circuits, causing damage to equipment and even posing risks to personal and property safety [3,4]. Timely localization of fault occurrences is essential for rapid risk mitigation, holding significant theoretical and practical importance.

The structure of the power distribution network is often in a radial pattern, characterized by multiple branches and short line lengths. When a small-current ground fault occurs, the fault signal tends to exhibit non-linear, weak, and complex characteristics. Existing fault localization methods may struggle to meet the accuracy requirements for localization. At current, the main research methods for fault location can be roughly divided into several types, such as the fault analysis method, artificial intelligence method, signal injection method, traveling-wave method, and impedance method [5,6]. One of the most effective methods to calculate the fault distance is the traveling-wave method [7,8]. However, due to the intricate line structure of the distribution network, it is challenging to differentiate and recognize the wave head type and time information. Karmacharya and Gokaraju [9] employed wavelet transformation to decompose the monitoring signal and extract fault features, facilitating the utilization of a three-layer feedforward artificial neural network classifier for automated fault localization. Nevertheless, manual extraction of fault features is imperative, with the precision of outcomes being heavily reliant on the scale of decomposition and wavelet basis functions. Elkalashy [10] utilized a controlled thyristor to ground the neutral point and generate traveling waves for fault distance estimation. However, this approach is limited to neutral ground systems and necessitates signal injection. Sun [11] proposed a method for calculating the fault area by establishing an adjacency table of distribution network equipment to illustrate the relationship between each piece of equipment. However, this approach requires a substantial amount of electrical data from customers, making the collection process cumbersome. Liao [12] proposed a novel integrated fault location solution for overhead distribution systems, contingent upon the prior knowledge of network parameters and topology. Hua Fu et al. [13] proposed a traveling-wave fault detection method that combines variational mode decomposition (VMD) and synchrosqueezing wavelet transform (SWT). However, the VMD algorithm lacks adaptability as it requires a manual setting of decomposition levels. Peng Hua et al. [14] utilized the full-phase fast Fourier transform spectrum correction to extract the fundamental effective values and phase information of voltage and current at measurement points as feature vectors. They established a fault locator using the extreme gradient boosting method to achieve fault location and distance measurement. However, in the case of single-phase grounding faults in low-current grounded systems, the effective value of the power frequency current changes minimally. This effect is especially pronounced when there is a large transition resistance, leading to further weakening of the fundamental fault characteristics and affecting the distance measurement accuracy of this method. The impedance method calculates the impedance by measuring the voltage and current when a fault occurs in the circuit. Since the line impedance is directly proportional to the length of the line, this method can be used to determine the distance between the measuring device and the fault point [15]. Zheng Tao et al. [16] used a node impedance matrix and network equivalence method for fault location. This algorithm utilizes the node impedance matrix formed after a distribution network fault to establish a distance measurement expression based on the physical significance of node impedance. Qi Zheng et al. [17] proposed a fault location technique for distribution networks based on the zero-sequence impedance method. This technique utilizes the zero-sequence voltage on both sides of the distribution network lines and the zero-sequence current on the busbar side to establish distance-related measurement equations for each section of the network. However, these methods require prior knowledge of the distribution network parameters and topology, making them difficult to apply to increasingly complex distribution network structures. In recent years, with the development of artificial intelligence, machine learning has been widely used in the field of fault diagnosis, and many new fault diagnosis models have been proposed [18,19]. Researchers have integrated neural network technology into the field of distribution network fault location. They use artificial intelligence algorithms to address the challenges in fault location within distribution networks. Refs. [20–22] propose the utilization of artificial intelligence algorithms for distribution network fault location. These approaches integrate traditional methods with artificial intelligence algorithms, utilizing AI to predict fault location, streamline the complex steps of traditional fault location algorithms, and demonstrate certain resistance to interference. However, Ref. [20] artificially decomposes fault signals and extracts fault features using wavelet packets, which introduces a subjective element. In Ref. [21], neural networks are employed for automatic extraction of fault features; however, the samples used for training do not fully capture fault information. Ref. [22] utilizes a backpropagation (BP) neural network for fault localization; nevertheless, the BP neural network is susceptible to local minima, gradient vanishing or exploding, overfitting, and other issues. Additionally, the BP neural network is sensitive to input data, limiting its generalization ability in processing noise or unseen data.

In summary, in response to the current issues of complex and inaccurate fault localization in fault location methods, this paper proposes a new approach for predicting fault positions using Markov transition fields and deep learning, effectively achieving fault distance prediction. Firstly, a new phase-shifting matrix is used to extract the modulus 1 component of the fault current in the distribution network, ensuring that this modulus 1 component can represent single-phase ground faults for all phases; then, the extracted current modulus 1 component is transformed into a Markov transition field, which is visually encoded as an image using pseudo-colors; finally, this image is used as input for the Darknet-19 model, which automatically extracts fault features of the line through multilayer convolution and pooling operations, and calculates fault distance through a regression model. Simulation results show that this approach has lower errors and stronger robustness. Compared with traditional methods, it improves detection reliability.

The paper is structured into the following sections. Section 2 introduces the phase-mode transformation. In Section 3, a signal-to-image conversion method is proposed. Section 4 describes fault location based on Darknet-19. The results of fault-ranging experiments are presented in Section 5.

2. Phase-Mode Transformation

The parameters of the ABC three-phase current in the power distribution network exhibit complex electromagnetic coupling, making their calculation complex. However, the phase-shifting transformation can simplify this and avoid complex calculations in the complex domain, making it suitable for decoupling electrical quantities from discrete sampling [23]. The relationship between phase-mode transformation and inverse transformation in the time domain is as follows:

$$\begin{cases} \begin{pmatrix} i_{\mathrm{m}}{}^{(0)} & i_{\mathrm{m}}{}^{(1)} & i_{\mathrm{m}}{}^{(2)} \end{pmatrix}^{\mathrm{T}} = S^{-1}\begin{pmatrix} i_{\mathrm{a}} & i_{\mathrm{b}} & i_{\mathrm{c}} \end{pmatrix}^{\mathrm{T}} \\ \begin{pmatrix} i_{\mathrm{a}} & i_{\mathrm{b}} & i_{\mathrm{c}} \end{pmatrix}^{\mathrm{T}} = S\begin{pmatrix} i_{\mathrm{m}}{}^{(0)} & i_{\mathrm{m}}{}^{(1)} & i_{\mathrm{m}}{}^{(2)} \end{pmatrix}^{\mathrm{T}} \end{cases} \tag{1}$$

where $i_{\mathrm{m}}{}^{(0)}$, $i_{\mathrm{m}}{}^{(1)}$, and $i_{\mathrm{m}}{}^{(2)}$ represent the current modulus components of 0, 1, and 2.

The ABC three-phase parameters, after undergoing phase-mode transformation, are converted into modulus 0, modulus 1, and modulus 2 components. Because the modulus 0 component is connected to the ground, its loop parameters are affected by complex factors related to the ground, such as resistivity and grounding conditions. Therefore, for fault analysis problems, most researchers use the modulus 1 or modulus 2 components.

The commonly used phase-mode transformation methods include the Clarke transformation, the Karenbauer transformation, and the Wedpohl transformation. These three methods demonstrate good analytical capabilities in certain fields, but they are unable to achieve a single modal component that reflects all types of faults in fault analysis problems. The decision has been made to implement a new phase-mode transformation matrix, which not only retains the advantages of the time-domain matrix but also achieves the objective of single-modulus response for all types of faults [23]. The original matrix is represented by Equation (2).

$$S = \frac{1}{15}\begin{pmatrix} 5 & 5 & 5 \\ 5 & -1 & -4 \\ 5 & -4 & -1 \end{pmatrix}; S^{-1} = \begin{pmatrix} 1 & 1 & 1 \\ 1 & 2 & -3 \\ 1 & -3 & 2 \end{pmatrix} \tag{2}$$

The phase-mode transformation matrix S^{-1} can transform the current vectors into a modal form, as follows:

$$\begin{pmatrix} i_{\mathrm{m}}{}^{(0)} \\ i_{\mathrm{m}}{}^{(1)} \\ i_{\mathrm{m}}{}^{(0)} \end{pmatrix} = \begin{pmatrix} 1 & 1 & 1 \\ 1 & 2 & -3 \\ 1 & -3 & 2 \end{pmatrix}\begin{pmatrix} i_{\mathrm{a}} \\ i_{\mathrm{b}} \\ i_{\mathrm{c}} \end{pmatrix} \tag{3}$$

Table 1 provides the mode components obtained using the phase-mode transformation matrix for various fault types. From this table, we can observe that the mode components for all types of faults are non-zero, indicating that their modulus 1 and modulus 2 components can individually reflect all fault types.

Table 1. Current modes of different faults.

Fault Type	Boundary Condition	Modulus 1	Modulus 2
AG [1]	$i_{\text{fb}} = i_{\text{fc}} = 0$	i_{fa}	i_{fa}
BG [2]	$i_{\text{fa}} = i_{\text{fc}} = 0$	$2i_{\text{fb}}$	$-3i_{\text{fb}}$
CG [3]	$i_{\text{fa}} = i_{\text{fb}} = 0$	$-3i_{\text{fc}}$	$2i_{\text{fc}}$
AB [4]	$i_{\text{fc}} = 0; i_{\text{fa}} = -i_{\text{fb}}$	i_{fb}	$-4i_{\text{fb}}$
BC [5]	$i_{\text{fa}} = 0; i_{\text{fb}} = -i_{\text{fc}}$	$5i_{\text{fb}}$	$-5i_{\text{fb}}$
CA [6]	$i_{\text{fb}} = 0; i_{\text{fa}} = -i_{\text{fc}}$	$4i_{\text{fa}}$	$-i_{\text{fa}}$
ABG [7]	$i_{\text{fc}} = 0$	$i_{\text{fa}} + 2i_{\text{fb}}$	$i_{\text{fa}} - 3i_{\text{fb}}$
BCG [8]	$i_{\text{fa}} = 0$	$2i_{\text{fb}} - 3i_{\text{fc}}$	$2i_{\text{fc}} - 3i_{\text{fb}}$
CAG [9]	$i_{\text{fb}} = 0$	$i_{\text{fa}} - 3i_{\text{fc}}$	$i_{\text{fa}} + 2i_{\text{fc}}$
ABC [10]	$i_{\text{fa}} + i_{\text{fb}} + i_{\text{fc}} = 0$	$i_{\text{fa}} + 2i_{\text{fb}} - 3i_{\text{fc}}$	$i_{\text{fa}} - 3i_{\text{fb}} + 2i_{\text{fc}}$

[1] Phase A single phase to ground; [2] Phase B single phase to ground; [3] Phase C single phase to ground; [4] Phase A is connected to phase B; [5] Phase B is connected to phase C; [6] Phase C is connected to phase A; [7] Phase A and phase B are simultaneously grounded; [8] Phase B and phase C are simultaneously grounded; [9] Phase C and phase A are simultaneously grounded; [10] Phase A, phase B, and phase C are interconnected with each other.

3. Markov Transition Field

To maximize the convolutional neural network's ability to extract image features, an algorithm can be used to transform one-dimensional time-series signals into two-dimensional matrices. Markov transition field (MTF) [24] is one such method, wherein the transition probabilities of a Markov process are sequentially represented, allowing the signal to be transformed into an image while retaining the temporal information.

The principle of MTFs involves first identifying Q quantile bins based on the given one-dimensional time-series signal $X = \{x_1, x_2, ..., x_n\}$ and assigning each value x_i to its corresponding unit $q_j (j \in [1, Q])$, expressing relationships in terms of single-step transition probabilities and multi-step transition probabilities defined in Markov chains.

$$\begin{cases} P_{i,i-1} = p_{i,i-1}(x_{\text{t}} \in q_i | x_{\text{t}-1} \in q_{i-1}) \\ P_{i,j} = p_{i,j}(x_t \in q_i | x_{\text{t}-1} \in q_j)(i - j > 1) \end{cases} \tag{4}$$

where $P_{i,j}$ represents the multi-step transition probabilities. It represents the probability that an element located in the q_j quantile bin region will multi-step to the q_i quantile bin at the next moment. Then, the transition probabilities between quantile bins can be calculated using a first-order Markov chain method along the time axis. By arranging all the transition probabilities of the Markov chain according to the transition rules, a $Q \times Q$ weighted adjacency matrix, i.e., the Markov transition matrix (MTM) W, can be constructed, as shown in Equation (5). From the equation, it is evident that the MTM is entirely determined by the Markov chain, indicating a strong correspondence between the two [25].

$$W = \begin{pmatrix} w_{1,1}(x_t \in q_1 | x_{t-1} \in q_1) & \cdots & w_{1,Q}(x_t \in q_1 | x_{t-1} \in q_Q) \\ w_{2,1}(x_t \in q_2 | x_{t-1} \in q_1) & \cdots & w_{2,Q}(x_t \in q_2 | x_{t-1} \in q_Q) \\ \cdots & \ddots & \cdots \\ w_{Q,1}(x_t \in q_Q | x_{t-1} \in q_1) & \cdots & w_{Q,Q}(x_t \in q_Q | x_{t-1} \in q_Q) \end{pmatrix} \tag{5}$$

Due to the Markov chain's lack of memory, whereby the current state depends only on the previous state, so $p(x \in \sum_1^Q q_j | x_{\text{t}-1} \in \sum_1^Q q_j, \ldots, x_1 \in \sum_1^Q q_j) = p(x_{\text{t}-1} \in \sum_1^Q q_j | x_{\text{t}-1} \in \sum_1^Q q_j)$, the MTM also exhibits this lack of memory. This characteristic causes it to lose the dependence on the time steps of the one-dimensional time series X. Directly using the Markov matrix would result in the loss of much information from the one-dimensional time series.

Conversely, the improved MTF, as the sequence follows a time-ordered arrangement, can effectively utilize the sequential signal. The definition of the MTF is shown in Equation (6).

$$M = \begin{pmatrix} w_{ij}|x_1 \in q_i, x_1 \in q_j & \cdots & w_{ij}|x_1 \in q_i, x_n \in q_j \\ w_{ij}|x_2 \in q_i, x_1 \in q_j & \cdots & w_{ij}|x_2 \in q_i, x_n \in q_j \\ \vdots & \ddots & \vdots \\ w_{ij}|x_n \in q_i, x_1 \in q_j & \cdots & w_{ij}|x_n \in q_i, x_n \in q_j \end{pmatrix} \quad (6)$$

Here, w_{ij} represents the transition probability of the quantile relationship between q_i and q_j on the matrix W, while the elements on the diagonal represent the self-transition probabilities. Consequently, the information derived from the Markov chain can be expressed on the MTF M, constructed based on the sequence of data length. Finally, by visually encoding the obtained Markov field matrix using pseudo-colors, a two-dimensional image containing fault information can be obtained. The transformation process is illustrated in Figure 1.

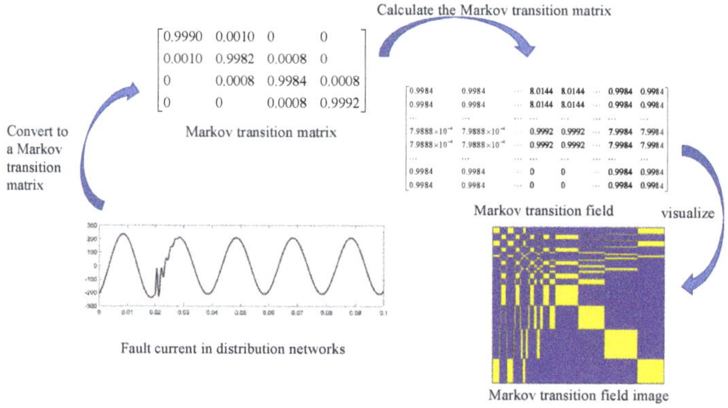

Figure 1. The MTF transformation process.

4. Fault Distance Measurement Based on Logistic Regression

Convolutional neural networks (CNNs) not only possess strong feature extraction capabilities, widely used in image classification, but also harbor powerful advantages for handling regression problems [26]. However, conventional convolutional neural networks are prone to issues such as gradient saturation and local optima. To address these problems, it is important to sensibly design the neural network's structure. Darknet-19 [27] incorporates the advantages of VGG-16 [28] while discarding unnecessary complex structures. It primarily utilizes convolutional layers with filters, doubling the number of channels after each pooling step. Following the network-in-network (NIN) operation, global average pooling is performed for prediction, and filters are used to compress feature representations between the convolutions. Lastly, batch normalization is employed to stabilize training, accelerate convergence, and regularize the model. The network structure is depicted in Figure 2, with detailed explanations provided in Table 2.

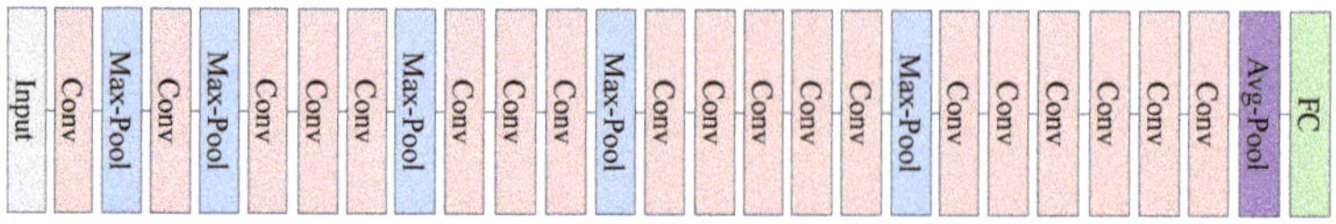

Figure 2. The Darknet-19 network model.

Table 2. Parameters of the Darknet-19 network structure.

Layer	Filters	Size/Stride	Input	Output
0 conv	32	(3,3)/1	(256,256,3)	(256,256,32)
1 max		(2,2)/2	(256,256,32)	(128,128,32)
2 conv	64	(3,3)/1	(128,128,32)	(128,128,64)
3 max		(2,2)/2	(128,128,64)	(64,64,64)
4 conv	128	(3,3)/1	(64,64,64)	(64,64,128)
5 conv	64	(1,1)/1	(64,64,128)	(64,64,64)
6 conv	128	(3,3)/1	(64,64,64)	(64,64,128)
7 max		(2,2)/2	(64,64,128)	(32,32,128)
8 conv	256	(3,3)/1	(32,32,128)	(32,32,256)
9 conv	128	(1,1)/1	(32,32,256)	(32,32,128)
10 conv	256	(3,3)/1	(32,32,128)	(32,32,256)
11 max		(2,2)/2	(32,32,256)	(16,16,256)
12 conv	512	(3,3)/1	(16,16,256)	(16,16,512)
13 conv	256	(1,1)/1	(16,16,512)	(16,16,256)
14 conv	512	(3,3)/1	(16,16,256)	(16,16,512)
15 conv	256	(1,1)/1	(16,16,512)	(16,16,256)
16 conv	512	(3,3)/1	(16,16,256)	(16,16,512)
17 max		(2,2)/2	(16,16,512)	(8,8,512)
18 conv	1024	(3,3)/1	(8,8,512)	(8,8,1024)
19 conv	512	(1,1)/1	(8,8,1024)	(8,8,512)
20 conv	1024	(3,3)/1	(8,8,512)	(8,8,1024)
21 conv	512	(1,1)/1	(8,8,1024)	(8,8,512)
22 conv	1024	(3,3)/1	(8,8,512)	(8,8,1024)
23 conv	1000	(1,1)/1	(8,8,1024)	(8,8,1000)
24 avg			(8,8,1000)	1000
25 fc				1

Figure 3 demonstrates the process of image feature extraction using Darknet-19. As shown in Figure 3, it is evident that the features extracted from lower layers are relatively elementary. As the network deepens and new layers are added, the receptive field mapped to the input layer expands. The output of the preceding convolutional layer acts as the input for the subsequent convolutional layer, enabling feature accumulation. Consequently, features extracted by later convolutional layers gradually become more sophisticated, equipping the network with enhanced capability to model complex functions and extract robust features.

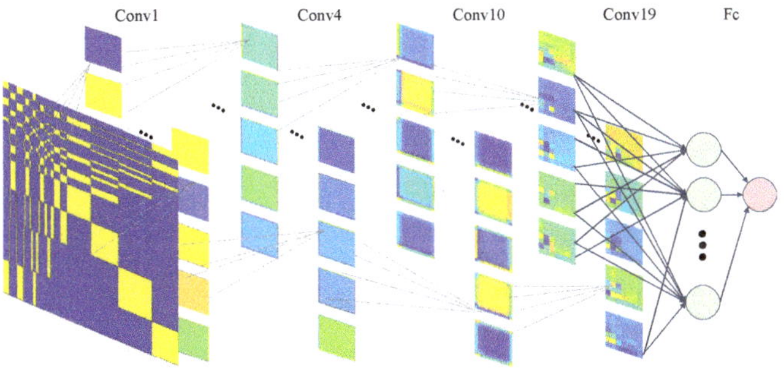

Figure 3. The feature extraction process in Darknet-19.

5. Experimental Validation and Analysis

5.1. Experimental Simulation Model and Data Sampling

Training deep neural networks necessitates a substantial quantity of samples for iteration. MATLAB/SIMULINK is employed to conduct simulations on various types of faults within the distribution network. The simulated power line operates at a voltage of 10 kV and a frequency of 50 Hz, encompassing pure cable, pure overhead line, and hybrid line configurations with both cable and overhead components, spanning a total length of 10 km.

The zero-sequence and positive-sequence parameters of the overhead line are given in Equation (7).

$$\begin{cases} R_0 = 0.251\ \Omega/\text{km} & L_0 = 4.560 \times 10^{-3}\ \text{H/km} \\ C_0 = 0.0056 \times 10^{-6}\ \text{F/km} & R_1 = 0.178\ \Omega/\text{km} \\ L_1 = 1.250 \times 10^{-6}\ \text{H/km} & C_1 = 0.0098 \times 10^{-6}\ \text{F/km} \end{cases} \tag{7}$$

The zero-sequence and positive-sequence parameters of the cable are shown in Equation (8).

$$\begin{cases} R_0 = 2.850\ \Omega/\text{km} & L_0 = 1.218 \times 10^{-3}\ \text{H/km} \\ C_0 = 0.490 \times 10^{-6}\ \text{F/km}, & R_1 = 0.288\ \Omega/\text{km} \\ L_1 = 0.266 \times 10^{-6}\ \text{H/km} & C_1 = 0.538 \times 10^{-6}\ \text{F/km} \end{cases} \tag{8}$$

Next, on the established simulation model, fault current data are sampled to create a training dataset. The total number of samples is 6000, with fault types set as A, B, and C single-phase grounding faults. The fault angles are 0°, 90°, 180°, and 270°, with fault resistance ranging from 1 to 1500 Ω. Five fault points are uniformly distributed along the 10 km distribution network line. Detailed information about the dataset is provided in Table 3.

Table 3. Parameters of the training sample dataset.

Fault Types	AG, BG, CG
Fault Resistance (Ω)	1–1500
Fault Angle	0°, 90°, 180°, 270°
Line Type	Overhead Line, Cable, Overhead Line and Cable Hybrid
Size of the Dataset	6000

Finally, the time-series current data are transformed into a two-dimensional image using MTFs. To reduce the computational load of the MTF, the data from two periods before and after the occurrence of the fault are taken, and the difference in current data between these two periods is used for the MTF transformation. This not only reduces the computational load but also highlights the fault characteristics. Figure 4 shows partial images of the transformation of the distribution network after ground fault occurrence at different distances.

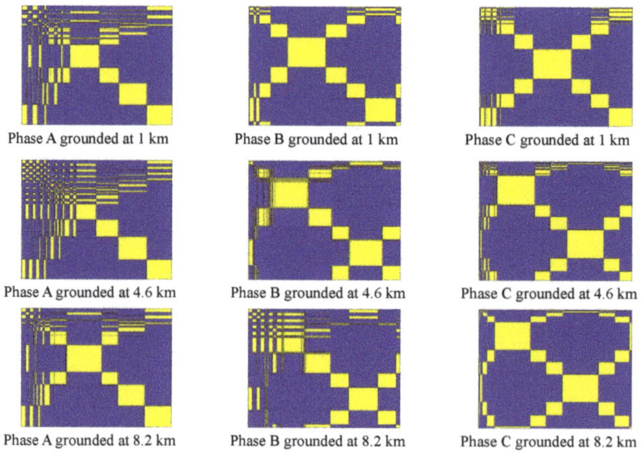

Figure 4. MTF images of distribution network ground faults at different distances.

5.2. Building a Fault Distance Measurement Model

Based on the solution for the regression problem, it is only necessary to build a single-output Darknet-19 neural network. After the convolution calculation, the Darknet-19 analyzes and calculates the predicted distance through a fully connected layer. In this article, the current signal of the distribution network is first collected, and its phase transformation is performed to obtain the modulus 1 component. Then, the obtained component is used to intercept the data of the current for two cycles before and after the occurrence of the fault. The difference between the current data of these two cycles is used to perform an MTF transformation. First, the Markov matrix is calculated, and then, it is transformed into an MTF. Finally, Darknet-19 is used to predict the fault distance. The model flowchart is shown in Figure 5.

The prepared dataset is imported into the Darknet-19 model for training. The learning rate during training is set to 0.0001, using the mean square error loss function, and the Adam optimizer is used to optimize the gradient descent process. A total of 30 epochs are trained, and the gradient descent process is shown in Figure 6. From Figure 6, it can be observed that the network convergence speed is very fast during the first training iteration. However, as the number of iterations increases, the convergence speed decreases. The training sample loss function and the validation sample loss function gradually approach zero. At the same time, the loss function of the validation sample dataset also gradually decreases in the same trend, indicating that the training model continuously fits the fault distance model without overfitting. Ultimately, a stable, fast, and highly accurate fault distance prediction model is obtained.

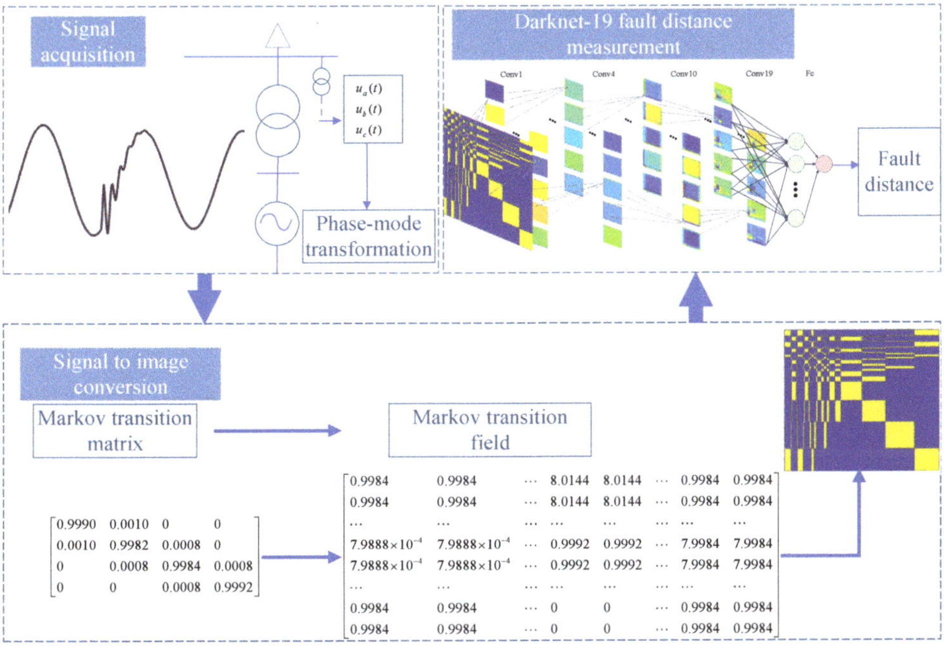

Figure 5. Fault distance measurement process.

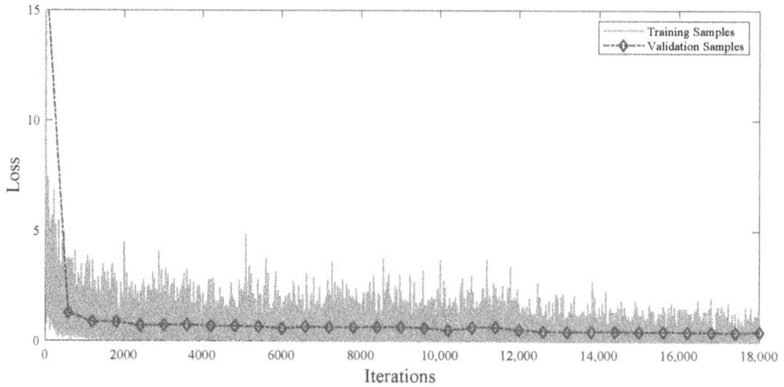

Figure 6. Training and validation loss function curves of the Darknet-19 model.

5.3. Analysis of Test Sample Results

To verify the experimental results, the fault data were resampled, and the same method was used to convert them into an MTF. The trained neural network was then used for testing, with the results shown in Table 4. From Table 4, it can be seen that the predicted results of the test samples have a relatively high accuracy and a small range of prediction errors. This demonstrates that the method can fully leverage the feature extraction ability of the convolutional neural network to extract fault characteristics from the MTF images, thereby predicting the distance of the fault occurrence and avoiding the issues of detecting the traveling-wave head and predicting traveling-wave speed. Compared to traditional traveling-wave distance measurement methods, this approach has a certain advantage in distance measurement accuracy.

Table 4. Prediction results of fault position under different conditions.

Fault Angle	Fault Types	Fault Distance	PFD [1]	Error
0°	AG	6.2	6.2102	0.0102
		3	3.0740	0.0740
0°	BG	4.5	4.5926	0.0926
		6.2	6.0879	−0.1121
0°	CG	4.5	4.4904	−0.0096
		6.6	6.5543	−0.0457
90°	AG	4.5	4.4982	−0.0018
		6.6	6.4959	−0.1041
90°	BG	3	2.9966	−0.0034
		1.2	1.1788	−0.0212
90°	CG	3	3.1047	0.1047
		0.9	0.9189	0.0189
180°	AG	1.2	1.1343	−0.0657
		8.3	8.3005	0.0005
180°	BG	1.2	1.1008	−0.0992
		4.5	4.6239	0.1239
180°	CG	1.2	1.2005	0.0005
		8.3	8.3167	0.0167
270°	AG	3	2.8889	−0.1111
		6.2	6.2829	0.0829
270°	BG	1.2	1.4509	0.2509
		6.2	5.9876	−0.2124
270°	CG	0.9	0.9173	0.0173
		4.5	4.6401	0.1401

[1] Predicted fault distance. Distance units are kilometers.

Different phasor transformation methods have a significant impact on fault distance estimation. To compare the fault distance estimation performance under different phasor transformation methods, the Clarke transformation, the Schmidt orthogonalization matrix of the new phasor transformation, and the transformation matrix used in this study were selected for comparison. The results in Table 5 show that the fault distance estimation performance under the Clarke transformation is poor. This is because when phase B of the distribution network is single-phase grounded, the modulus 2 component remains zero according to the Clarke transformation matrix. However, the method used in this study can uniquely identify the fault regardless of the phase in which the fault occurs, thereby having a lower prediction error.

Table 5. Fault distance estimation performance under different phasor transformation matrices.

Fault Types	Fault Distance	Clarke Transformation		Proposed Method	
		PFD [1]	Error	PFD	Error
AG	0.9	1.2354	0.3354	0.9637	0.0637
	1.2	2.2067	1.0067	1.0999	−0.1001
	3	2.5721	−0.4279	3.0355	0.0355
	4.5	5.1885	0.6885	4.6337	0.1337
	6.2	6.3321	0.1321	6.2102	0.0102
	8	6.0578	−1.9422	7.867	−0.133
BG	0.9	1.3433	0.4433	0.9595	0.0595
	1.2	1.9279	0.7279	1.0321	−0.1679
	3	4.5361	1.5361	2.9007	−0.0933
	4.5	3.5951	−0.9049	4.3358	−0.1642
	6.2	4.0899	−2.1101	6.0346	−0.1654
	8	5.6227	−2.3773	8.3237	0.3237
CG	0.9	2.3222	1.4222	0.9647	0.0647
	1.2	0.926	−0.2704	1.3775	0.1775
	3	3.5651	0.5651	3.0293	0.0293
	4.5	4.6647	0.1647	4.5468	0.0468
	6.2	5.6867	−0.5133	6.2735	0.0735
	8	6.5404	−1.4596	7.8009	−0.1991

[1] Predicted fault distance. Distance units are kilometers.

In actual distribution network lines, current signals are susceptible to noise interference, and as a result, the prediction results are also affected by the noise. To verify the advantages of the method proposed in this paper, a comparison was made between the MTM and the MTF under four different signal-to-noise ratios (SNRs): 10 dB, 20 dB, 30 dB, and 40 dB. As shown in Table 6, the traveling-wave fault distance estimation method shows unstable performance. The results for samples at different signal-to-noise ratios and different phases and fault distances show significant variations. While the method accurately predicts the distance for samples with an actual fault distance of 1 km, the prediction errors for other samples are large. This is because the traveling-wave fault distance estimation algorithm has strict requirements for various parameters of the actual system. The speed of the traveling-wave front differs for different distribution network line parameters, so the prediction algorithm needs to be modified according to the actual line. Additionally, the method is highly reliant on empirical selection for the detection range and lacks reliable methods for range selection, making the method's conditions for use strict and inflexible, and thus, difficult to effectively apply in practice.

The algorithm transforms the current signal into an MTM and an MTF. and then, uses a neural network for fault distance prediction. Both methods outperform the traveling-wave fault detection method. However, due to the MTF incorporating temporal information under the premise of the MTM, it effectively utilizes sequential signals and exhibits stronger resistance to noise interference. This results in the MTF generally demonstrating lower fault distance prediction errors than the MTM under various degrees of noise impact.

To validate the effectiveness of the method proposed in this paper, we compared it with two other fault location methods. As shown in Table 7, the results obtained using our method exhibit lower errors. This is due to the fact that the method proposed in this paper does not require the detection of the wavefront and wave speed of traveling waves, and it can automatically extract fault features, instead of relying on manual extraction.

Table 6. Resistance to interference in fault distance measurement under different methods.

Fault Types	SNR	Fault Distance	TW [1]		MTM		MTF	
			PFD [2]	Error	PFD	Error	PFD	Error
AG	10 dB	1	0.7352	−0.2648	0.6332	−0.3668	1.7009	0.7009
		6.4	1.1259	−5.2741	5.0566	−1.3434	6.7567	−1.3434
	20 dB	2.8	0.6452	−2.1548	3.8229	1.0229	3.0667	1.0229
		4.6	0.733	−3.867	3.917	−0.683	4.4469	−0.683
	30 dB	1	0.9898	−0.0102	1.782	0.782	0.8517	0.782
		2.8	0.6052	−2.1948	3.6214	0.8214	2.6883	−0.1117
	40 dB	4.6	0.6057	−3.9943	4.1397	−0.4603	4.5495	−0.0505
		8.2	0.8724	−7.3276	7.7062	−0.4938	8.2631	0.0631
BG	10 dB	1	0.6716	−0.3284	0.6946	−0.3054	1.4819	0.4819
		6.4	0.6386	−5.7614	7.218	0.818	6.9242	0.5242
	20 dB	2.8	0.7594	−2.0406	3.6459	0.8459	2.5137	−0.2863
		4.6	0.7835	−3.8165	5.3376	0.7376	4.3951	−0.2049
	30 dB	1	1.06	0.06	1.572	0.572	0.8517	−0.1483
		2.8	0.7725	−2.0275	2.475	−0.325	1.966	−0.834
	40 dB	4.6	0.6716	−3.9284	4.8053	0.2053	4.5233	−0.0767
		8.2	0.8976	−7.3024	8.3398	0.1398	8.314	0.114
CG	10 dB	1	0.8263	−0.1737	0.7619	−0.2381	2.0776	1.0776
		6.4	1.0315	−5.3685	5.4536	−0.9464	7.1384	0.7384
	20 dB	2.8	0.665	−2.135	3.4514	0.6514	2.6055	−0.1945
		4.6	0.9964	−3.6036	3.8594	−0.7406	4.6252	0.0252
	30 dB	1	0.6979	−0.3021	2.4312	1.4312	0.9356	−0.0644
		2.8	0.6863	−2.1137	2.1011	−0.6989	2.9104	0.1104
	40 dB	4.6	1.0095	−3.5905	4.0632	−0.5368	4.6597	0.0597
		8.2	0.9174	−7.2826	4.5419	−3.6581	8.2511	0.0511

[1] Traveling wave. [2] Predicted fault distance. Distance units are kilometers.

Table 7. Results of fault location under three different kinds of methods.

Fault Types	Fault Distance	Ref. [29]	Ref. [30]	Proposed Method
		Error	Error	Error
AG	1.2	0.968	2.374	−0.100
	3.6	1.126	1.562	0.090
BG	5	1.413	1.827	0.274
	4.3	1.237	1.635	0.133
CG	6.2	1.819	2.078	0.010
	2.6	1.068	1.235	0.251

Distance units are kilometers.

To validate the practical application value of the proposed method, the trained model was tested on an embedded device. The raw fault current data obtained from the simulation platform were imported into a Raspberry Pi, where they were converted into an MTF. The fault distance prediction was then made using the fault distance estimation method proposed in this paper. The results presented in Table 8 demonstrate that the method exhibits minimal error across various fault angles and ground fault types, indicating its significant practical applicability. The experimental setup is depicted in Figure 7.

Table 8. Raspberry Pi device fault prediction results.

Fault Angle	Fault Types	Fault Distance	Predicted Fault Distance	Error
0	BG	3	3.1104	−0.1104
90	AG	8.3	8.4258	−0.1258
270	CG	3	2.8469	0.1531

Distance units are kilometers.

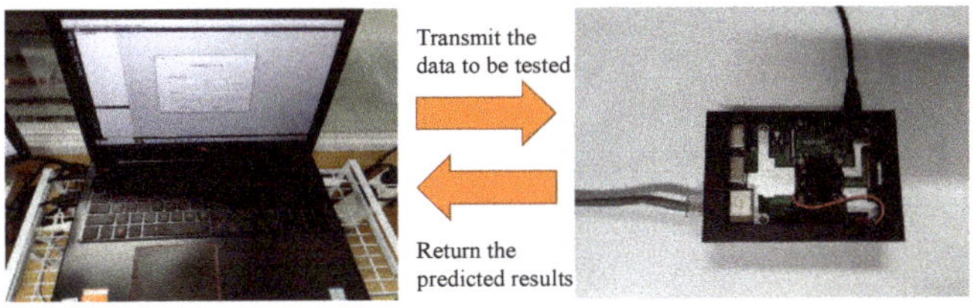

Figure 7. Physical simulation of fault distance detection.

6. Conclusions

This paper proposes a novel method for accurately and simply predicting the distance of single-phase grounding faults in distribution networks, leveraging the ground regression capability of neural networks and the reliable and anti-interference characteristics of MTF. This study presents a prediction method for single-phase grounding fault distances in distribution networks based on MTF and Darknet-19, and conducts simulation experiments using MATLAB. The final experimental conclusions are validated accordingly.

(1) The new phase-mode transformation matrix can effectively capture all types of fault separately in the distribution network, reflecting both the modulus 1 and modulus 2 components of the fault current. This enables a comprehensive expression of fault features in the sample.

(2) The MTF is capable of effectively extracting the fault features from one-dimensional signals, demonstrating a certain degree of resistance to interference. Furthermore, the visual representation produced can accurately convey the fault information present in the sample.

(3) The fault distance regression model of the Darknet-19 neural network was trained using MTF images. The entire system exhibits strong noise robustness. In simulated verification, the average prediction error is 330 m under a 40 dB noise condition. Additionally, test samples generated by the simulation platform at various distances demonstrate that the constructed regression model can predict labels that were not present during training, indicating its strong generalization ability.

Author Contributions: Conceptualization, Y.S., W.G., and H.W.; methodology, W.G.; software, H.W.; validation, W.G. and H.W.; formal analysis, H.W.; investigation, H.W.; resources, Y.S., W.G., and H.W.; data curation, W.G. and H.W.; writing—original draft preparation, H.W.; writing—review and editing, W.G. and H.W.; visualization, H.W.; supervision, H.W.; project administration, Y.S. and H.W.; funding acquisition, Y.S. and W.G. All authors have read and agreed to the published version of the manuscript.

Funding: This work was sponsored by the National Natural Science Foundation of China (62373006).

Data Availability Statement: The results/data/figures in this manuscript have not been published elsewhere, nor are they under consideration by another publisher.

Conflicts of Interest: The authors declare no conflicts of interest.

References

1. Hojabri, M.; Nowak, S.; Papaemmanouil, A. ML-Based Intermittent Fault Detection, Classification, and Branch Identification in a Distribution Network. *Energies* **2023**, *16*, 6023. [CrossRef]
2. Mahmoud, T.; Dong, Z.Y.; Ma, J. Integrated Optimal Active and Reactive Power Control Scheme for Grid Connected Permanent Magnet Synchronous Generator Wind Turbines. *IET Electr. Power Appl.* **2018**, *12*, 474–485. [CrossRef]
3. Yong, W.; Yongbin, B.; Pengtian, H.; Shouling, N.; Shenghai, H.; Bochao, P.; Ruini, F.; Xiaohui, W. Recognition of Single-Phase-to-Ground Fault Section of Distribution Line Based Phase Current Variation. In Proceedings of the 2021 IEEE/IAS Industrial and Commercial Power System Asia (I&CPS Asia), Chengdu, China, 18–21 July 2021; pp. 1138–1144. Available online: https://ieeexplore.ieee.org/abstract/document/9621573 (accessed on 10 May 2024). [CrossRef]
4. Niu, L.; Wu, G.; Xu, Z. Single-Phase Fault Line Selection in Distribution Network Based on Signal Injection Method. *IEEE Access* **2021**, *9*, 21567–21578. [CrossRef]
5. Zhang, X.; Xu, C.; Ma, X.; Wang, Z.; Lin, D.; Lin, X.; Li, Z. Research on the Precise Fault Location Scheme for Distribution Network with Multiple Branches Independent of Time Synchronization. *Power Syst. Prot. Control.* **2019**, *47*, 56–63.

6. Feng, X.; Qi, L.; Pan, J. A Novel Fault Location Method and Algorithm for DC Distribution Protection. *IEEE Trans. Ind. Appl.* **2017**, *53*, 1834–1840. [CrossRef]
7. Qi, Z.; Zhuang, S.; He, X.; Huang, Z. Traveling Wave Fault Location Technology for Hybrid Lines in Distribution Network Based on Disturbance Signal Injection at Busbar. *AEPS* **2019**, *43*, 124. [CrossRef]
8. Kong, F.; Hao, Z.; Zhang, B. A Novel Traveling-Wave-Based Main Protection Scheme for ±800 kV UHVDC Bipolar Transmission Lines. *IEEE Trans. Power Deliv.* **2016**, *31*, 2159–2168. [CrossRef]
9. Karmacharya, I.M.; Gokaraju, R. Fault Location in Ungrounded Photovoltaic System Using Wavelets and ANN. *IEEE Trans. Power Deliv.* **2018**, *33*, 549–559. [CrossRef]
10. Elkalashy, N.I.; Sabiha, N.A.; Lehtonen, M. Earth Fault Distance Estimation Using Active Traveling Waves in Energized-Compensated MV Networks. *IEEE Trans. Power Deliv.* **2015**, *30*, 836–843. [CrossRef]
11. Sun, K.; Chen, Q.; Gao, Z. An Automatic Faulted Line Section Location Method for Electric Power Distribution Systems Based on Multisource Information. *IEEE Trans. Power Deliv.* **2016**, *31*, 1542–1551. [CrossRef]
12. Liao, Y. Generalized Fault-Location Methods for Overhead Electric Distribution Systems. *IEEE Trans. Power Deliv.* **2011**, *26*, 53–64. [CrossRef]
13. Fu, H.; Liu, C.; Zhang, S.; Xu, Y.; Feng, S. Application of VMD-SWT Joint Algorithm in Fault Traveling Wave Detection. *Proc. CSU-EPSA* **2020**, *32*, 55–61. [CrossRef]
14. Peng, H.; Zhu, Y. Single Phase Grounding Fault Location for Power Lines of Wind Farm Based on apFFT Spectrum Correction and XGBoost Algorithm. *Trans. China Electrotech. Soc.* **2020**, *35*, 4931–4939.
15. Zhang, J.; Zhou, P.; Chen, H. Simulation of Transmission Line Single-Phase Ground Fault Location Based on Improved Impedance Method. *Electr. Meas. Instrum.* **2018**, *55*, 84–87.
16. Zheng, T.; Pan, Y.; Guo, K.; Wang, Z.; Sun, J. A Nodal Impedance Matrix Based Fault Location Algorithm for Distribution Network. *Power Syst. Technol.* **2013**, *37*, 3233–3240. [CrossRef]
17. Qi, Z.; Huang, Z.; Chen, Y. Impedance Fault Location Technology for a Distribution Network Based on a Zero-Sequence Component. *Power Syst. Prot. Control.* **2023**, *51*, 54–62. [CrossRef]
18. Keerqinhu; Qi, G.; Tsai, W.-T.; Hong, Y.; Wang, W.; Hou, G.; Zhu, Z. Fault-Diagnosis for Reciprocating Compressors Using Big Data. In Proceedings of the 2016 IEEE Second International Conference on Big Data Computing Service and Applications (BigDataService), Oxford, UK, 29 March–1 April 2016; pp. 72–81.
19. Huang, X.; Qi, G.; Mazur, N.; Chai, Y. Deep Residual Networks-Based Intelligent Fault Diagnosis Method of Planetary Gearboxes in Cloud Environments. *Simul. Model. Pract. Theory* **2022**, *116*, 102469. [CrossRef]
20. Xu, Y.; Feng, M.; Liang, X.; Gao, Y. Fault Location Method with the Combination of Wavelet Packet and PSO-RBF. *Proc. CSU-EPSA* **2019**, *31*, 127–132. [CrossRef]
21. Meng, Z.; Du, W.; Wang, H. Distribution Network Fault Area Location Based on Deep Convolution Neural Network with Transfer Learning. *South. Power Syst. Technol.* **2019**, *13*, 25–33. [CrossRef]
22. Zhang, C.; Peng, K.; Li, H.; Xu, B.; Chen, Y. Fault Calculation Method of Distribution Network Based on Deep Learning. *Symmetry* **2021**, *13*, 1086. [CrossRef]
23. Song, G.; Li, S.; Kang, X.; Zhou, D.; Yang, Z.; Suonan, J. A Novel Phase-Mode Transformation Matrix. *Autom. Electr. Power Syst.* **2007**, *31*, 57–60.
24. Wang, Z.; Oates, T. Encoding Time Series as Images for Visual Inspection and Classification Using Tiled Convolutional Neural Networks. In Proceedings of the Workshops at the Twenty-Ninth AAAI Conference on Artificial Intelligence, Austin, TX, USA, 25–30 January 2015.
25. Luo, Y.; Li, K.; Xiao, X.; Yin, C.; Li, B.; Li, X. Multi-Label Classification of Power Quality Composite Disturbances Based on Markov Transfer Field and Resnet. *Proc. CSEE* **2024**, *44*, 2519–2531. [CrossRef]
26. Abdel-Hamid, O.; Mohamed, A.; Jiang, H.; Deng, L.; Penn, G.; Yu, D. Convolutional Neural Networks for Speech Recognition. *IEEE/ACM Trans. Audio Speech Lang. Process.* **2014**, *22*, 1533–1545. [CrossRef]
27. Redmon, J.; Farhadi, A. YOLO9000: Better, Faster, Stronger. In Proceedings of the 2017 IEEE Conference on Computer Vision and Pattern Recognition (CVPR), Honolulu, HI, USA, 21–26 July 2017; pp. 6517–6525. [CrossRef]
28. Simonyan, K.; Zisserman, A. Very Deep Convolutional Networks for Large-Scale Image Recognition. *arXiv* **2015**, arXiv:1409.1556. [CrossRef]
29. Wang, Y.; Zheng, T.; Yang, C.; Yu, L. Traveling-Wave Based Fault Location for Phase-to-Ground Fault in Non-Effectively Earthed Distribution Networks. *Energies* **2020**, *13*, 5028. [CrossRef]
30. Hou, S.; Guo, X. Research on Fault Location of Distribution Lines Based on the Standing Wave Principle. *Processes* **2021**, *9*, 1436. [CrossRef]

mathematics

MDPI

Review

Review on System Identification, Control, and Optimization Based on Artificial Intelligence

Pan Yu [1,2,*], Hui Wan [2], Bozhi Zhang [2], Qiang Wu [2], Bohao Zhao [2], Chen Xu [2] and Shangbin Yang [2]

1 School of Information Science and Technology, Beijing University of Technology, Beijing 100124, China
2 Beijing Institute of Artificial Intelligence, Beijing University of Technology, Beijing 100124, China; huiwan@emails.bjut.edu.cn (H.W.); zhangbozhi@emails.bjut.edu.cn (B.Z.); wuqiang@emails.bjut.edu.cn (Q.W.); zhaobohao@emails.bjut.edu.cn (B.Z.); chenxu@emails.bjut.edu.cn (C.X.); yangshangbin@emails.bjut.edu.cn (S.Y.)
* Correspondence: panyu@bjut.edu.cn

Abstract

Control engineering plays an indispensable role in enhancing safety, improving comfort, and reducing fuel consumption and emissions for various industries, for which system identification, control, and optimization are primary topics. Alternatively, artificial intelligence (AI) is a leading, multi-disciplinary technology, which tries to incorporate human learning and reasoning into machines or systems. AI exploits data to improve accuracy, efficiency, and intelligence, which is beneficial, especially in complex and challenging cases. The rapid progress of AI facilitates major changes in control engineering and is helping advance the next generation of system identification, control, and optimization methods. In this study, we review the developments, key technologies, and recent advancements of AI-based system identification, control, and optimization methods, as well as present potential future research directions.

Keywords: artificial intelligence (AI); control engineering; model prediction control; optimization; parameter estimation; reinforcement learning; system identification; neural networks

MSC: 93-02

1. Introduction

Figuring out models from observations and unearthing their properties is really what science is about, and system identification is an important object of this process. System identification deals with the problem of figuring out mathematical models (such as deterministic models, stochastic models, non-parametric models, and parametric models) of dynamical systems based on the observed input-output data [1].

Although the term system identification was introduced by Lotfi Zadeh in the late 1950s [2], some progress (such as continuous functional [3], analytic functional [4]) was made by Maurice Fréchet and Vito Volterra before then. Since then, system identification has become an established research area within automatic control [5]. Considerable research has been conducted on this. Integral models can be used to describe the evolution of nonlinear dynamical systems [6]. Volterra series can be used to identify nonlinear dynamical systems [7], where integral equations play a key role in system analysis [8]. Moreover, it has been revealed that by using polynomial kernels, Volterra series can be represented implicitly as elements of a reproducing kernel Hilbert space [9]. The convex majorants method can be used to construct main solutions to nonlinear Volterra Equations [10]. A method was developed to compute the solution boundary of an interval outside which blow-up phenomena occur [11].

It is well known that when the essence, basic principles, or fundamental laws are known, mechanistic models (also called first-principles models, analytical models, or knowledge-based models) can be derived for dynamical systems. However, when dynamical systems are too complex to be understood at a fundamental level, data-driven approaches are a highly practical alternative to the first-principles approaches, which leverage computational algorithms or mathematical statistics to identify patterns in input-output data.

In general, the mechanism of dynamical systems is clear according to mechanistic models, while data-driven models are opaque because they are largely developed using mathematical methods. For this reason, mechanistic models are termed white-box models and data-driven models as black-box models. Integrating the traits of both modeling approaches yields hybrid modeling [12], which can be viewed as gray-box models. The structure of a hybrid model usually contains one part derived from first principles and the other part derived from data.

In addition to describing system dynamics, there may be other requirements, including the active manipulation of system behaviors. Control engineering involves applying control methods to design systems such that the systems behave in a desired manner, which has a wide range of applications, including aerospace [13], manufacturing [14], automotive [15], and robotics [16], where precision and reliability are imperative.

There are two main types of control methods, namely, open-loop control and closed-loop control. For simplicity, open-loop control imposes certain preplanned control logic to manipulate the systems. There is no feedback from the states or outputs of the systems. Closed-loop control uses sensors to measure the systems and then make decisions based on how the systems are responding, which allows one to deal with uncertainty and error by introducing feedback. Many methodologies have been developed for feedback control system design.

Mathematical models can be viewed as an interface between a real-world phenomenon and a mathematical world of control theory, which can be used to achieve specific control tasks by control methods. For the period of classical and/or modern control theory, model-based control is the dominant paradigm, and the framework of its control system design is shown in Figure 1. In general, mathematical models are only approximations of real plants, which cannot capture all the features. For example, high-frequency unmodeled dynamics like residual vibration modes were not considered in robotic and spacecraft models [17]. Therefore, although a model-based controller can be designed to achieve satisfactory performance in a simulation environment, it does not necessarily satisfy the predefined requirements for the real plant in practical applications due to various modeling errors or invalid prior assumptions.

Data-driven control is a promising alternative approach to control system design, using the input-output data of a plant to directly design the controller. It circumvents the necessity of system identification and has proliferated rapidly in recent decades. Consequently, data-driven control approaches are basically model-free designs, which can greatly alleviate the theory-practice gap.

Optimization refers to the problem of choosing a set of arguments that maximize or minimize a cost function or multiple cost functions. In the control community, arguments are usually related to control inputs, control parameters, etc., and a cost function or cost functions are related to the performance or requirements of a control system, like estimation errors and tracking errors. Due to various uncertainties in system dynamics, analytical solutions usually cannot be obtained for the formulated optimization problem. Various numerical optimization methods can be used to derive numerical solutions.

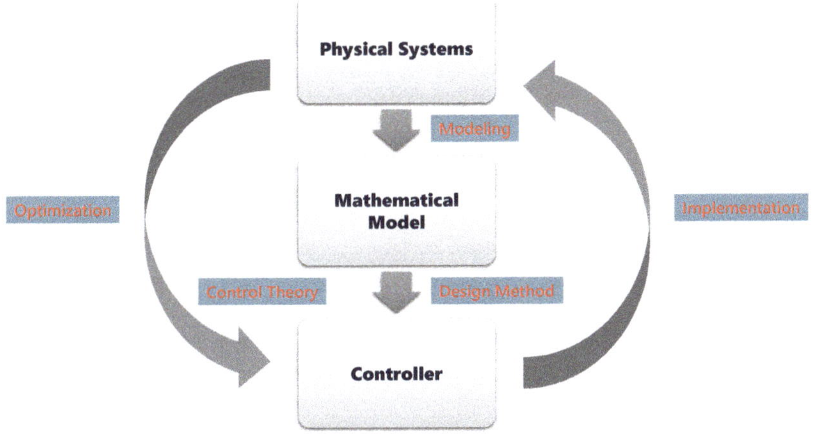

Figure 1. Framework for model-based control system design.

Alternatively, as one of the most highlighted research areas during the past decades, artificial intelligence (AI) is expanding rapidly [18,19], aiming to enable the use of systems or machines with the capability of mimicking human learning and reasoning. Much progress has been made with the help of AI technology in diversified industrial fields, including natural language processing [20], pattern recognition [21], autonomous cars [22], computer vision [23], robotics [24], etc. As the access to the data information of various sensors continues to expand and computing power becomes increasingly accessible, AI-aided or AI-based approaches have gained significant momentum. System identification, control, and optimization benefit greatly from the development of AI.

In this paper, a literature review of AI-based system identification, control, and optimization methods together with their applications and research challenges are presented. The paper is arranged as follows. The review of AI-based system identification methods is presented in Section 2. Section 3 reviews the control methods by integrating AI technology. Optimization methods are reviewed in Section 4. Section 5 presents the challenges and prospects.

2. AI-Based System Identification

In this section, we discuss parameter estimation, data-driven modeling, and hybrid modeling approaches together. Moreover, the advantages and disadvantages are discussed from a control-oriented point of view.

2.1. Parameter Estimation

To ensure mathematical models from mechanistic or data-driven modeling are capable of reflecting their physical counterparts, the parameters need to be precisely estimated. Parameter estimation usually involves the procedures of collecting data, devising estimation algorithms, and optimizing parameters to maximize the likelihood between the prediction and the observation or to minimize the error between the prediction and the observation. Although physics is able to provide knowledge for parameter estimation, the simultaneous estimation of potentially various parameters poses an exceptional challenge for high-dimensional complex systems. AI opens new avenues for the parameter estimation of dynamical systems [25].

By virtue of computational intractability, machine learning algorithms were used for the parameter estimation of complex systems following a transformation to large-scale inverse problems [26]. The stability to small changes in the data is an important property for solutions. Inverse problems that fail to satisfy this stability condition are called ill-posed as per Hadamard [27]. The strategies to solve inverse problems usually involve statistics, optimization, and regularization. Probabilistic tools (such as Bayesian inference and stochastic regularization) were mathematically introduced to address uncertainty, thus transforming ill-posedness into statistically stable solutions [28]. A neural parameter calibration method was developed to estimate parameter probability densities for large-scale multi-agent models [29]. By combining neural ordinary differential equations with physical prior knowledge, a new parameter estimation method was presented [30], which achieved a robust and accurate parameter estimation with a small sample and high noise condition. Deep learning provides an attractive strategy for solving parameter estimation problems by optimization. Regularization is usually used to avoid the ill-posed problem of parameter estimation for a large number of parameters [31]. By introducing additional constraints, a method was developed to regularize ill-posed problems into well-posed formulations [32]. A DeepBayes-based parameter estimator was devised for stochastic nonlinear dynamical models [33].

2.2. Data-Driven Modeling

The increasing complexity of dynamical systems has rendered mechanistic modeling gradually insufficient to meet the requirements due to its inherent limitations. Data-driven modeling does not rely on any prior knowledge or theoretical assumptions. It automatically learns and extracts features from a large amount of data through algorithms to establish models, which makes up for the deficiencies of mechanistic modeling. Therefore, it is increasingly favored in studies and more widely used in various industries.

2.2.1. Machine Learning

The main task of machine learning is to guide computers to learn from data and then use that experience to improve their own performance without explicit programming. In data-driven modeling, as a main learning mode of machine learning, supervised learning algorithms aim to establish the mapping and functional relationships between the inputs and outputs implicitly, with the training dataset consisting of input-and-output pairs.

Neural networks (NNs), support vector machines, logistic regression, etc., and they are supervised learning techniques with shallow structures. NNs were used to predict urban noise and to simulate car tailgating models, respectively [34,35]. Owing to the high approximation capability and the lower reliance on prior knowledge, NNs can handle more variables than traditional mathematical models, and they can deal with the nonlinear factors of dynamical systems. Due to their chaotic, unstable, or time-varying behaviors, it is more challenging to identify a dynamical system for which the observed data is nonstationary. A review about parametric system identification using neural networks was reported by [36], where the model interpretability of three types of NNs (i.e., feedforward NNs, recurrent NNs and encoder–decoder models) was summarized in modeling nonstationary time series. Support vector machines were used to model nonlinear systems [37], which reduced the impact of sample size and noise on system modeling. Furthermore, a bilinear logistic regression approach was proposed for smart grid fault modeling [38], where the parameters were trained using a real-world power grid failure dataset.

2.2.2. Deep Learning

As a breakthrough in AI, deep learning allows for the automatic processing of data by multi-level concatenation to refine highly nonlinear and complex features. Different deep learning based modeling techniques and architectures are used for system identification.

Feed-forward neural networks (FFNNs) are widely used. FFNN training entails random parameter initialization, gradient computation via back-propagation (BP) algorithms, and iterative parameter updates using stochastic gradient descent to minimize the loss function and optimize model performance. This was used to obtain the total nitrogen prediction model of effluents, with significantly improved prediction accuracy [39]. Recurrent neural networks (RNNs) have directed topological connections between neurons for learning features from sequential data [40], which were used for modeling the forward dynamics of soft robots [41]. Long and short-term memory networks are an improved version of RNNs, which were designed to solve the gradient vanishing problem and deal with complex time-series data [42]. Long and short-term memory networks were proposed to predict the acceleration distribution in car-following behavior [43]. Convolutional neural networks (CNNs) especially excel in the field of image recognition [44], where feature learning is achieved by stacking convolutional layers and pooling layers.

2.2.3. Transfer Learning

It is clear that a vast amount of data used for training is necessary for deep learning technology. When it is difficult to find sufficient training data, transfer learning is a good alternative, as it uses models trained from other data sources with certain modifications and improvements for similar fields.

Most data-driven approaches use online data to retrain models. However, unnecessary data updates and retraining are often costly and time consuming. When the studied wind–heat hybrid power system faced the issue of limited input-output data in the current scenario, transfer learning was proposed to utilize the data collected in the historical scenario to construct an online aggregated system frequency response model of the wind–heat hybrid power system operating in the current scenario [45]. A dynamic multi-source transfer learning model was proposed to effectively utilize rather than discard knowledge of historical data under similar working conditions or equipment to solve the defect of the neural network that was difficult to extrapolate [46]. Moreover, transfer learning was used in the initial feature extraction phase, where features were extracted by a pre-trained model, enabling the model to capture complex patterns in videos and extract deep features from video frames [47].

2.3. Hybrid Modeling

The idea of combining mechanistic modeling with data-driven models has emerged in the 1990s [48–50]. Since then, a significant amount of research has been published using the term hybrid modeling in process engineering-related research fields and gray-box modeling in the control and automation fields. Advantages with respect to modeling complex, high-dimensional, and/or computationally expensive systems could greatly benefit from hybrid modeling techniques. Hybrid modeling methodologies are reviewed from the aspect of the structure or typology of hybrid models. The relation between mechanistic modeling and data-driven modeling is shown in Figure 2.

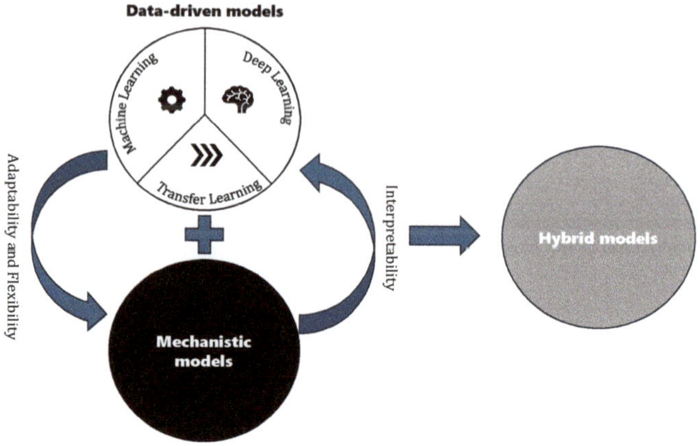

Figure 2. System identification methods.

2.3.1. Parallel Structures

When the performance of a mechanistic model is unsatisfactory due to oversimplifications, unreasonable assumptions, and unmodeled effects [51], hybrid models with parallel structures are usually appropriate. More specifically, mechanistic and data-driven models are executed simultaneously, and then, their outputs are combined in a way (e.g., voting and weighted averaging). It is well known that a mechanistic model represents the dynamics independently of a data-driven model. Consequently, a hybrid model serves to improve the quality of the predictions of the mechanistic model. Moreover, the performance of a hybrid model of a parallel structure depends on the quality of the data-driven model.

Parallel structures are able to reduce the potential bias of a single model by combining the outputs of different models. For example, a hybrid model of a mechanistic model and an FFNN for the wastewater treatment process worked well in parallel, where the output of the mechanistic model served as an input to the neural network and compensated for the model prediction error [52]. A multi-stage model consisting of a mechanistic model and a bi-directional gated recurrent unit model was developed [53], where the outputs of both models were passed by a dense neural network regressor to generate the final predictions.

Another common scenario where a parallel structure is widely used is to embed physical properties into loss functions. The loss function of a traditional data-driven model emphasizes the reduction of the loss between the estimate and the actual observation. However, it ignores the inherent physical properties, which could result in a model that is not consistent with the physics. Physics-informed loss functions are developed to address this challenge. They are constructed to constrain data-driven models to physically consistent spaces [54]. For example, Bayesian optimization algorithms were used to adjust the weighting factors in a loss function, thus optimizing model accuracy [55,56].

2.3.2. Serial Structures

Data-driven models can be advantageous when a mechanistic model is unavailable or too complex to be described mathematically [57]. Therefore, a serial structure can be chosen when a mechanistic model cannot fully map the relation between inputs and outputs because of the complexity, where the mechanistic and data-driven models are executed sequentially with the output of one model serving as the input of the other model. The performance of hybrid models of serial structures depends on how well a mechanistic model represents real phenomena. When the mechanistic model is reliable, the predictive properties of serial structures are usually better than those of parallel structures. However, parallel structures have better generalization because first-principles knowledge usually generalizes better than pure data.

A physically guided CNN was developed for the fault diagnosis of rolling element bearings [58], where the output of a mechanistic model was used as the input of a data-driven model. Deformation data were obtained by finite element simulation under different geometric gaps, and then, an FFNN prediction model was constructed for the deformation of a typical weld structure [59].

Physical information neural networks (PINNs) are a new type of networks that embed physical principles as a priori knowledge into the training process of NNs. To enable the NNs to fit the data while satisfying physical constraints, some strategies and techniques for incorporating the underlying first principles of the power grid into different types of machine learning approaches were reviewed [60]. PINNs are particularly well suited for scientific computing and engineering problems that involve solving partial differential equations or ordinary differential equations. Some newly developed techniques to enhance PINN performance while reducing training costs have been reviewed [61]. A PINN-based approach was proposed for modeling friction-inclusive dynamics of industrial robots [62], which ensured modeling accuracy while avoiding reliance on joint torque component labels and enhancing its ability to learn nonlinear features.

3. AI-Based Control Methods

The combination of AI and feedback control is an emerging research area, aiming to achieve more efficient and intelligent control systems by integrating the learning and decision-making capabilities of AI with the stability and accuracy of feedback control. The prevailing control methods have been studied extensively with the aid of AI.

3.1. Neural Network Control

Owing to universal approximation, parallel distributed processing, hardware implementation, learning and adaptation, and multivariable systems [63], neural networks are becoming particularly attractive and promising in control system design. Many neural networks with different structures have been introduced, like FFNNs [64–68], radial basis function neural networks (RBFNNs) [69–74], RNNs [75–78], and CNNs [79,80]. The key or challenge of using a neural network for feedback control is to select a suitable control system structure and then demonstrate how the weights of neural networks can be tuned to ensure the control performances (including stability, robustness, dynamic performance, steady-state performance, etc.) of the developed closed-loop feedback systems. Some prevailing control approaches are reviewed in the following.

3.1.1. Neural Network-Based Adaptive Control

Conventional adaptive control without neural networks is usually vulnerable to uncertainties or unknown dynamics and is challenging to deal with complex nonlinear systems. Neural network-based adaptive control is able to directly approximate unknown dynamics using neural networks, which removes the need for precise mathematical models. This is also the main reason why neural network-based adaptive control is especially suitable for complex nonlinear systems or uncertain dynamical systems.

Although promising results can be obtained for the neural network-based adaptive control methods, the closed-loop stability analysis is a burdensome task. Therefore, most of the existing neural network-based adaptive control methods rely on the Lyapunov direct method to guarantee stability. More specifically, a suitable Lyapunov candidate function is chosen first, which relates to both the neural network weights and tracking/estimation errors. Then, the update rules for the network weights are derived such that the time derivative of the Lyapunov candidate function becomes negative definite or negative semi-definite [81]. By the implicit function theorem, an observer-based direct adaptive fuzzy neural control scheme was proposed for non-affine nonlinear systems with unknown nonlinear structures [82], for which fuzzy neural networks were used to estimate the unknown nonlinear dynamics of the error system while ensuring the boundedness of all system signals by the strictly positive real Lyapunov theory. Furthermore, for highly nonlinear systems, with an online update of the layer width (e.g., neuron numbers) of the neural networks, a direct adaptive state feedback controller was used to approximate and adaptively compensate for unknown nonlinearities [83], whereby the uniform asymptotic stability of tracking errors were guaranteed via the incorporation of robust control terms.

3.1.2. Neural Network-Based Sliding-Mode Control

Owing to its robustness against structured and unstructured uncertainties, as well as its ease of implementation, sliding-mode control (SMC) has gained significant attention in the nonlinear systems control community. However, prior knowledge of the upper bounds of uncertainties or disturbances is usually required for conventional SMC methods, which may be impractical for some applications. Moreover, a large switching gain could bring about significant chattering. Therefore, numerous attempts have been made to integrate neural networks to make SMC more intelligent [84,85]. These can be mainly categorized into two types, namely, model-based and model-free ones.

Based on a mathematical model that may be inaccurate, some neural network-based adaptive SMC methods were designed for robots [86–88], vehicles [89,90], and aircraft [74], where the neural network was used to compensate for model uncertainties or other non-linearities. Compared with the conventional SMC, the developed method was able to reduce chattering and improve control performance. Alternatively, to remove the prior requirement of an upper bound of uncertainties and disturbances, rather than estimating the real value, neural networks were utilized to estimate the bounds [73,91–94].

For model-free control, neural networks are designed to estimate the whole dynamics of control systems. Although there is no need to calculate mathematical models for model-free control methods, the computation complexity is challenging. For example, a recurrent fuzzy wavelet neural network was integrated into robust adaptive SMC for industrial robot manipulators [95]. An RBFNN was combined with fuzzy sliding mode to tackle the trajectory tracking control [70].

3.1.3. Neural Network-Based Backstepping Control

It is well known that it is challenging to find a suitable control Lyapunov function for a general nonlinear control system. However, for nonlinear systems of a strict feedback form, the backstepping control method is a good solution. More specifically, a recursive design procedure is used, which links finding a control Lyapunov function with the design of a feedback controller. Moreover, the global asymptotic stability of strict feedback systems is guaranteed. By integrating neural networks to estimate unknown dynamics, nonlinearities, or virtual control laws, effective control strategies have been developed for nonlinear systems with uncertainties [96,97].

Owing to their universal approximation property, neural networks were employed to construct the nonlinear mapping online in backstepping control schemes. In earlier research, an RBFNN was used for the online approximation of a linear parametric model for a nonlinear system [71]. For the case where obtaining system states was difficult or costly in practice, neural network-based observers were developed to estimate the unavailable states, which broadened the application of backstepping control [98,99]. To remove the problem of the explosion of complexity of the traditional backstepping design, neural network techniques were combined with the command-filtered control method to achieve a robust and excellent performance [100–102]. Virtual control laws were approximated step-by-step by neural networks and then incorporated in backstepping control design based on the Lyapunov stability method [103,104].

3.1.4. Neural Network-Based Iterative Learning Control

Iterative learning control (ILC) is widely used in practical applications, such as manufacturing [105], robotics [106], and chemical processing [107], where mass production entails repeated operations on an assembly line. It learns error knowledge from the previous iteration to improve the next iteration [108]. However, it is difficult for conventional ILCs to cope with strong nonlinearities and uncertainties in practice. Therefore, neural networks are also incorporated into ILCs to solve practical difficulties and enhance control performance.

An RBFNN was used to automatically adjust the ILC gain of a nonlinear system by a dynamic linearization technique [109]. A generalized regression neural network was developed as an estimator to calculate key parameters, and then an RBFNN was designed to find the control input by iterative training [110]. Two neural networks were used to model a nonlinear process and as a learning controller, respectively, [111]. Moreover, the convergence analysis was conducted for both P-type and D-type learning controllers. A data-driven prediction model was established by a new RBFNN to estimate non-repeating external disturbances along the iterative learning axis [112]. Based on the previous iterative control input and output error, a BP neural network was used to learn system uncertainties and disturbances and then to compensate for them [113]. To solve the zero tracking problem with inherent noise tolerance, an ILC was proposed based on a modified zeroing neural network [114], which can not only theoretically converge to the exact solution of the zero tracking problem but also eliminate the strict assumptions on the initialization conditions of each iteration [115]. Neural networks were used to estimate the nonlinear portion of an ILC output and then predicted the ILC output for multiple tasks [116]. An inverse model-based ILC method was developed for a multiple input and multiple output (MIMO) nonlinear system, for which a neural network was constructed to observe the system [117].

3.1.5. Summary

The adaptation property arises from the many characteristics of neural networks, which include learnable weights and flexible architectures. According to the mechanism of the weight update policies, neural network control methods can be broadly categorized into two types, which can be seen from Figure 3. The weight update policy of the first type is based on BP algorithms [118,119], and the second type utilizes the Lyapunov stability theory [72]. It is important to mention that the BP algorithm is a class of optimization methods based on gradient information, which is one of the core algorithms in neural network training and is very popular in the control community. Besides the gradient-based methods explained in Section 4.1, second-order optimization methods (such as Newton's method [120], quasi-Newton methods [121]), metaheuristic optimization presented in Section 4.2, and Bayesian optimization [122] can be used to train neural networks. Furthermore, the selection of the number of hidden layers and neurons of a neural network is also important. In general, a neural network with more hidden layers and neurons is capable of providing a better control performance at the cost of higher complexity and computational cost.

Alternatively, it is clear that all the controllers mentioned above are based on standard neural networks. There are a few works based on neural ordinary differential equations. For example, a recurrent wavelet first-order neural network was developed for the multistability control of an erbium-doped fiber laser [123]. Similarly, the selection of the order number of a neural ordinary differential equation is a trade-off between performance and complexity.

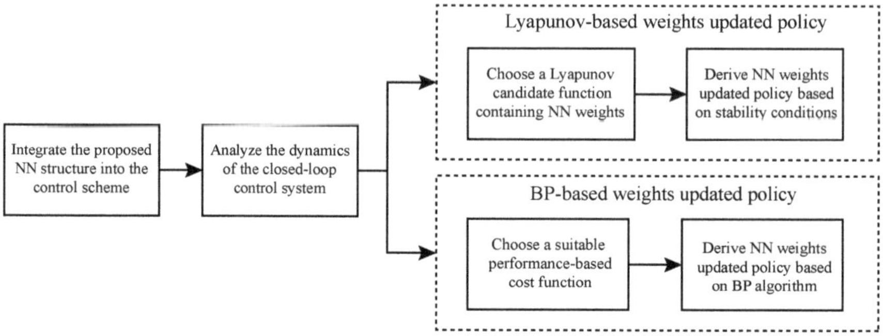

Figure 3. Two types of weight update policies for neural network control.

3.2. Model Prediction Control

Model predictive control (MPC) is also known as receding horizon control, which belongs to the intersection fields of optimization and control. There are several notable advantages for MPC. First, it can seamlessly deal with MIMO systems, which are the main system types in complex industries. Second, various constraints including physical limitations can be well handled for MPC. Third, noting that MPC not only considers the current states and inputs but also takes into account the future states and inputs to achieve optimization control at every sampling time, it is adaptive or robust to future effects. The implementation of MPC includes three key components, namely, model prediction, optimization in a receding horizon, and feedback correction.

However, for dynamical systems requiring high-frequency control, MPC may be infeasible, especially when complex MPC schemes such as nonlinear MPC or robust MPC are used, or when the controller needs to be implemented in a low-cost embedded platform. So, the main challenge of the design and real-time implementation of MPC in practical applications is to have an accurate enough predictive model with a real-time computation capability for large-scale optimization problems. In the past two decades, a great deal of research has been carried out to utilize AI technology to facilitate the design of MPC, for which most works focus on prediction models and fast optimization for high-lever controllers.

3.2.1. Model Prediction

Machine Learning can be used to provide an accurate model at a decreased computational cost and with improved MPC performance [124]. An RNN enjoys the advantages of both high scalability and the capability of modeling multiple-output data. Therefore, RNNs have been widely used in model prediction. For example, to address the limitation of adaptive algorithms based on continuous model update processes and MPC policy redesign, which are constrained to systems with long sampling times, a novel nonlinear system identification and adaptive control method leveraging integrated neural networks was proposed [125]. Addressing at the challenges of nonlinearity, noise, and time delay in industrial processes, and a method of using RNN architectures to solve the problem of modeling and control of complex dynamical systems in industrial processes was proposed [126]. Addressing the challenge of significant hysteresis and unknown state interactions in soft robot systems, a deep-neural network-based method was proposed for modeling and controlling soft robots [127].

A nonlinear auto-regressive predictive model was built for MPC by utilizing a neural network to learn exogenous inputs, and the input-to-state stability of the closed-loop system was ensured [128]. A path-tracking MPC algorithm was developed for a vision-based mobile robot, where the disturbance was modeled as a Gaussian process [129]. To ensure the safety of the robot when operating under new conditions, a learning probabilistic model was developed by comparing a Gaussian process with a specific form of local linear regression [130]. A novel parameter adaptive MPC architecture was proposed, which enabled online tuning without recomputing large datasets and retraining [131]. To solve the problem related to the fact that the performance of nonlinear MPC models depends on the quality of the underlying model, and that the closed-loop behavior of systems may be difficult to analyze formally, a data-driven economic nonlinear MPC strategy was presented to support parameterization and approximate the action value functions [132].

3.2.2. Fast Optimization

To enable MPC strategies with fast optimization, two types of approaches are developed. The first type includes the development of fast solvers and tailored implementations to calculate formulated optimization problems in real time [133,134]. Machine learning was used to accelerate the original active set to solve the developed quadratic programming-based MPC problem [135], where a state-dependent warm-start was designed by solving the parameterized program offline.

The second type is usually called explicit MPC [136]. With feasibility and stability guarantees, a sampling-based explicit nonlinear MPC was developed for nonlinear systems, for which a support vector machine classifier was used to approximate the feasible region [137]. Neural networks were used to compute the approximate explicit MPC laws, and the feasible control inputs were generated by projecting onto a multifaceted region that was derived from the maximum control invariant set [138]. A deep-learning-based method was developed to efficiently represent an approximation of the MPC laws [133]. Neural networks with modified rectified linear units were constructed to approximate the piecewise affine explicit control laws of MPC, which allowed the approximations to effectively address large-scale problems involving thousands of parameter variables [136].

3.3. *Reinforcement Learning Control*

As another learning mode of machine learning, unlike supervised learning, which relies on a training dataset with predefined answers and unsupervised learning without desired answers, reinforcement learning (RL) learns a task through a lot of trials. RL is a field closely related to control theory. From the perspective of control theory, the relation of RL with dynamic programming is reviewed first. Through model-based and model-free learning, recent developments in RL in control science are summarized.

3.3.1. Approximate Dynamic Programming

Optimal control is an important branch of control theory, aiming to design controllers to optimize dynamical systems under certain performance metrics [139]. There are three pillars in optimal control, i.e., calculus of variations, Pontryagin's maximum principle, and dynamic programming [140]. Dynamic programming was proposed by Richard Bellman to solve the Bellman equation for a discrete-time system or the Hamilton-Jacobi-Bellman (HJB) for a continuous-time system [141]. However, in practice, directly solving these equations often leads to the curse of dimensionality. In other words, it is computationally large and difficult to realize for high-dimensional systems [140].

To solve this problem, heuristic dynamic programming was developed in 1990, which approximated an optimal value function of the Bellman equation by using approximation functions or models [142]. Then HDP was developed into approximate dynamic programming [143], which is essentially equivalent to the temporal difference methods in RL [144]. In 1989, the proposal of the Q-learning approach combining dynamic programming with online learning marked the emergence of RL in the field of optimal control [145]. As a result, RL and optimal control theory began to integrate, providing a new way to solve complex optimal control problems.

In the context of the optimal control of continuous stochastic processes, the HJB equation and dynamic programming can solve the optimal solution. However, theoretical solutions are difficult to find. Thus, numerical methods such as gradient descent were employed to approximate the optimal solution [146].

3.3.2. Model-Based RL Control

In the field of control systems, with a known system model, the model information can be fully used in the RL algorithm to accelerate the learning process. Given a system model, the value and corresponding reward of each state are accurately calculated, and then, the state transfer probability matrix can be constructed [147]. Using value iteration or policy iteration, the optimal policy can be solved. When the system model is completely known, model-based RL algorithms have been widely used to solve the optimal stabilization problem [148,149], the control problem [150,151], and the tracking problem [152].

3.3.3. Model-Free RL Control

However, in practical applications, it is difficult to obtain an accurate mathematical model for an environment or a dynamic system. Even if an accurate model is obtained, it would be too complex to be used directly. Model-free RL algorithms become particularly important. They perform policy learning through interaction with the environment or system and collect data samples from interaction processes, without relying on an accurate model. There are mainly three categories of model-free RL algorithms [153], including value-based, policy-based, and actor-critic algorithms.

For value-based algorithms, a value function is estimated to evaluate the system states or control actions. An agent or controller selects the optimal policy based on the value function [139]. For example, the Q-learning algorithm is a typical value-based model-free RL algorithm [153]. It is widely used in optimal regulation control [154,155] and optimal tracking control [156,157] for nonlinear systems with unknown models. The deep Q-learning algorithm was used to optimize the energy storage management system of a wind power generator [158].

Unlike value-based algorithms, policy-based algorithms directly learn the mapping relation from states to actions, i.e., the policy function. Instead of explicitly estimating the value function, such methods maximize the long-term cumulative reward by optimizing the policy function [153]. For example, the policy gradient algorithm is a commonly used model-free RL algorithm, which uses gradient descent to optimize parameterized policies [159]. In the gait control for bipedal robots, the policy gradient algorithm learned an optimal gait control strategy in different terrains and motion states by interacting with the environment [160,161].

The actor-critic algorithm combines the advantages of both value and policy functions and learns both value and policy functions to achieve policy optimization. An actor-critic online optimal control algorithm with three neural networks was proposed for the robust control of unknown nonlinear systems [162]. To achieve the optimal synchronous tracking control of heterogeneous multi-agent systems with input-constrained and unknown nonlinearities, an off-policy RL algorithm was proposed, which utilized neural networks to build critic and actor networks, trained them by an actor-critic algorithm, and then obtained the optimal control policy [163]. An actor-critic algorithm was developed to evaluate different control strategies by learning the value function and optimizing the policy function to achieve an optimal active suspension adjustment to meet the comfort and handling requirements of the vehicle [164].

4. Performance Optimization

Satisfactory performance is one of the end goals of system design or control. Moreover, most system design or control problems can be formulated as optimization tasks. Although gradient-based algorithms are typically recognized because of their computational speed and efficiency, gradients and Hessian matrices are required for the iteration. However, the information is unavailable for black-box cases. Alternatively, when the computational cost is very cheap, the design space is noisy or discontinuous, there may be multiple optima, or when derivatives can not be calculated efficiently, gradient-free optimizers are recommended.

4.1. Gradient-Based Optimization

Gradient-based optimization is the backbone of modern machine learning. It is based on gradient descent and is crucial for training neural networks, deep learning models, and many other machine learning models.

The key idea of gradient descent is that a loss function $J(\theta)$ of parameters θ can be minimized along with the direction of the negative gradient $-\nabla J(\theta)$. In other words, the loss function value can be decreased when θ takes a step in the negative gradient direction. Gradient descent optimizers are based on first-order derivatives, which are more practical than high-order derivative-based algorithms, e.g., Newton's method, for deep models.

Many variants are proposed. The vanilla batch gradient descent algorithm renews the parameters via the gradient of the entire training set, and while simple, it is slow for large datasets and models. Stochastic gradient descent (SGD) addresses this by updating based on the gradient of individual training examples, introducing stochasticity that can help escape suboptimal local minima. In practice, mini-batch SGD that computes the gradient over small subsets of the data is used as a happy medium.

In practice, the gradients are computed by the BP algorithm by utilizing the chain rule. The BP algorithm together with automatic differentiation tools has made gradient-based optimization the default choice for training machine learning models.

4.2. Metaheuristic Optimization

Metaheuristic optimization algorithms are a kind of computational technique widely used in complex optimization problems [165], seeking an approximate optimal solution by imitating the evolution of social behavior or natural phenomena. Moreover, they usually do not rely on the gradient information of the problems considered. Through global or local search, they reach a balance between exploration and development in search space, so as to avoid falling into a local optimal solution. Evolutionary algorithms, particle swarm optimization, ant colony optimization, and simulated annealing are examples of metaheuristic optimization algorithms. Their features are summarized in Table 1.

Genetic algorithms (GAs) are inspired by biological evolution, which simulates natural selection and genetic mechanisms to find optimal solutions. A GA was applied to automatically search for the optimal key hyperparameters of deep RL models [166], such as learning rates, discount factors, and exploration–exploitation trade-offs, which were typically difficult to fine-tune manually. A GA was used for the parameter identification of vapor-liquid thermodynamic models [167]. Differential evolution (DE) is a population-based evolutionary algorithm that guides the optimization process by exploiting the differences between solutions in a population. DE is widely used in the design optimization of power electronic systems, such as the parameter estimation of inverters [168], power converters [169], and solar photovoltaic models [170].

Particle swarm optimization (PSO) methods iteratively solve problems by moving a swarm of particles around the design space until convergence is reached [171,172]. PSO emerges as a powerful optimization technique in fields such as power system state estimation [173]. Ant colony optimization (ACO) is a kind of optimization algorithm inspired by ant foraging behavior, which is mainly used to solve combinatorial optimization problems, such as power scheduling [174], optimal path selection [175], and so on. ACO was used to identify the natural frequencies and damping ratios of mechanical systems [176]. Simulated annealing (SA) solves optimization problems iteratively by simulating the physical annealing process, which is suitable for large-scale, complex nonlinear problems and has been applied in power electronics system design [177] and other fields.

Table 1. Metaheuristic optimization algorithms.

Algorithms	Inspiration	Feature	References
GA	Evolutionary	Robust Global Search	[166,167]
DE	Evolutionary	Efficient Mutation	[168–170]
PSO	Swarm Intelligence	Fast Convergence	[173]
ACO	Swarm Intelligence	Positive Feedback	[177]
SA	Physics	Escape Local Optima	[174,175]

5. Challenges and Prospects

Some future challenges and directions are discussed as follows based on this literature review.

5.1. Challenges

(1) AI models or algorithms usually rely on a large amount of high-quality training data. The means for obtaining these data, especially in dynamic and complex environments, are a significant challenge.

(2) Data-driven techniques for system identification rely on extracted patterns from historical or experimental data. The reasoning mechanism has yet to be fully understood or explained by physics and may thus be opaque to engineers. In other words, interpretability could be a concern due to its black-box nature.

(3) Since the mathematical foundations of AI are yet to be fully established, a practice guide to facilitate the architecture designs and implementation of AI models or algorithms for system identification, control, and optimization is still an open issue.

(4) Although AI models or algorithms can improve the modeling accuracy or control performance of dynamical systems, computational complexity becomes correspondingly more complex. Ways to deal with the trade-off are also a crucial challenge.

5.2. Future Directions

AI is capable of making feedback control loops smarter and more adaptive to uncertainties. Several promising directions to make full use of AI in control systems are given as follows.

(1) More models and learning methods can be used to improve the generalization ability of deep learning. Future efforts should prioritize multi-modal learning architectures that integrate heterogeneous data sources (e.g., multi-modal sensor fusion of vision, LiDAR, and inertial measurement units) to create more comprehensive system representations. Meta-learning approaches, particularly few-shot and zero-shot learning paradigms, could enable control systems to adapt rapidly to novel scenarios with

minimal retraining. Foundation-scale models pre-trained on multi-domain physical system datasets demonstrate transformative potential. They can serve as universal priors for low-level control tasks while retaining domain-specific knowledge through lightweight fine-tuning. For instance, a physics-informed large language model could interpret system dynamics from textual maintenance logs and simultaneously process numerical sensor data, enabling cross-domain knowledge transfer in industrial control engineering applications.

(2) Developing a new, effective, and more interpretable architecture to implement AI models or algorithms in feedback control systems could make the decision-making process of control systems more transparent, ensuring stability and real-time guarantees. Neural ordinary differential equation networks could be synergistically integrated with traditional MPC frameworks, where the neural component learns residual dynamics while the MPC core provides stability guarantees through convex optimization constraints. Furthermore, attention mechanisms and symbolic regression layers should be incorporated into control strategies to produce human-understandable explanations for control actions. Moreover, the integration of performance assessment tools, such as reachability analysis and Lyapunov functional synthesis, with neural network-based controllers will be essential for safety-critical applications like autonomous vehicles and medical robotics.

(3) Exploring strategies regarding the ways machine learning is used to model and handle uncertainties can achieve more robust control. For most mechanical systems, the dominant dynamics can be obtained by first principles. Uncertainties including parameter variations (e.g., the moment of the inertia of robotic arms) and unmodeling dynamics (e.g., the aerodynamic disturbances of unmanned aerial vehicles) are the main causes of performance deterioration. A hierarchical learning framework could be developed where Bayesian neural networks quantify uncertainty distributions, while adversarial reinforcement learning agents train controllers to cope optimally under worst-case uncertainty scenarios. Physics-guided uncertainty propagation methods should be investigated, whereby learned uncertainty bounds are systematically incorporated into robust control strategies such as H infinity control and SMC. For distributed systems, federated learning architectures could enable collaborative uncertainty modeling across fleets of cyber-physical systems while preserving data privacy.

(4) Most works focus on uncertainty estimation and compensation without considering the learning performance. Utilizing AI-based optimization algorithms to calculate the control input could be a more efficient and direct control method. Implicit neural representation networks could parameterize entire families of optimal control laws, enabling real-time solutions for nonlinear MPC problems without iterative computations. Evolutionary strategies enhanced by neural surrogates may discover non-conventional control strategies that outperform conventional PID or linear quadratic Gaussian designs in complex multi-objective scenarios. For large-scale systems, graph neural networks could solve distributed optimization problems by learning message-passing mechanisms between subsystems. Crucially, these approaches must address the duality between learning performance and control stability through novel loss functions that penalize Lyapunov function derivatives or contraction metric violations.

Author Contributions: Conceptualization, P.Y.; methodology, P.Y. and H.W.; software, B.Z. (Bozhi Zhang) and Q.W.; validation, P.Y., H.W. and B.Z.; formal analysis, B.Z. (Bohao Zhao) and B.Z. (Bozhi Zhang); investigation, C.X., S.Y. and B.Z. (Bozhi Zhang); resources, H.W., B.Z. (Bozhi Zhang) and B.Z. (Bohao Zhao); data curation, C.X.; writing—original draft preparation, P.Y. and B.Z. (Bozhi Zhang); writing—review and editing, Q.W. and H.W.; visualization, B.Z. (Bozhi Zhang) and H.W.;

supervision, P.Y.; project administration, P.Y.; funding acquisition, P.Y. All authors have read and agreed to the published version of the manuscript.

Funding: This work was partly supported by the National Natural Science Foundation of China under Grant 62003010 and the Scientific Research Project of the Beijing Educational Committee under Grant KM202410005036.

Conflicts of Interest: The authors declare no conflicts of interest.

References

1. Ljung, L. Perspectives on system identification. *Annu. Rev. Control* **2010**, *34*, 1–12. [CrossRef]
2. Zadeh, L. On the identification problem. *IRE Trans. Circuit Theory* **1956**, *3*, 277–281. [CrossRef]
3. Fréchet, M. Sur les fonctionnelles continues. *Ann. Sci. L'éCole Norm. SupéRieure* **1910**, *27*, 193–216. [CrossRef]
4. Volterra, V. *Theory of Functionals and of Integral and Integro-Differential Equations;* Dover Publications, Inc.: New York, NY, USA, 1958.
5. Ljung, L. *System Identification—Theory for the User*, 2nd ed.; Prentice-Hall: Hoboken, NJ, USA, 1999.
6. Sidorov, D. *Integral Dynamical Models: Singularities, Signals and Control;* World Scientific: Singapore, 2014.
7. Sidorov, D.; Tynda, A.; Muratov, V.; Yanitsky, E. Volterra Black-Box Models Identification Methods: Direct Collocation vs. Least Squares. *Mathematics* **2024**, *12*, 227.[CrossRef]
8. Apartsyn, A.S. *Nonclassical Linear Volterra Equations of the First Kind;* De Gruyter: Berlin, Germany, 2011.
9. Franz, M.O.; Schölkopf, B. A unifying view of Wiener and Volterra theory and polynomial kernel regression. *Neural Comput.* **2006**, *18*, 3097–3118. [CrossRef]
10. Sidorov, D.; Sidorov, N.A. Convex majorants method in the theory of nonlinear Volterra equations. *Banach J. Math. Anal.* **2012**, *6*, 1–10. [CrossRef]
11. Sidorov, D. Existence and blow-up of Kantorovich principal continuous solutions of nonlinear integral equations. *Differ. Equ.* **2014**, *50*, 1175–1182. [CrossRef]
12. Schweidtmann, A.M.; Zhang, D.D.; Stosch, M.V. Review and perspective on hybrid modeling methodologies. *Digit. Chem. Eng.* **2024**, *10*, 100136. [CrossRef]
13. Chernyshev, S.; Sypalo, K.; Bazhenov, S. Intelligent control algorithms to ensure the flight safety of aerospace vehicles. *Acta Astronaut.* **2025**, *226*, 782–790. [CrossRef]
14. Monostori, L.; Kádár, B.; Bauernhansl, T. Cyber-physical systems in manufacturing. *CIRP Ann.* **2016**, *65*, 621–641. [CrossRef]
15. Liu, F.Y.; Jin, L.; Shang, M.; Wang, X. ACP-Incorporated Perturbation-Resistant Neural Dynamics Controller for Autonomous Vehicles. *IEEE Trans. Intell. Veh.* **2024**, *9*, 4675–4686. [CrossRef]
16. Huang, X.; Rong, Y.; Gu, G. High-Precision Dynamic Control of Soft Robots with the Physics-Learning Hybrid Modeling Approach. *IEEE/ASME Trans. Mechatron.* 2024, *early access*. [CrossRef]
17. Khaki-Sedigh A. *An Introduction to Data-Driven Control Systems;* John Wiley & Sons, Inc.: Hoboken, NJ, USA, 2023.
18. Bishop, C.M. *Pattern Recognition and Machine Learning;* Springer: Berlin/Heidelberg, Germany, 2006.
19. Goodfellow, I.; Bengio, Y.; Courville, A. *Deep Learning;* MIT Press: Cambridge, MA, USA, 2016.
20. Liu, D. Design Information Extraction and Visual Representation based on Artificial Intelligence Natural Language Processing Techniques. In Proceedings of the International Conference on Computer Vision, Image and Deep Learning, Zhuhai, China, 12–14 May 2023; pp. 154–158.
21. Zimo, Y.; Jian, P.; Ru, W.; Xiang, Y.X. Embrace sustainable AI: Dynamic data subset selection for image classification. *Pattern Recognit.* **2024**, *151*, 110392.
22. Kashyap, A.; Ray, A.; Kalyan, B.; Bhushan, P. A Minimalistic Model for Converting Basic Cars Into Semi-Autonomous Vehicles Using AI and Image Processing. In Proceedings of the 2023 International Conference on Applied Intelligence and Sustainable Computing, Dharwad, India, 16–17 June 2023; pp. 1–6.
23. Bhamare, A.; Upadhyay, V.; Bansal, P. AI based Plant Growth Monitoring System using Computer Vision. In Proceedings of the 2023 IEEE Technology & Engineering Management Conference—Asia Pacific, Bengaluru, India, 14–16 December 2023; pp. 1–5.
24. Jorge, R.; Rui, L.; Tiago, E.; Sara, P. Robotic Process Automation and Artificial Intelligence in Industry 4.0—A Literature review. *Procedia Comput. Sci.* **2021**, *181*, 51–58.
25. Kutz, J. Machine learning for parameter estimation. *Proc. Natl. Acad. Sci. USA* **2023**, *120*, e2300990120. [CrossRef]
26. Richard, C.A.; Brian, B.; Clifford, H.T. *Parameter Estimation and Inverse Problems*, 2nd ed.; Academic Press: Cambridge, MA, USA, 2013; pp. 93–127.
27. Kabanikhin, S.I. *Inverse and Ill-Posed Problems;* de Gruyter: Berlin, Germany, 2008.
28. Lavrentiev, M.M. *Some Improperly Posed Problems of Mathematical Physics;* Springer: Berlin/Heidelberg, Germany, 1967.
29. Gaskin, T.; Pavliotis, G.A.; Girolami, M. Neural parameter calibration for large-scale multi-agent models. *Proc. Natl. Acad. Sci. USA* **2023**, *120*, e2216415120. [CrossRef]

30. Yong, Y.; Haibin, L. Neural ordinary differential equations for robust parameter estimation in dynamic systems with physical priors. *Appl. Soft Comput.* **2025**, *169*, 112649. [CrossRef]
31. Pillonetto, G.; Chen, T.; Chiuso, A.; Nicolao, G.; Ljung, L. *Regularized System Identification: Learning Dynamic Models from Data*; Springer: Cham, Switzerland, 2022.
32. Tikhonov, A.N.; Arsenin, V.Y. *Solutions of Ill-Posed Problems*; Halsted Press: Ultimo, Australia, 1977.
33. Anubhab, G.; Mohamed, A.; Saikat, C.; Håkan, H. DeepBayes—An estimator for parameter estimation in stochastic nonlinear dynamical models. *Automatica* **2024**, *159*, 111327.
34. Genaro, N.; Torija, A.; Ramos, A.; Requena, I.; Ruiz, D.P.; Zamorano, M. Modeling environmental noise using artificial neural networks. In Proceedings of the International Conference on Intelligent Systems Design and Applications, Pisa, Italy, 30 November–2 December 2009; pp. 215–219.
35. Khodayari, A.; Ghaffari, A.; Kazemi, R.; Braunsting, R. A modified car-following model based on a neural network model of the human driver effects. *IEEE Trans. Syst.* **2012**, *42*, 1440–1449. [CrossRef]
36. Dong, A.; Starr, A.; Zhao, Y. Neural network-based parametric system identification: A review. *Int. J. Syst. Sci.* **2023**, *54*, 2676–268. [CrossRef]
37. Zhang, H.R.; Wang, X.S.; Zhang, C.J.; Xu, X.L. Modeling nonlinear dynamical systems using support vector machine. In Proceedings of the International Conference on Machine Learning and Cybernetics, Guangzhou, China, 18–21 August 2005; pp. 3204–3209.
38. De Santis, E.; Rizzi, A. Modeling failures in smart grids by a bilinear logistic regression approach. *Neural Netw.* **2024**, *174*, 106245. [CrossRef] [PubMed]
39. Zhao, Z.H.; Wang, Z.H.; Yuan, J.L.; Ma, J.; He, Z.L.; Xu, Y.L.; Shen, X.J.; Zhu, L. Development of a novel feedforward neural network model based on controllable parameters for predicting effluent total nitrogen engineering. *Engineering* **2021**, *7*, 195–202. [CrossRef]
40. Hihi, S.E.; Bengio, Y. Hierarchical recurrent neural networks for long-term dependencies. *Int. Conf. Neural Inf. Process. Syst.* **1995**, *8*, 493–499.
41. Thuruthel, T.G.; Falotico, E.; Renda, F.; Laschi, C. Model-based reinforcement learning for closed-loop dynamic control of soft robotic manipulators. *IEEE Trans. Robot.* **2019**, *35*, 124–134. [CrossRef]
42. Wang, J.J.; Ma, Y.; Zhang, L.B.; Gao, R.X.; Wu, D.Z. Deep learning for smart manufacturing: Methods and applications. *J. Manuf. Syst.* **2018**, *48*, 144–156. [CrossRef]
43. Morton, J.; Wheeler, T.A.; Kochenderfer, M.J. Analysis of recurrent neural networks for probabilistic modeling of driver behavior. *IEEE Trans. Intell. Transp. Syst.* **2017**, *18*, 1289–1298. [CrossRef]
44. Yu, M.; Zhang, G.; Li, Q.; Chen, F. PGMM—Pre-trained gaussian mixture model based convolution neural network for electroencephalography imagery analysis. *IEEE Access* **2020**, *8*, 157418–157426. [CrossRef]
45. Zhang, J. Sfr modeling for hybrid power systems based on deep transfer learning. *IEEE Trans. Ind. Inform.* **2024**, *20*, 399–410. [CrossRef]
46. Zhou, X.; Zhai, N.; Li, S.; Shi, H. Time series prediction method of industrial process with limited data based on transfer learning. *IEEE Trans. Ind. Inform.* **2023**, *19*, 6872–6882. [CrossRef]
47. Hassan, N.; Miah, A.; Shin, J. A deep bidirectional LSTM model enhanced by transfer-learning-based feature extraction for dynamic human activity recognition. *Appl. Sci.* **2024**, *14*, 603. [CrossRef]
48. Psichogios, D.C.; Ungar, L.H. A hybrid neural network-first principles approach to process modeling. *AIChE J.* **1992**, *38*, 1499–1511. [CrossRef]
49. Su, H.T.; Bhat, N.; Minderman, P.A.; McAvoy, T.J. Integrating neural networks with first principles models for dynamic modeling. In *Dynamics and Control of Chemical Reactors, Distillation Columns and Batch Processes*; Elsevier: Amsterdam, The Netherlands, 1993; pp. 327–332.
50. Thompson, M.L.; Kramer, M.A. Modeling chemical processes using prior knowledge and neural networks. *AIChE J.* **1994**, *40*, 1328–1340. [CrossRef]
51. Yang, S.; Pranesh, N.; Sambit, G.; Wayne, B. Hybrid modeling in the era of smart manufacturing. *Comput. Chem. Eng.* **2020**, *140*, 106874. [CrossRef]
52. Chen, Z.; Zhang, J.; Chu, Q.; Wang, Y. Study on hybrid modeling of urban wastewater treatment process. In Proceedings of the 2022 34th Chinese Control and Decision Conference, Hefei, China, 15–17 August 2022; pp. 792–797.
53. Wang, J.J.; Li, Y.L.; Zhao, R.; Gao, R.X. Physics guided neural network for machining tool wear prediction. *J. Manuf. Syst.* **2020**, *57*, 298–310. [CrossRef]
54. Wang, J.J.; Li, Y.L.; Gao, R.X.; Zhang, F.L. Hybrid physics-based and data-driven models for smart manufacturing: Modelling, simulation, and explainability. *J. Manuf. Syst.* **2022**, *63*, 381–391. [CrossRef]
55. Wei, C.J.; Zhang, J.X.; Liechti, M.; Wu, C.L. Data-driven modeling of interfacial traction–separation relations using a thermodynamically consistent neural network. *Comput. Methods Appl. Mech. Eng.* **2023**, *404*, 115826. [CrossRef]

56. Gao, T.; Zhu, H.; Wu, J. Hybrid physics data-driven model-based fusion framework for machining tool wear prediction. *Int. J. Adv. Manuf. Technol.* **2024**, *132*, 1481–1496. [CrossRef]
57. Zendehboudi, S.; Rezaei, N.; Lohi, A. Applications of hybrid models in chemical, petroleum, and energy systems: A systematic review. *Appl. Energy* **2018**, *228*, 2539–2566. [CrossRef]
58. Sadoughi, M.; Hu, C. Physics-based convolutional neural network for fault diagnosis of rolling element bearings. *IEEE Sens. J.* **2019**, *19*, 4181–4192. [CrossRef]
59. Wang, J.M.; Liu, J.Y.; Hou, X.J. A hybrid mechanics-data modeling approach for predicting the accuracy of train body flexible assembly. *Mech. Syst. Signal Process.* **2024**, *202*, 111242.
60. Jabbari, Z.M.; Chatterjee, P.; Srivastava, A.K. Physics informed machine learning for data anomaly detection, classification, localization, and mitigation: A review, challenges, and path forward. *J. Mech. Eng.* **2024**, *60*, 177–186.
61. Lawal, Z.K.; Lai, D.T.C.; Cheldris, A. Physics-informed neural network (PINN) evolution and beyond: A systematic literature review and bibliometric analysis. *Big Data Cogn. Comput.* **2022**, *26*, 140. [CrossRef]
62. Hu, H.; Shen, Z.; Zhuang, C. A PINN-based friction-inclusive dynamics modeling method for industrial robots. *IEEE Trans. Ind. Electron.* 2024, *early access*. [CrossRef]
63. Hunt, K.J.; Sbarbaro, D.; Zbikowski, R.; Gawthrop, P.J. Neural networks for control systems—A survey. *Automatica* **1992**, *28*, 1083–1112. [CrossRef]
64. Zhan, X.; Wang, W.; Chung, H. A neural-network-based color control method for multi-color LED systems. *IEEE Trans. Power Electron.* **2019**, *34*, 7900–7913. [CrossRef]
65. Wang, W.; Chung, H.S.; Cheng, R.; Leung, C.S.; Zhan, X.; Lo A.W.; Kwok, J.; Xue, C.J.; Zhang, J. Training neural-network-based controller on distributed machine learning platform for power electronics systems. In Proceedings of the 2017 IEEE Energy Conversion Congress and Exposition, Cincinnati, OH, USA, 1–5 October 2017; pp. 3083–3089.
66. Novak, M.; Dragicevic, T. Supervised imitation learning of finite-set model predictive control systems for power electronics. *IEEE Trans. Ind. Electron.* **2021**, *68*, 1717–1723. [CrossRef]
67. Lin, C.M.; Hung, K.N.; Hsu, C.F. Adaptive neuro-wavelet control for switching power supplies. *IEEE Trans. Power Electron.* **2007**, *22*, 87–95. [CrossRef]
68. Zhao, J.; Bose, B. Neural-network-based waveform processing and delayless filtering in power electronics and AC drives. *IEEE Trans. Ind. Electron.* **2004**, *51*, 981–991. [CrossRef]
69. Lin, F.J.; Teng, L.T.; Yu, M.H. Radial basis function network control with improved particle swarm optimization for induction generator system. *IEEE Trans. Power Electron.* **2008**, *23*, 2157–2169. [CrossRef]
70. Wang, F.; Chao, Z.Q.; Huang, L.B.; Li, H.Y.; Zhang, C.Q. Trajectory tracking control of robot manipulator based on RBF neural network and fuzzy sliding mode. *Clust. Comput.* **2019**, *22*, 5799–5809. [CrossRef]
71. Polycarpou, M. Stable adaptive neural control scheme for nonlinear systems. *IEEE Trans. Autom. Control* **1996**, *41*, 447–451. [CrossRef]
72. Seshagiri, S.; Khalil, H. Output feedback control of nonlinear systems using RBF neural networks. *IEEE Trans. Neural Netw.* **2000**, *11*, 69–79. [CrossRef] [PubMed]
73. Fei, J.; Ding, H. Adaptive sliding mode control of dynamic system using RBF neural network. *Nonlinear Dyn.* **2012**, *70*, 1563–1573. [CrossRef]
74. Li, S.; Wang, Y.; Tan, J.; Zheng, Y. Adaptive RBFNNs/integral sliding mode control for a quadrotor aircraft. *Neurocomputing* **2016**, *216*, 126–134. [CrossRef]
75. Lin, W.M.; Hong, C.M. A new Elman neural network-based control algorithm for adjustable-pitch variable-speed wind-energy conversion systems. *IEEE Trans. Power Electron.* **2011**, *26*, 473–481. [CrossRef]
76. Lin, F.J.; Teng, L.T.; Chu, H. A robust recurrent wavelet neural network controller with improved particle swarm optimization for linear synchronous motor drive. *IEEE Trans. Power Electron.* **2008**, *23*, 3067–3078. [CrossRef]
77. Lin, F.J.; Huang, P.K.; Wang, C.C.; Teng, L.T. An induction generator system using fuzzy modeling and recurrent fuzzy neural network. *IEEE Trans. Power Electron.* **2007**, *22*, 260–271. [CrossRef]
78. Chen, C.S. TSK-type self-organizing recurrent-neural-fuzzy control of linear microstepping motor drives. *IEEE Trans. Power Electron.* **2010**, *25*, 2253–2265. [CrossRef]
79. Bose, B.K. Neural network applications in power electronics and motor drives—An introduction and perspective. *IEEE Trans. Ind. Electron.* **2007**, *54*, 14–33. [CrossRef]
80. Kiranyaz, S.; Gastli, A.; Ben-Brahim, L.; Al-Emadi, N.; Gabbouj, M. Real-time fault detection and identification for MMC using 1-D convolutional neural networks. *IEEE Trans. Ind. Electron.* **2019**, *66*, 8760–8771. [CrossRef]
81. Esfandiari K.; Abdollahi, F.; Talebi, H.A. *Neural Network-Based Adaptive Control of Uncertain Nonlinear Systems*; Springer International Publishing: Berlin/Heidelberg, Germany, 2022.
82. Leu, Y.G.; Wang, W.Y.; Lee, T.T. Observer-based direct adaptive fuzzy-neural control for nonaffine nonlinear systems. *IEEE Trans. Neural Netw.* **2005**, *16*, 853–861. [CrossRef] [PubMed]

83. Park, J.H.; Huh, S.H.; Kim, S.H.; Seo, S.J.; Park, G.T. Direct adaptive controller for nonaffine nonlinear systems using self-structuring neural networks. *IEEE Trans. Neural Netw.* **2005**, *16*, 414–422. [CrossRef] [PubMed]
84. Wang, S.; Hui, Y.; Sun, X.; Shi, D. Neural network sliding mode control of intelligent vehicle longitudinal dynamics. *IEEE Access* **2019**, *7*, 162333–162342. [CrossRef]
85. Bao, Y.; Thesma, V.; Velni, J.M. Physics-guided and neural network learning-based sliding mode control. *IFAC-PapersOnLine* **2021**, *54*, 705–710. [CrossRef]
86. Sun, T.; Pei, H.; Pan, Y.; Zhou, H.; Zhang, C. Neural network-based sliding mode adaptive control for robot manipulators. *Neurocomputing* **2011**, *74*, 2377–2384. [CrossRef]
87. Yen, V.T.; Nan, W.Y.; Van Cuong, P.; Quynh, N.X.; Thich, V.H. Robust adaptive sliding mode control for industrial robot manipulator using fuzzy wavelet neural networks. *Int. J. Control Autom. Syst.* **2017**, *15*, 2930–2941. [CrossRef]
88. Yen, V.T.; Nan, W.Y.; Van Cuong P. Robust adaptive sliding mode neural networks control for industrial robot manipulators. *Int. J. Control Autom. Syst.* **2019**, *17*, 783–792. [CrossRef]
89. Lu, X.; Zhang, X.; Zhang, G.; Fan, J.; Jia, S. Neural network adaptive sliding mode control for omnidirectional vehicle with uncertainties. *ISA Trans.* **2019**, *86*, 201–214. [CrossRef]
90. Sun, Z.; Zou, J.; He, D.; Zhu, W. Path-tracking control for autonomous vehicles using double-hidden-layer output feedback neural network fast nonsingular terminal sliding mode. *Neural Comput. Appl.* **2021**, *34*, 5135–5150. [CrossRef]
91. Liu, H.; Gong, Z. Upper bound adaptive learning of neural network for the sliding mode control of underwater robot. In Proceedings of the 2008 International Conference on Advanced Computer Theory and Engineering, Phuket, Thailand, 20–22 December 2008; pp. 276–280.
92. Bagheri, A.; Moghaddam, J.J. Simulation and tracking control based on neural-network strategy and sliding-mode control for underwater remotely operated vehicle. *Neurocomputing* **2009**, *72*, 1934–1950. [CrossRef]
93. Tlijani, H.; Jouila, A.; Nouri, K. Wavelet neural network sliding mode control of two rigid joint robot manipulator. *Adv. Mech. Eng.* **2022**, *14*, 16878132221119886. [CrossRef]
94. Boukens, M.; Boukabou, A.; Chadli, M. Robust adaptive neural network-based trajectory tracking control approach for nonholonomic electrically driven mobile robots. *Robot. Auton. Syst.* **2017**, *92*, 30–40. [CrossRef]
95. Yen, V.T.; Nan, W.Y.; Van, C.P. Recurrent fuzzy wavelet neural networks based on robust adaptive sliding mode control for industrial robot manipulators. *Neural Comput. Appl.* **2018**, *31*, 6945–6958. [CrossRef]
96. Lai, G.; Tao, G.; Zhang, Y.; Liu, Z. Adaptive control of noncanonical neural-network nonlinear systems with unknown input dead-zone characteristics. *IEEE Trans. Neural Netw. Learn. Syst.* **2020**, *31*, 3346–3360. [CrossRef] [PubMed]
97. El-Sousy, F.F.M.; Abuhasel, K.A. Adaptive nonlinear disturbance observer using a double-loop self-organizing recurrent wavelet neural network for a two-axis motion control system. *IEEE Trans. Ind. Appl.* **2018**, *54*, 764–786. [CrossRef]
98. Choi, J.Y.; Farrell, J. Adaptive observer backstepping control using neural networks. *IEEE Trans. Neural Netw.* **2001**, *12*, 1103–1112. [CrossRef]
99. Xi, R.D.; Ma, T.N.; Xiao, X.; Yang, Z.X. Design and implementation of an adaptive neural network observer–based backstepping sliding mode controller for robot manipulators. *Trans. Inst. Meas. Control* **2024**, *46*, 1093–1104. [CrossRef]
100. Zhou, Z.; Yu, J.; Yu, H.; Lin, C. Neural network-based discrete-time command filtered adaptive position tracking control for induction motors via backstepping. *Neurocomputing* **2017**, *260*, 203–210. [CrossRef]
101. Zhang, C.; Wang, C.; Wei, Y.; Wang, J. Neural-based command filtered backstepping control for trajectory tracking of underactuated autonomous surface vehicles. *IEEE Access* **2020**, *8*, 42481–42490. [CrossRef]
102. Niu, S.; Wang, J.; Zhao, J.; Shen, W. Neural network-based finite-time command-filtered adaptive backstepping control of electro-hydraulic servo system with a three-stage valve. *ISA Trans.* **2024**, *144*, 419–435. [CrossRef]
103. Zhou, Q.; Zhao, S.; Li, H.; Lu, R.; Wu, C. Adaptive neural network tracking control for robotic manipulators with dead zone. *IEEE Trans. Neural Netw. Learn. Syst.* **2019**, *30*, 3611–3620. [CrossRef] [PubMed]
104. Zong, G.; Xu, Q.; Zhao, X.; Su, S.F.; Song, L. Output-feedback adaptive neural network control for uncertain nonsmooth nonlinear systems with input deadzone and saturation. *IEEE Trans. Cybern.* **2023**, *53*, 5957–5969. [CrossRef] [PubMed]
105. Armstrong, A.A.; Alleyne, A.G. A multi-input single-output iterative learning control for improved material placement in extrusion-based additive manufacturing. *Control Eng. Pract.* **1990**, *111*, 104783. [CrossRef]
106. Schwegel, M.; Kugi, A. A simple computationally efficient path ILC for industrial robotic manipulators. In Proceedings of the IEEE International Conference on Robotics and Automation, Yokohama, Japan, 13–17 May 2024; pp. 2133–2139.
107. Hao, S.L.; Liu, T.; Rogers, E. Extended state observer based indirect-type ILC for single-input single-output batch processes with time- and batch-varying uncertainties. *Automatica* **2020**, *112*, 108673. [CrossRef]
108. Bristow, D.A.; Tharayil, M.; Alleyne, A.G. A survey of iterative learning control. *IEEE Control Syst. Mag.* **2006**, *26*, 96–114.
109. Yu, X.; Hou, Z.; Polycarpou, M.M. Controller-dynamic-linearization-based data-driven ILC for nonlinear discrete-time systems with RBFNN. *IEEE Trans. Syst. Man Cybern. Syst.* **2022**, *52*, 4981–4992. [CrossRef]

110. Shi, Q.; Huang, X.; Meng, B. Neural network-based iterative learning control for trajectory tracking of unknown SISO nonlinear systems. *Expert Syst. Appl.* **2023**, *232*, 120863. [CrossRef]
111. Patan, K.; Patan, M. Neural-network-based iterative learning control of nonlinear systems. *ISA Trans.* **2020**, *98*, 445–453. [CrossRef]
112. Yu, Q.; Hou, Z.; Bu, X.; Yu, Q. RBFNN-based data-driven predictive iterative learning control for nonaffine nonlinear systems. *IEEE Trans. Neural Netw. Learn. Syst.* **2020**, *31*, 1170–1182. [CrossRef]
113. Chen, Z.; Hou, Y.; Huang, R. Neural network compensator-based robust iterative learning control scheme for mobile robots nonlinear systems with disturbances and uncertain parameters. *Appl. Math. Comput.* **2024**, *469*, 128549. [CrossRef]
114. Zhang, Y.; Ge, S.S. Design and analysis of a general recurrent neural network model for time-varying matrix inversion. *IEEE Trans. Neural Netw.* **2005**, *16*, 1477–1490. [CrossRef] [PubMed]
115. Hu, Y. Noise-tolerant ZNN-based data-driven iterative learning control for discrete nonaffine nonlinear MIMO repetitive systems. *IEEE/CAA J. Autom. Sin.* **2024**, *11*, 344–361. [CrossRef]
116. Zhang, D.; Wang, Z.; Masayoshi, T. Neural-network-based iterative learning control for multiple tasks. *IEEE Trans. Neural Netw. Learn. Syst.* **2021**, *32*, 4178–4190. [CrossRef]
117. Lv, Y.; Ren, X.; Tian, J. Inverse-model-based iterative learning control for unknown MIMO nonlinear system with neural network. *Neurocomputing* **2023**, *519*, 187–193. [CrossRef]
118. Abdollahi, F.; Talebi, H.; Patel, R. Stable identification of nonlinear systems using neural networks: Theory and experiments. *IEEE Trans. Mechatron.* **2006**, *11*, 488–495. [CrossRef]
119. Chen, F.C.; Liu, C.C. Adaptively controlling nonlinear continuous-time systems using multilayer neural networks. *IEEE Trans. Autom. Control* **1994**, *39*, 1306–1310. [CrossRef]
120. Wang, C.C.; Tan, K.L.; Chen, C.T.; Lin, Y.H.; Keerthi, S.S.; Mahajan, D.; Sundararajan, S.; Lin, C.J. Distributed Newton Methods for Deep Neural Networks. *Neural Comput.* **2018**, *30*, 1673–1724. [CrossRef]
121. Indrapriyadarsini, S.; Mahboubi, S.; Ninomiya, H.; Kamio, T.; Asai, H. Accelerating Symmetric Rank-1 Quasi–Newton Method with Nesterov's Gradient for Training Neural Networks. *Algorithms* **2022**, *15*, 6. [CrossRef]
122. Guilhoto, L.F.; Perdikaris, P. Composite Bayesian Optimization in function spaces using NEON—Neural Epistemic Operator Networks. *Sci. Rep.* **2024**, *14*, 29199. [CrossRef]
123. Magallón, D.A.; Jaimes, R.R.; García, J.H.; Huerta, C.G.; López, M.D.; Pisarchik, A.N. Control of Multistability in an Erbium-Doped Fiber Laser by an Artificial Neural Network: A Numerical Approach. *Mathematics* **2022**, *10*, 3140. [CrossRef]
124. Norouzi, A.; Heidarifar, H.; Borhan, H.; Shahbakhti, M.; Koch, C.R. Integrating machine learning and model predictive control for automotive applications: A review and future directions. *Eng. Appl. Artif. Intell.* **2023**, *120*, 105878. [CrossRef]
125. Akpan, V.A.; Hassapis, G.D. Nonlinear model identification and adaptive model predictive control using neural networks. *IEEE Robot. Autom. Lett.* **2011**, *4*, 177–194. [CrossRef] [PubMed]
126. Lanzetti, N.; Lian, Y.Z.; Cortinovis, A.; Dominguez, L.; Mercangoz, M.; Jones, C. Recurrent neural network based MPC for process industries. *Eur. Control Conf.* **2019**, *6*, 1005–1010.
127. Gillespie, M.T.; Best, C.M.; Townsend, E.C.; Wingate, D.; Killpack, M.D. Learning nonlinear dynamic models of soft robots for model predictive control with neural networks. *Proc. IEEE Int. Conf. Soft Robot.* **2018**, *7*, 568–581.
128. Seel, K.; Grotli, E.I.; Moe, S.; Gravdahl, J.T.; Pettersen, K.Y. Neural network-based model predictive control with input-to-state stability. *Proc. Am. Control Conf.* **2021**, *5*, 3556–3563.
129. Ostafew, C.J.; Schoellig, A.P.; Barfoot, T.D. Learning-based nonlinear model predictive control to improve vision-based mobile robot path-tracking in challenging outdoor environments. *Proc. IEEE Int. Conf. Robot. Autom.* **2014**, *5*, 4029–4036.
130. McKinnon, C.D.; Schoellig, A.P. Learning probabilistic models for safe predictive control in unknown environments. *Proc. IEEE Int. Conf. Robot. Autom.* **2019**, *6*, 2472–2479.
131. Hose, H.; Gräfe, A.; Trimpe, S. Parameter-adaptive approximate MPC: Tuning neural-network controllers without retraining. *Annu. Learn. Dyn. Control. Conf.* **2024**, *242*, 349–360.
132. Gros, S.; Zanon, M. Data-driven economic NMPC using reinforcement learning. *IEEE Trans. Autom. Control* **2020**, *2*, 636–648. [CrossRef]
133. Karg, B.; Lucia, S. Efficient representation and approximation of model predictive control laws via deep learning. *IEEE Trans. Cybern.* **2020**, *9*, 3866–3878. [CrossRef]
134. Lovelett, R.J.; Dietrich, F.; Lee, S.; Kevrekidis, I.G. Some manifold learning considerations towards explicit model predictive control. *AIChE J.* **2019**, *66*, 16881. [CrossRef]
135. Klaučo, M.; Kalúz, M.; Kvasnica, M. Machine learning-based warm starting of active set methods in embedded model predictive control. *Eng. Appl. Artif. Intell.* **2019**, *1*, 1–8. [CrossRef]
136. Chen, S.W.; Wang, T.; Atanasov, N.; Kumar, V.; Morari, M. Large scale model predictive control with neural networks and primal active sets. *Automatica* **2022**, *1*, 109947. [CrossRef]
137. Chakrabarty, A.; Dinh, V.; Corless, M.J.; Rundell, A.E.; Zak, S.H.; Buzzard, G.T. Support vector machine informed explicit nonlinear model predictive control using low-discrepancy sequences. *IEEE Trans. Autom. Control* **2017**, *1*, 135–148. [CrossRef]

138. Chen, S.; Saulnier, K.; Atanasov, N.; Lee, D.D.; Kumar, V.; Pappas, G.J.; Morari, M. Approximating explicit model predictive control using constrained neural networks. *Proc. Annu. Am. Control Conf.* **2018**, *6*, 1520–1527.
139. Sutton, R.S.; Barto, A.G. *Reinforcement Learning: An Introduction*; MIT Press: Cambridge, MA, USA, 2018.
140. Li, S.E. *Reinforcement Learning for Sequential Decision and Optimal Control*; Springer: Berlin/Heidelberg, Germany, 2023.
141. Bellman, R.E. *Dynamic Programming*; Princeton University Press: Princeton, NJ, USA, 1957.
142. Werbos, P. Consistency of HDP applied to a simple reinforcement learning problem. *Neural Netw.* **1990**, *3*, 179–189. [CrossRef]
143. Werbos, P. Approximate dynamic programming for real-time control and neural modeling. In *Handbook of Intelligent Control*; Van Nostrand Reinhold: New York, NY, USA, 1992.
144. Sutton, R.S. Learning to predict by the methods of temporal differences. *Mach. Learn.* **1988**, *3*, 9–44. [CrossRef]
145. Watkins, C. Learning from Delayed Rewards. Ph.D. Thesis, University of Cambridge, Cambridge, UK, 1989.
146. Wang, Z.H.; Justin, S. Continuous-time stochastic gradient descent for optimizing over the stationary distribution of stochastic differential equations. *Math. Financ.* **2023**, *34*, 348–424. [CrossRef]
147. Moerl, T.M.; Broekens, J.; Plaat, A. Model-based reinforcement learning: A survey. *Found. Trends Mach. Learn.* **2023**, *16*, 1–118.
148. Vamvoudakis, K.G.; Lewis, F.L. Online actor-critic algorithm to solve the continuous-time infinite horizon optimal control problem. *Automatica* **2010**, *46*, 878–888. [CrossRef]
149. Liu, D.; Wei, Q. Finite-approximation-error-based optimal control approach for discrete-time nonlinear systems. *IEEE Trans. Cybern.* **2013**, *43*, 779–789. [PubMed]
150. Abu-Khalaf, M.; Lewis, F.L.; Huang, J. Neuro dynamic programming and zero-sum games for constrained control systems. *IEEE Trans. Neural Netw.* **2008**, *19*, 1243–1252. [CrossRef]
151. Feng, Y.; Anderson, B.D.O.; Rotkowitz, M. A game theoretic algorithm to compute local stabilizing solutions to HJBI equations in nonlinear H∞ control. *Automatica* **2009**, *45*, 881–888. [CrossRef]
152. Wang, D.; Liu, D.; Wei, Q. Finite-horizon neuro-optimal tracking control for a class of discrete-time nonlinear systems using adaptive dynamic programming approach. *Neurocomputing* **2012**, *78*, 14–22. [CrossRef]
153. Garaffa, L.C.; Basso, M.; Konzen, A.A.; de Freitas, E.P. Reinforcement Learning for Mobile Robotics Exploration: A Survey. *IEEE Trans. Neural Netw. Learn. Syst.* **2023**, *34*, 3796–3810. [CrossRef]
154. Liu, D.; Zhang, H. A neural dynamic programming approach for learning control of failure avoidance problems. *Int. J. Intell. Control Syst.* **2005**, *10*, 21–32.
155. Si, J.; Wang, Y.T. Online learning control by association and reinforcement. *IEEE Trans. Neural Netw.* **2001**, *12*, 264–276. [CrossRef]
156. Long, M.; Su, H.; Zeng, Z. Output-feedback global consensus of discrete-time multiagent systems subject to input saturation via Q-Learning method. *IEEE Trans. Cybern.* **2022**, *52*, 1661–1670. [CrossRef]
157. Song, S.; Zhu, M.; Dai, X.; Gong, D. Model-free optimal tracking control of nonlinear input-affine discrete-time systems via an iterative deterministic Q-learning algorithm. *IEEE Trans. Neural Netw. Learn. Syst.* **2024**, *35*, 999–1012. [CrossRef]
158. Liu, F.; Liu, Q.; Tao, Q. Deep reinforcement learning based energy storage management strategy considering prediction intervals of wind power. *Int. J. Electr. Power Energy Syst.* **2023**, *145*, 108608. [CrossRef]
159. Xu, X.; Hu, D.; Lu, X. Kernel-based least squares policy iteration for reinforcement learning. *IEEE Trans. Neural Netw.* **2007**, *18*, 973–992. [CrossRef] [PubMed]
160. Sartoretti, G.; Paivine, W.; Shi, Y.; Wu, Y.; Choset, H. Distributed learning of decentralized control policies for articulated mobile robots. *IEEE Trans. Robot.* **2019**, *35*, 1109–1122. [CrossRef]
161. Zhang, M.; Geng, X.; Bruce, J.; Caluwaerts, K.; Vespignani, M.; SunSpiral, V.; Abbeel, P.; Levine, S. Deep reinforcement learning for tensegrity robot locomotion. In Proceedings of the IEEE International Conference on Robotics and Automation, Singapore, 29 May–3 June 2017; pp. 634–641.
162. Wang, X.; Deng, H.; Ye, X. Model-free nonlinear robust control design via online critic learning. *ISA Trans.* **2022**, *129*, 446–459. [CrossRef]
163. Xia, L.; Li, Q.; Song, R.; Modares, H. Optimal synchronization control of heterogeneous asymmetric input constrained unknown nonlinear MASs via reinforcement learning. *IEEE/CAA J. Autom. Sin.* **2022**, *9*, 520–532. [CrossRef]
164. Yong, H.; Seo, J.; Kim, J.; Kim, M.; Choi, J. Suspension control strategies using switched soft actor-critic models for real roads. *IEEE Trans. Ind. Electron.* **2023**, *70*, 824–832. [CrossRef]
165. Nassef, A.M.; Abdelkareem, M.A.; Maghrabie, H.M.; Baroutaji, A. Review of metaheuristic optimization algorithms for power systems problems. *Sustainability* **2023**, *15*, 9434. [CrossRef]
166. Sehgal, A.; Ward, N.; La H.; Louis, S. Automatic parameter optimization using genetic algorithm in deep reinforcement learning for robotic manipulation tasks. *arXiv* **2022**, arXiv:2204.03656.
167. Erodotou, P.; Voutsas, E.; Sarimveis, H. A genetic algorithm approach for parameter estimation in vapour-liquid thermodynamic modelling problems. *Comput. Chem. Eng.* **2020**, *134*, 106684. [CrossRef]
168. Qian, S.; Ye, Y.; Liu, Y.; Xu, G. An improved binary differential evolution algorithm for optimizing PWM control laws of power inverters. *Optim. Eng.* **2018**, *19*, 271–296. [CrossRef]

169. Godoy, R.B.; Pinto, J.O.; Canesin, C.A.; Coelho, E.A.; Pinto, A.M. Differential-evolution-based optimization of the dynamic response for parallel operation of inverters with no controller interconnection. *IEEE Trans. Ind. Electron.* **2011**, *59*, 2859–2866. [CrossRef]
170. Wang, D.; Sun, X.; Kang, H.; Shen, Y.; Chen, Q. Heterogeneous differential evolution algorithm for parameter estimation of solar photovoltaic models. *Energy Rep.* **2022**, *8*, 4724–4746. [CrossRef]
171. Shi, J.; Mi, Q.; Cao, W.; Zhou, L. Optimizing BLDC motor drive performance using particle swarm algorithm-tuned fuzzy logic controller. *SN Appl. Sci.* **2022**, *4*, 293. [CrossRef]
172. Hafez, I.; Dhaouadi, R. Parameter identification of DC motor drive systems using particle swarm optimization. In Proceedings of the 2021 International Conference on Engineering and Emerging Technologies, Istanbul, Turkey, 27–28 October 2021; pp. 1–6.
173. Tungadio, D.H.; Numbi, B.P.; Siti, M.W.; Jimoh, A.A. Particle swarm optimization for power system state estimation. *Neurocomputing* **2015**, *148*, 175–180. [CrossRef]
174. Foong, W.K.; Maier, H.R.; Simpson, A.R. Ant colony optimization for power plant maintenance scheduling optimization. In Proceedings of the 7th Annual Conference on Genetic and Evolutionary Computation, Washington, DC, USA, 25–29 June 2005; pp. 249–256.
175. Lee, K.Y.; Vlachogiannis, J.G. Optimization of power systems based on ant colony system algorithms: An overview. In Proceedings of the 13th International Conference on Intelligent Systems Application to Power Systems, Arlington, VA, USA, 6–10 November 2005; pp. 22–35.
176. Sitarz, P.; Powałka, B. Modal parameters estimation using ant colony optimisation algorithm. *Mech. Syst. Signal Process.* **2016**, *76*, 531–554. [CrossRef]
177. Zao, R.Z. Simulated annealing based multi-object optimal planning of passive power filters. In Proceedings of the 2005 IEEE/PES Transmission and Distribution Conference and Exposition: Asia and Pacific, Dalian, China, 18 August 2005; pp. 1–5.

MDPI AG
Grosspeteranlage 5
4052 Basel
Switzerland
Tel.: +41 61 683 77 34

Mathematics Editorial Office
E-mail: mathematics@mdpi.com
www.mdpi.com/journal/mathematics

www.ingramcontent.com/pod-product-compliance
Lightning Source LLC
LaVergne TN
LVHW070450061126
851858LV00011B/204